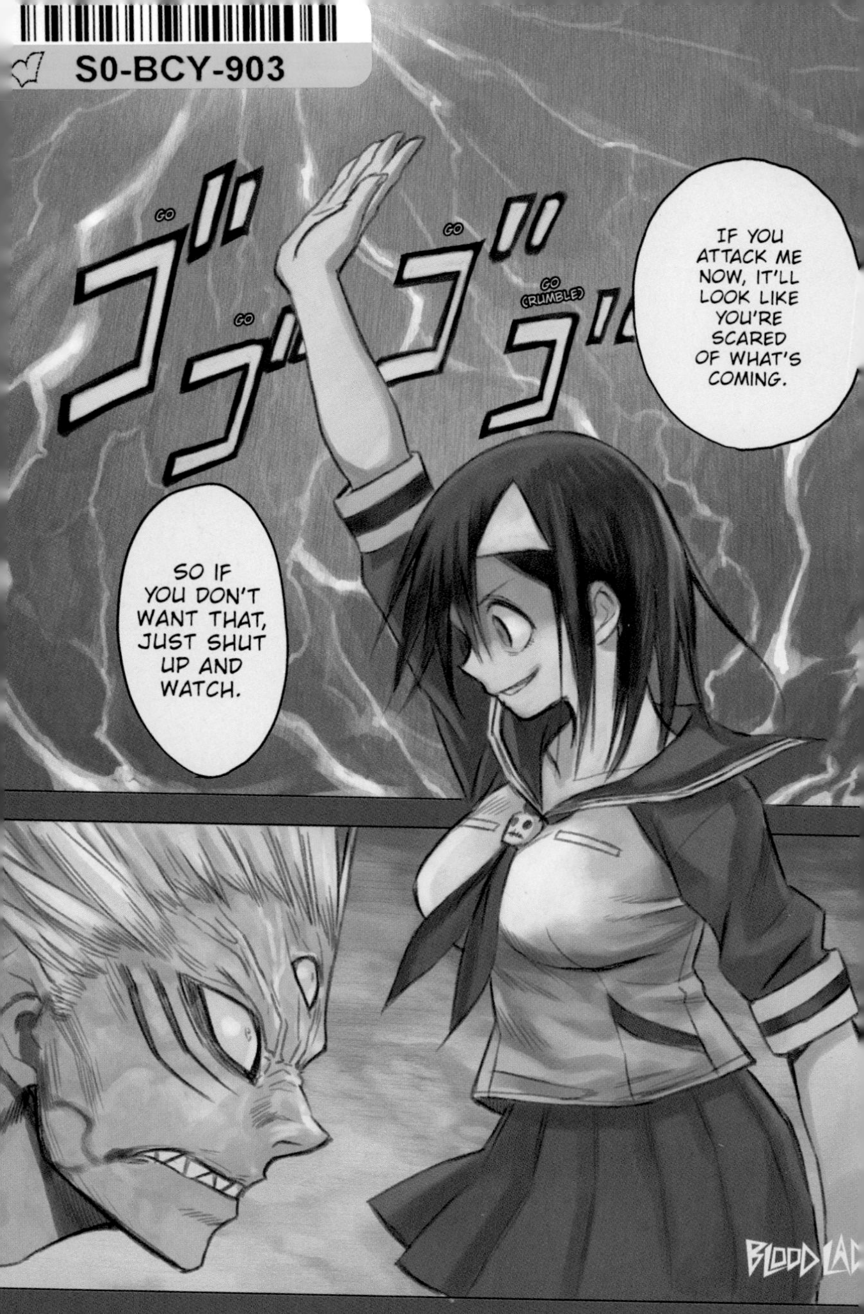
IF YOU ATTACK ME NOW, IT'LL LOOK LIKE YOU'RE SCARED OF WHAT'S COMING.
GO
GO (RUMBLE)
GO
GO
SO IF YOU DON'T WANT THAT, JUST SHUT UP AND WATCH.

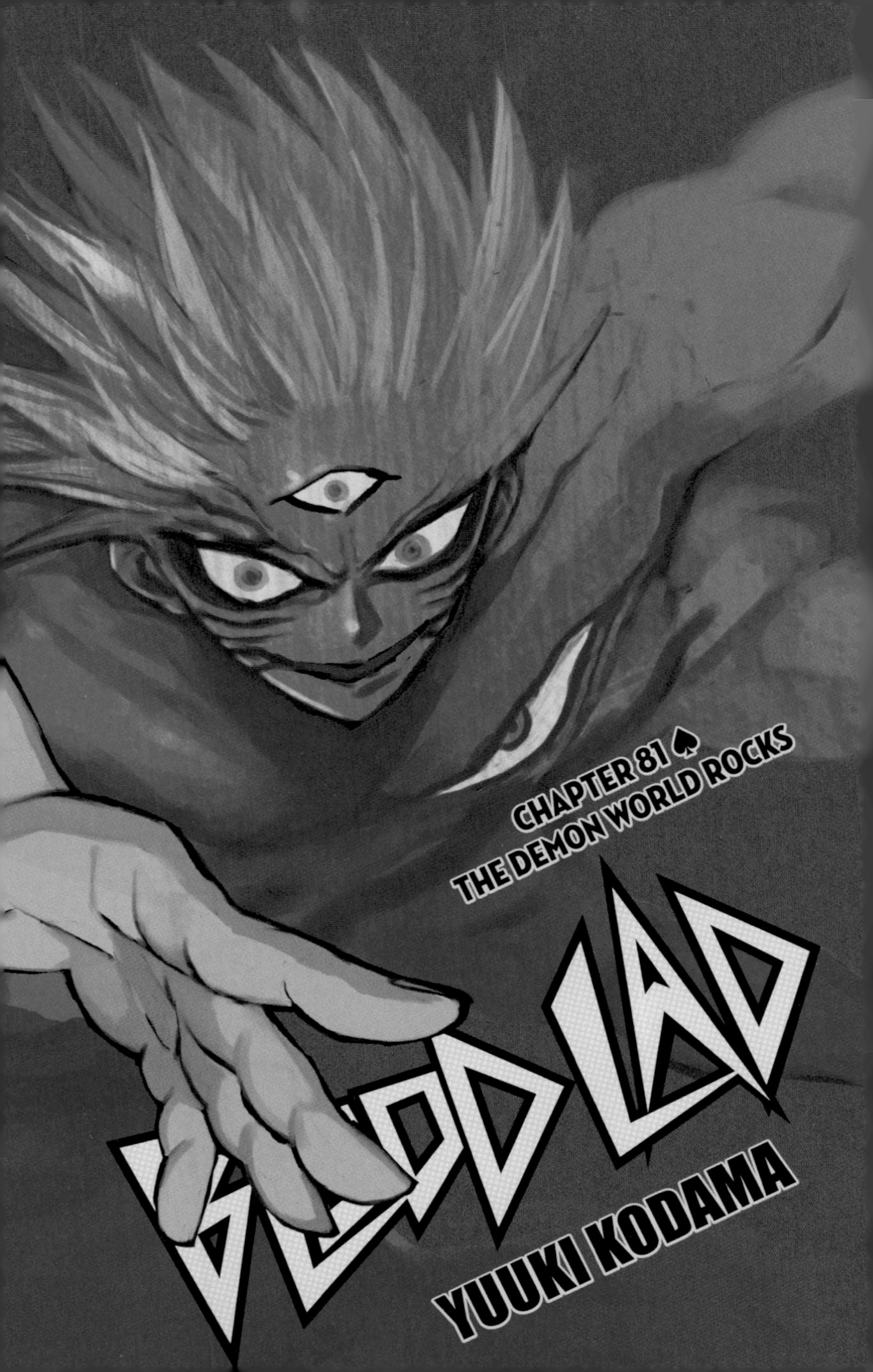
CHAPTER 81 ♠
THE DEMON WORLD ROCKS
BLOOD LAD
YUUKI KODAMA

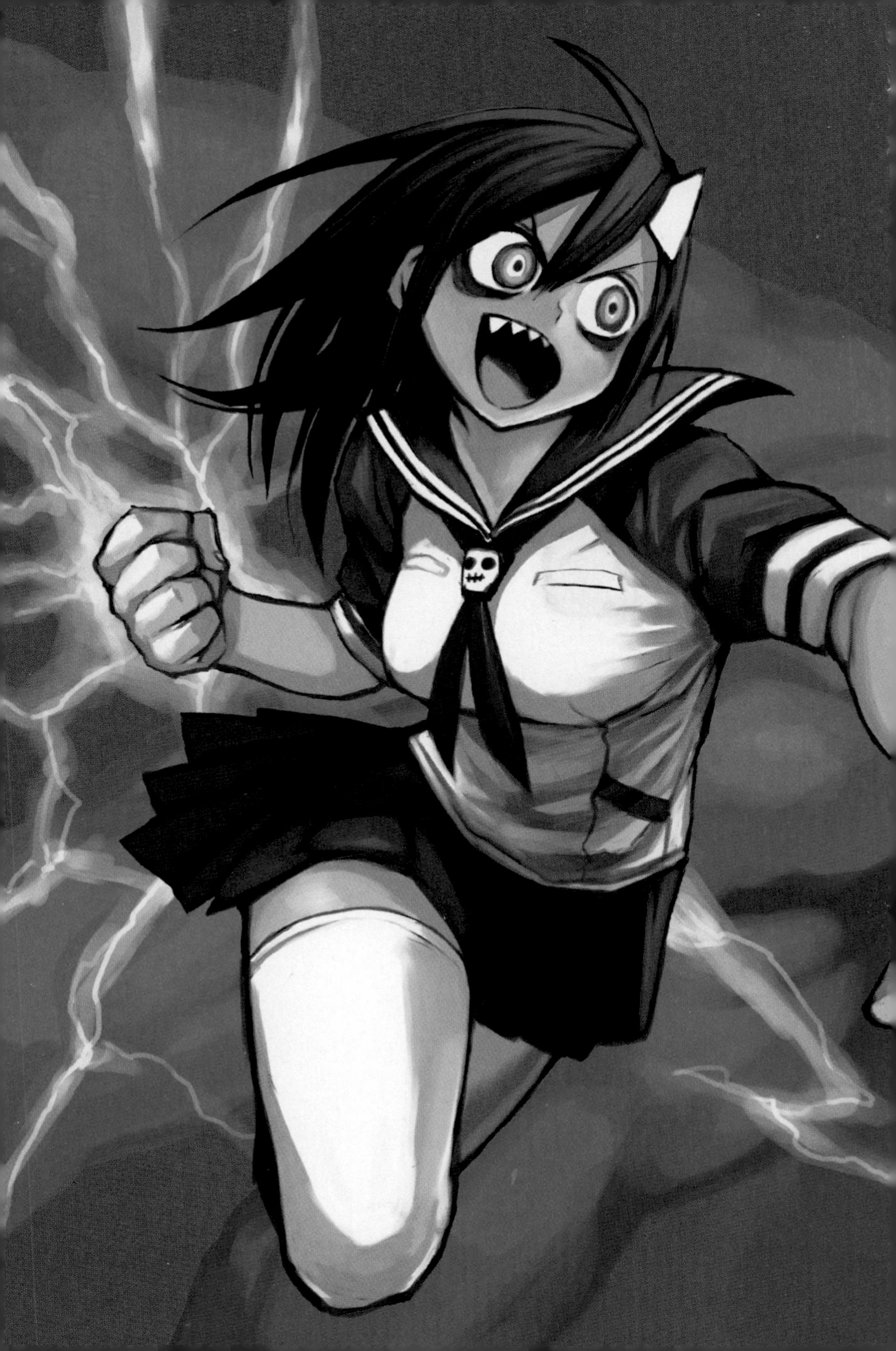

CONTENTS

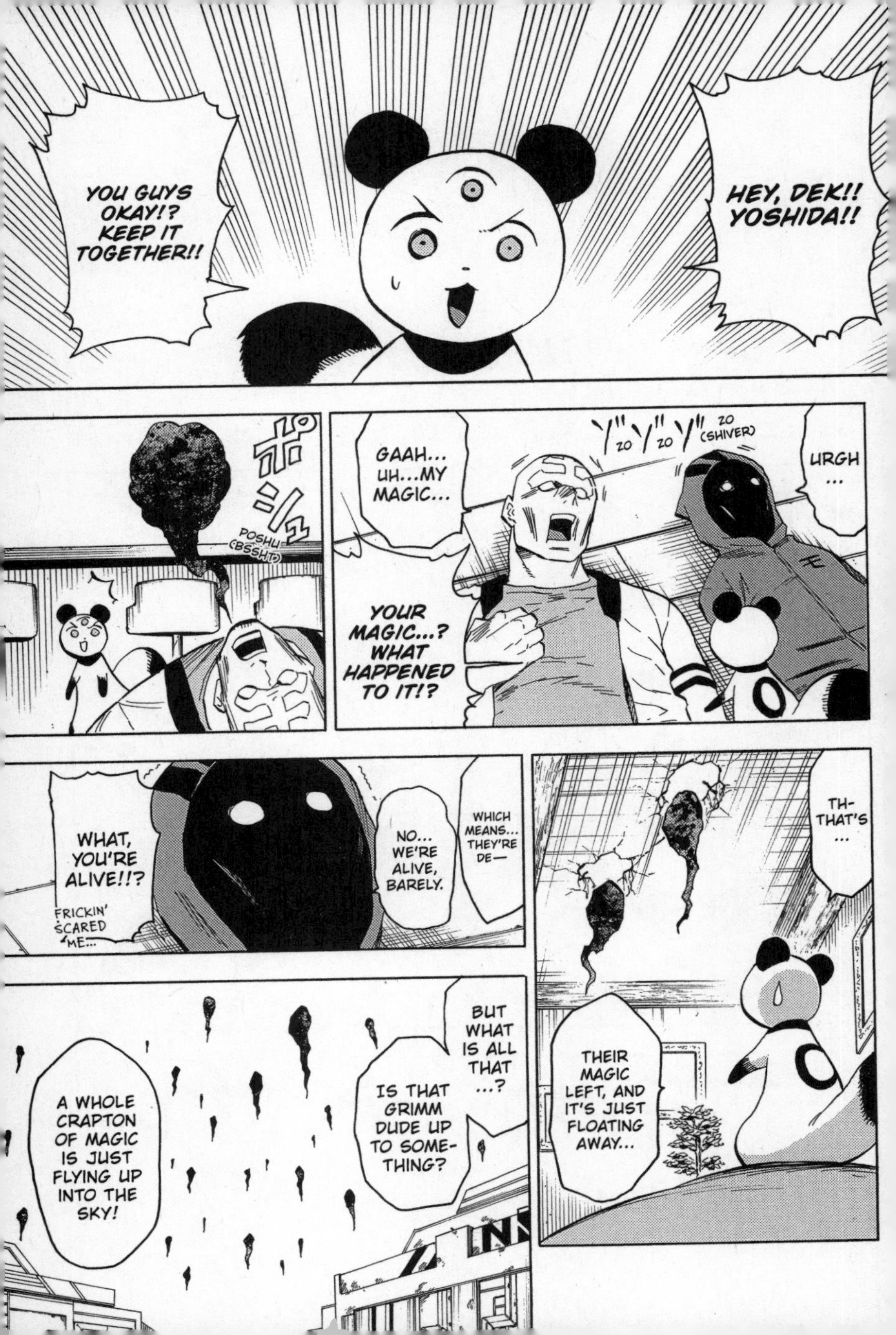
HEY, DEK!! YOSHIDA!!
YOU GUYS OKAY!? KEEP IT TOGETHER!!
URGH ...
ZO ZO ZO ZO (SHIVER)
GAAH... UH...MY MAGIC...
YOUR MAGIC...? WHAT HAPPENED TO IT!?
POSHU (BSSHT)
TH-THAT'S ...
THEIR MAGIC LEFT, AND IT'S JUST FLOATING AWAY...
WHICH MEANS... THEY'RE DE—
NO... WE'RE ALIVE, BARELY.
WHAT, YOU'RE ALIVE!!?
FRICKIN' SCARED ME...
BUT WHAT IS ALL THAT ...?
IS THAT GRIMM DUDE UP TO SOME-THING?
A WHOLE CRAPTON OF MAGIC IS JUST FLYING UP INTO THE SKY!

OOOOOOOO
(LOOOOM)

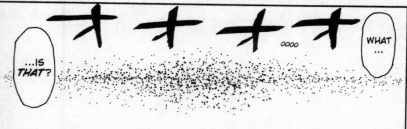

WHAT
...

...IS
THAT?

OOOO

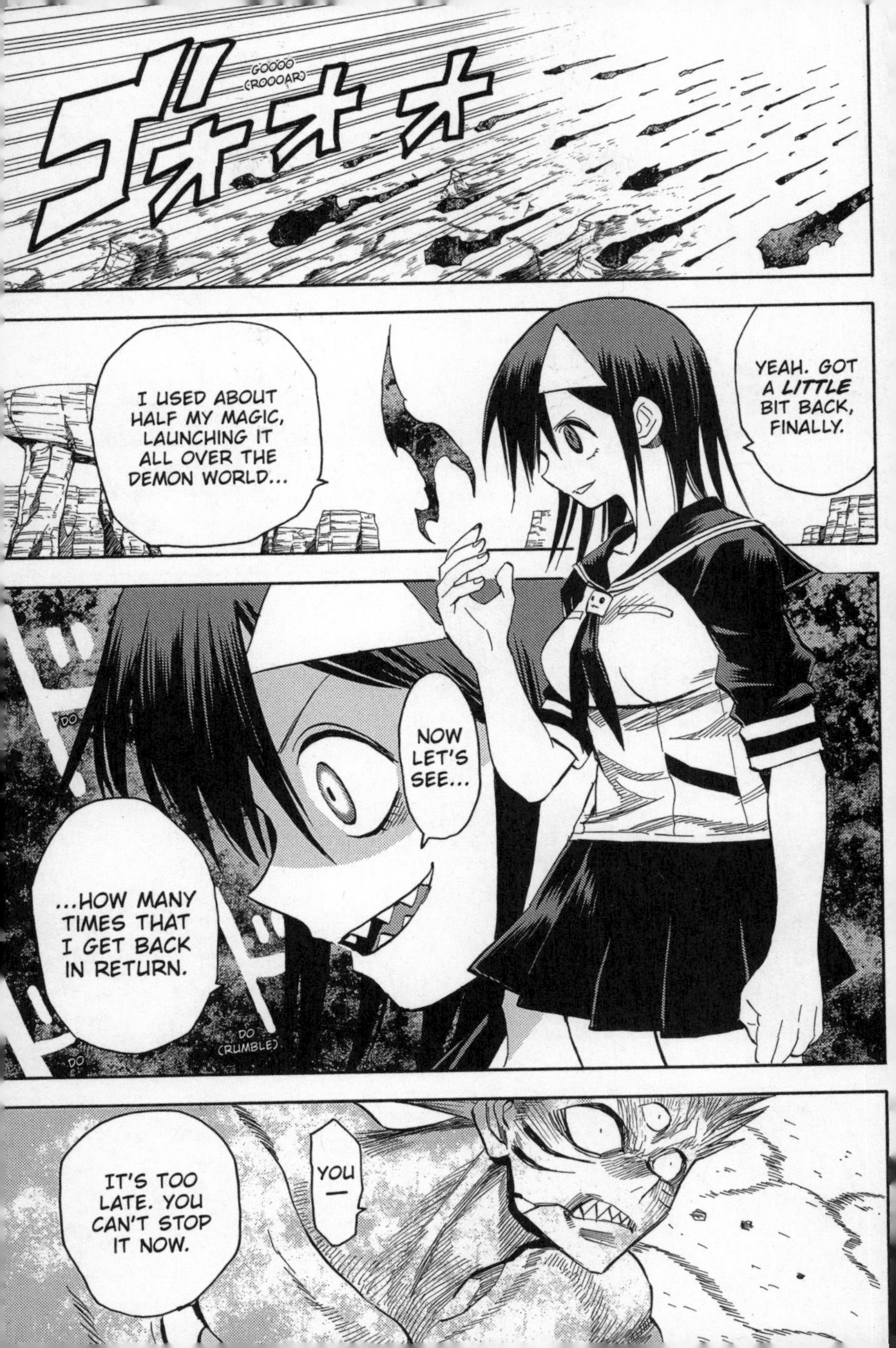
ゴォオオ
GOOOO (ROOOAR)
YEAH. GOT A *LITTLE* BIT BACK, FINALLY.
I USED ABOUT HALF MY MAGIC, LAUNCHING IT ALL OVER THE DEMON WORLD...
NOW LET'S SEE...
...HOW MANY TIMES THAT I GET BACK IN RETURN.
DO
DO (RUMBLE)
DO
YOU—
IT'S TOO LATE. YOU CAN'T STOP IT NOW.

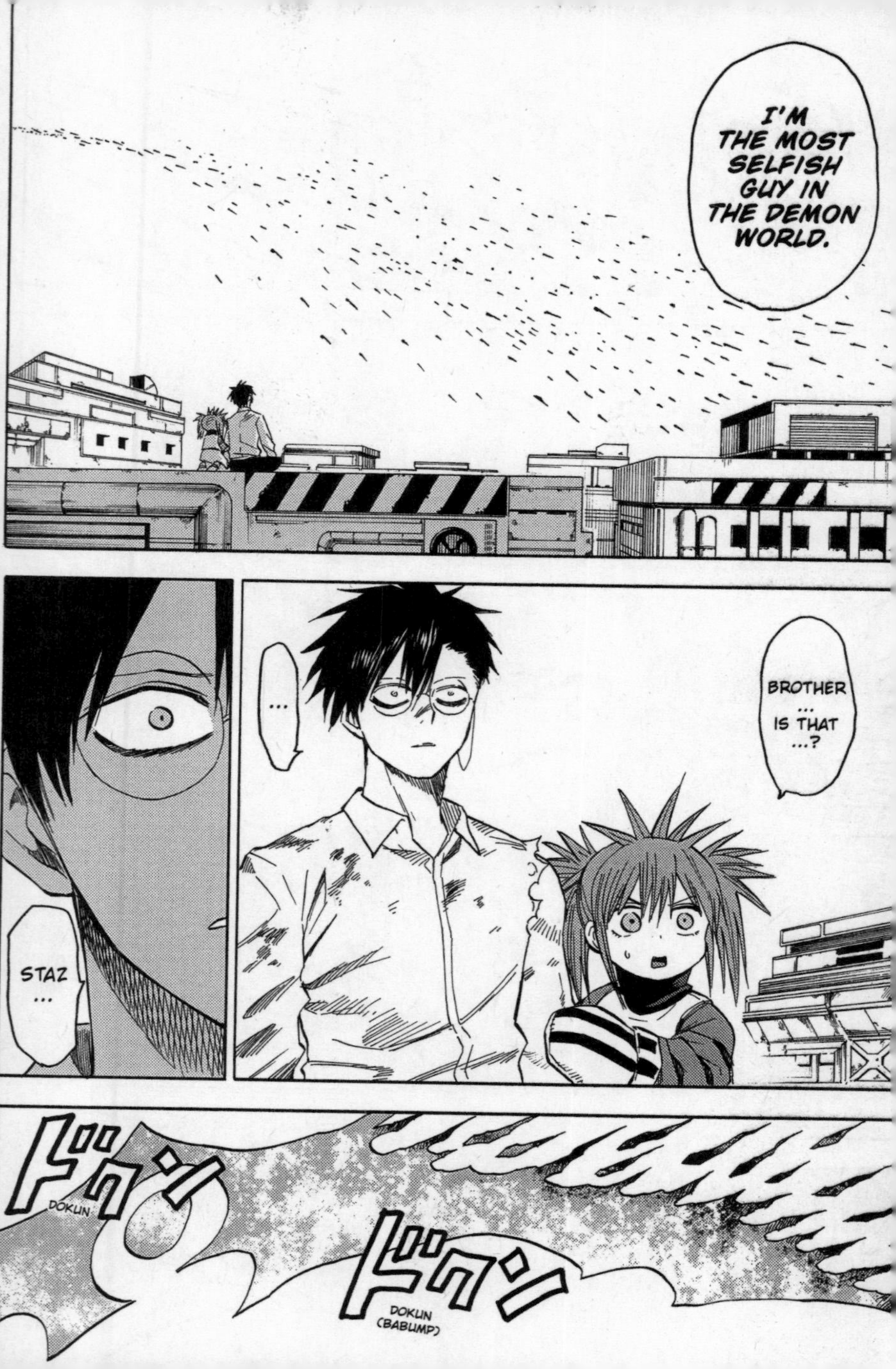
I'M THE MOST SELFISH GUY IN THE DEMON WORLD.
BROTHER ... IS THAT ...?
...
STAZ ...
DOKUN
DOKUN (BABUMP)

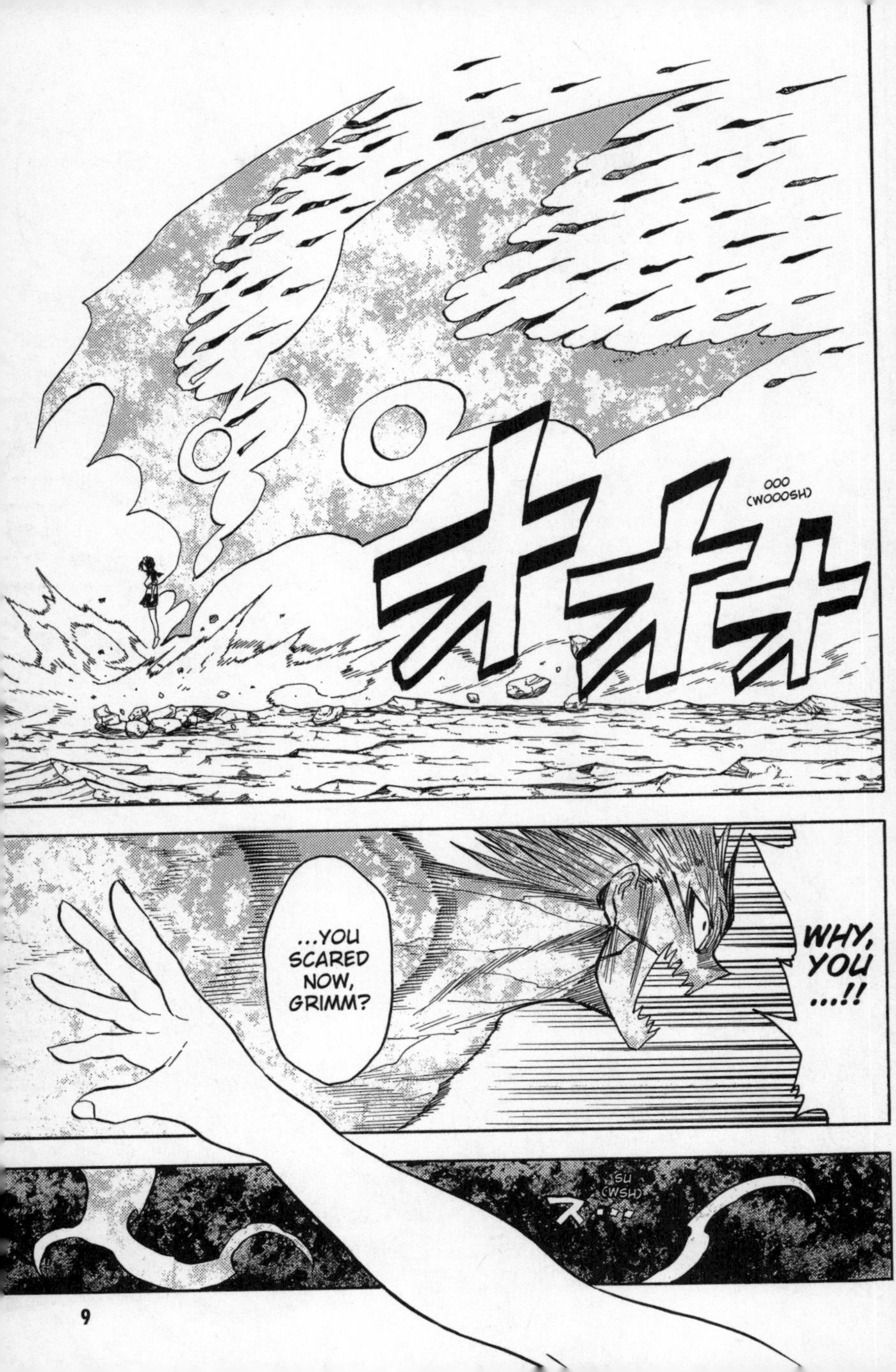
オォォ
OOO
(WOOOSH)
WHY, YOU ...!!
...YOU SCARED NOW, GRIMM?
ス...
SU
(WSH)

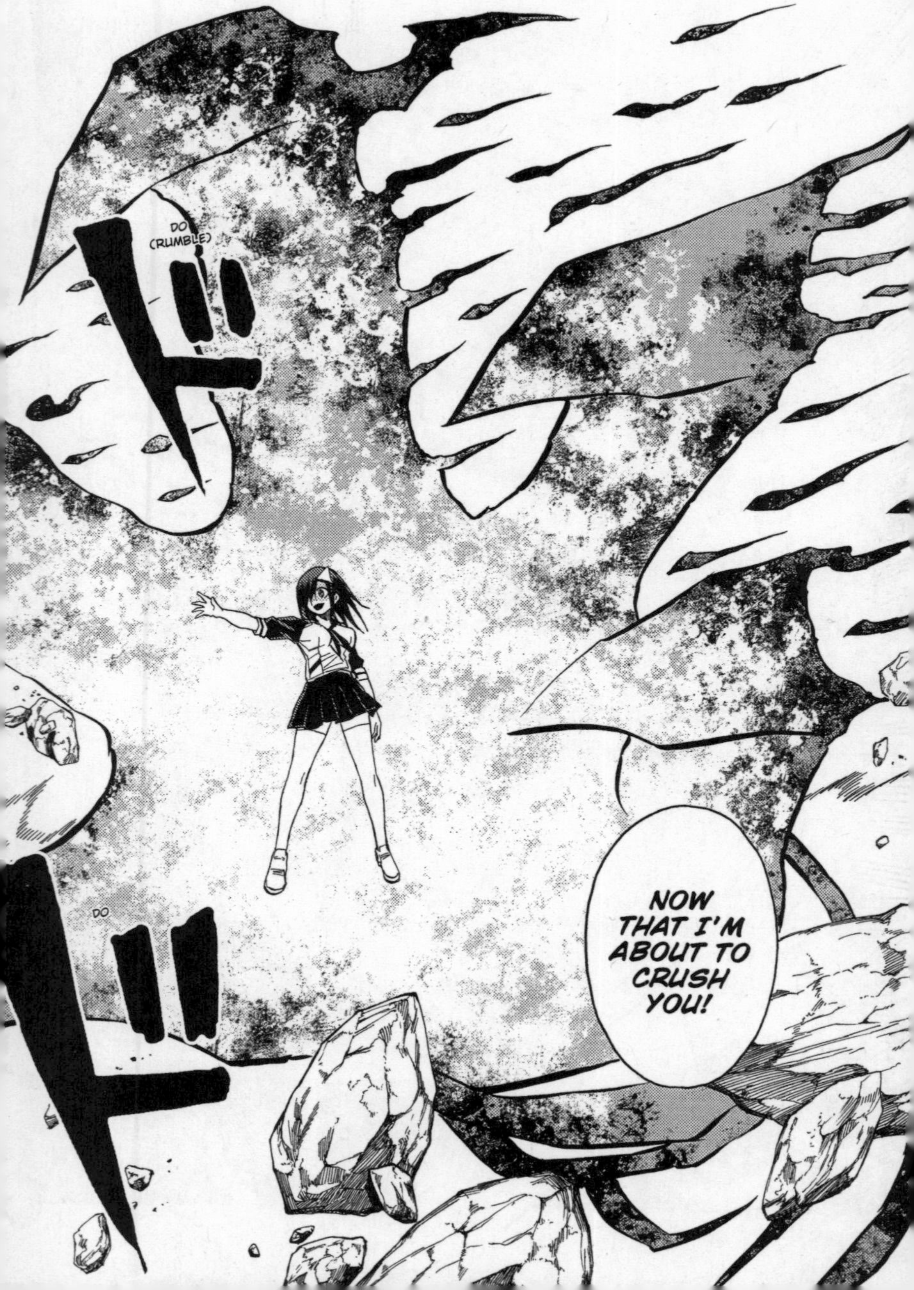

DO (RUMBLE)
NOW THAT I'M ABOUT TO CRUSH YOU!
DO

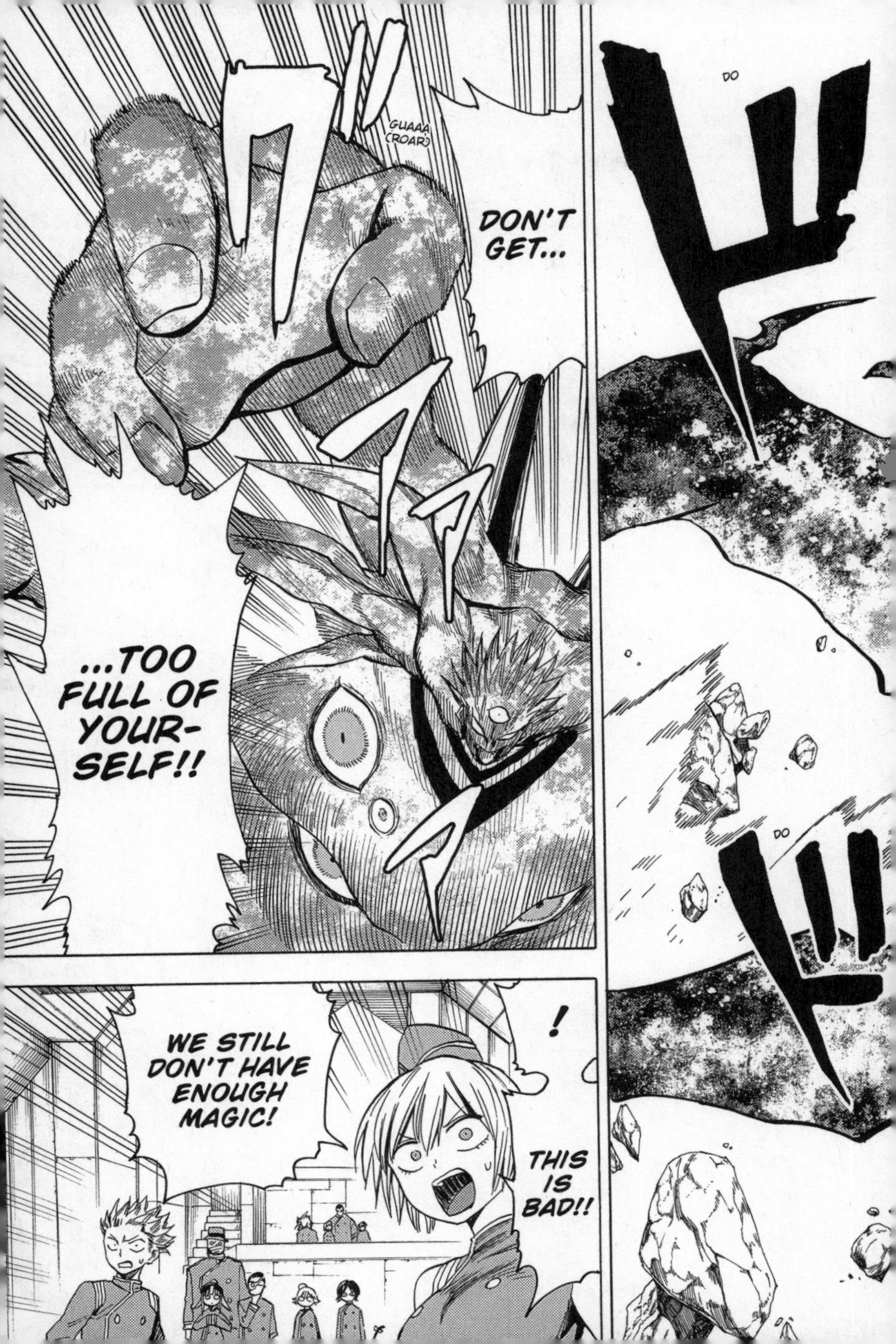
DO
DO
GUAAA (ROAR)
DON'T GET...
...TOO FULL OF YOURSELF!!
!
WE STILL DON'T HAVE ENOUGH MAGIC!
THIS IS BAD!!

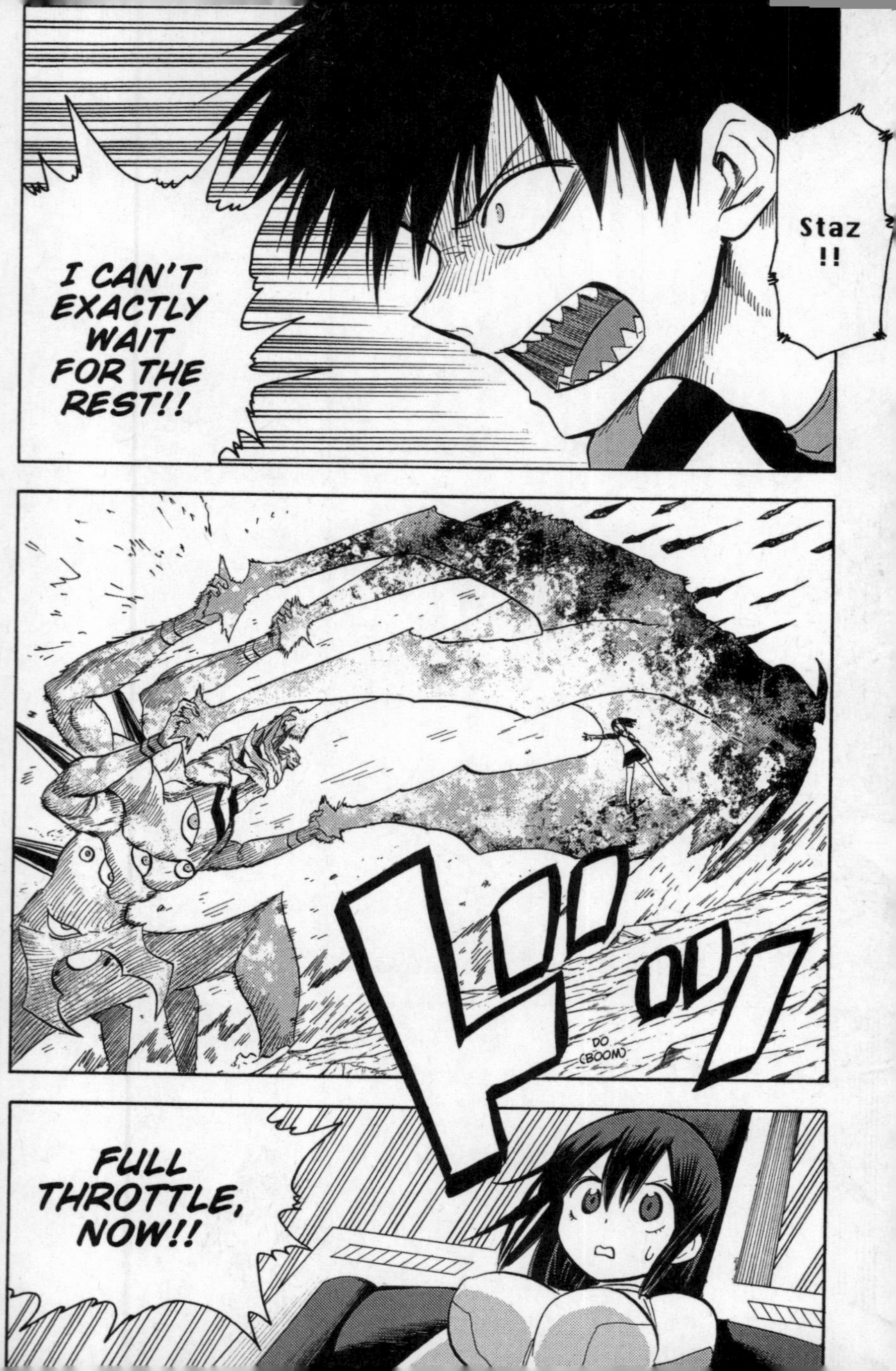
Staz !!
I CAN'T EXACTLY WAIT FOR THE REST!!
DO (BOOM)
FULL THROTTLE, NOW!!

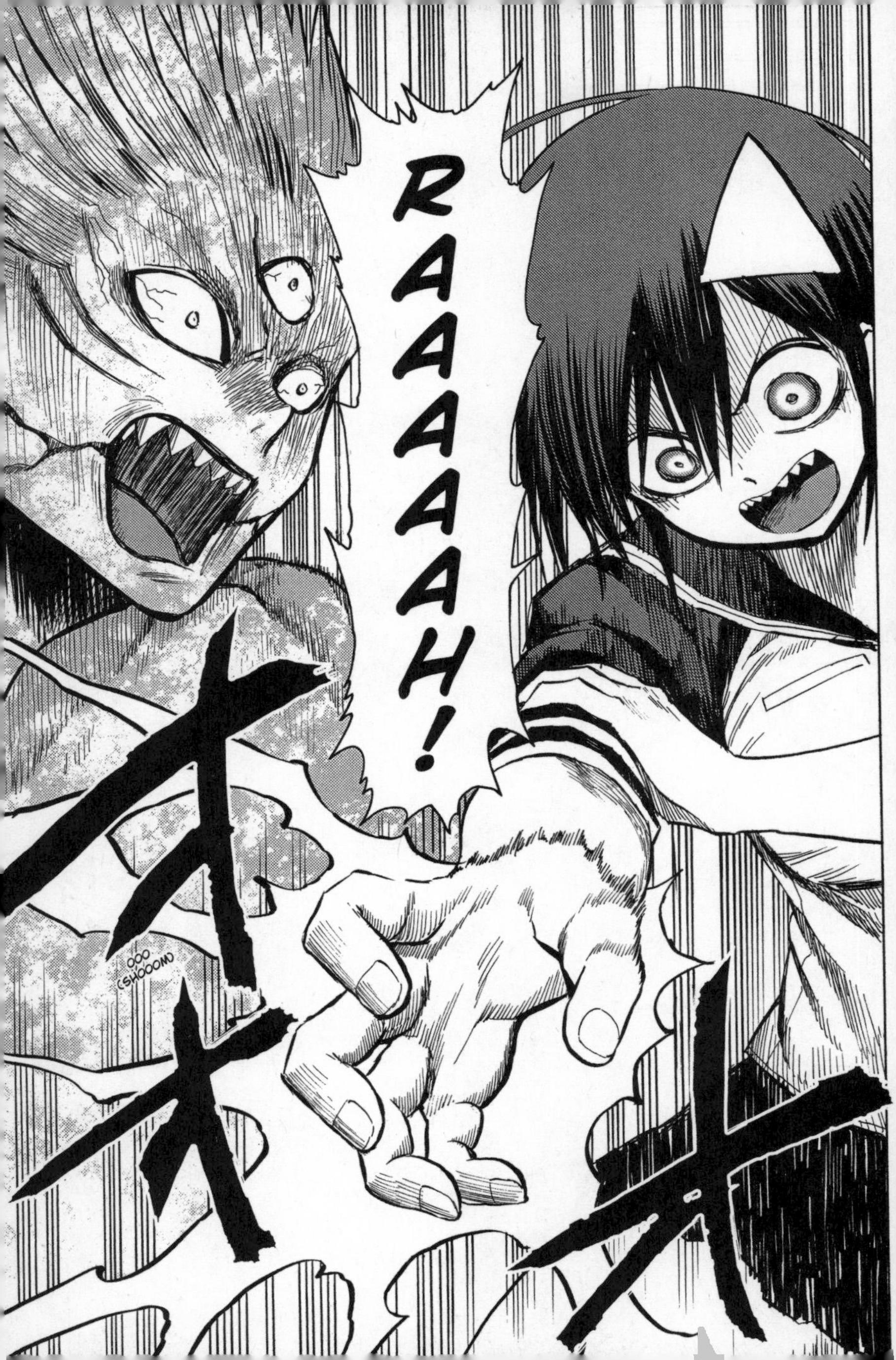
RAAAAAH!
OOO (SHOOOM)

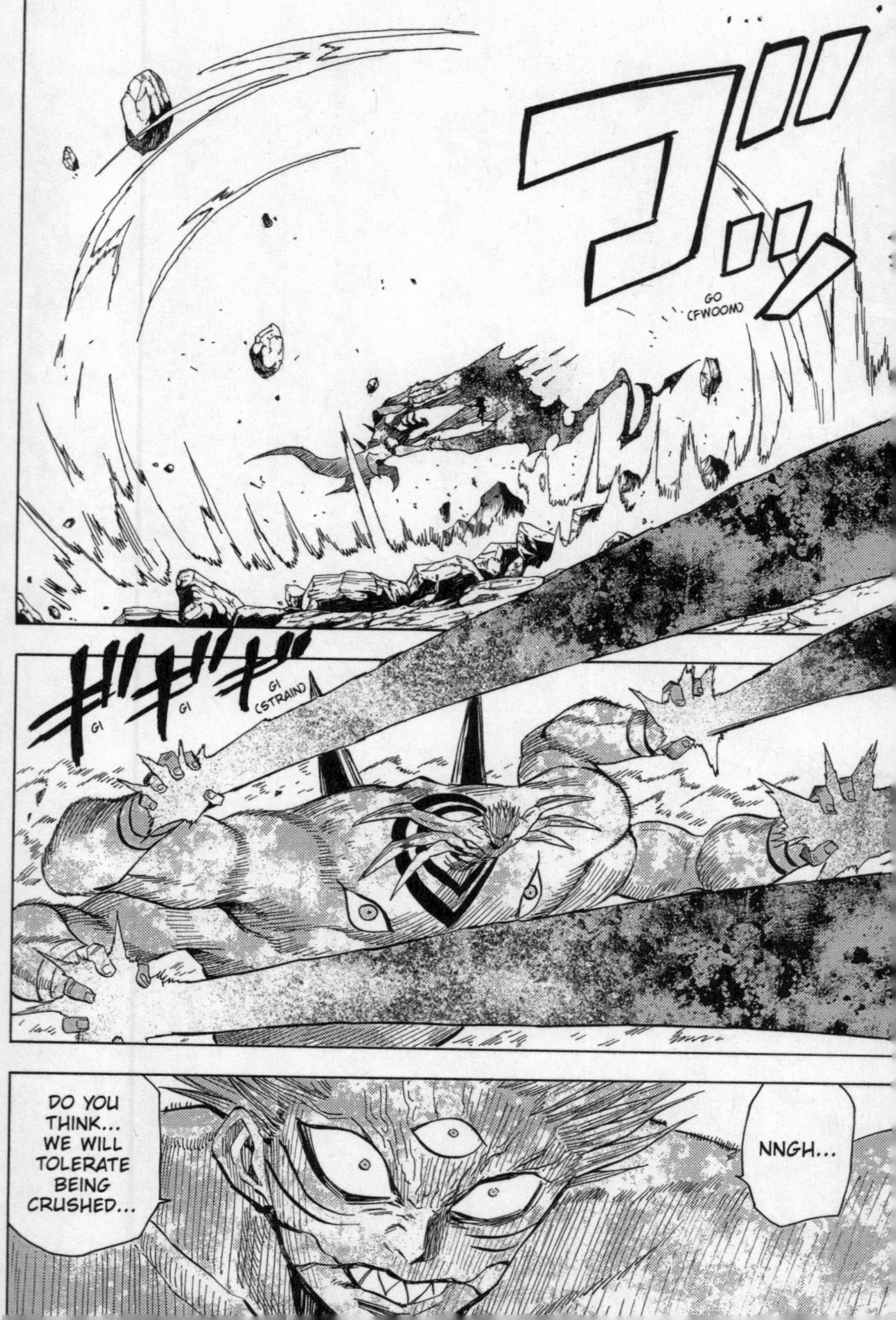
GO (FWOOM)
GI GI GI (STRAIN)
NNGH...
DO YOU THINK... WE WILL TOLERATE BEING CRUSHED...

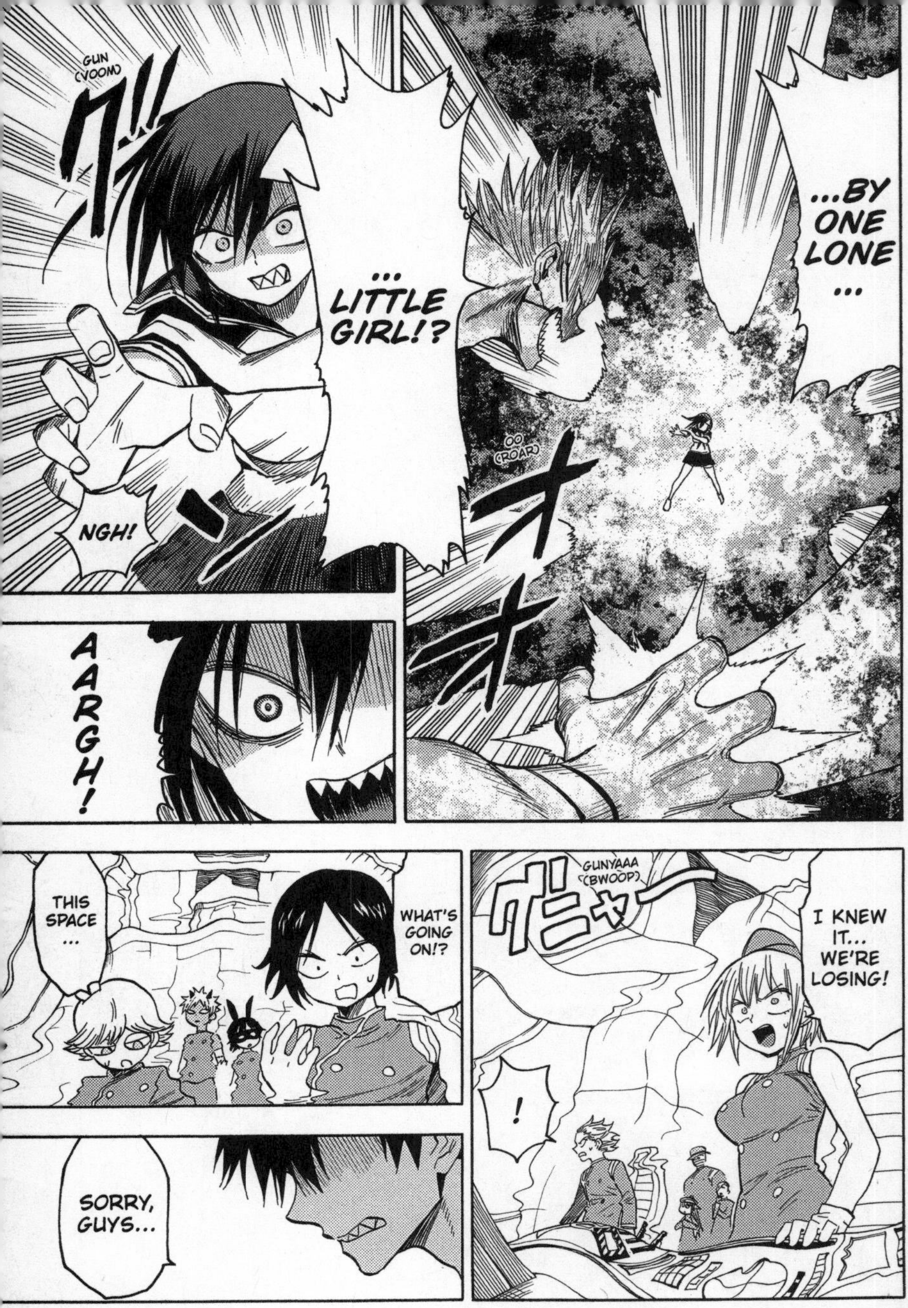
...BY ONE LONE ...
OO (ROAR)
GUN (VOOM)
... LITTLE GIRL!?
NGH!
AARGH!
GUNYAAA (BWOOP)
I KNEW IT... WE'RE LOSING!
!
WHAT'S GOING ON!?
THIS SPACE ...
SORRY, GUYS...

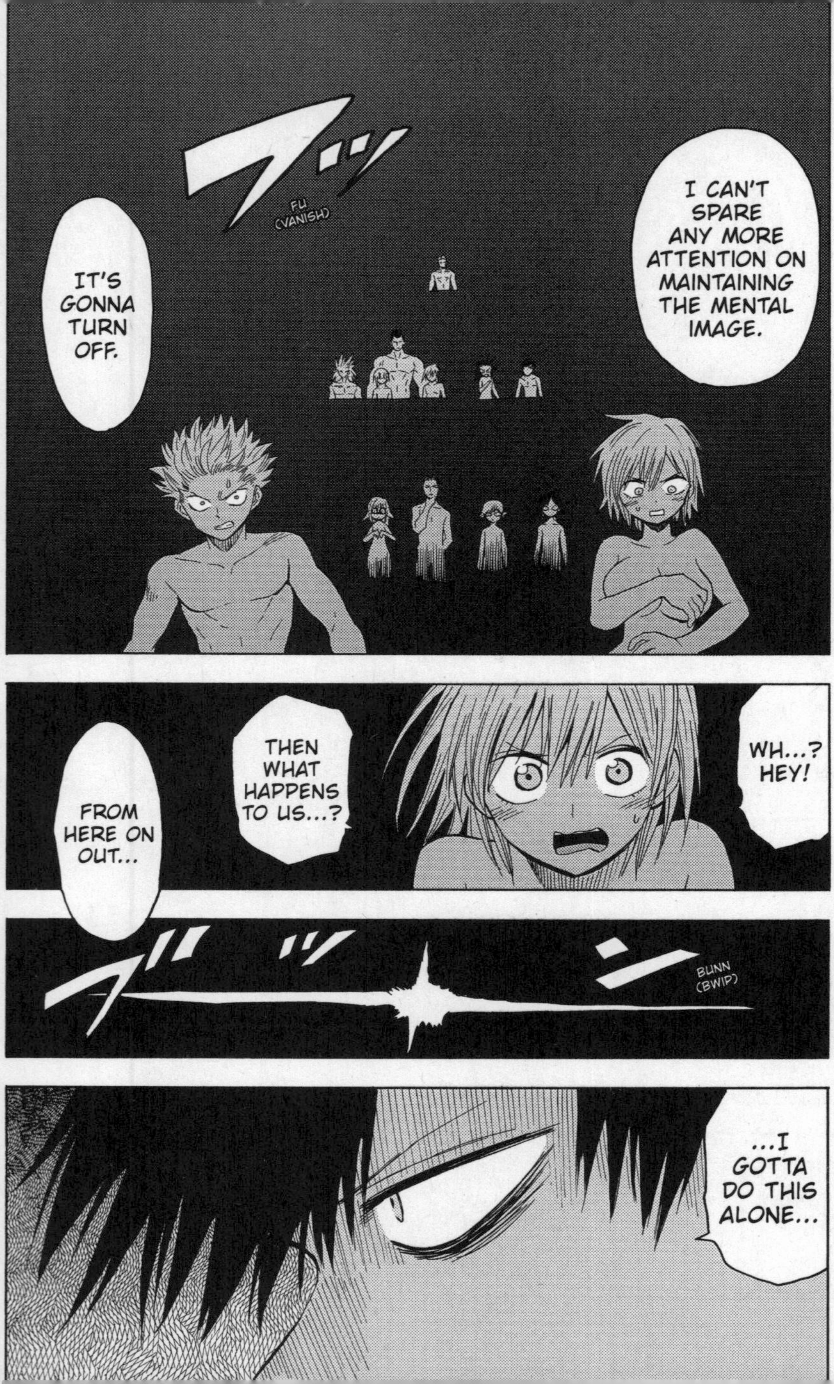
I CAN'T SPARE ANY MORE ATTENTION ON MAINTAINING THE MENTAL IMAGE.
FU (VANISH)
IT'S GONNA TURN OFF.
WH...? HEY!
THEN WHAT HAPPENS TO US...?
FROM HERE ON OUT...
BUNN (BWIP)
...I GOTTA DO THIS ALONE...

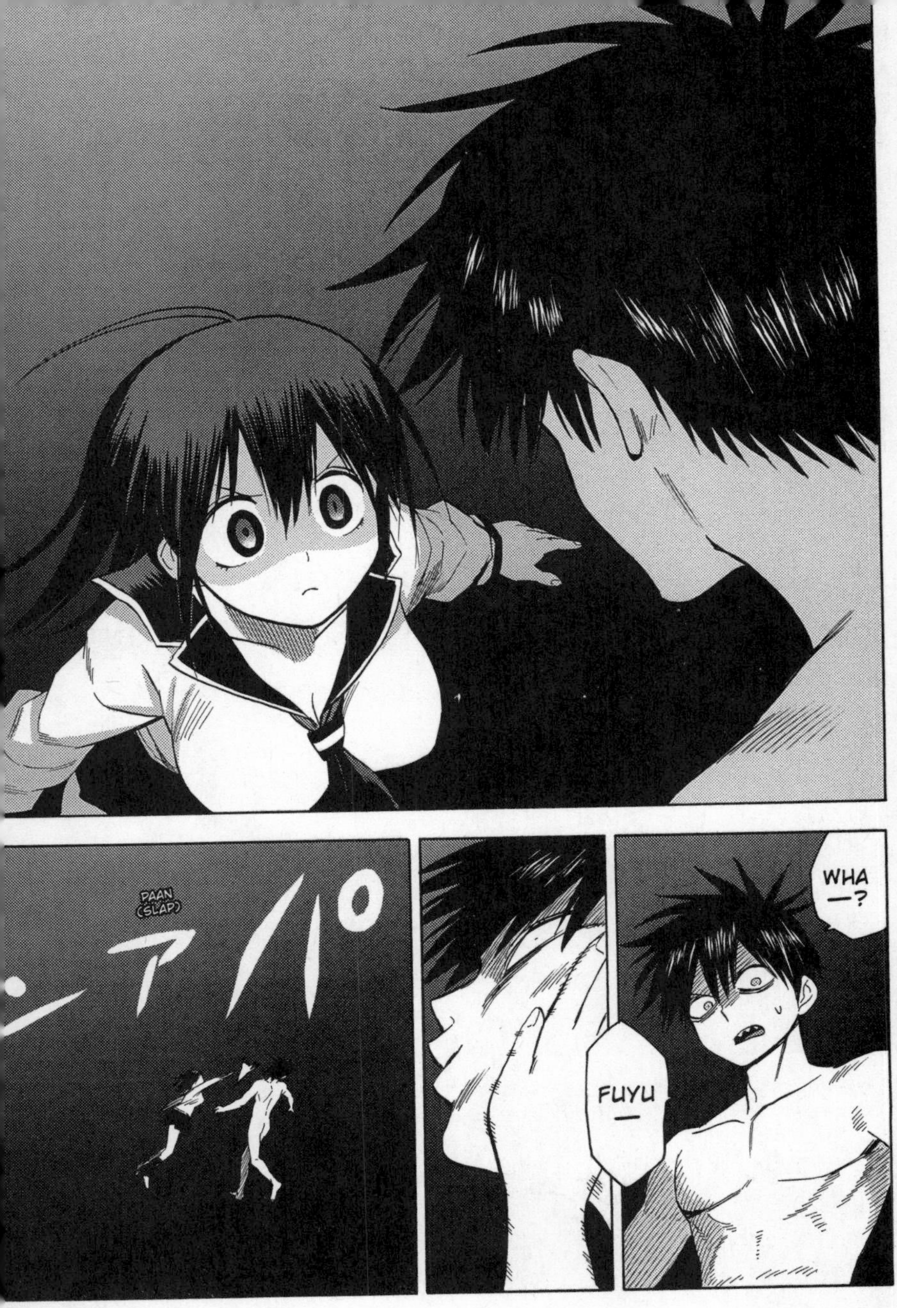
WHA—?
FUYU—
PAAN (SLAP)

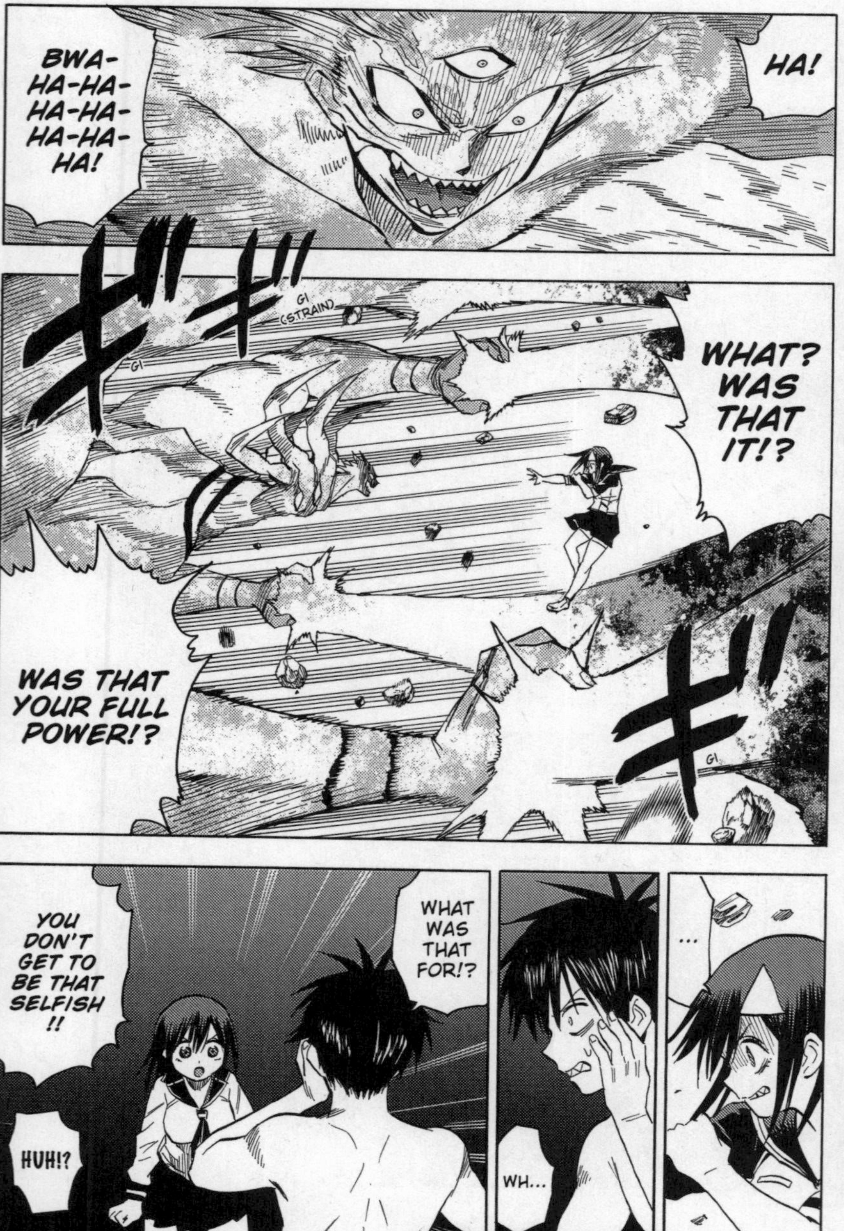
HA!
BWA-HA-HA-HA-HA-HA-HA-HA!
WHAT? WAS THAT IT!?
ギギ
GI (STRAIN)
GI
WAS THAT YOUR FULL POWER!?
ギ
GI
...
WH...
WHAT WAS THAT FOR!?
YOU DON'T GET TO BE THAT SELFISH!!
HUH!?

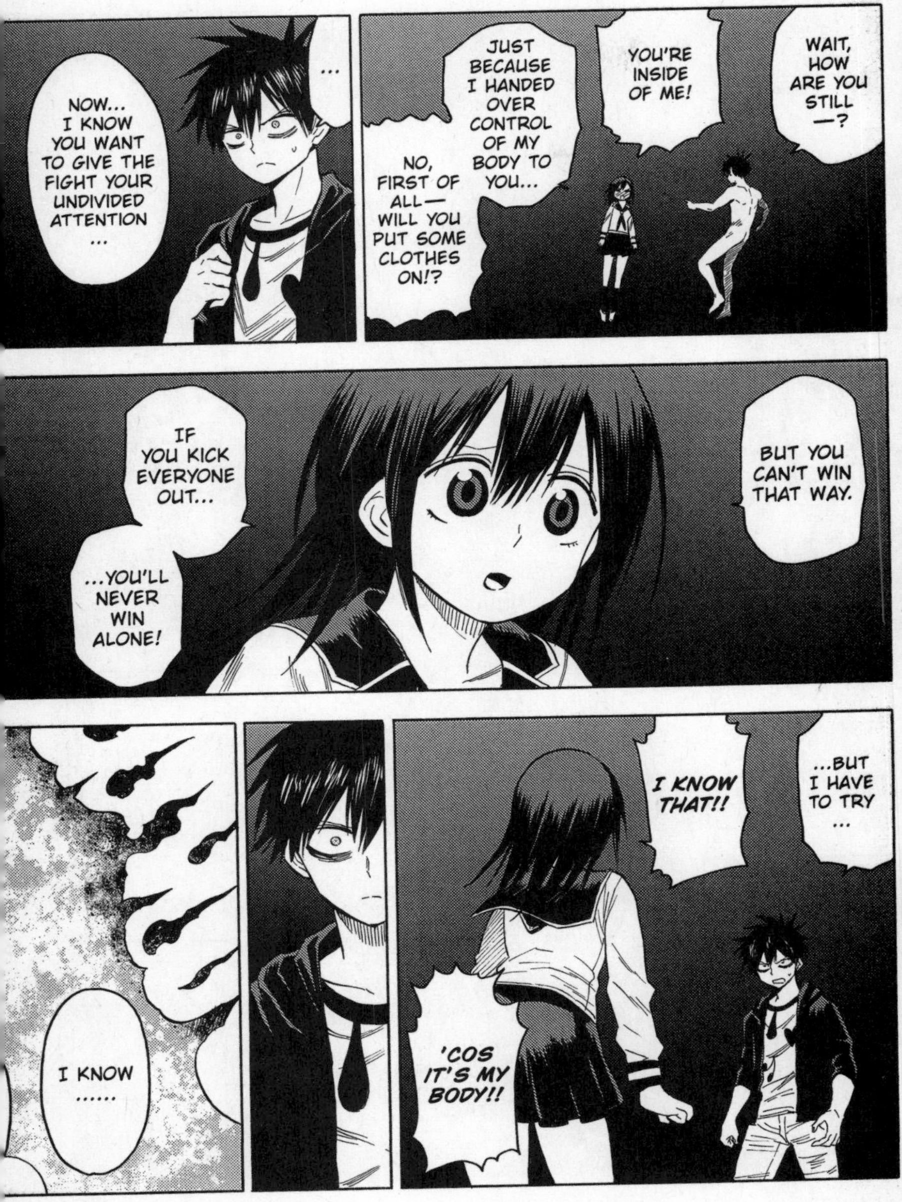
WAIT, HOW ARE YOU STILL —?
YOU'RE INSIDE OF ME!
JUST BECAUSE I HANDED OVER CONTROL OF MY BODY TO YOU...
NO, FIRST OF ALL— WILL YOU PUT SOME CLOTHES ON!?
...
NOW... I KNOW YOU WANT TO GIVE THE FIGHT YOUR UNDIVIDED ATTENTION ...
BUT YOU CAN'T WIN THAT WAY.
IF YOU KICK EVERYONE OUT...
...YOU'LL NEVER WIN ALONE!
...BUT I HAVE TO TRY ...
I KNOW THAT!!
'COS IT'S MY BODY!!
I KNOW ......

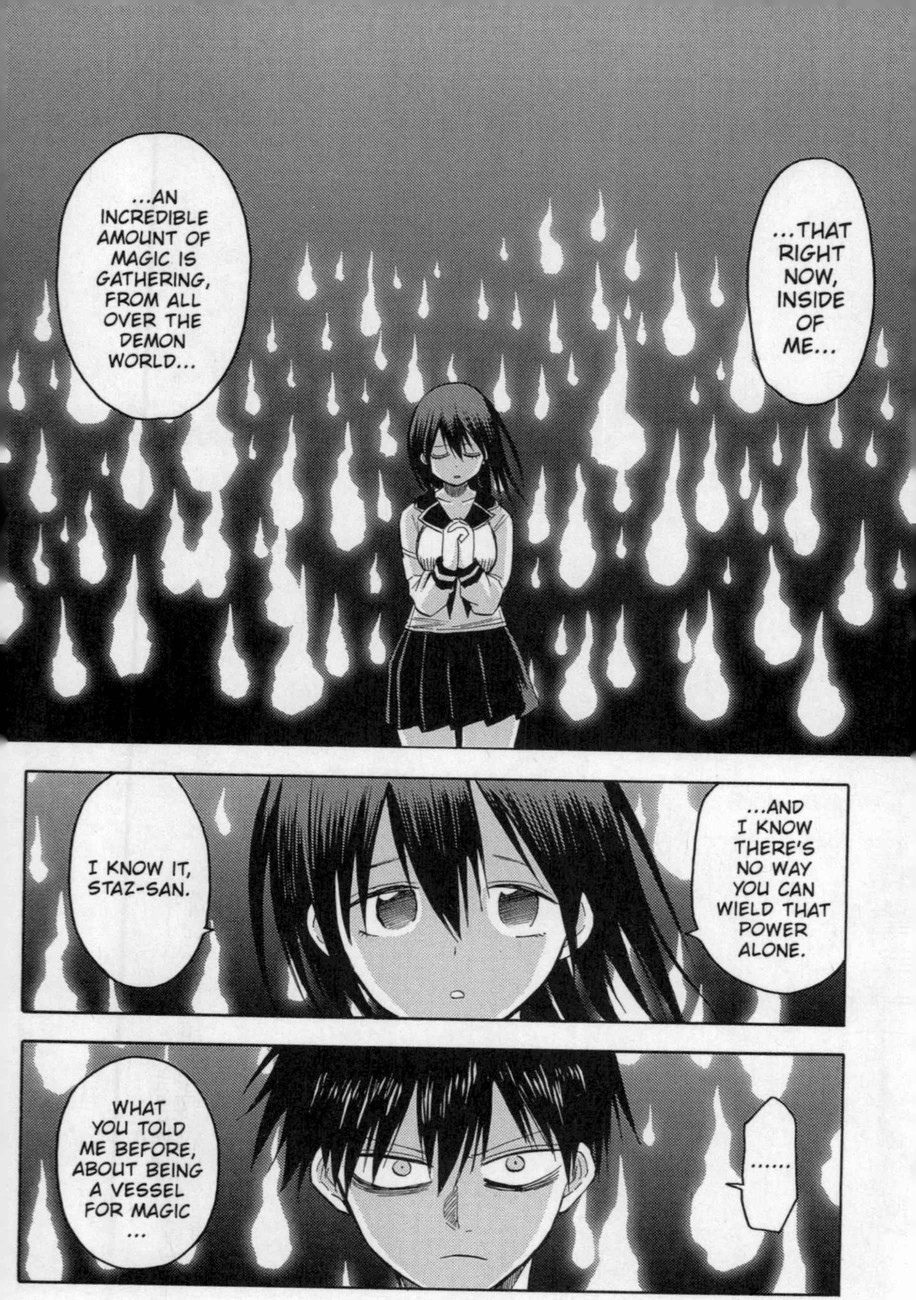
...THAT RIGHT NOW, INSIDE OF ME...
...AN INCREDIBLE AMOUNT OF MAGIC IS GATHERING, FROM ALL OVER THE DEMON WORLD...
...AND I KNOW THERE'S NO WAY YOU CAN WIELD THAT POWER ALONE.
I KNOW IT, STAZ-SAN.
......
WHAT YOU TOLD ME BEFORE, ABOUT BEING A VESSEL FOR MAGIC ...

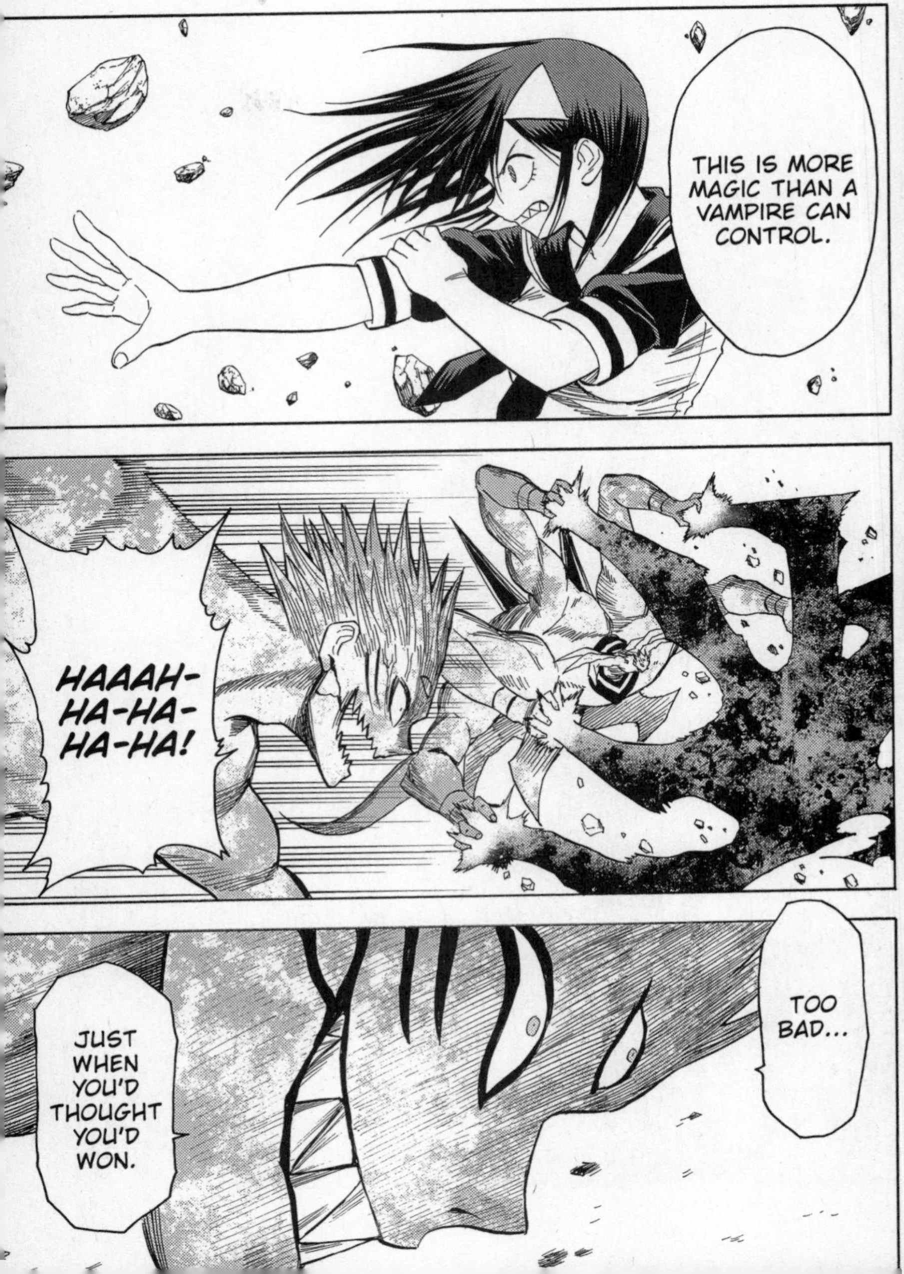
THIS IS MORE MAGIC THAN A VAMPIRE CAN CONTROL.
HAAAH-HA-HA-HA-HA!
TOO BAD...
JUST WHEN YOU'D THOUGHT YOU'D WON.

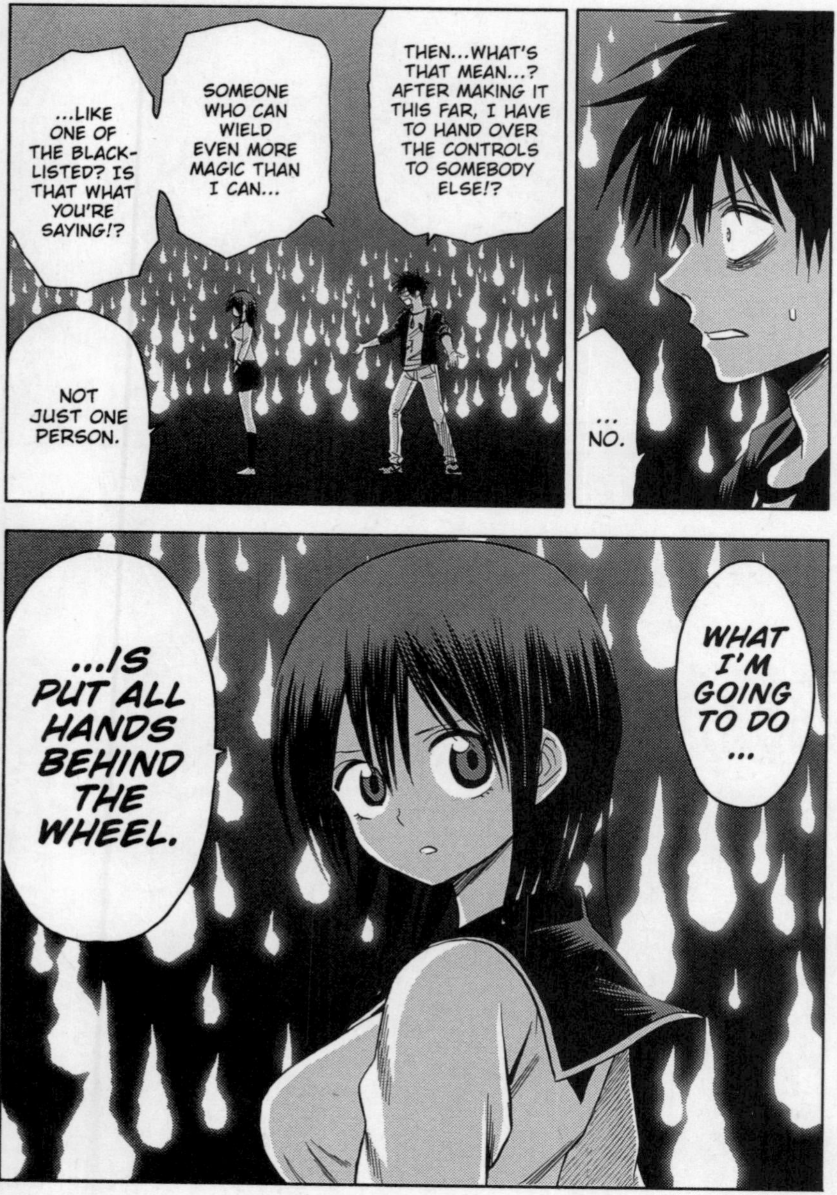
...
NO.
THEN...WHAT'S THAT MEAN...? AFTER MAKING IT THIS FAR, I HAVE TO HAND OVER THE CONTROLS TO SOMEBODY ELSE!?
SOMEONE WHO CAN WIELD EVEN MORE MAGIC THAN I CAN...
...LIKE ONE OF THE BLACK-LISTED? IS THAT WHAT YOU'RE SAYING!?
NOT JUST ONE PERSON.
WHAT I'M GOING TO DO ...
...IS PUT ALL HANDS BEHIND THE WHEEL.

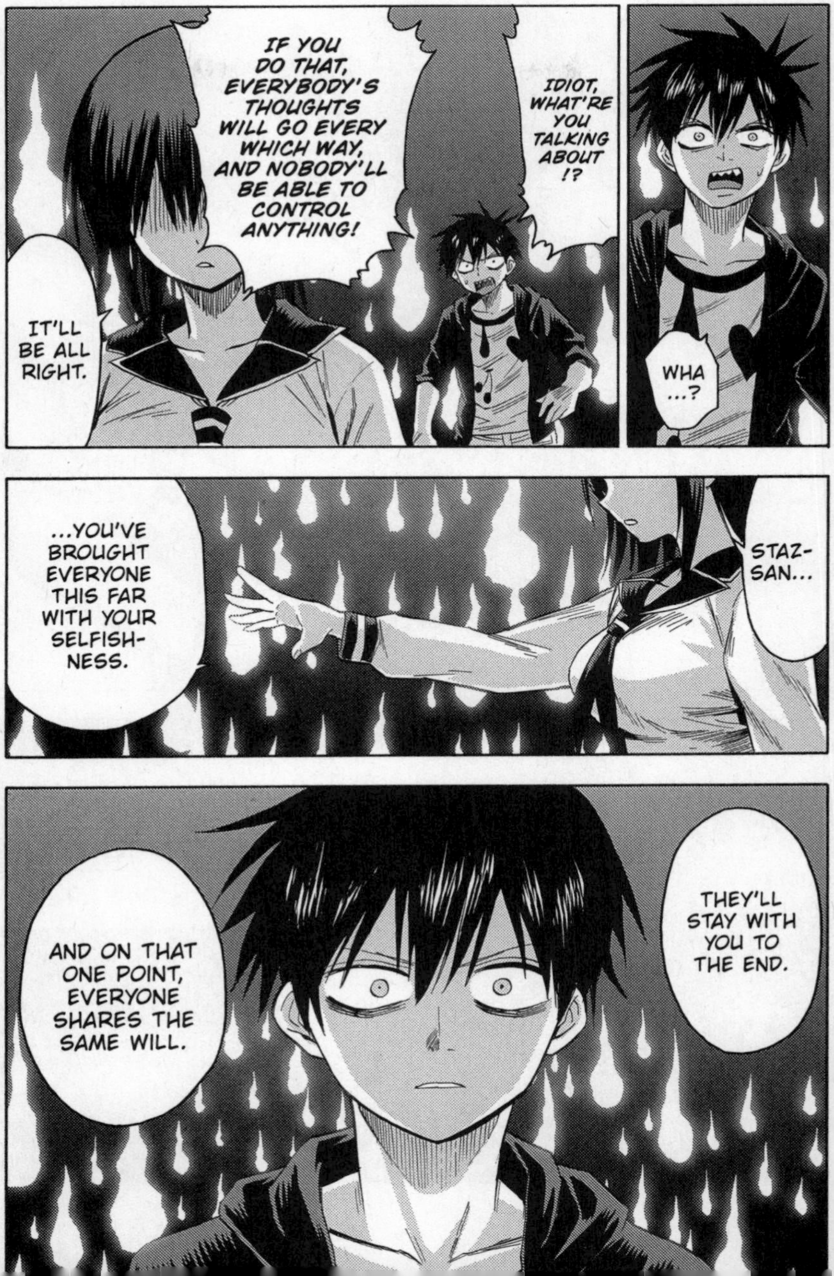
WHA ...?
IDIOT, WHAT'RE YOU TALKING ABOUT !?
IF YOU DO THAT, EVERYBODY'S THOUGHTS WILL GO EVERY WHICH WAY, AND NOBODY'LL BE ABLE TO CONTROL ANYTHING!
IT'LL BE ALL RIGHT.
STAZ-SAN...
...YOU'VE BROUGHT EVERYONE THIS FAR WITH YOUR SELFISH-NESS.
THEY'LL STAY WITH YOU TO THE END.
AND ON THAT ONE POINT, EVERYONE SHARES THE SAME WILL.

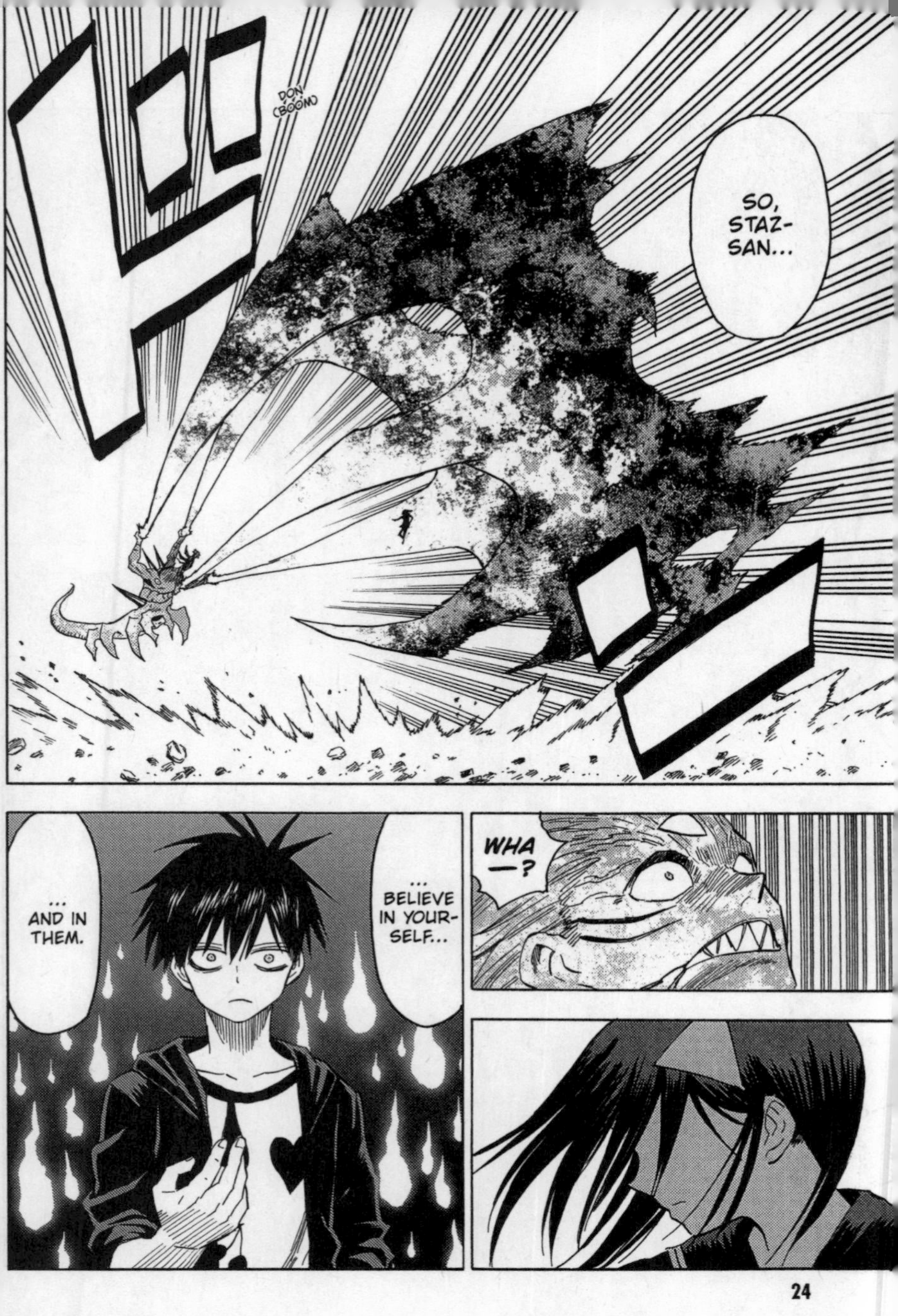
SO, STAZ-SAN...
DON (BOOM)
WHA—?
... BELIEVE IN YOURSELF...
... AND IN THEM.

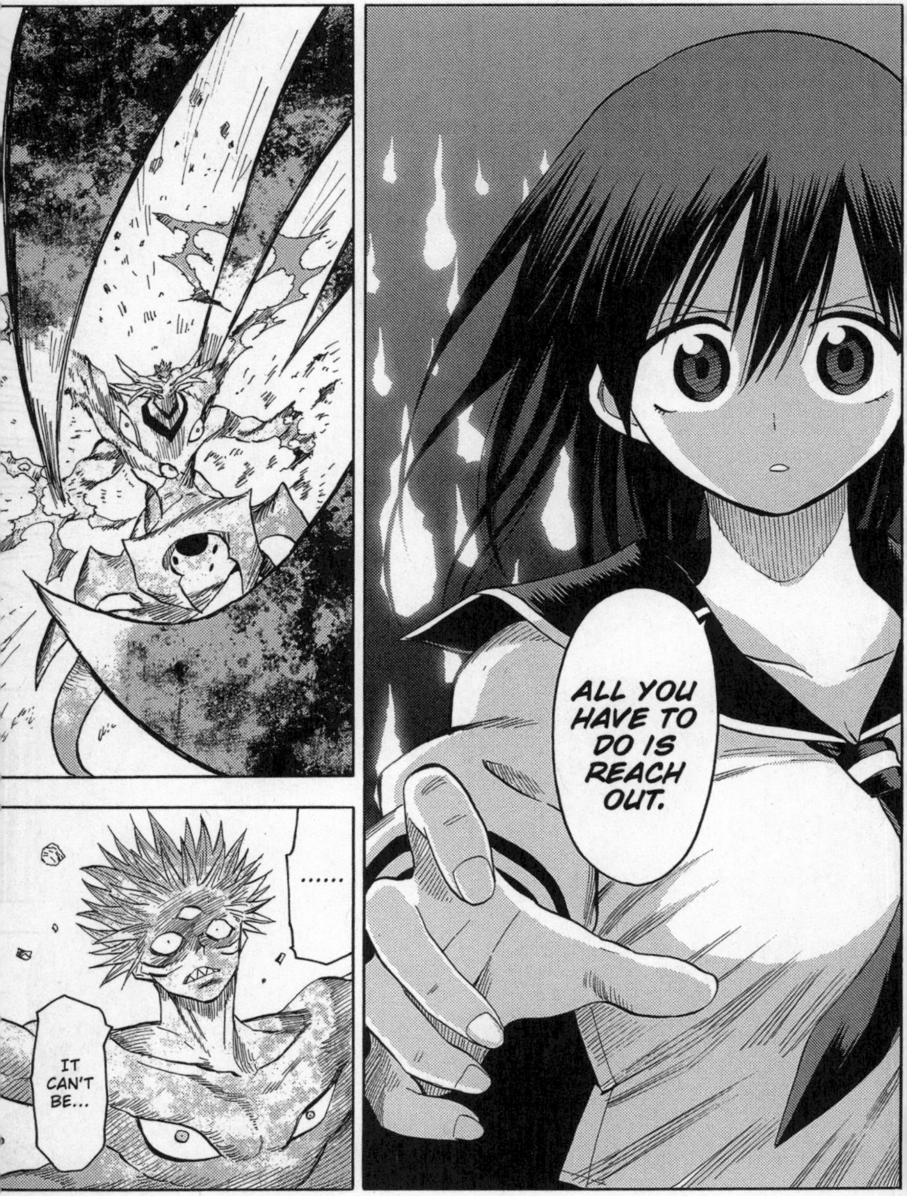
ALL YOU HAVE TO DO IS REACH OUT.
....
IT CAN'T BE...

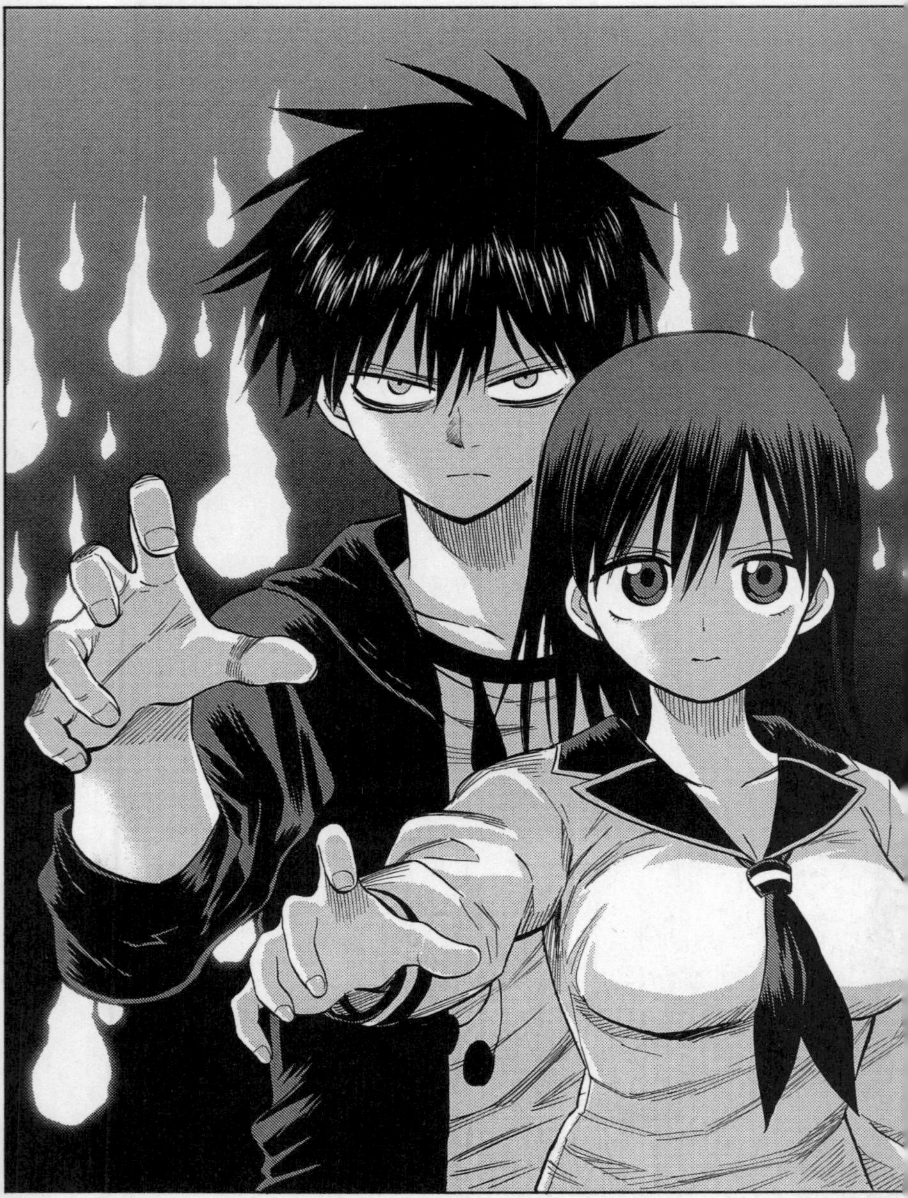

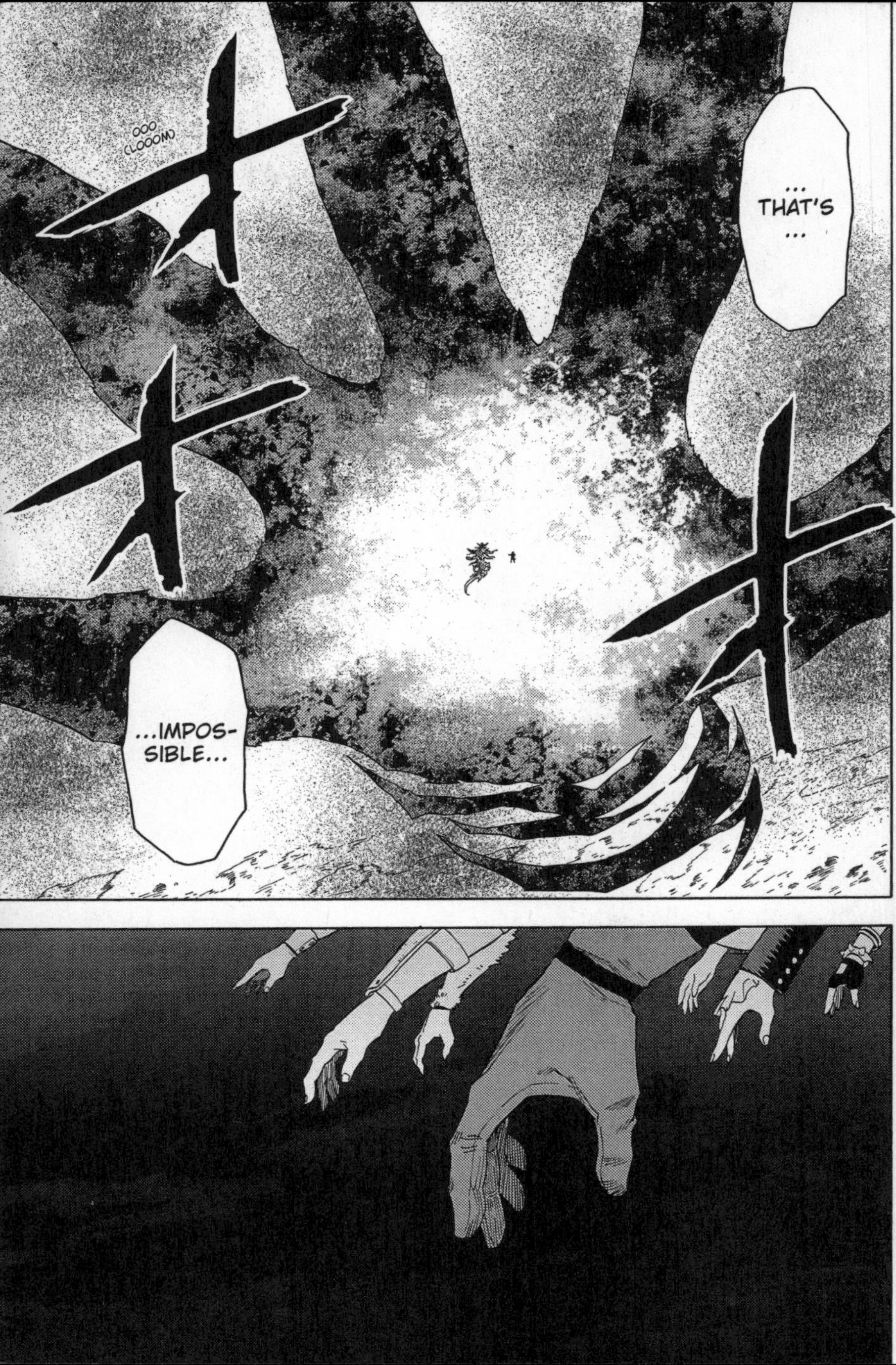
...THAT'S...
OOO (LOOOM)
...IMPOSSIBLE...

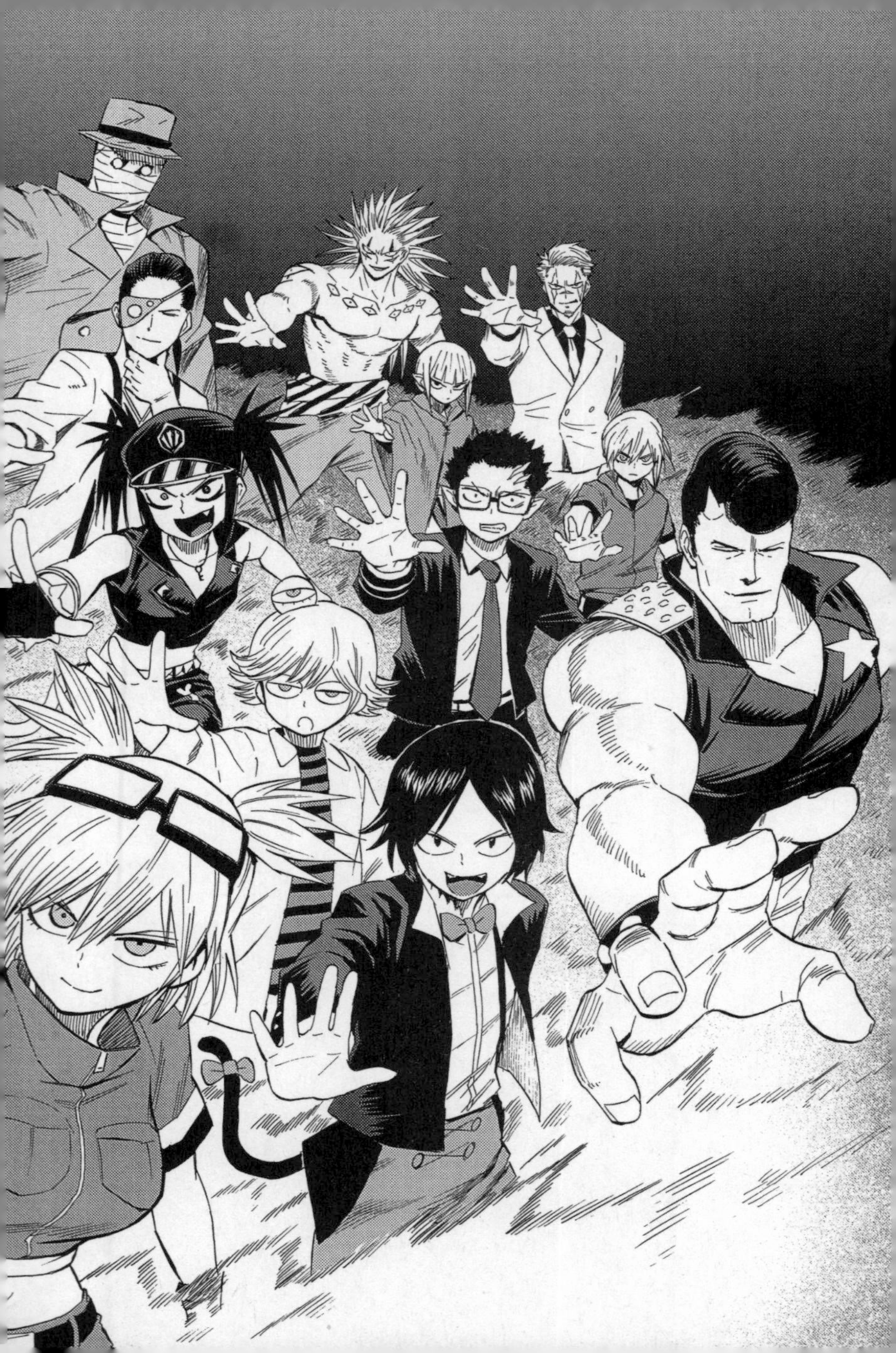

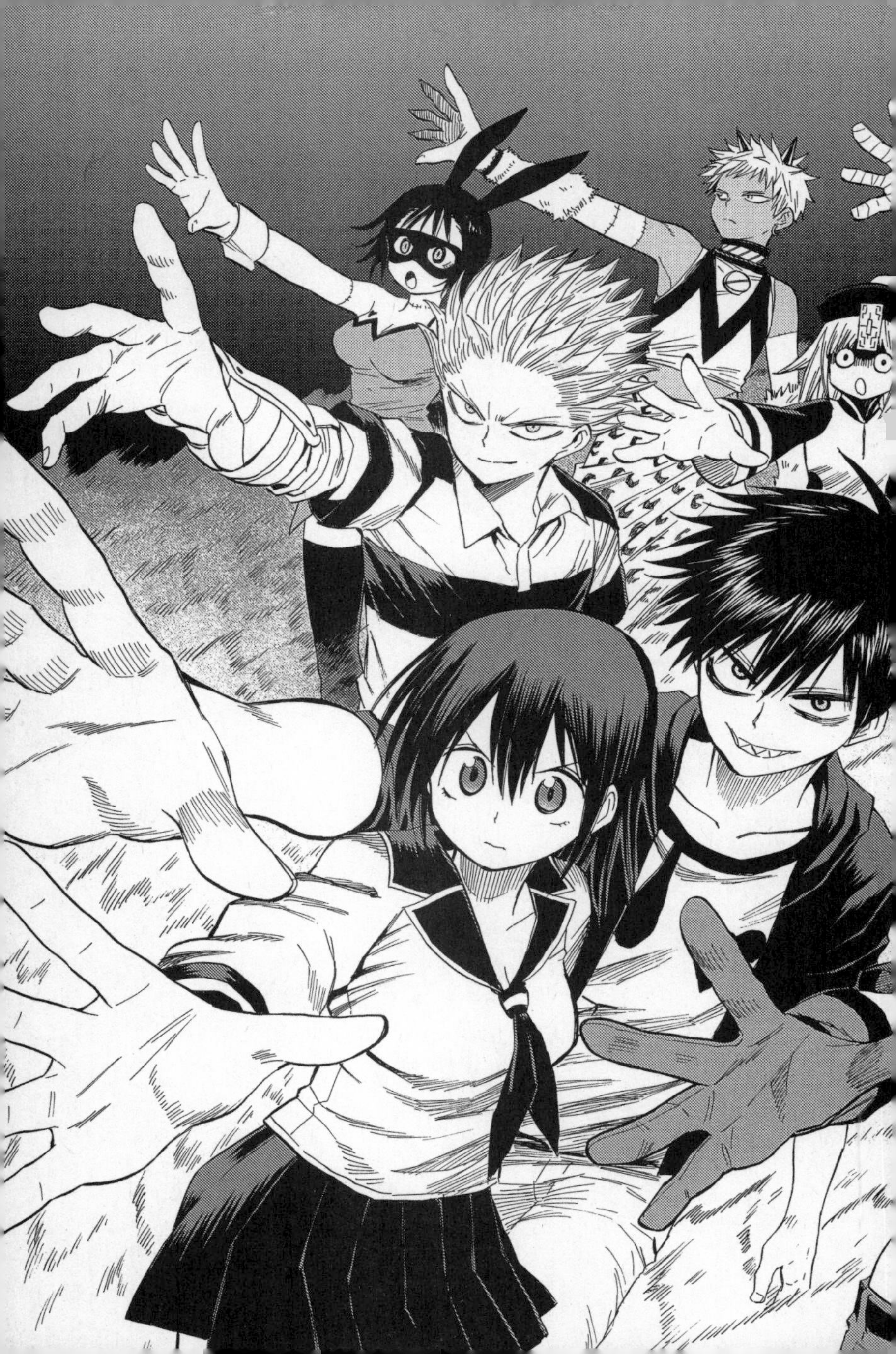

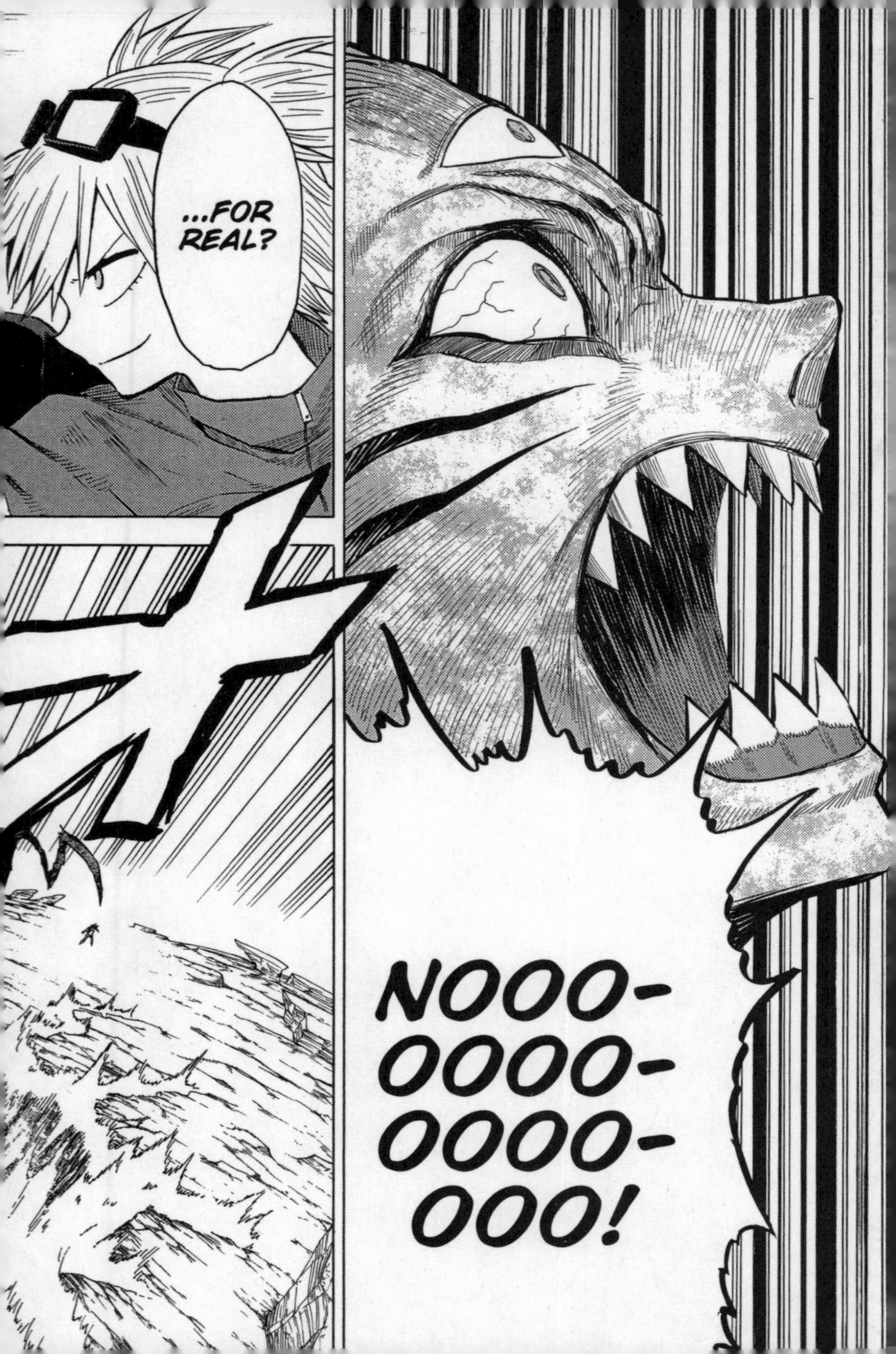
NOOO-OOOO-OOOO-OOO!
...FOR REAL?

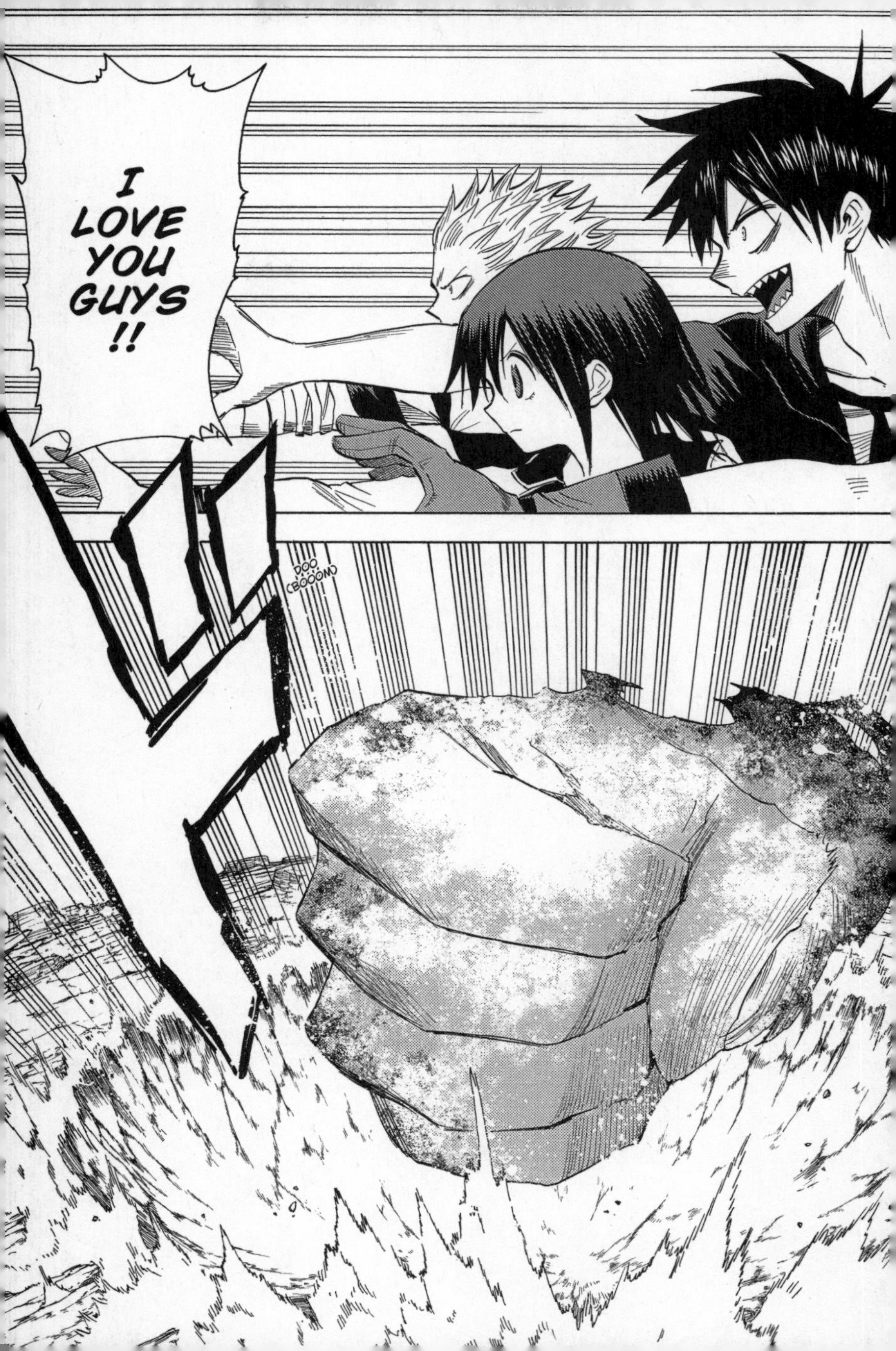
I LOVE YOU GUYS!!
DOO... (BOOOM)

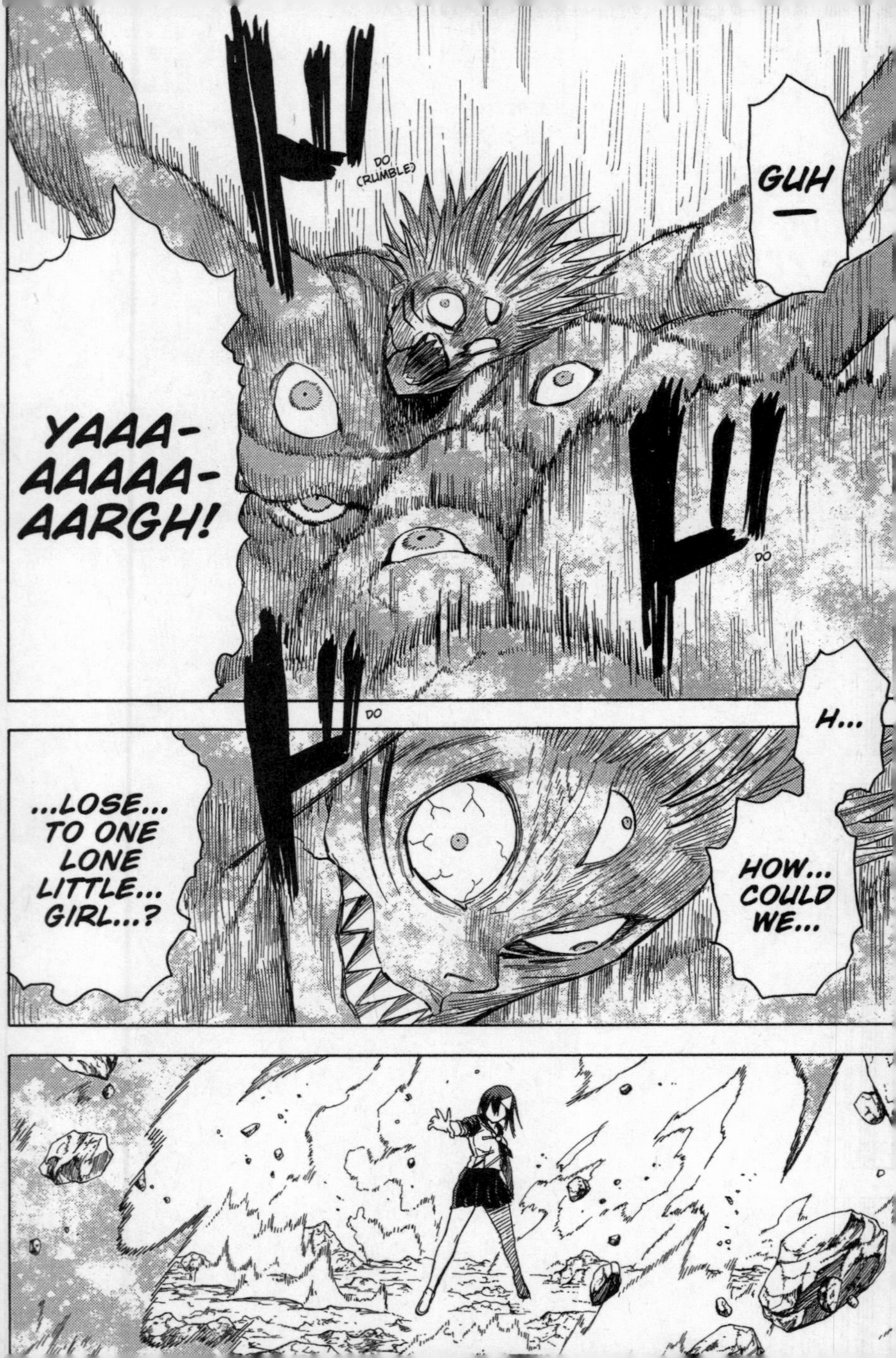
GUH —
DO (RUMBLE)
DO
YAAAA-AAAAA-AARGH!
DO
H...
HOW... COULD WE...
...LOSE... TO ONE LONE LITTLE... GIRL...?

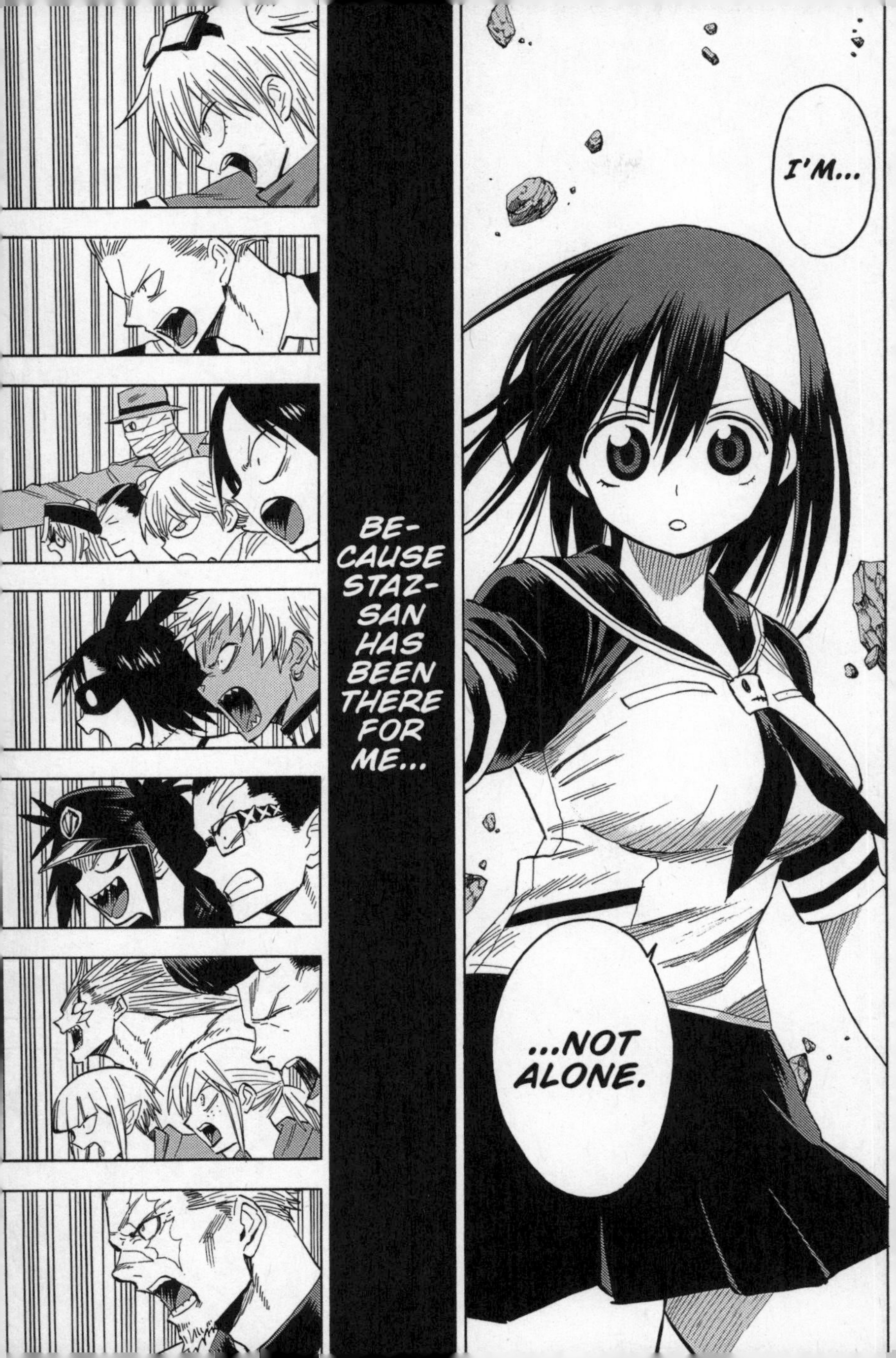
I'M...
...NOT ALONE.
BE-CAUSE STAZ-SAN HAS BEEN THERE FOR ME...

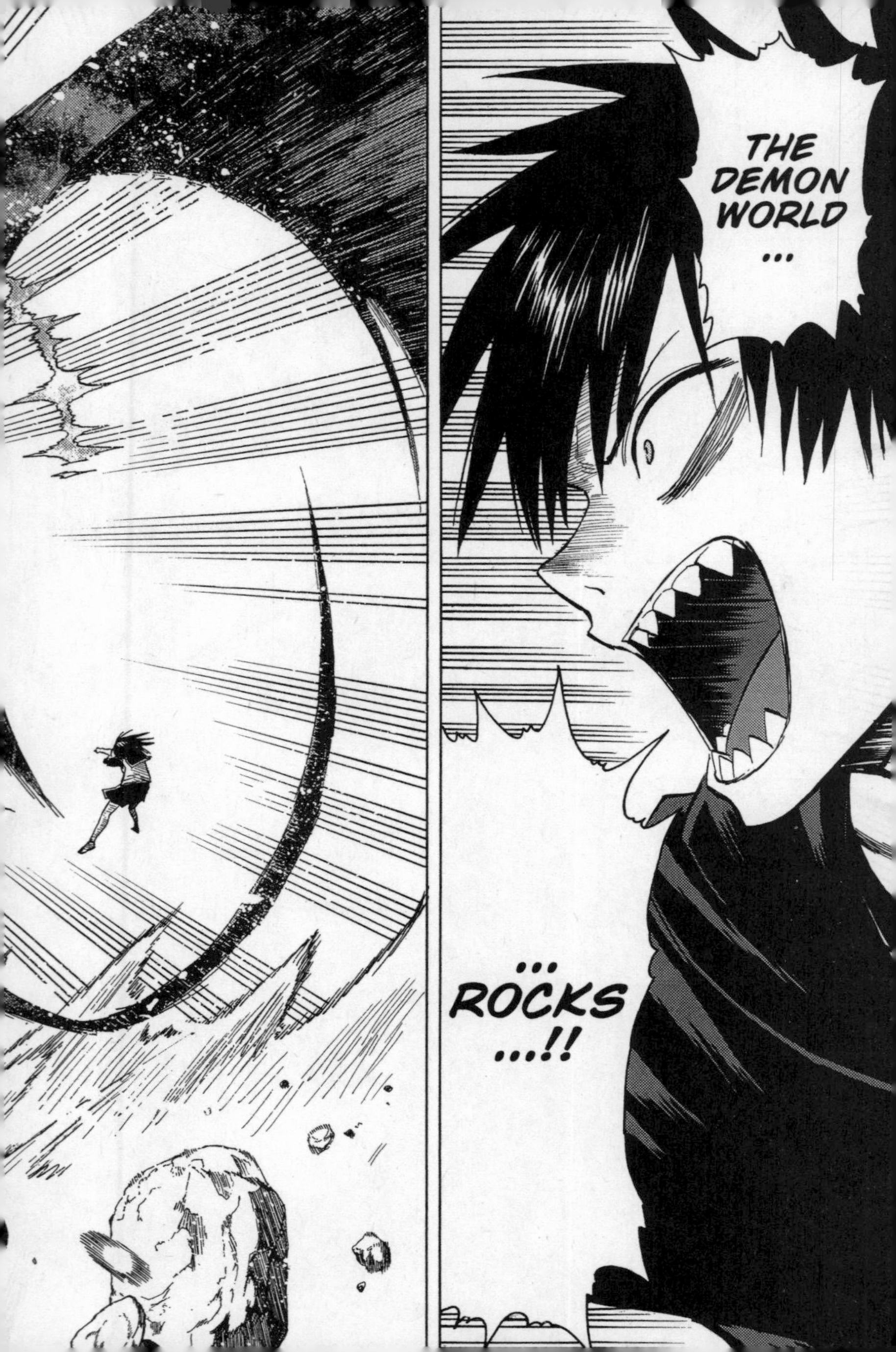
THE DEMON WORLD ...
... RÖCKS ...!!

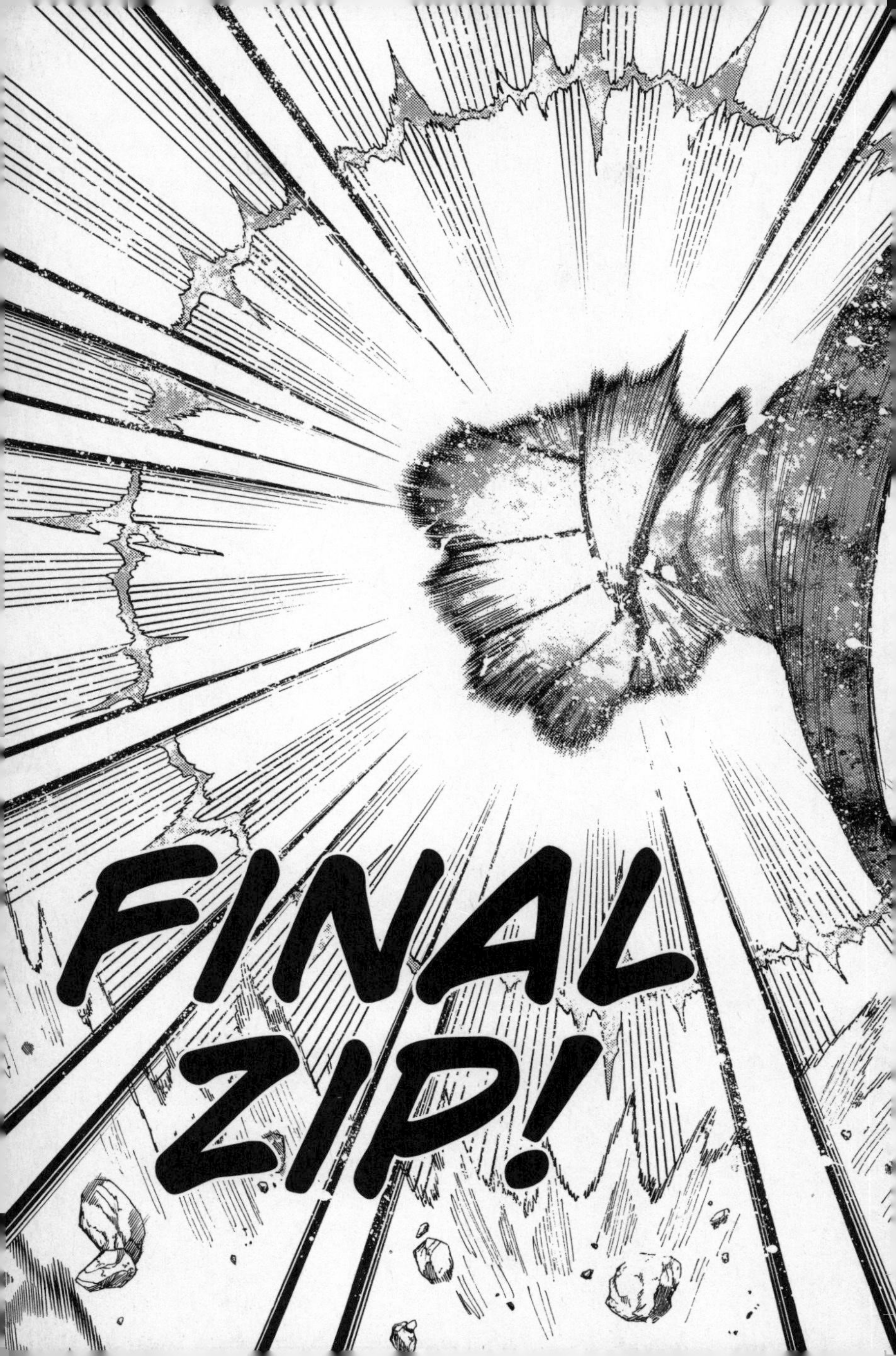
FINAL ZIP!

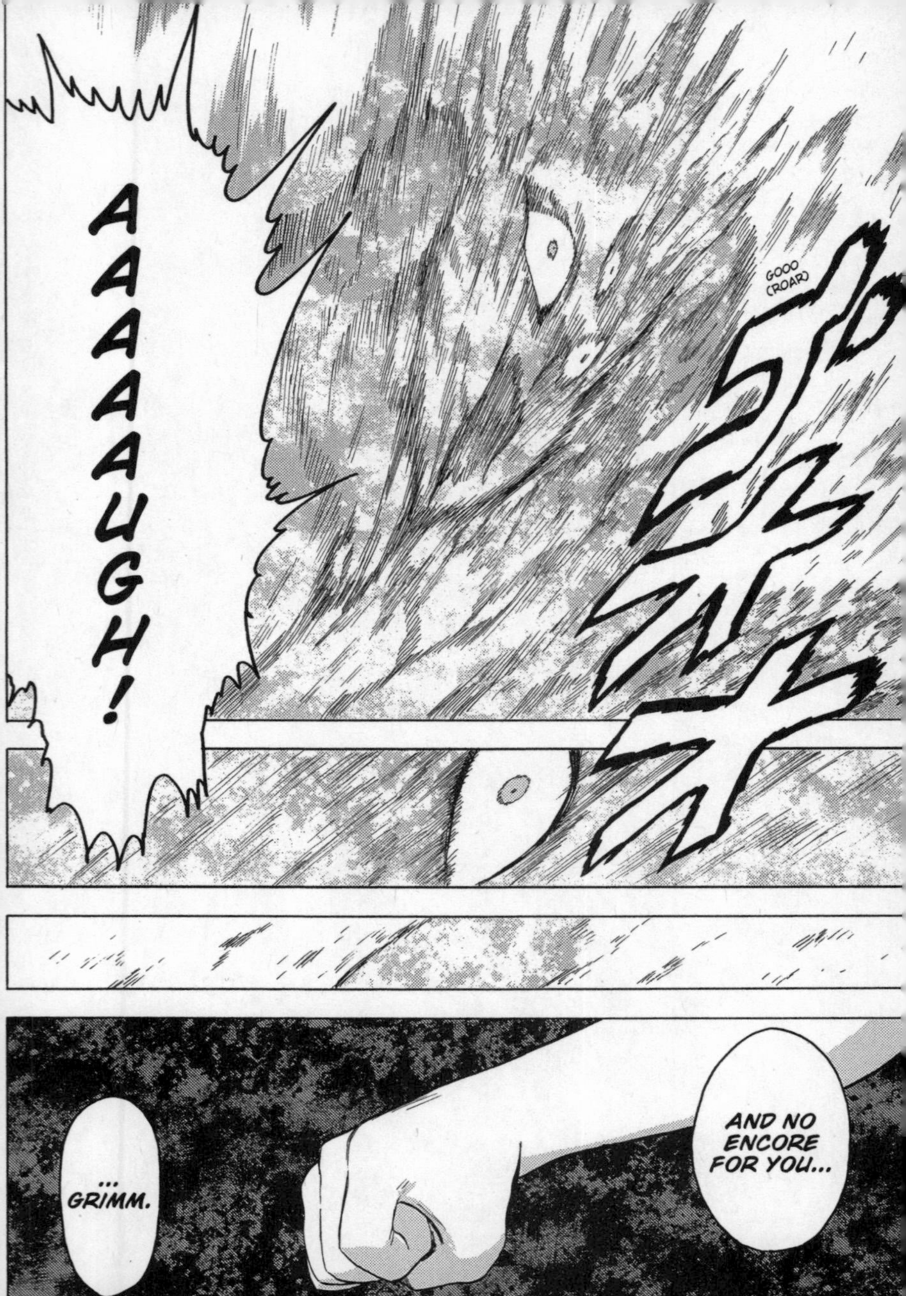
GOOO (ROAR)
AAAAAUGH!
AND NO ENCORE FOR YOU...
...GRIMM.
To Be Continued

BLOOD LAD

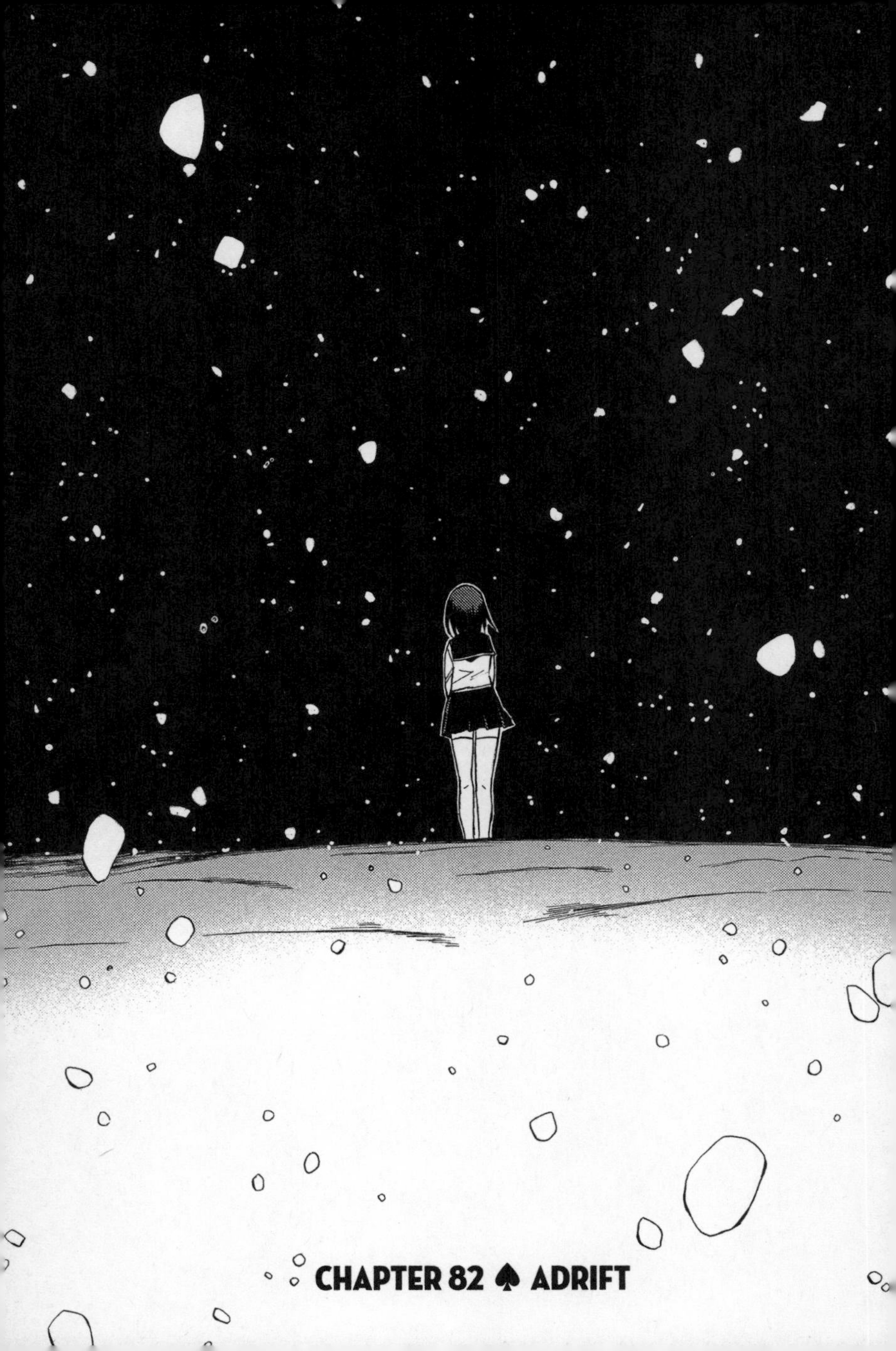
CHAPTER 82 ♠ ADRIFT

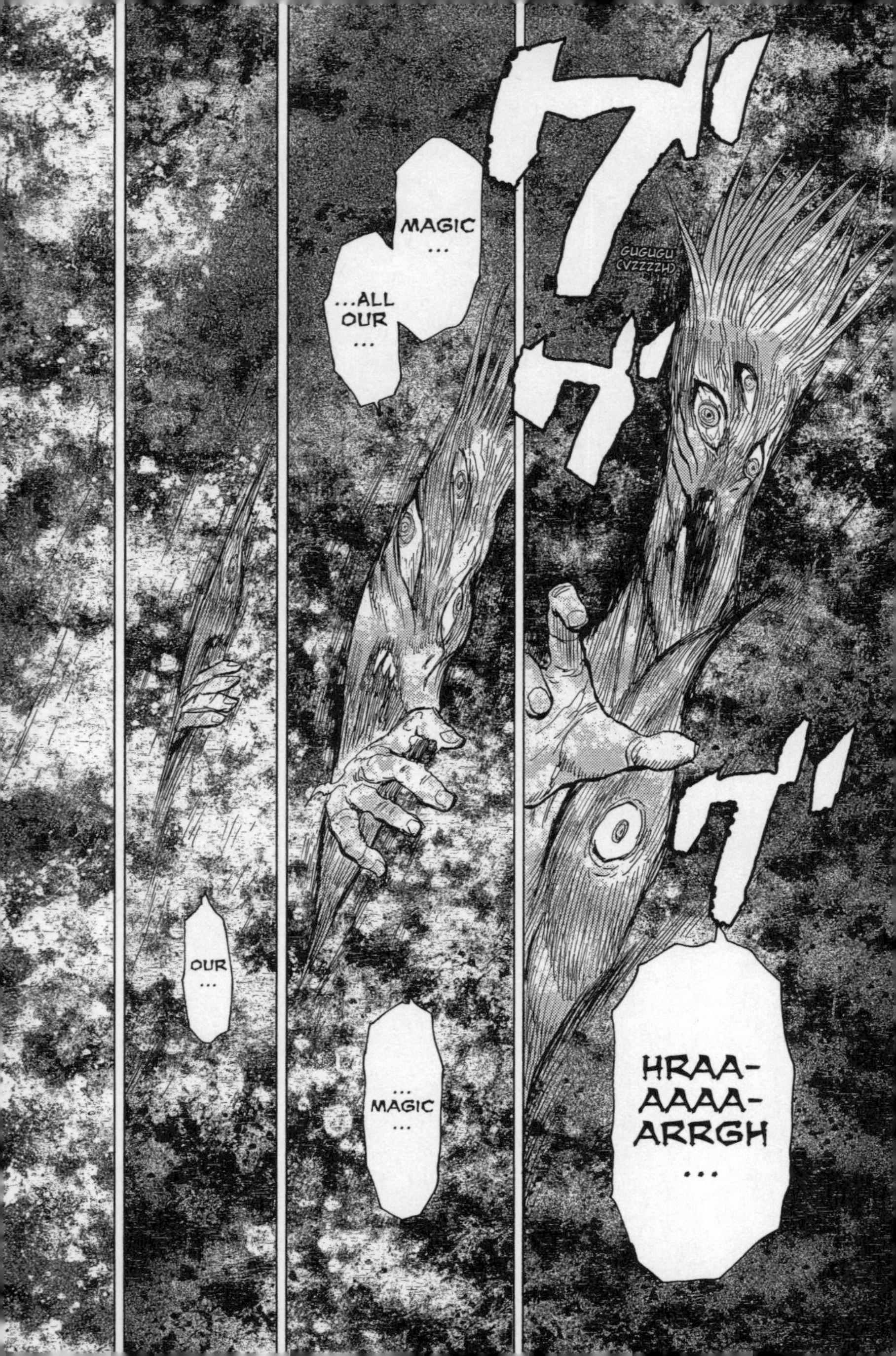
GUGUGU (VZZZZH)
HRAA-AAAA-ARRGH ...
MAGIC ...
...ALL OUR ...
... MAGIC ...
OUR ...

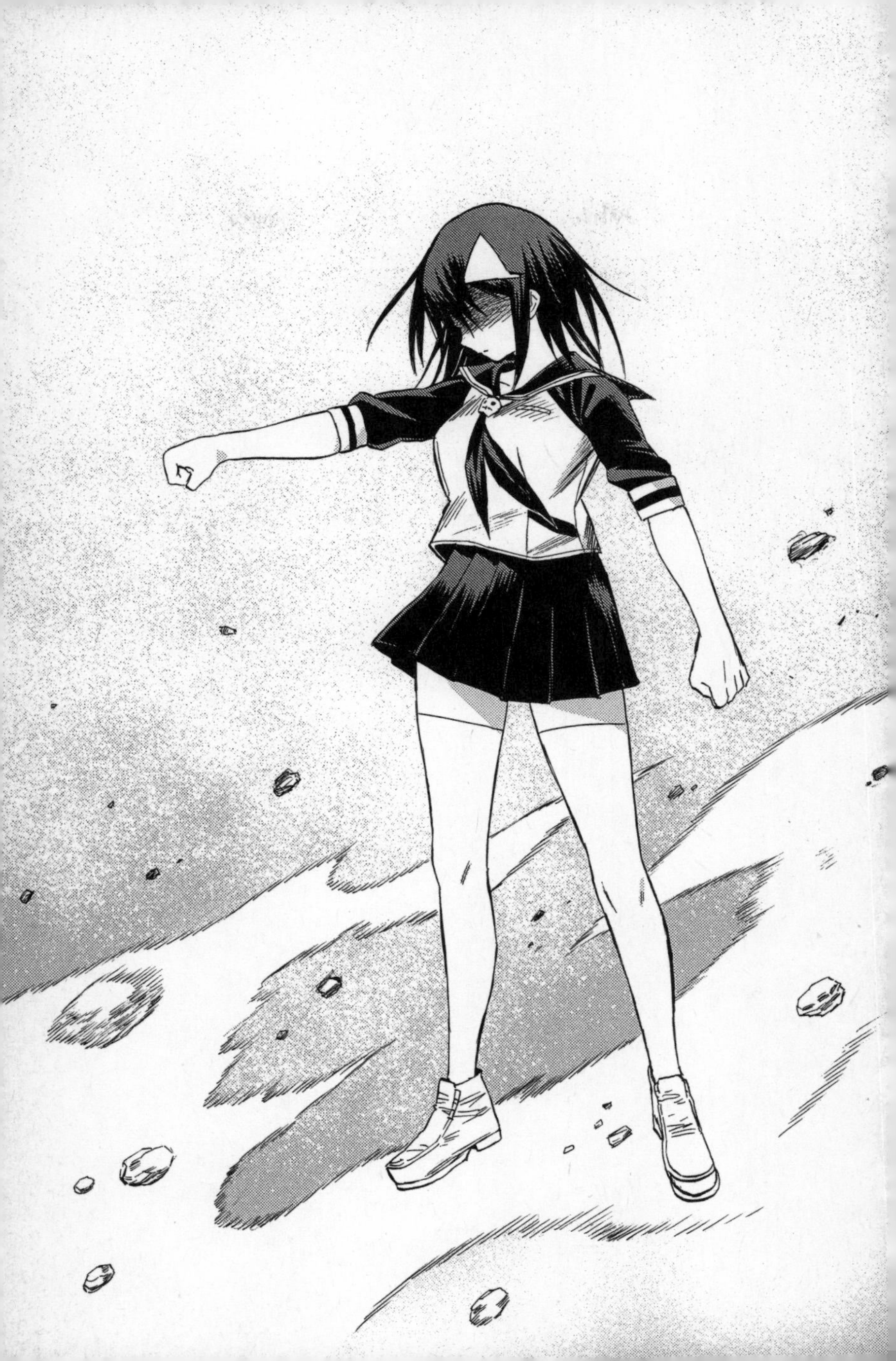

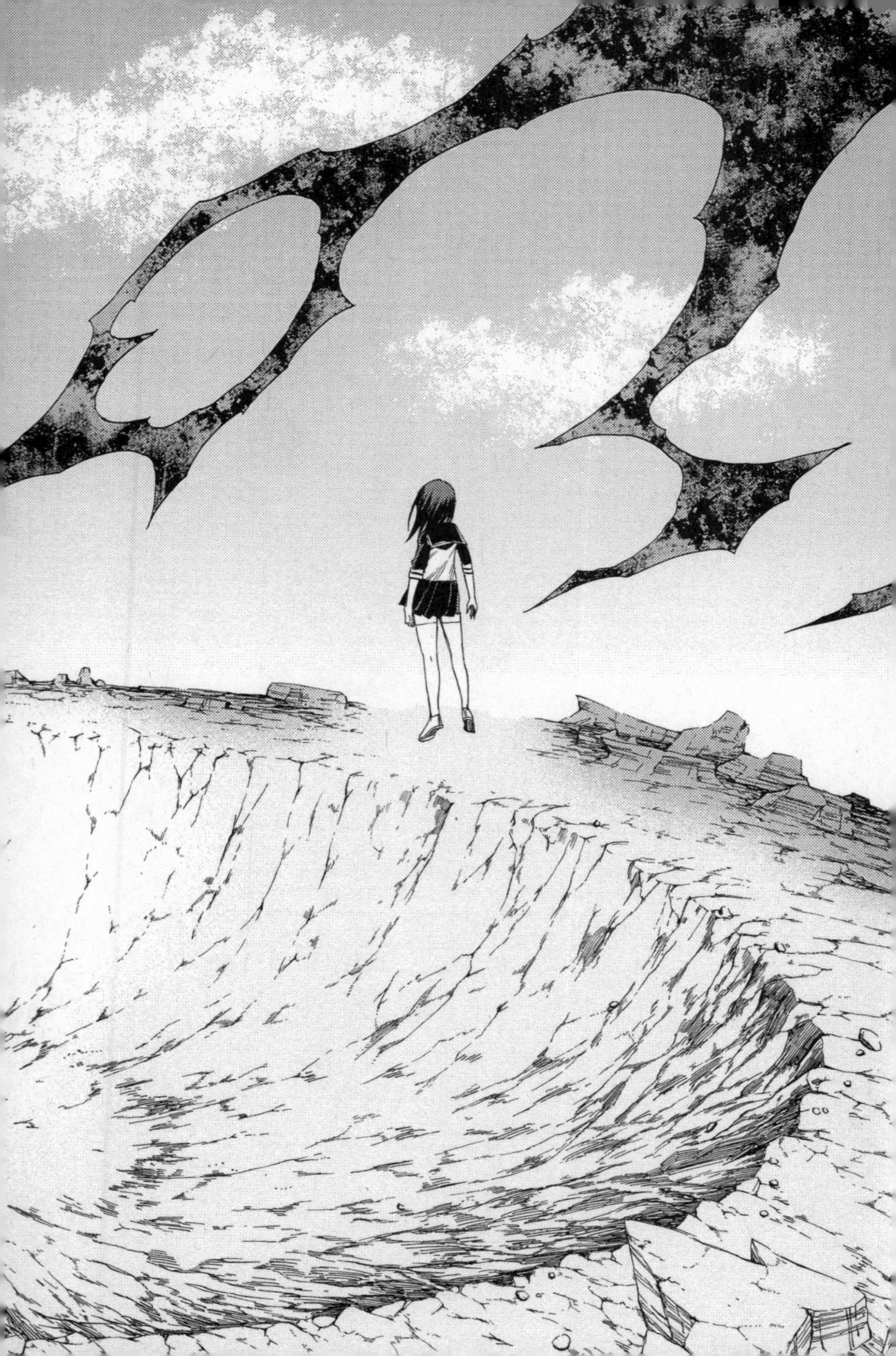

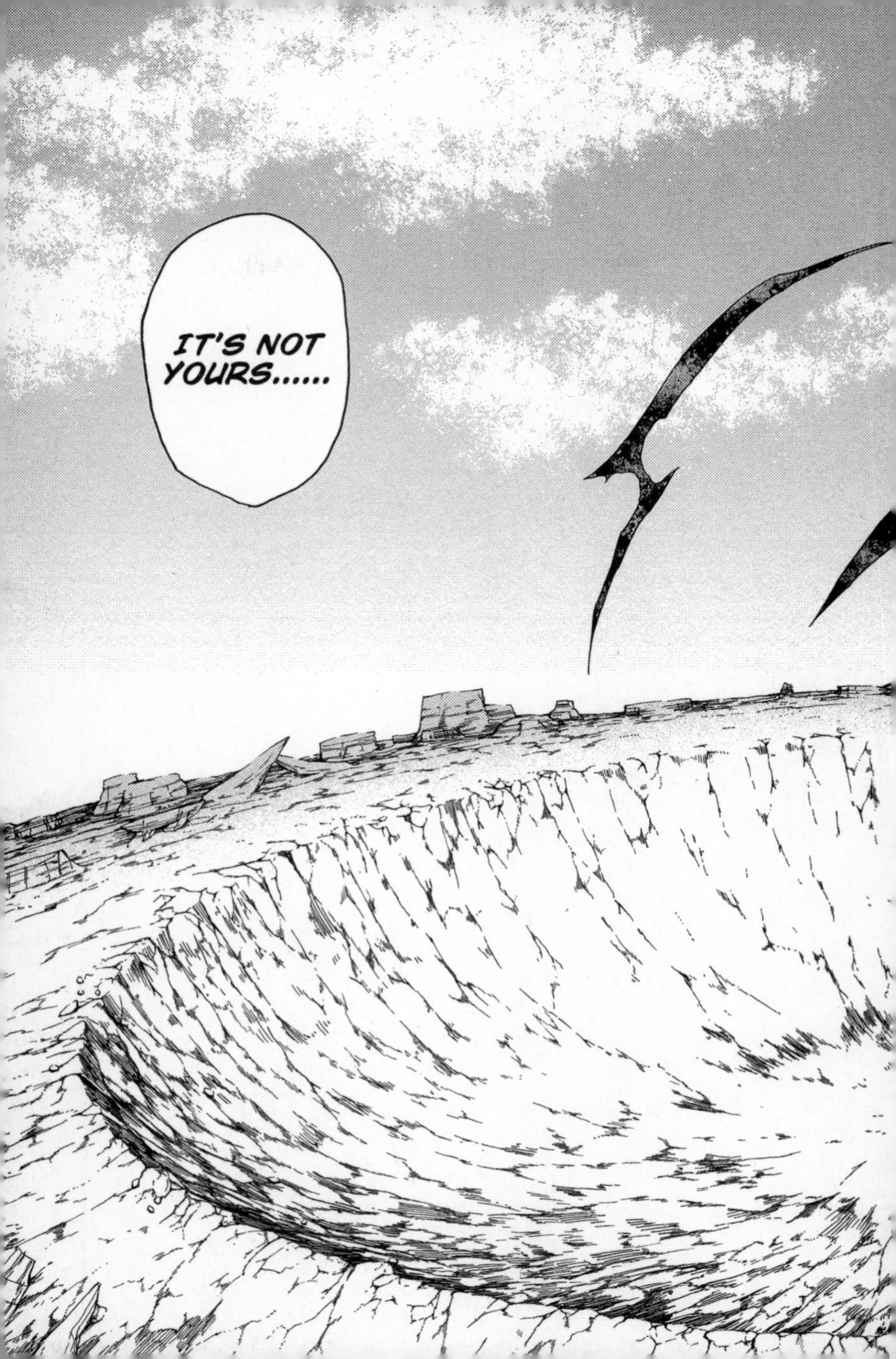
IT'S NOT YOURS......

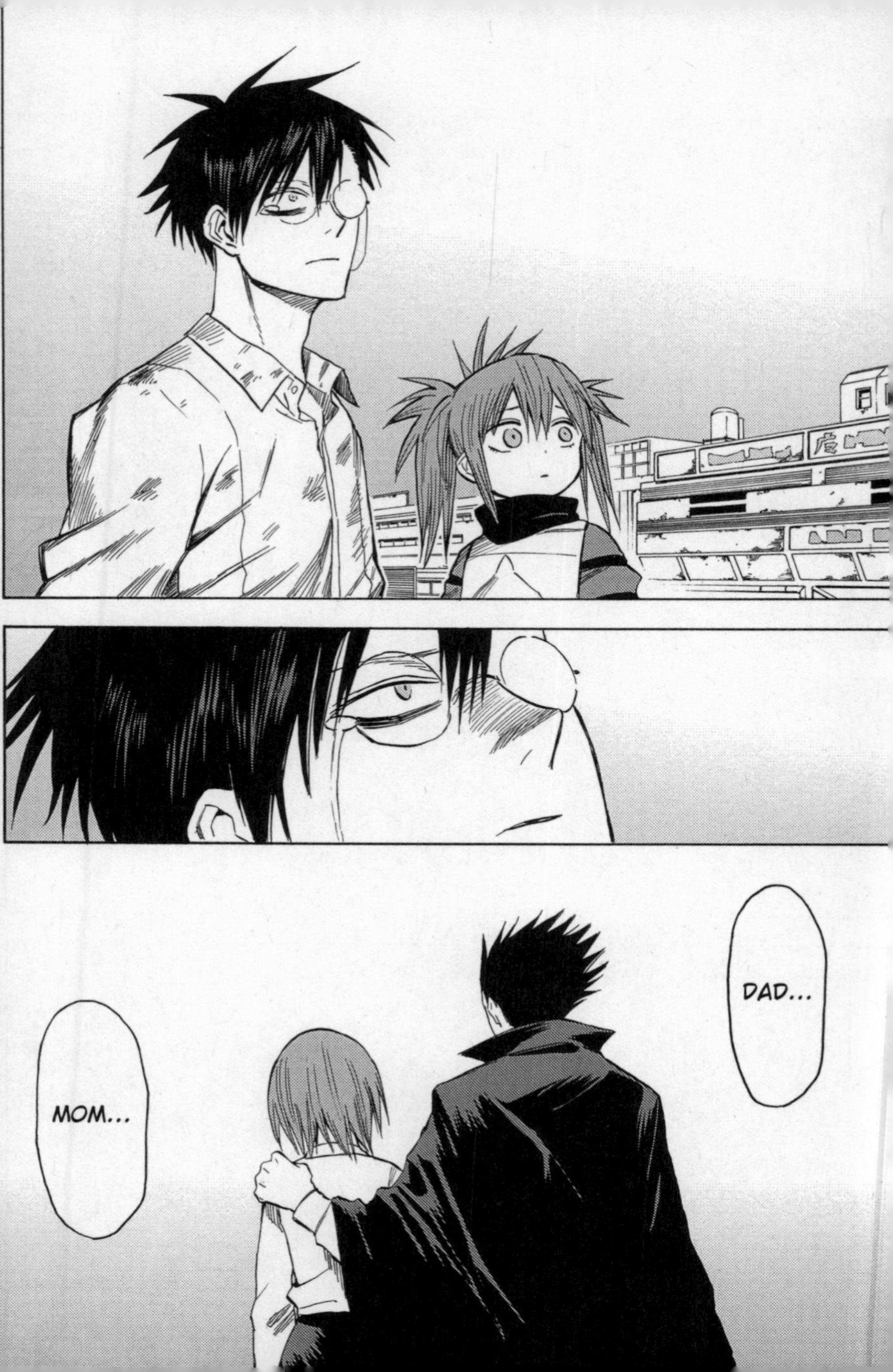
DAD...
MOM...

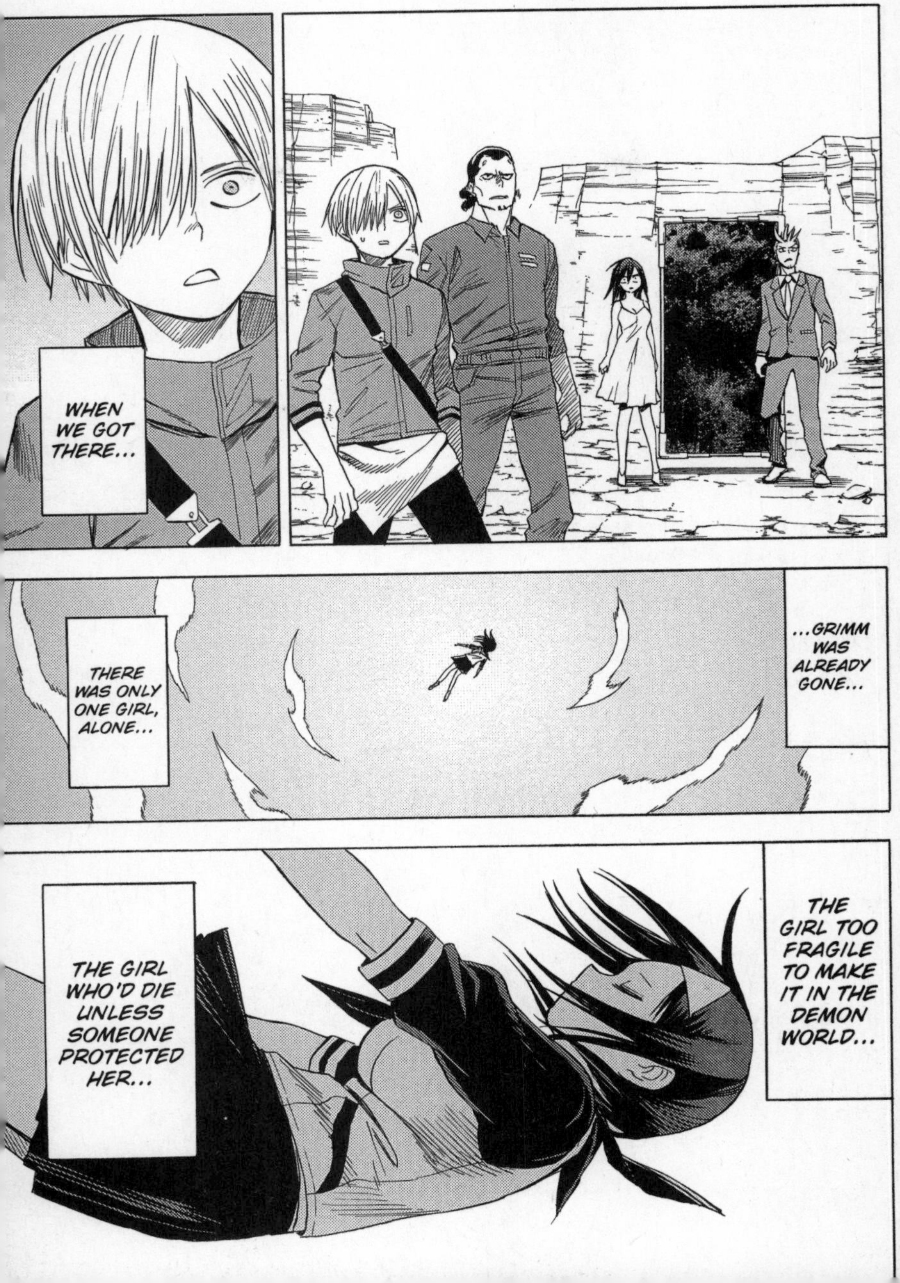
WHEN WE GOT THERE...
...GRIMM WAS ALREADY GONE...
THERE WAS ONLY ONE GIRL, ALONE...
THE GIRL TOO FRAGILE TO MAKE IT IN THE DEMON WORLD...
THE GIRL WHO'D DIE UNLESS SOMEONE PROTECTED HER...

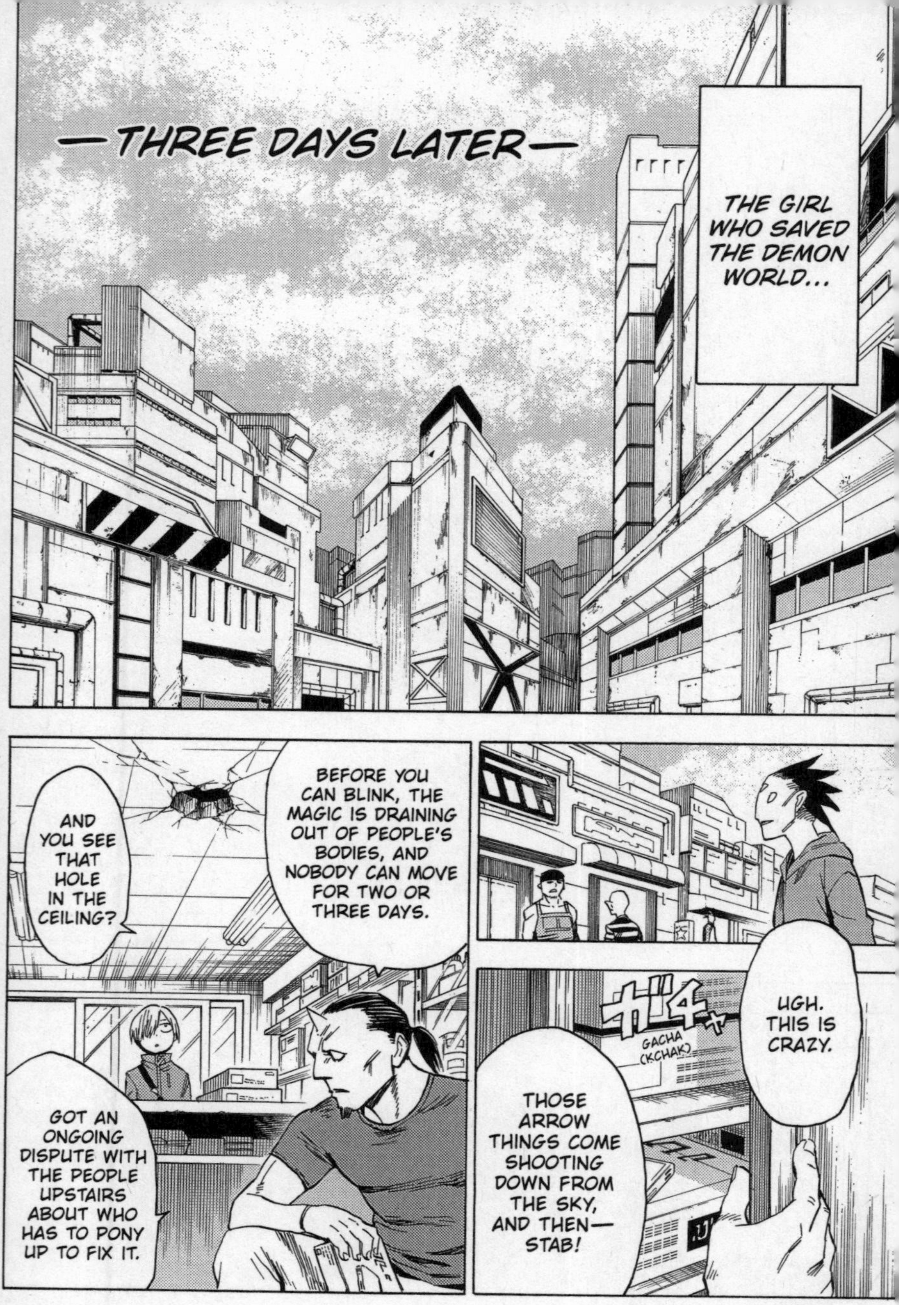
THE GIRL WHO SAVED THE DEMON WORLD...
—THREE DAYS LATER—
UGH. THIS IS CRAZY.
GACHA (KCHAK)
THOSE ARROW THINGS COME SHOOTING DOWN FROM THE SKY, AND THEN—STAB!
BEFORE YOU CAN BLINK, THE MAGIC IS DRAINING OUT OF PEOPLE'S BODIES, AND NOBODY CAN MOVE FOR TWO OR THREE DAYS.
AND YOU SEE THAT HOLE IN THE CEILING?
GOT AN ONGOING DISPUTE WITH THE PEOPLE UPSTAIRS ABOUT WHO HAS TO PONY UP TO FIX IT.

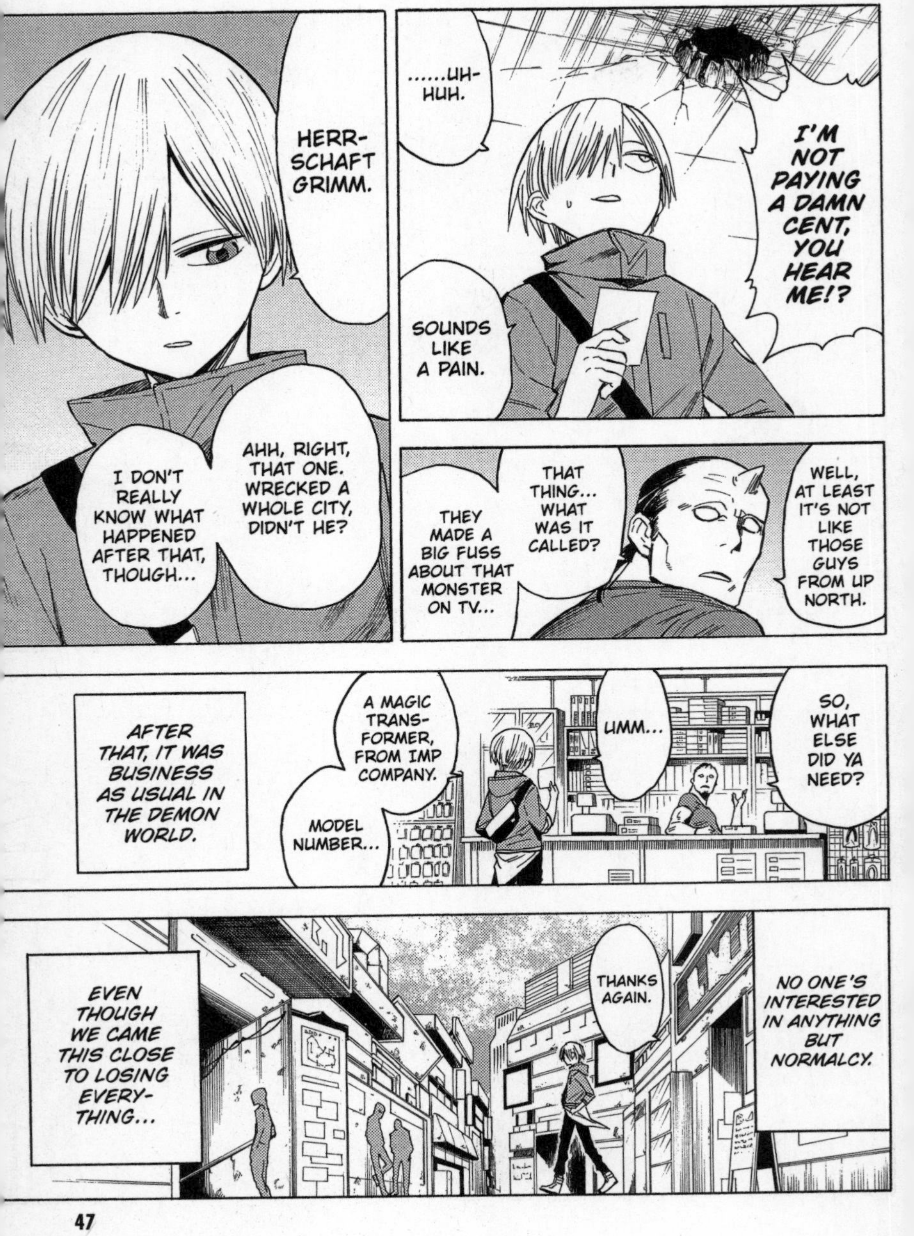
I'M NOT PAYING A DAMN CENT, YOU HEAR ME!?
......UH-HUH.
SOUNDS LIKE A PAIN.
WELL, AT LEAST IT'S NOT LIKE THOSE GUYS FROM UP NORTH.
THAT THING... WHAT WAS IT CALLED?
THEY MADE A BIG FUSS ABOUT THAT MONSTER ON TV...
HERR-SCHAFT GRIMM.
AHH, RIGHT, THAT ONE. WRECKED A WHOLE CITY, DIDN'T HE?
I DON'T REALLY KNOW WHAT HAPPENED AFTER THAT, THOUGH...
SO, WHAT ELSE DID YA NEED?
UMM...
A MAGIC TRANS-FORMER, FROM IMP COMPANY.
MODEL NUMBER...
AFTER THAT, IT WAS BUSINESS AS USUAL IN THE DEMON WORLD.
NO ONE'S INTERESTED IN ANYTHING BUT NORMALCY.
THANKS AGAIN.
EVEN THOUGH WE CAME THIS CLOSE TO LOSING EVERY-THING...

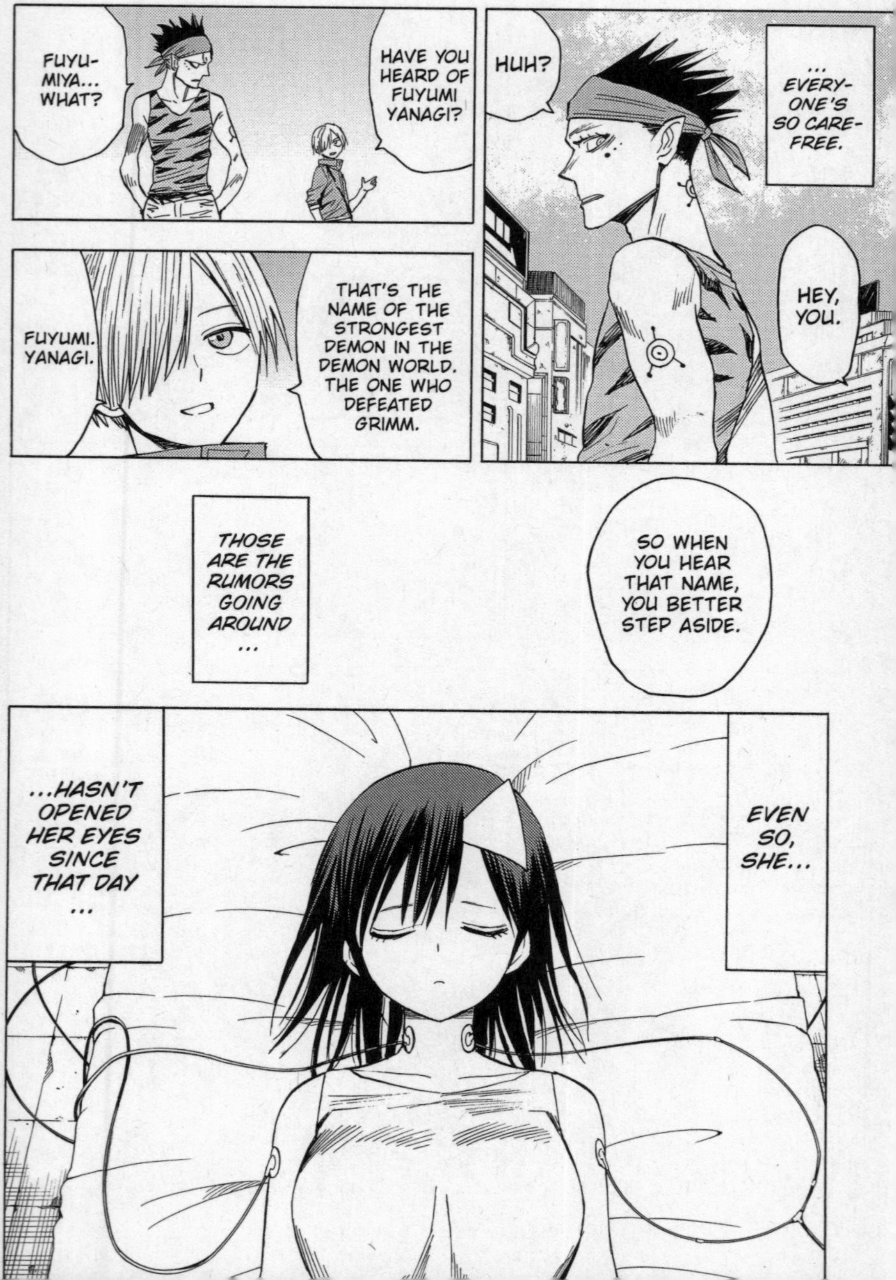
...EVERY-ONE'S SO CARE-FREE.
HUH?
HEY, YOU.
HAVE YOU HEARD OF FUYUMI YANAGI?
FUYU-MIYA... WHAT?
THAT'S THE NAME OF THE STRONGEST DEMON IN THE DEMON WORLD. THE ONE WHO DEFEATED GRIMM.
FUYUMI. YANAGI.
SO WHEN YOU HEAR THAT NAME, YOU BETTER STEP ASIDE.
THOSE ARE THE RUMORS GOING AROUND...
EVEN SO, SHE...
...HASN'T OPENED HER EYES SINCE THAT DAY...

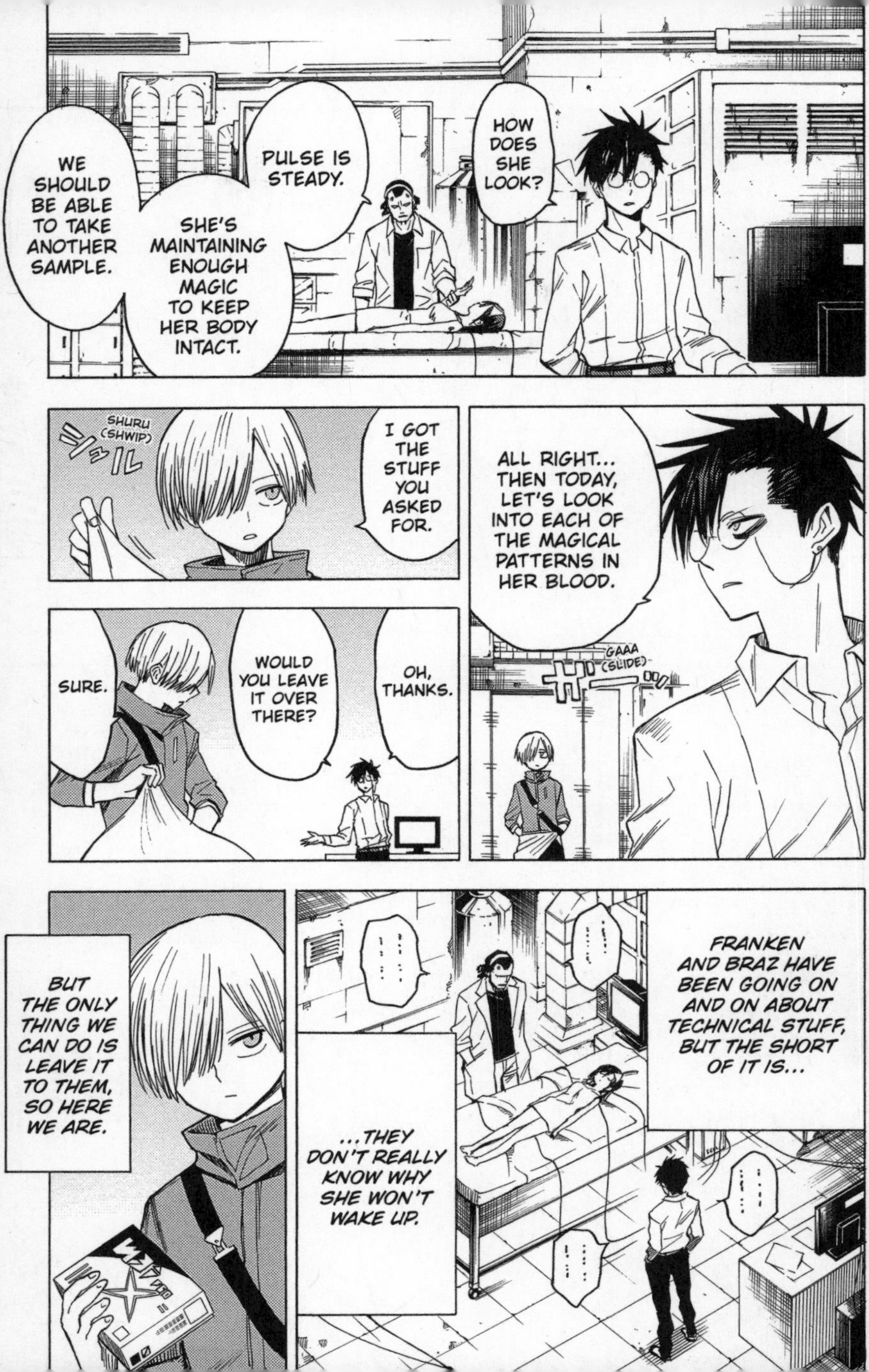
HOW DOES SHE LOOK?
PULSE IS STEADY.
SHE'S MAINTAINING ENOUGH MAGIC TO KEEP HER BODY INTACT.
WE SHOULD BE ABLE TO TAKE ANOTHER SAMPLE.
ALL RIGHT... THEN TODAY, LET'S LOOK INTO EACH OF THE MAGICAL PATTERNS IN HER BLOOD.
GAAA (SLIDE)
SHURU (SHWIP)
I GOT THE STUFF YOU ASKED FOR.
OH, THANKS.
WOULD YOU LEAVE IT OVER THERE?
SURE.
FRANKEN AND BRAZ HAVE BEEN GOING ON AND ON ABOUT TECHNICAL STUFF, BUT THE SHORT OF IT IS...
...THEY DON'T REALLY KNOW WHY SHE WON'T WAKE UP.
BUT THE ONLY THING WE CAN DO IS LEAVE IT TO THEM, SO HERE WE ARE.

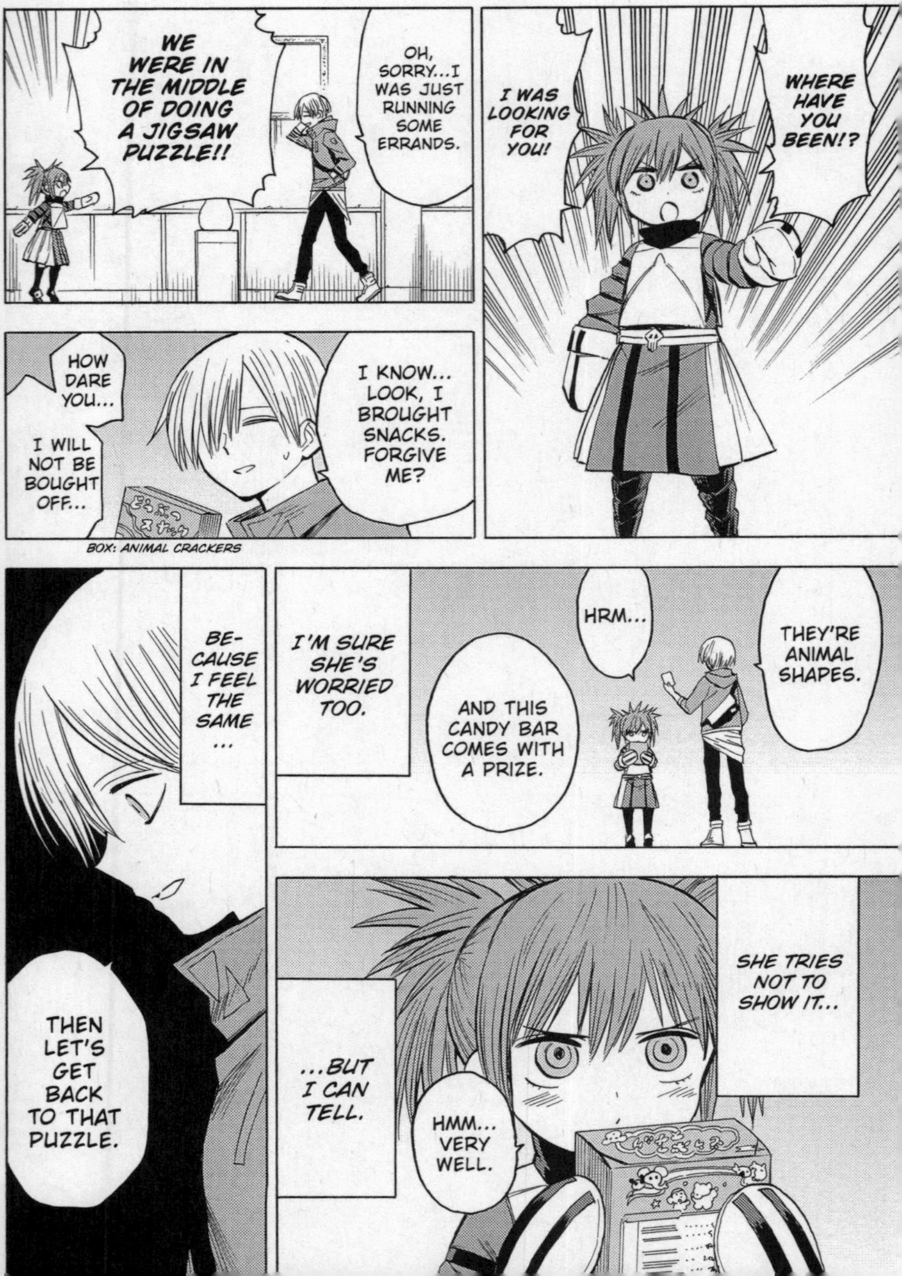
WHERE HAVE YOU BEEN!?
I WAS LOOKING FOR YOU!
OH, SORRY...I WAS JUST RUNNING SOME ERRANDS.
WE WERE IN THE MIDDLE OF DOING A JIGSAW PUZZLE!!
I KNOW... LOOK, I BROUGHT SNACKS. FORGIVE ME?
HOW DARE YOU...
I WILL NOT BE BOUGHT OFF...
BOX: ANIMAL CRACKERS
THEY'RE ANIMAL SHAPES.
HRM...
AND THIS CANDY BAR COMES WITH A PRIZE.
I'M SURE SHE'S WORRIED TOO.
SHE TRIES NOT TO SHOW IT...
...BUT I CAN TELL.
HMM... VERY WELL.
BE-CAUSE I FEEL THE SAME...
THEN LET'S GET BACK TO THAT PUZZLE.

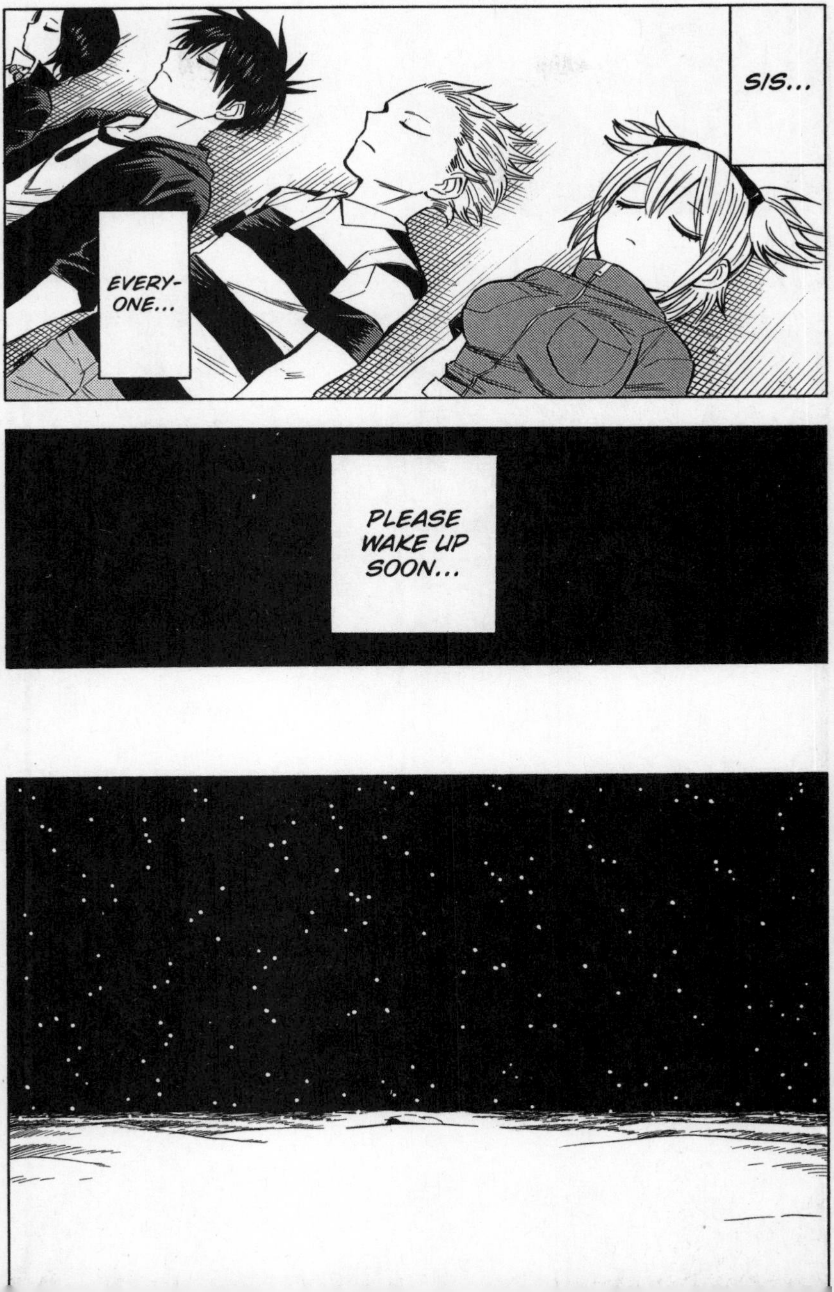
SIS...
EVERY-ONE...
PLEASE WAKE UP SOON...

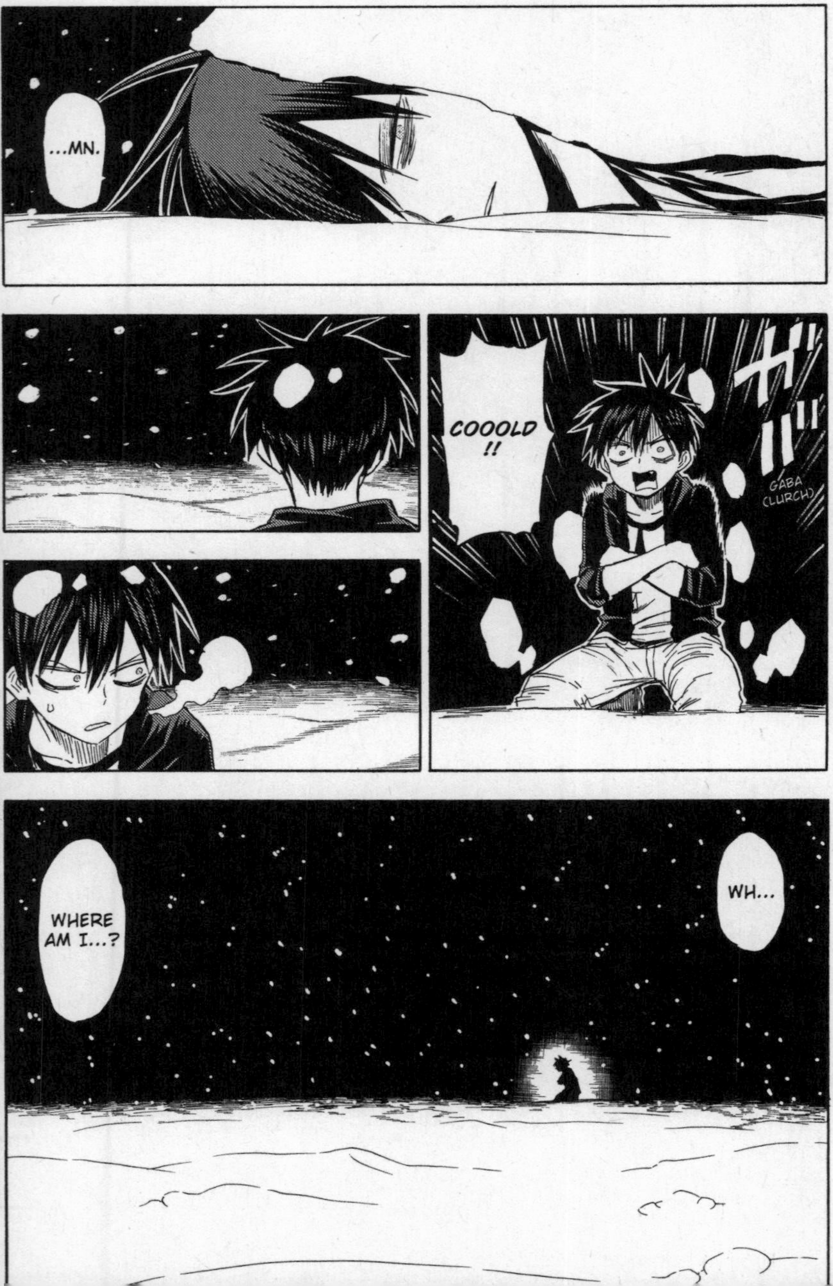
...MN.
COOOLD !!
GABA (LURCH)
WH...
WHERE AM I...?

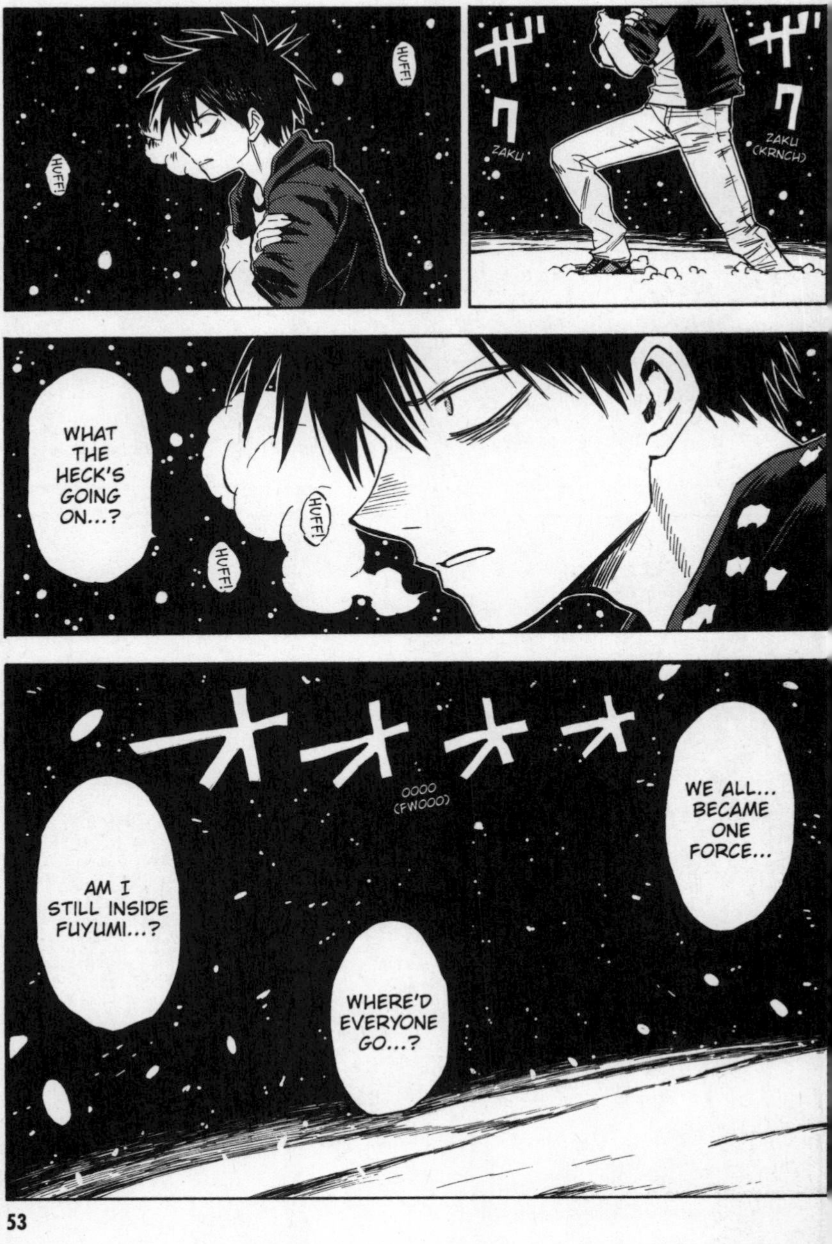
ザク
ZAKU (KRNCH)
ザク
ZAKU
HUFF!
HUFF!
WHAT THE HECK'S GOING ON...?
HUFF!
HUFF!
オオオオ
OOOO (FWOOO)
WE ALL... BECAME ONE FORCE...
WHERE'D EVERYONE GO...?
AM I STILL INSIDE FUYUMI...?

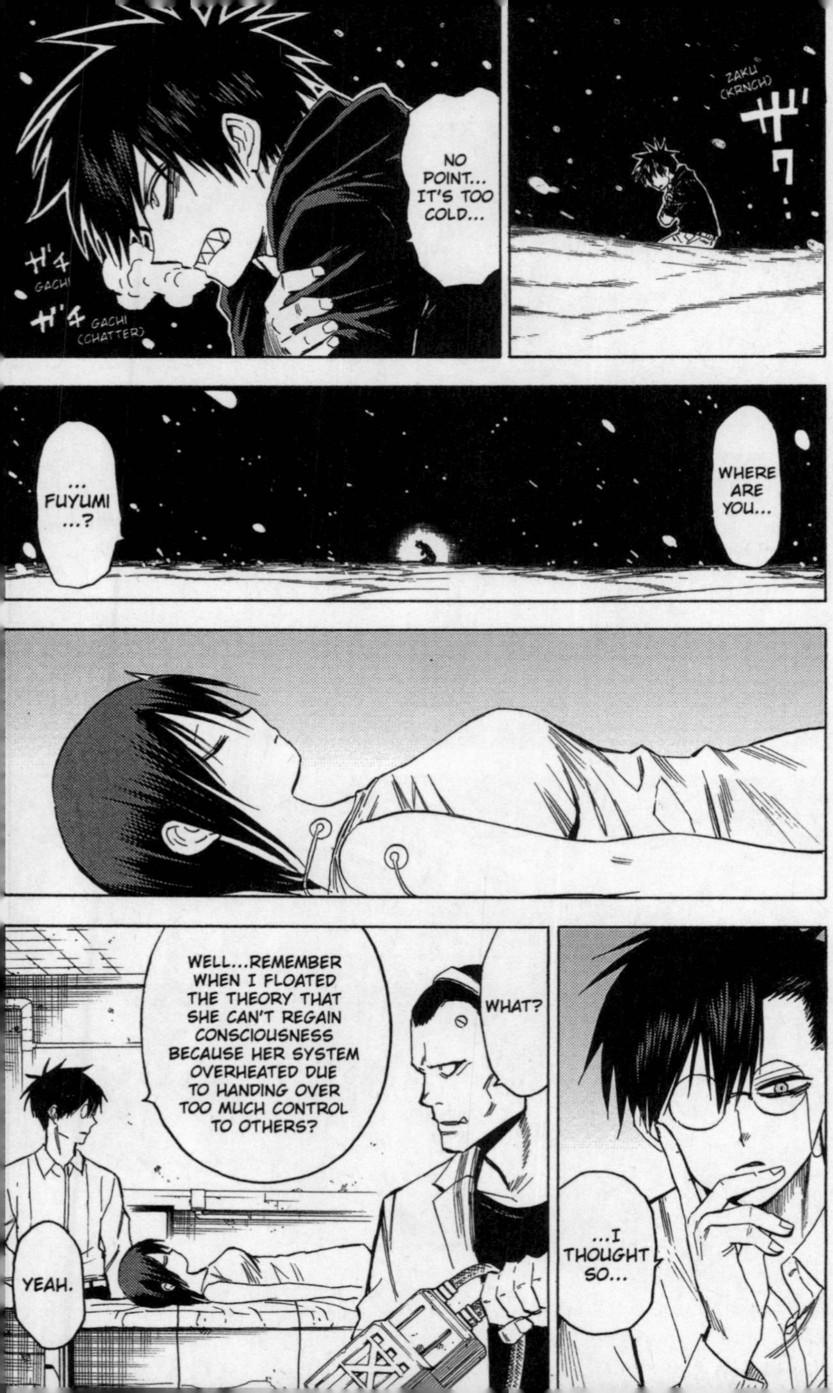
ZAKU (KRNCH)
ザク
NO POINT... IT'S TOO COLD...
GACHI
ガチ
GACHI (CHATTER)
ガチ
WHERE ARE YOU...
... FUYUMI ...?
...I THOUGHT SO...
WHAT?
WELL...REMEMBER WHEN I FLOATED THE THEORY THAT SHE CAN'T REGAIN CONSCIOUSNESS BECAUSE HER SYSTEM OVERHEATED DUE TO HANDING OVER TOO MUCH CONTROL TO OTHERS?
YEAH.

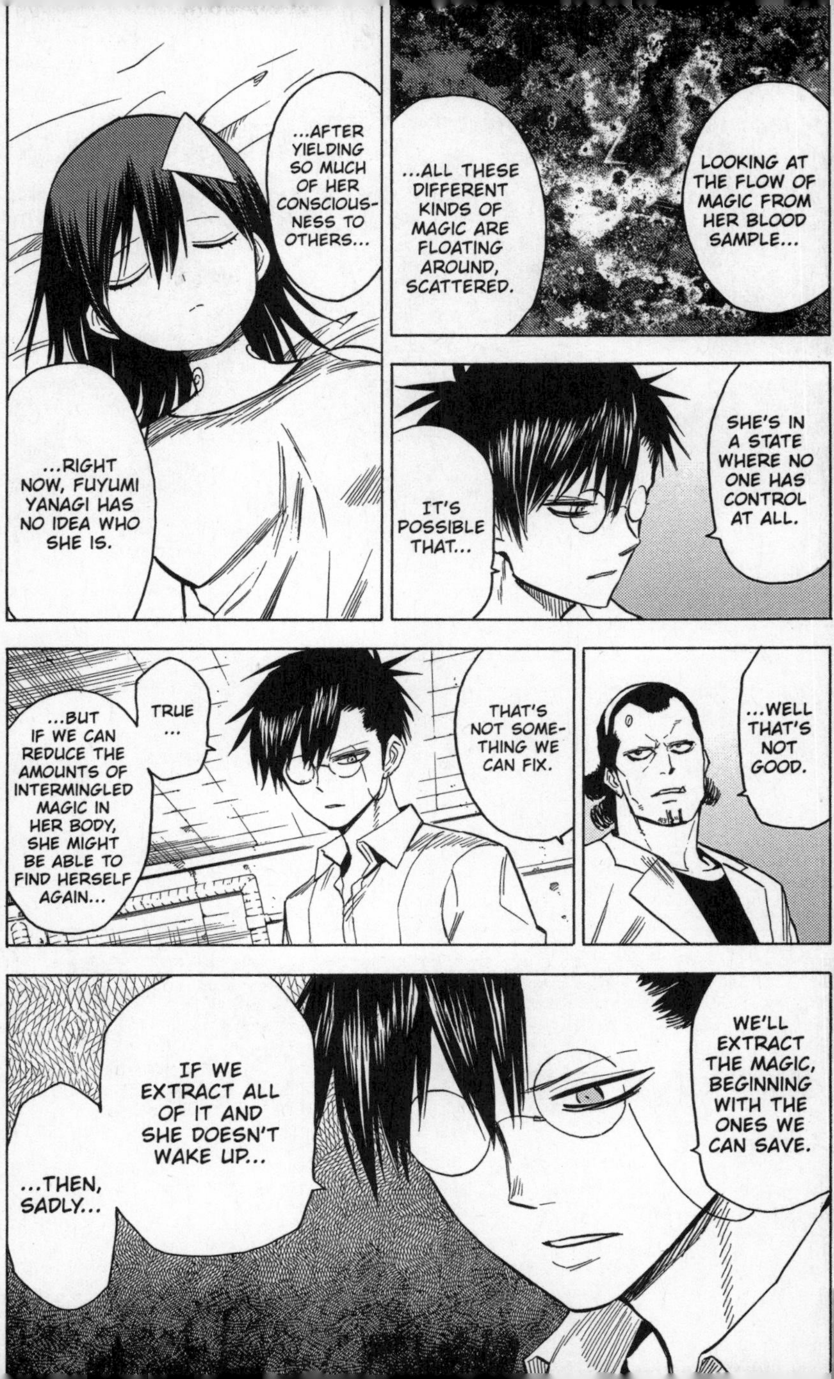
LOOKING AT THE FLOW OF MAGIC FROM HER BLOOD SAMPLE...
...ALL THESE DIFFERENT KINDS OF MAGIC ARE FLOATING AROUND, SCATTERED.
SHE'S IN A STATE WHERE NO ONE HAS CONTROL AT ALL.
IT'S POSSIBLE THAT...
...AFTER YIELDING SO MUCH OF HER CONSCIOUS-NESS TO OTHERS...
...RIGHT NOW, FUYUMI YANAGI HAS NO IDEA WHO SHE IS.
...WELL THAT'S NOT GOOD.
THAT'S NOT SOME-THING WE CAN FIX.
TRUE ...
...BUT IF WE CAN REDUCE THE AMOUNTS OF INTERMINGLED MAGIC IN HER BODY, SHE MIGHT BE ABLE TO FIND HERSELF AGAIN...
WE'LL EXTRACT THE MAGIC, BEGINNING WITH THE ONES WE CAN SAVE.
IF WE EXTRACT ALL OF IT AND SHE DOESN'T WAKE UP...
...THEN, SADLY...

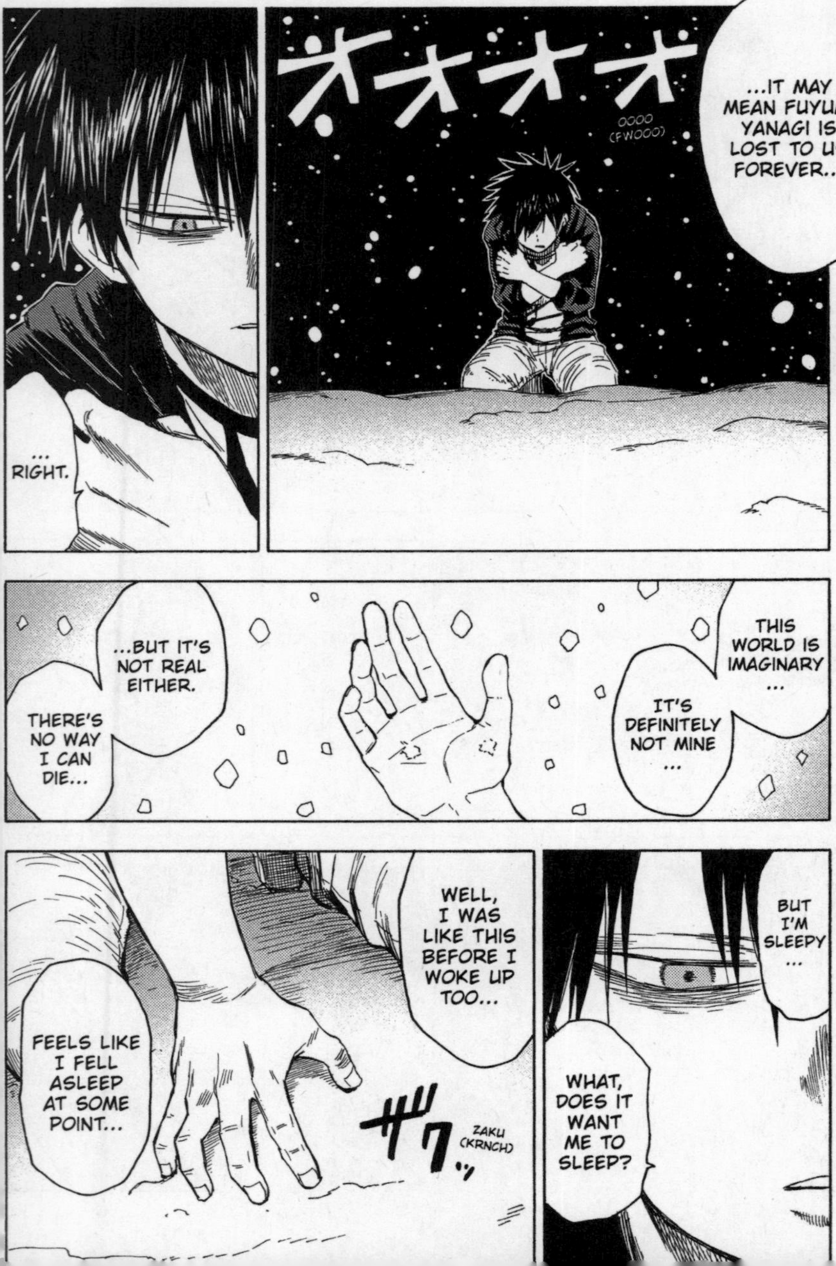
...IT MAY MEAN FUYUMI YANAGI IS LOST TO US FOREVER...
オオオオ
OOOO (FWOOO)
... RIGHT.
THIS WORLD IS IMAGINARY ...
IT'S DEFINITELY NOT MINE ...
...BUT IT'S NOT REAL EITHER.
THERE'S NO WAY I CAN DIE...
BUT I'M SLEEPY ...
WHAT, DOES IT WANT ME TO SLEEP?
WELL, I WAS LIKE THIS BEFORE I WOKE UP TOO...
ザクッ
ZAKU (KRNCH)
FEELS LIKE I FELL ASLEEP AT SOME POINT...

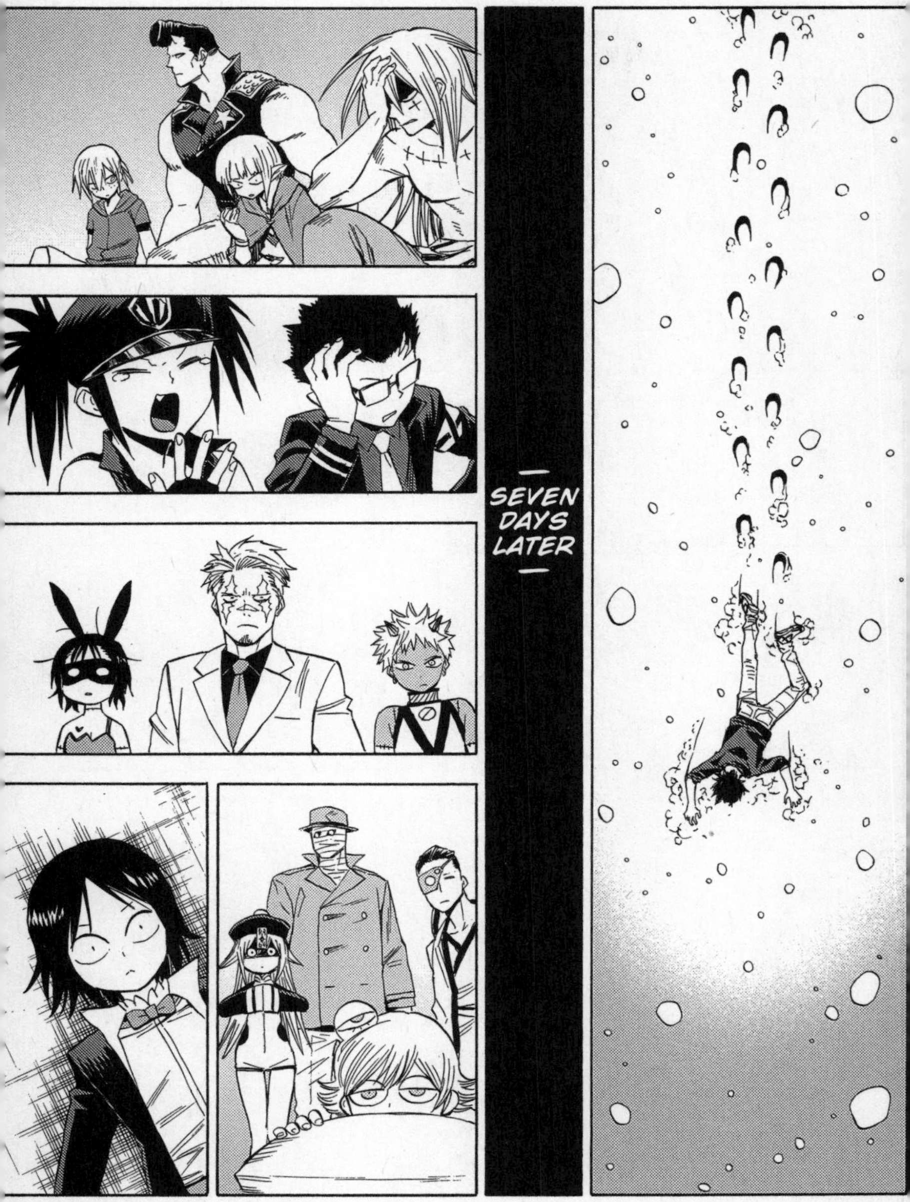
—SEVEN DAYS LATER—

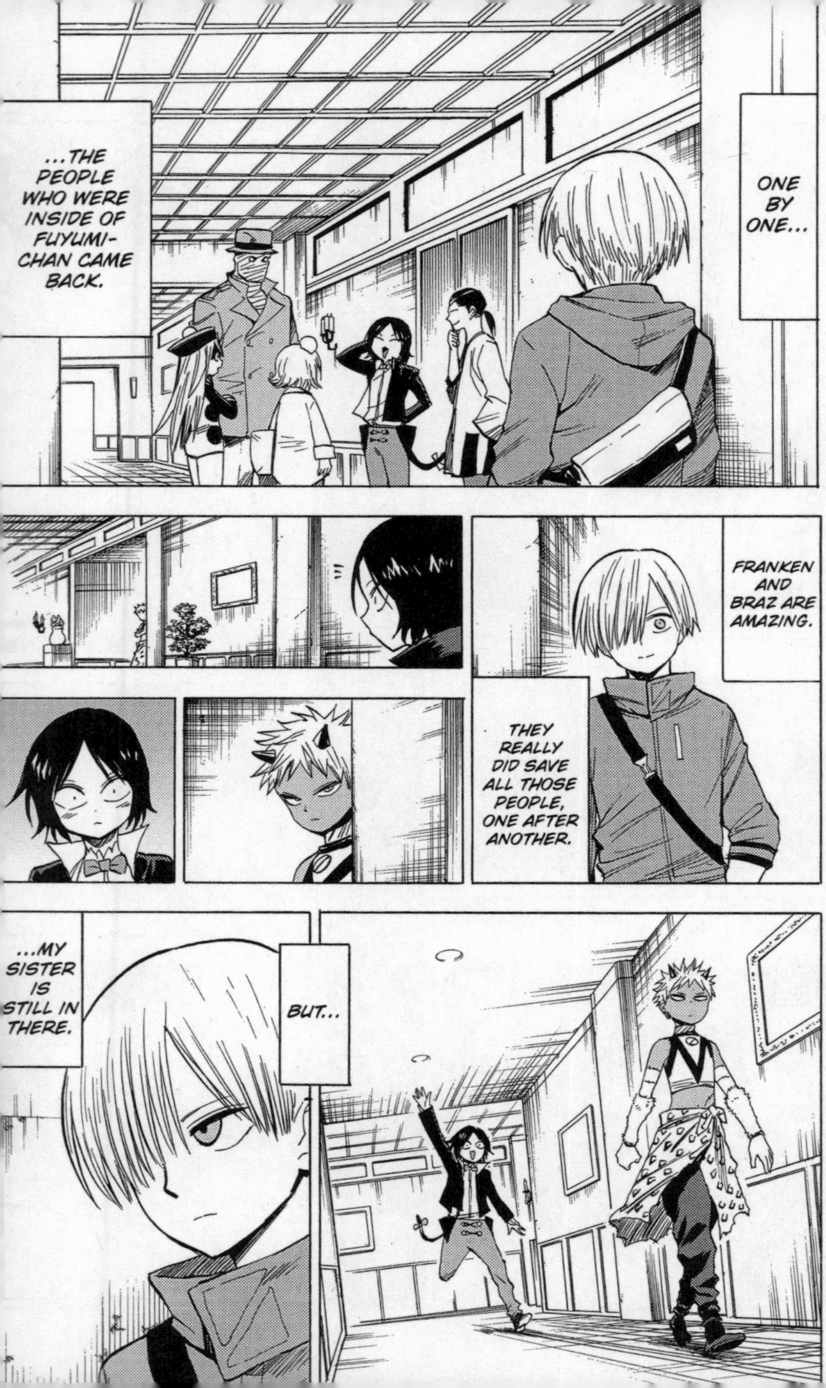
ONE BY ONE...
...THE PEOPLE WHO WERE INSIDE OF FUYUMI-CHAN CAME BACK.
FRANKEN AND BRAZ ARE AMAZING.
THEY REALLY DID SAVE ALL THOSE PEOPLE, ONE AFTER ANOTHER.
BUT...
...MY SISTER IS STILL IN THERE.

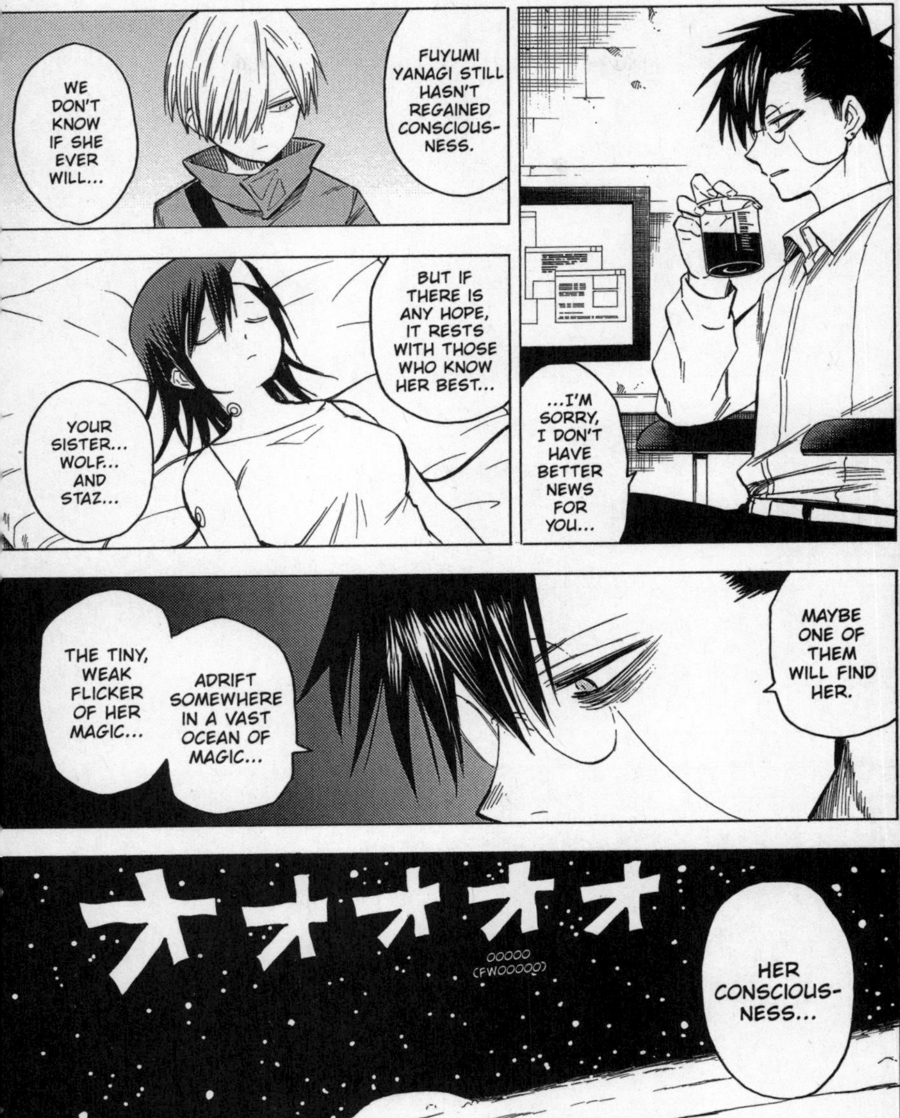
...I'M SORRY, I DON'T HAVE BETTER NEWS FOR YOU...
FUYUMI YANAGI STILL HASN'T REGAINED CONSCIOUS-NESS.
WE DON'T KNOW IF SHE EVER WILL...
BUT IF THERE IS ANY HOPE, IT RESTS WITH THOSE WHO KNOW HER BEST...
YOUR SISTER... WOLF... AND STAZ...
MAYBE ONE OF THEM WILL FIND HER.
THE TINY, WEAK FLICKER OF HER MAGIC...
ADRIFT SOMEWHERE IN A VAST OCEAN OF MAGIC...
HER CONSCIOUS-NESS...
オオオオオ
OOOOO (FWOOOOO)

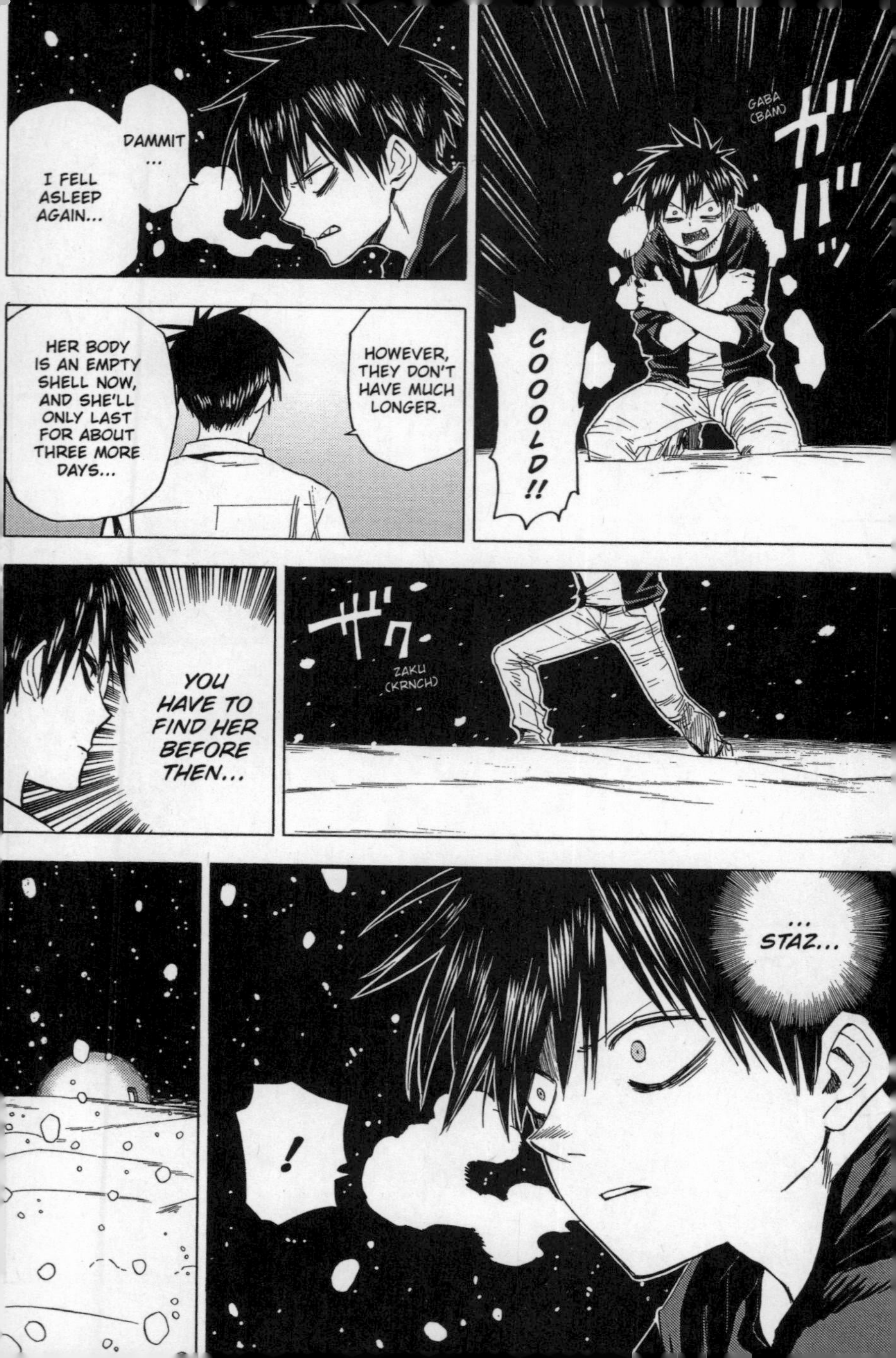
ガバッ
GABA (BAM)
COOOOLD!!
DAMMIT ... I FELL ASLEEP AGAIN...
HOWEVER, THEY DON'T HAVE MUCH LONGER.
HER BODY IS AN EMPTY SHELL NOW, AND SHE'LL ONLY LAST FOR ABOUT THREE MORE DAYS...
ザク
ZAKU (KRNCH)
YOU HAVE TO FIND HER BEFORE THEN...
... STAZ...
!

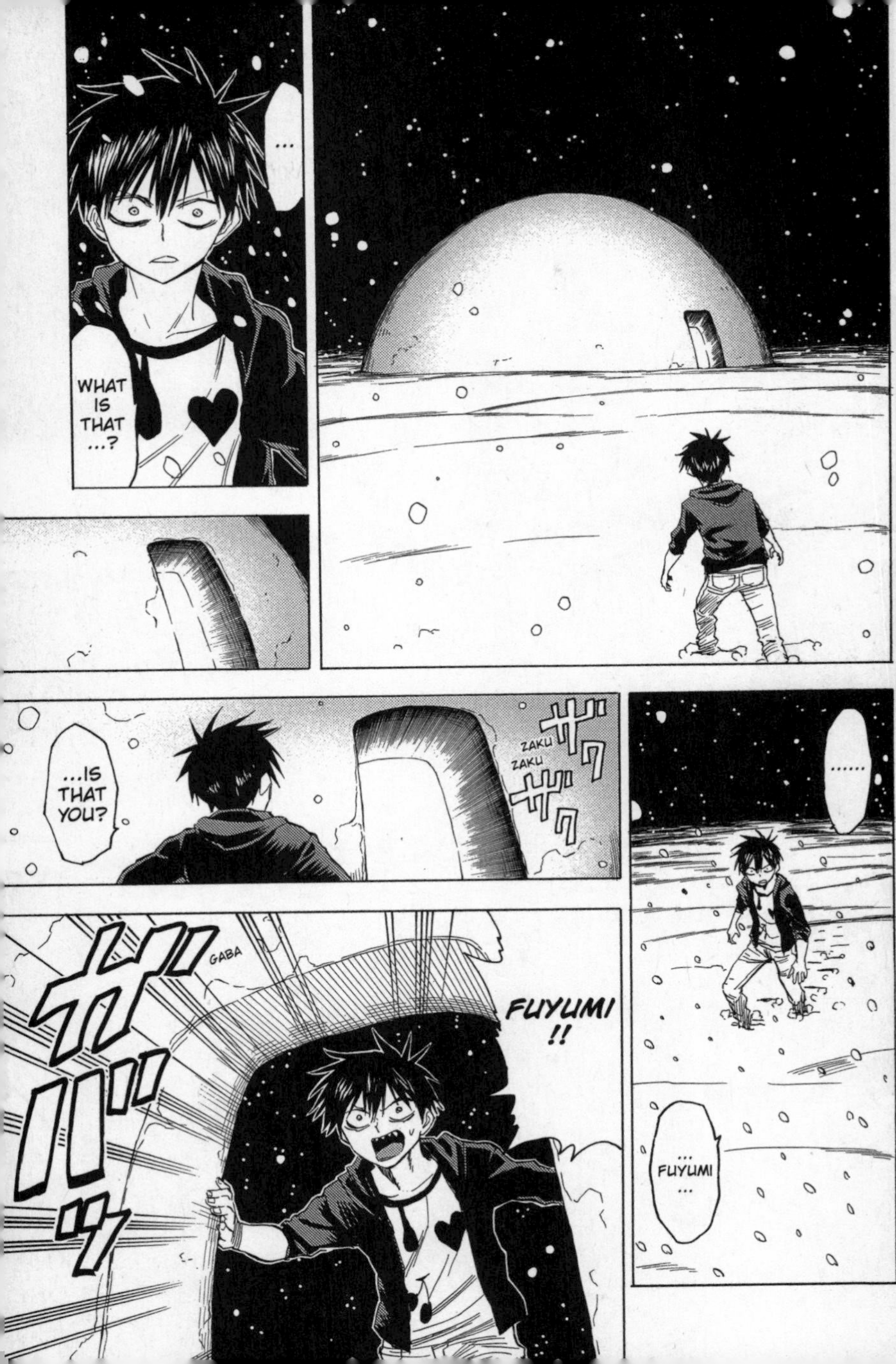

...
WHAT IS THAT ...?
......
... FUYUMI ...
ザク ザク
ZAKU ZAKU
...IS THAT YOU?
FUYUMI !!
ガバッ
GABA

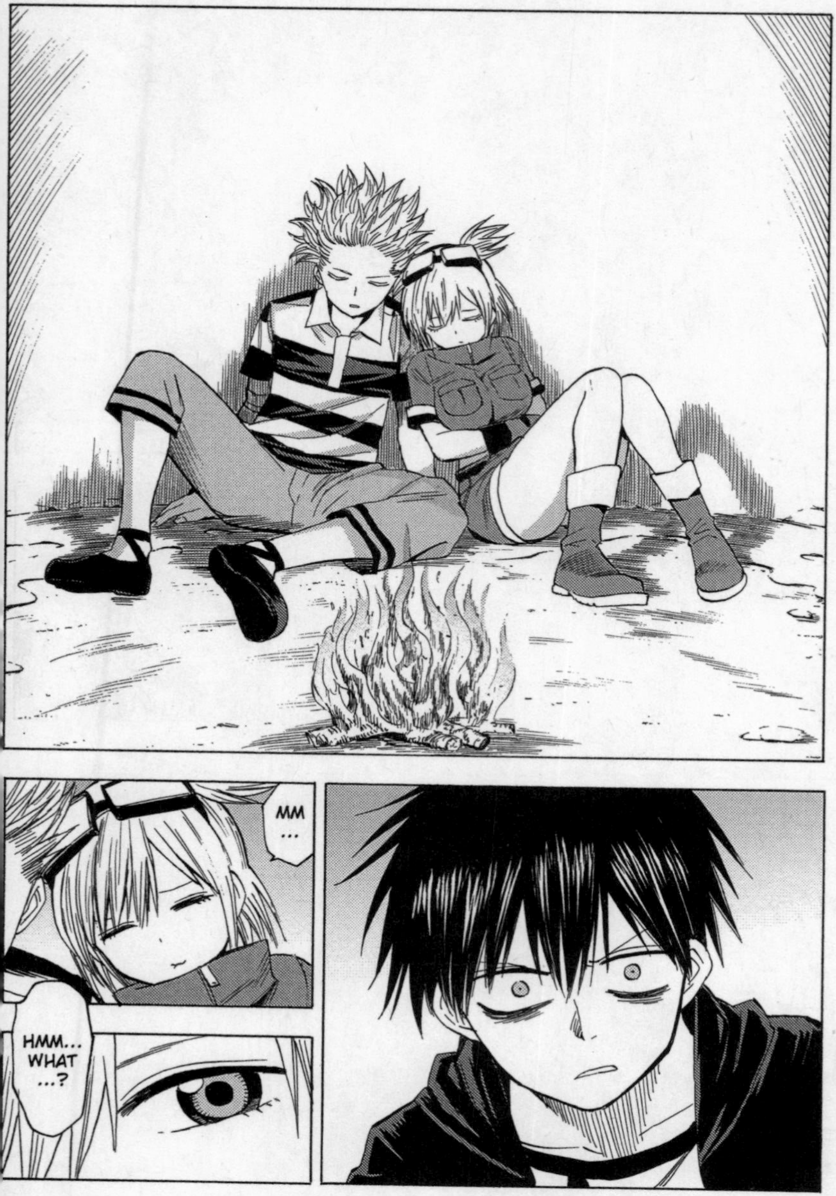
MM ...
HMM... WHAT ...?

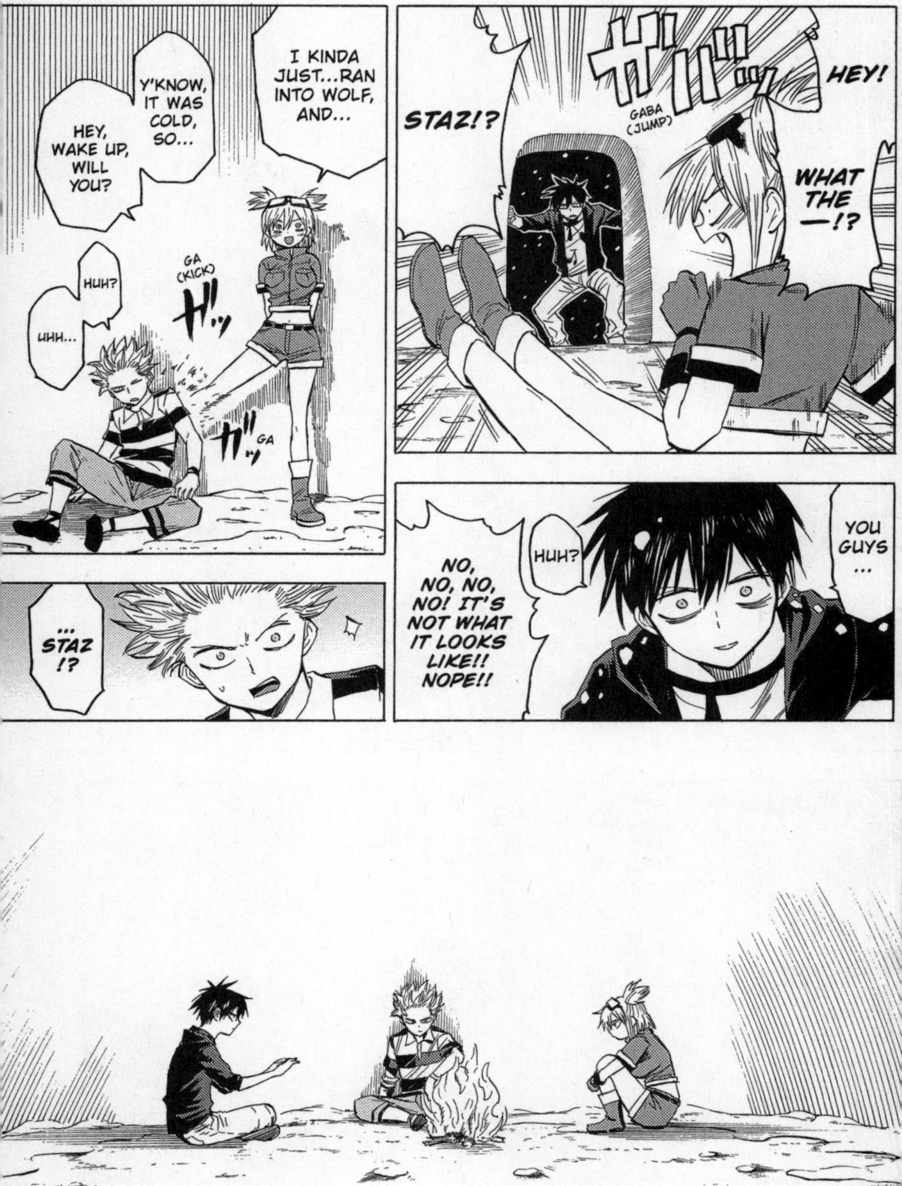
HEY!
WHAT THE—!?
GABA (JUMP)
STAZ!?
I KINDA JUST...RAN INTO WOLF, AND...
Y'KNOW, IT WAS COLD, SO...
HEY, WAKE UP, WILL YOU?
GA (KICK)
HUH?
UHH...
GA
YOU GUYS...
HUH?
NO, NO, NO, NO! IT'S NOT WHAT IT LOOKS LIKE!! NOPE!!
...STAZ!?

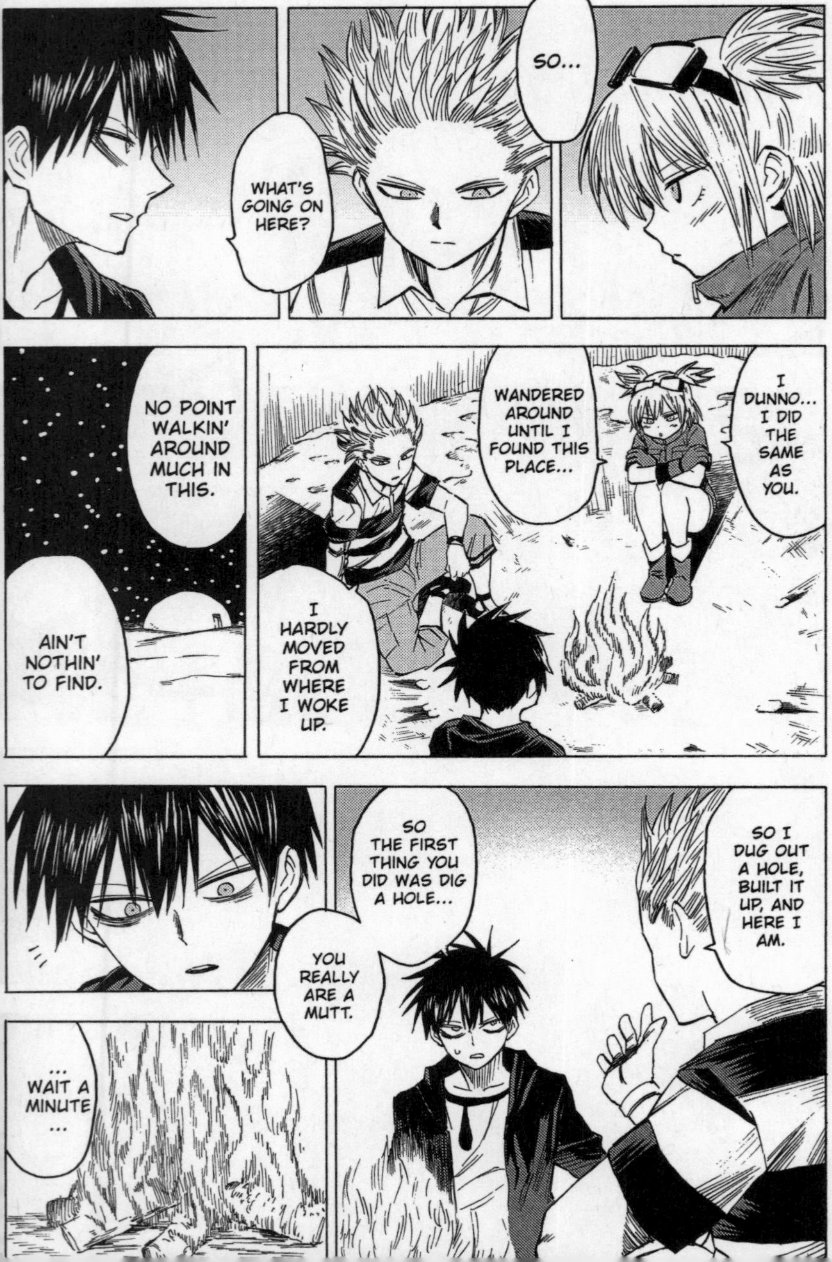
SO...
WHAT'S GOING ON HERE?
I DUNNO... I DID THE SAME AS YOU.
WANDERED AROUND UNTIL I FOUND THIS PLACE...
I HARDLY MOVED FROM WHERE I WOKE UP.
NO POINT WALKIN' AROUND MUCH IN THIS.
AIN'T NOTHIN' TO FIND.
SO I DUG OUT A HOLE, BUILT IT UP, AND HERE I AM.
SO THE FIRST THING YOU DID WAS DIG A HOLE...
YOU REALLY ARE A MUTT.
... WAIT A MINUTE ...

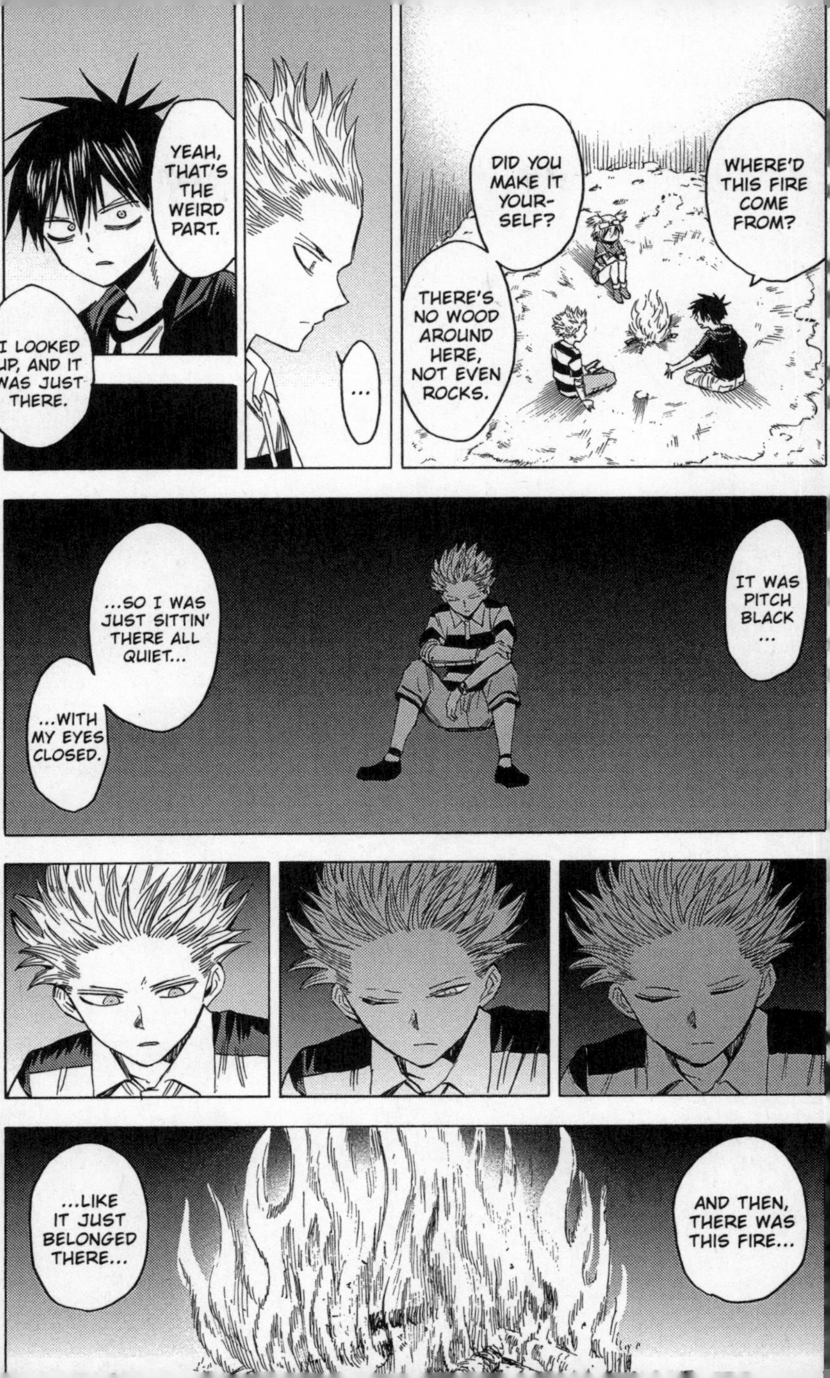
WHERE'D THIS FIRE COME FROM?
DID YOU MAKE IT YOUR-SELF?
THERE'S NO WOOD AROUND HERE, NOT EVEN ROCKS.
...
YEAH, THAT'S THE WEIRD PART.
I LOOKED UP, AND IT WAS JUST THERE.
IT WAS PITCH BLACK ...
...SO I WAS JUST SITTIN' THERE ALL QUIET...
...WITH MY EYES CLOSED.
AND THEN, THERE WAS THIS FIRE...
...LIKE IT JUST BELONGED THERE...

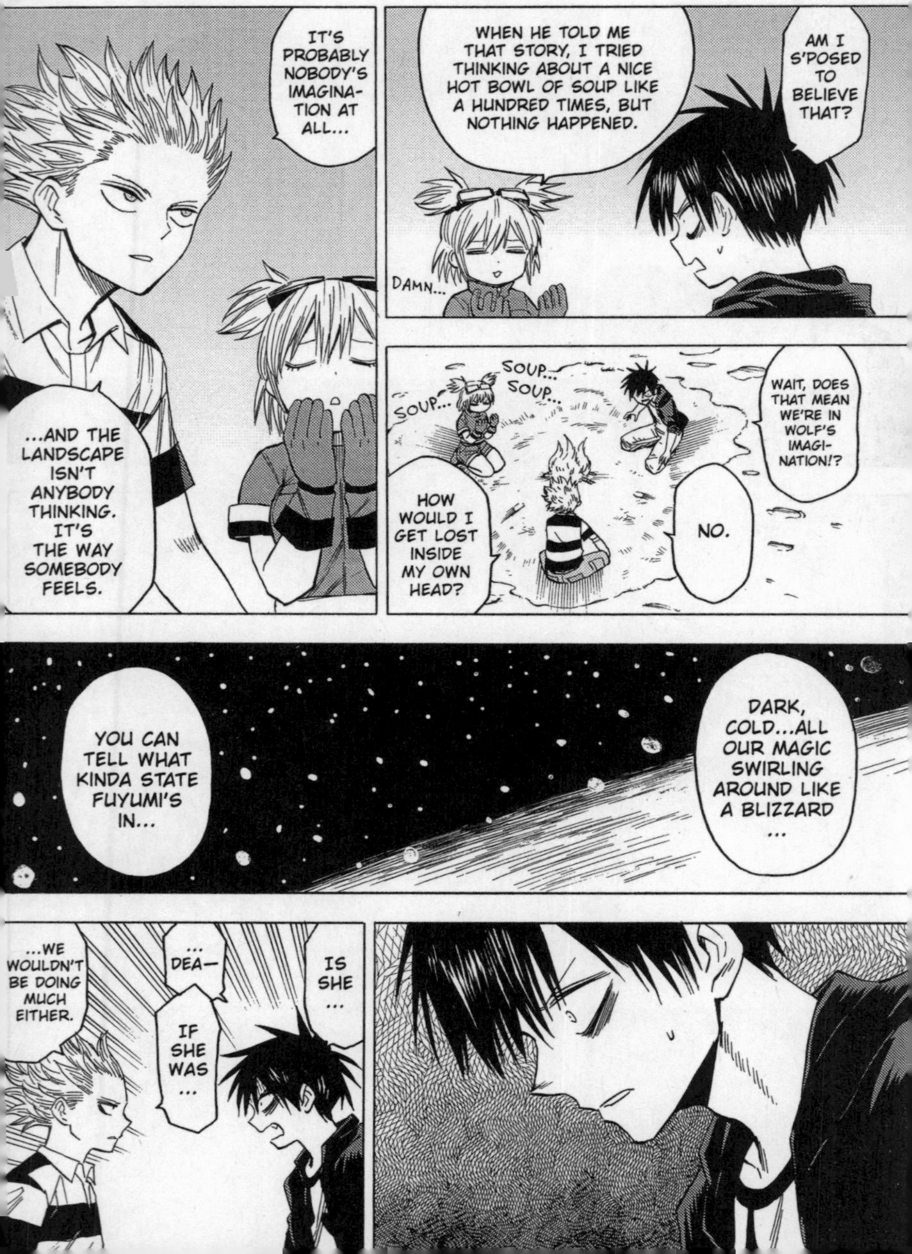
AM I S'POSED TO BELIEVE THAT?
WHEN HE TOLD ME THAT STORY, I TRIED THINKING ABOUT A NICE HOT BOWL OF SOUP LIKE A HUNDRED TIMES, BUT NOTHING HAPPENED.
DAMN...
WAIT, DOES THAT MEAN WE'RE IN WOLF'S IMAGI-NATION!?
SOUP...
SOUP...
SOUP...
NO.
HOW WOULD I GET LOST INSIDE MY OWN HEAD?
IT'S PROBABLY NOBODY'S IMAGINA-TION AT ALL...
...AND THE LANDSCAPE ISN'T ANYBODY THINKING. IT'S THE WAY SOMEBODY FEELS.
DARK, COLD...ALL OUR MAGIC SWIRLING AROUND LIKE A BLIZZARD ...
YOU CAN TELL WHAT KINDA STATE FUYUMI'S IN...
IS SHE ...
...DEA—
IF SHE WAS ...
...WE WOULDN'T BE DOING MUCH EITHER.

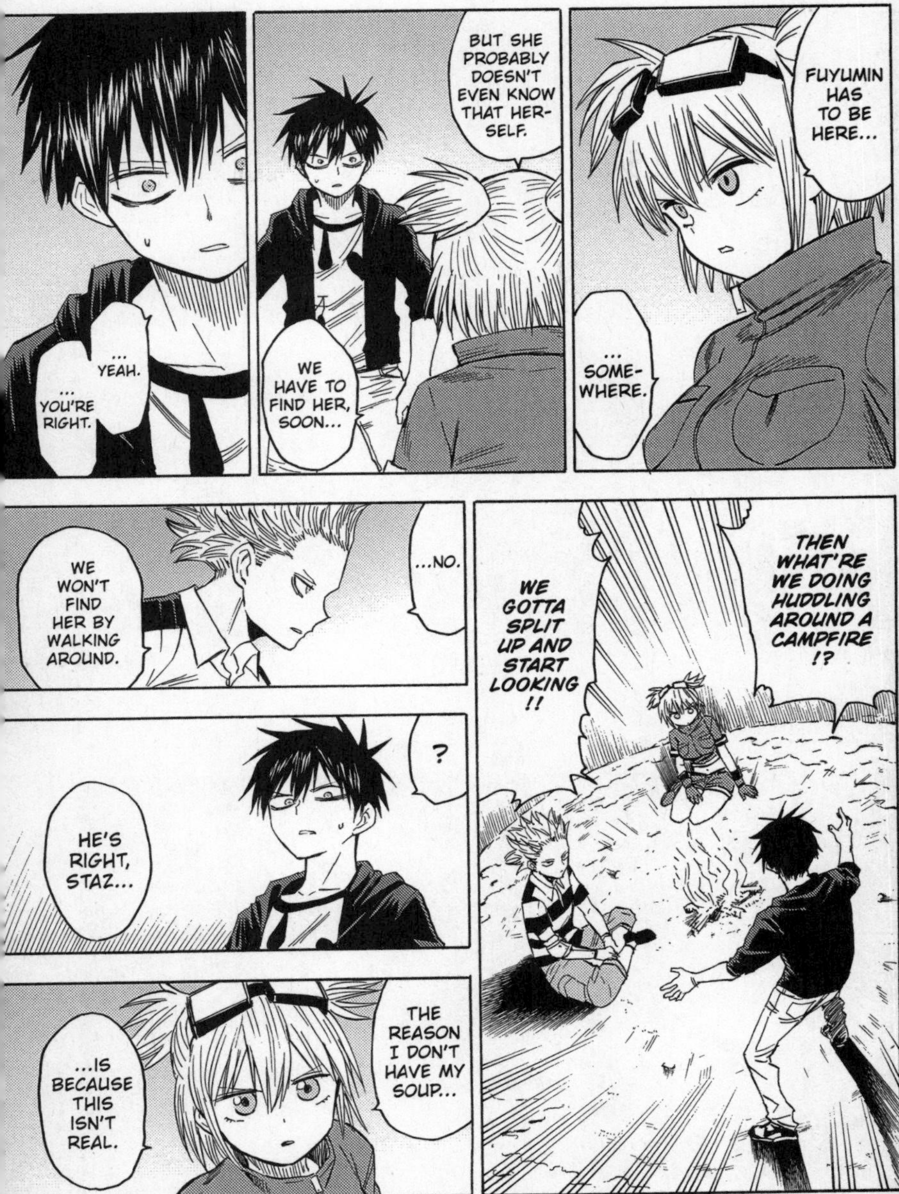
FUYUMIN HAS TO BE HERE...
...SOMEWHERE.
BUT SHE PROBABLY DOESN'T EVEN KNOW THAT HER-SELF.
WE HAVE TO FIND HER, SOON...
...YEAH.
...YOU'RE RIGHT.
THEN WHAT'RE WE DOING HUDDLING AROUND A CAMPFIRE!?
WE GOTTA SPLIT UP AND START LOOKING!!
...NO.
WE WON'T FIND HER BY WALKING AROUND.
?
HE'S RIGHT, STAZ...
THE REASON I DON'T HAVE MY SOUP...
...IS BECAUSE THIS ISN'T REAL.

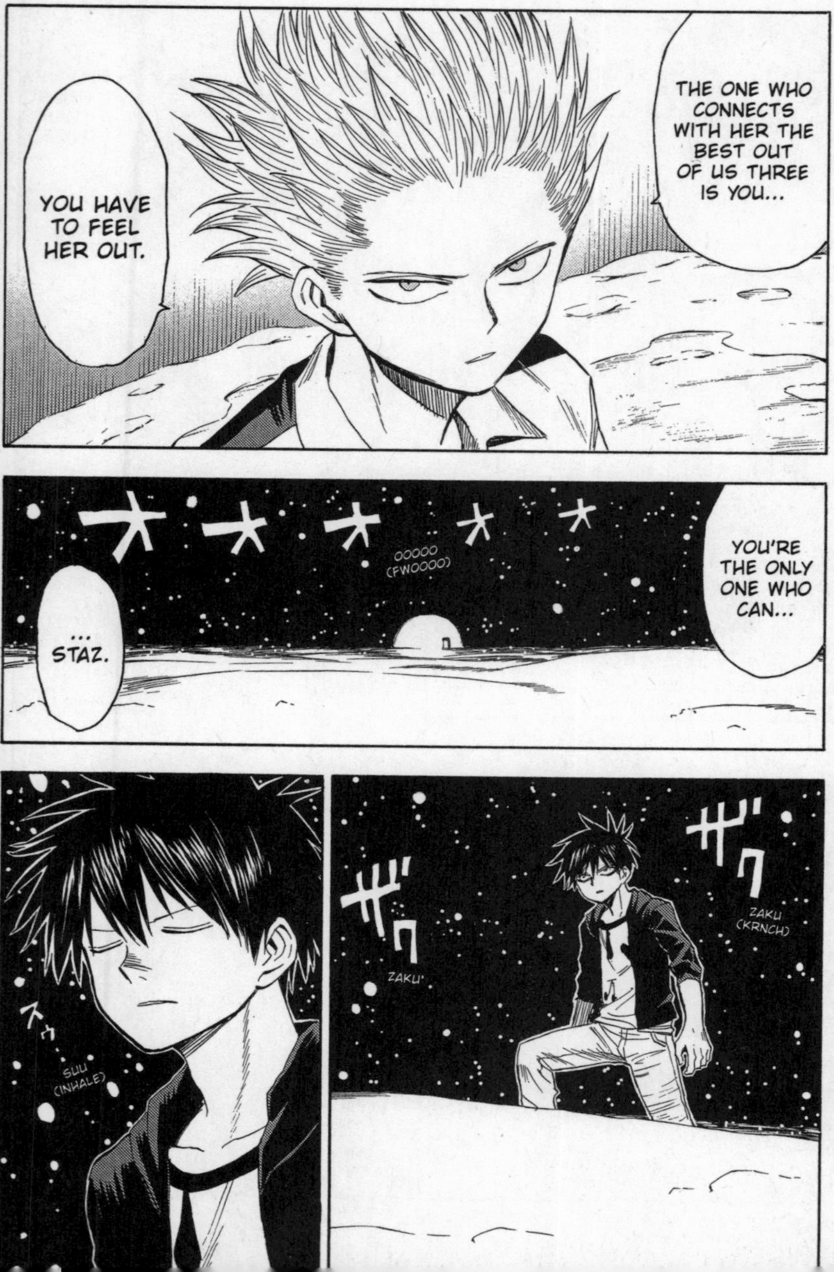
THE ONE WHO CONNECTS WITH HER THE BEST OUT OF US THREE IS YOU...
YOU HAVE TO FEEL HER OUT.
YOU'RE THE ONLY ONE WHO CAN...
OOOOO (FWOOOO)
... STAZ.
ZAKU (KRNCH)
ZAKU'
SUU (INHALE)

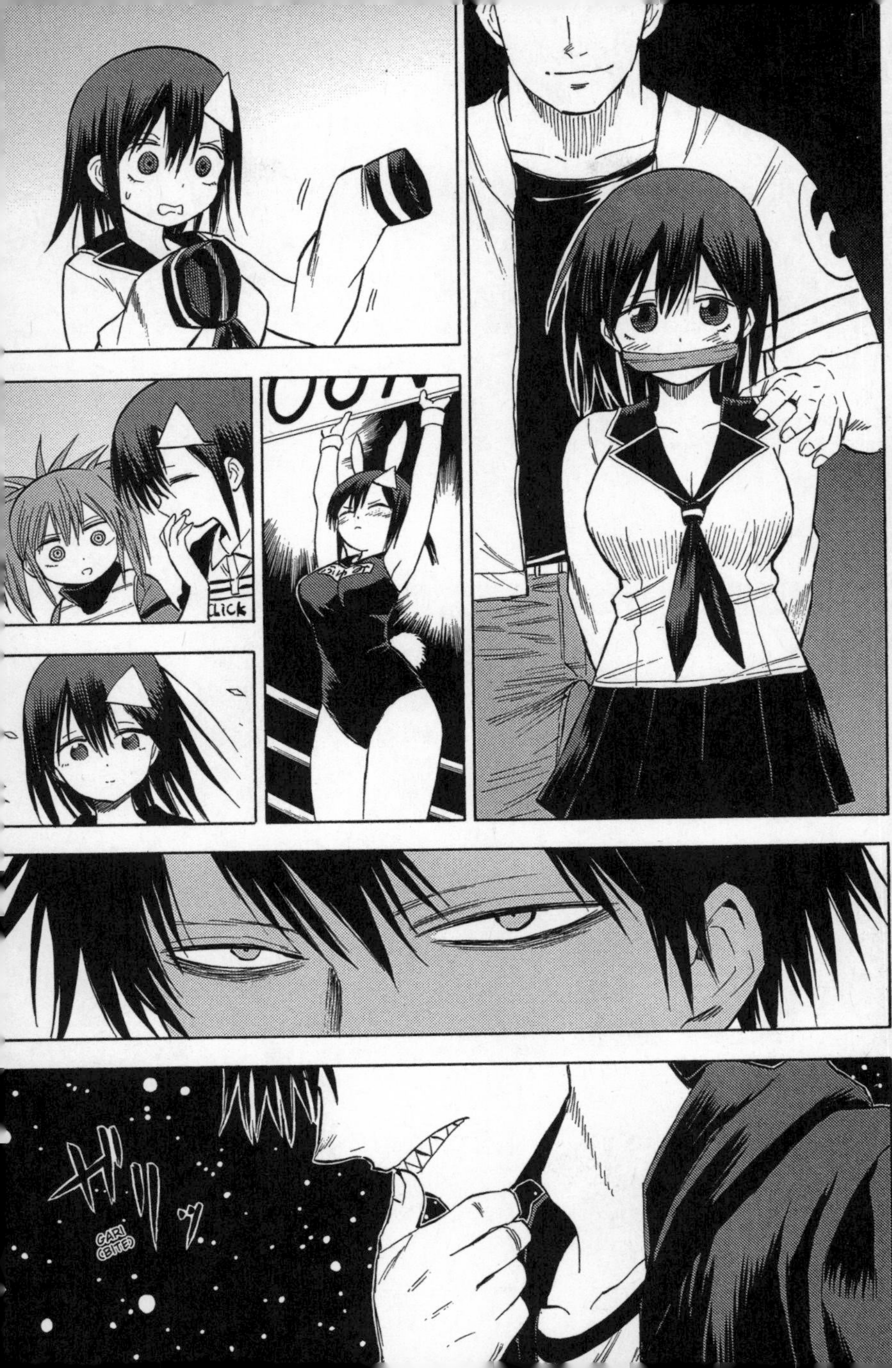
ガリッ
GARI (BITE)

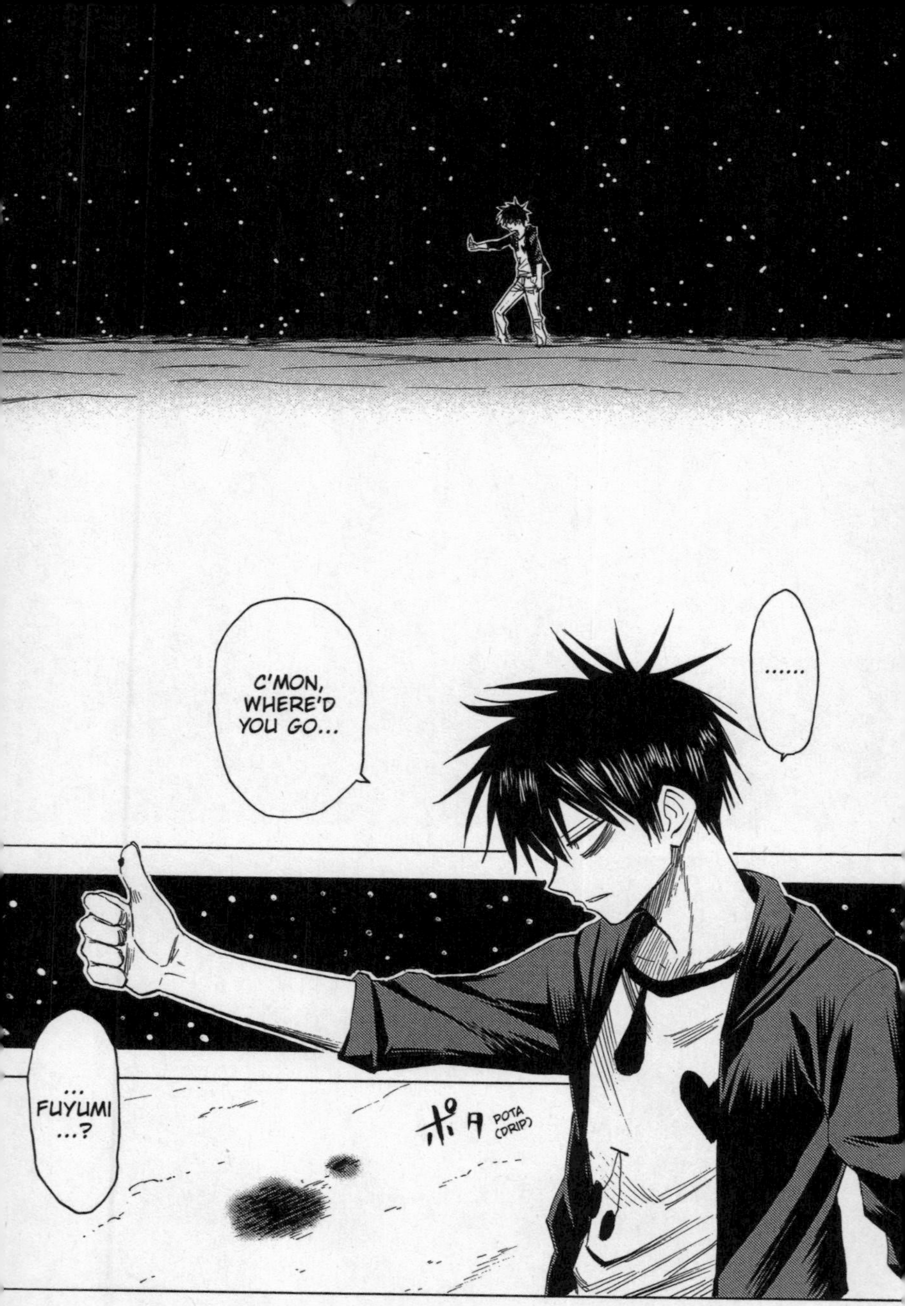
......
C'MON, WHERE'D YOU GO...
ポタ POTA (DRIP)
...FUYUMI...?

♠ To Be Continued ♠

BLOOD LAD

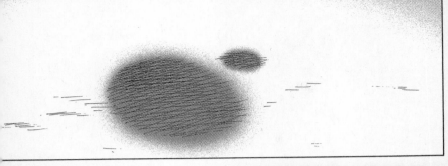

ZAKU
(KRNCH)

......

OH.
THAT'S
RIGHT...

YOU
DON'T NEED
MY MAGIC
ANYMORE...

CHAPTER 83 ◆ TRUE FEELINGS

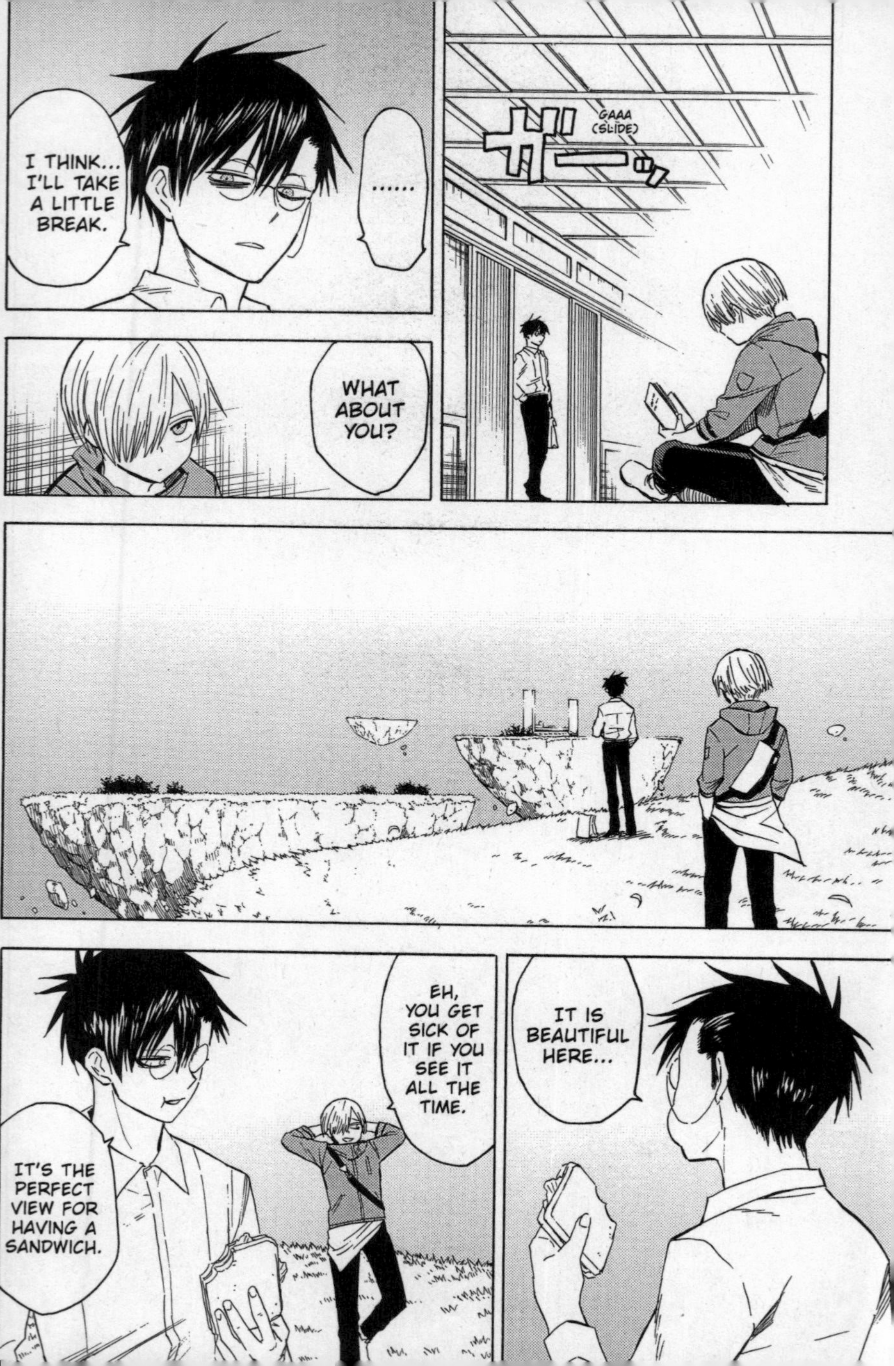
GAAA
(SLIDE)
......
I THINK... I'LL TAKE A LITTLE BREAK.
WHAT ABOUT YOU?
IT IS BEAUTIFUL HERE...
EH, YOU GET SICK OF IT IF YOU SEE IT ALL THE TIME.
IT'S THE PERFECT VIEW FOR HAVING A SANDWICH.

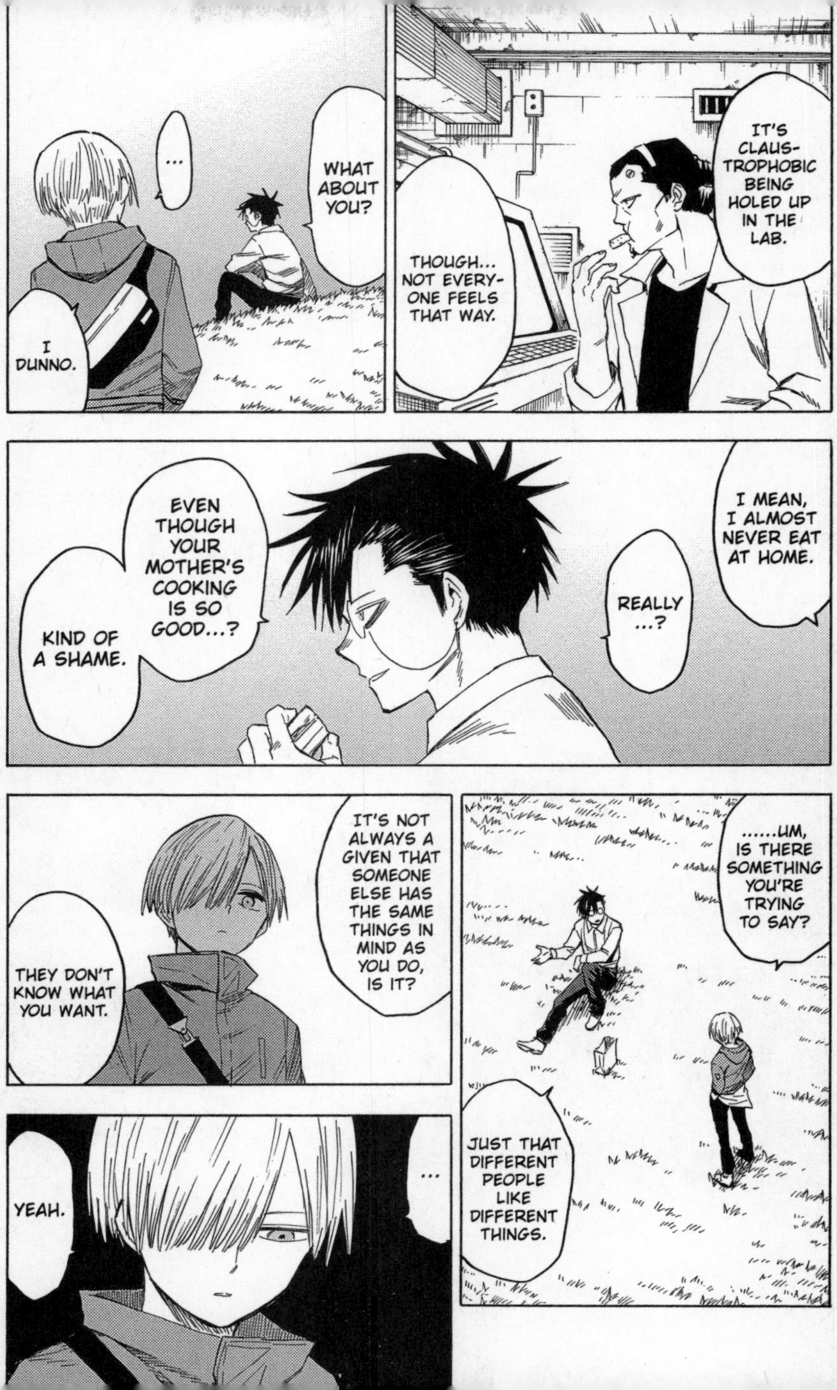
IT'S CLAUS-TROPHOBIC BEING HOLED UP IN THE LAB.
THOUGH... NOT EVERY-ONE FEELS THAT WAY.
WHAT ABOUT YOU?
...
I DUNNO.
I MEAN, I ALMOST NEVER EAT AT HOME.
REALLY ...?
EVEN THOUGH YOUR MOTHER'S COOKING IS SO GOOD...?
KIND OF A SHAME.
......UM, IS THERE SOMETHING YOU'RE TRYING TO SAY?
JUST THAT DIFFERENT PEOPLE LIKE DIFFERENT THINGS.
IT'S NOT ALWAYS A GIVEN THAT SOMEONE ELSE HAS THE SAME THINGS IN MIND AS YOU DO, IS IT?
THEY DON'T KNOW WHAT YOU WANT.
...
YEAH.

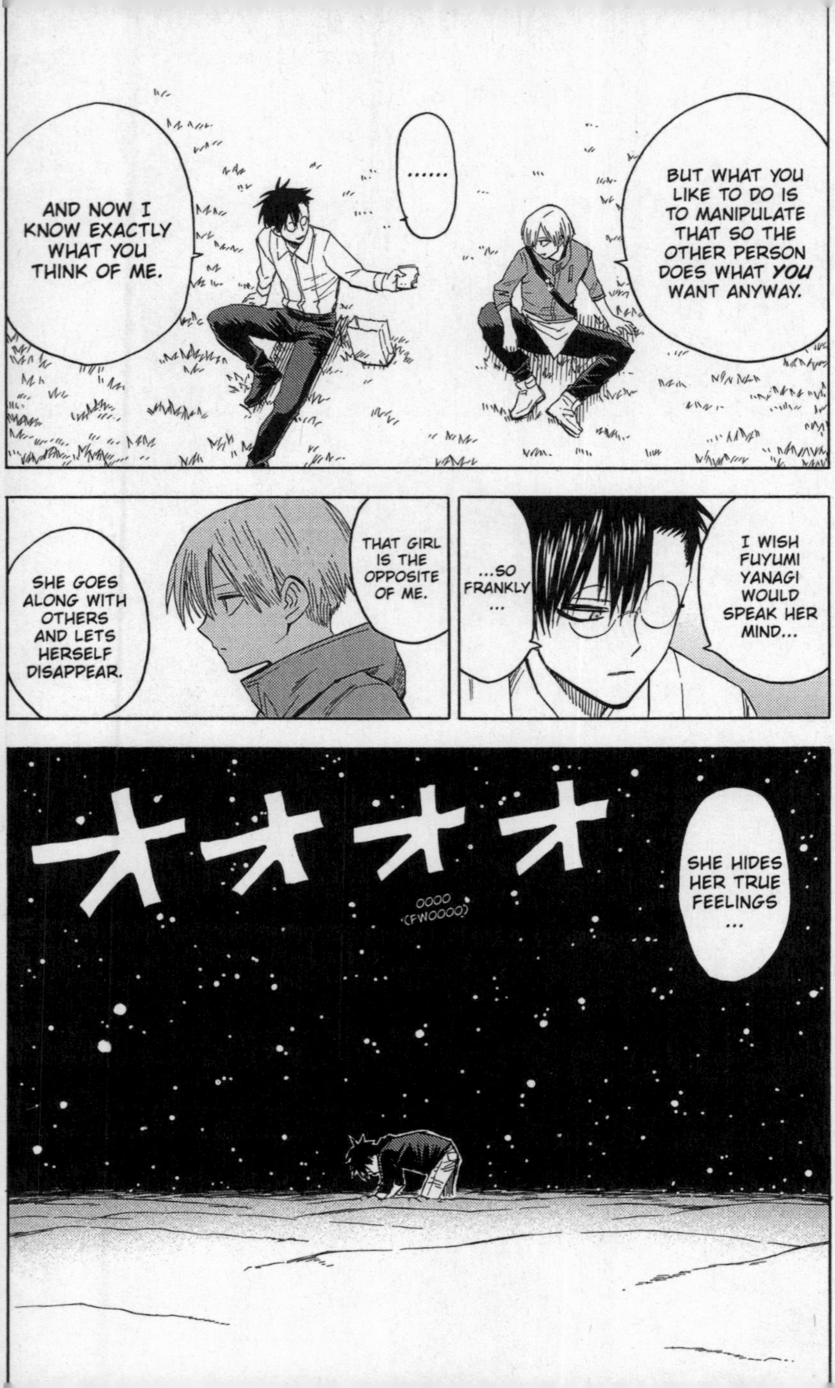
BUT WHAT YOU LIKE TO DO IS TO MANIPULATE THAT SO THE OTHER PERSON DOES WHAT *YOU* WANT ANYWAY.
......
AND NOW I KNOW EXACTLY WHAT YOU THINK OF ME.
I WISH FUYUMI YANAGI WOULD SPEAK HER MIND...
...SO FRANKLY ...
THAT GIRL IS THE OPPOSITE OF ME.
SHE GOES ALONG WITH OTHERS AND LETS HERSELF DISAPPEAR.
SHE HIDES HER TRUE FEELINGS ...
オオオオ
OOOO (FWOOOO)

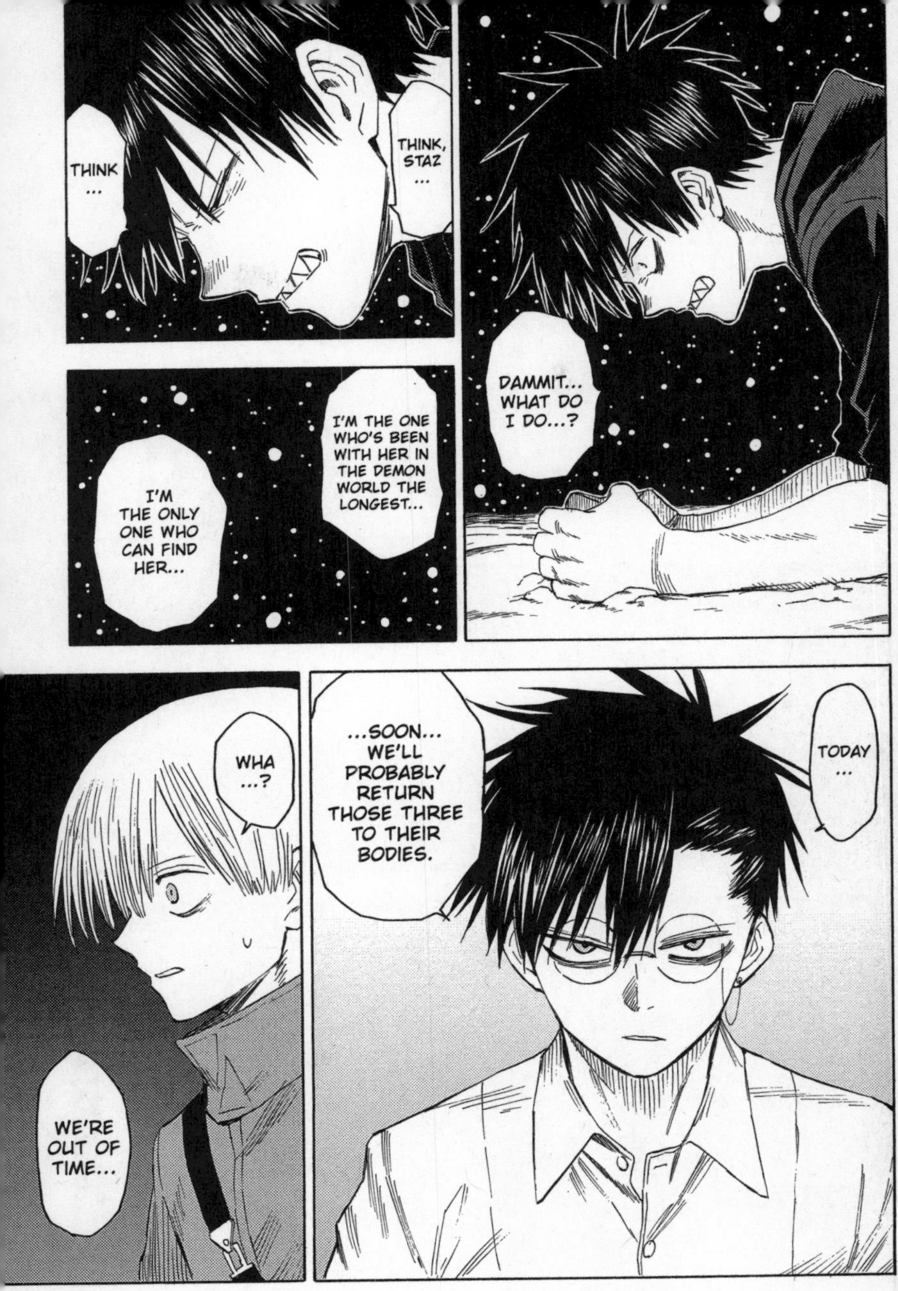
DAMMIT... WHAT DO I DO...?
THINK, STAZ...
THINK...
I'M THE ONE WHO'S BEEN WITH HER IN THE DEMON WORLD THE LONGEST...
I'M THE ONLY ONE WHO CAN FIND HER...
TODAY...
...SOON... WE'LL PROBABLY RETURN THOSE THREE TO THEIR BODIES.
WHA...?
WE'RE OUT OF TIME...

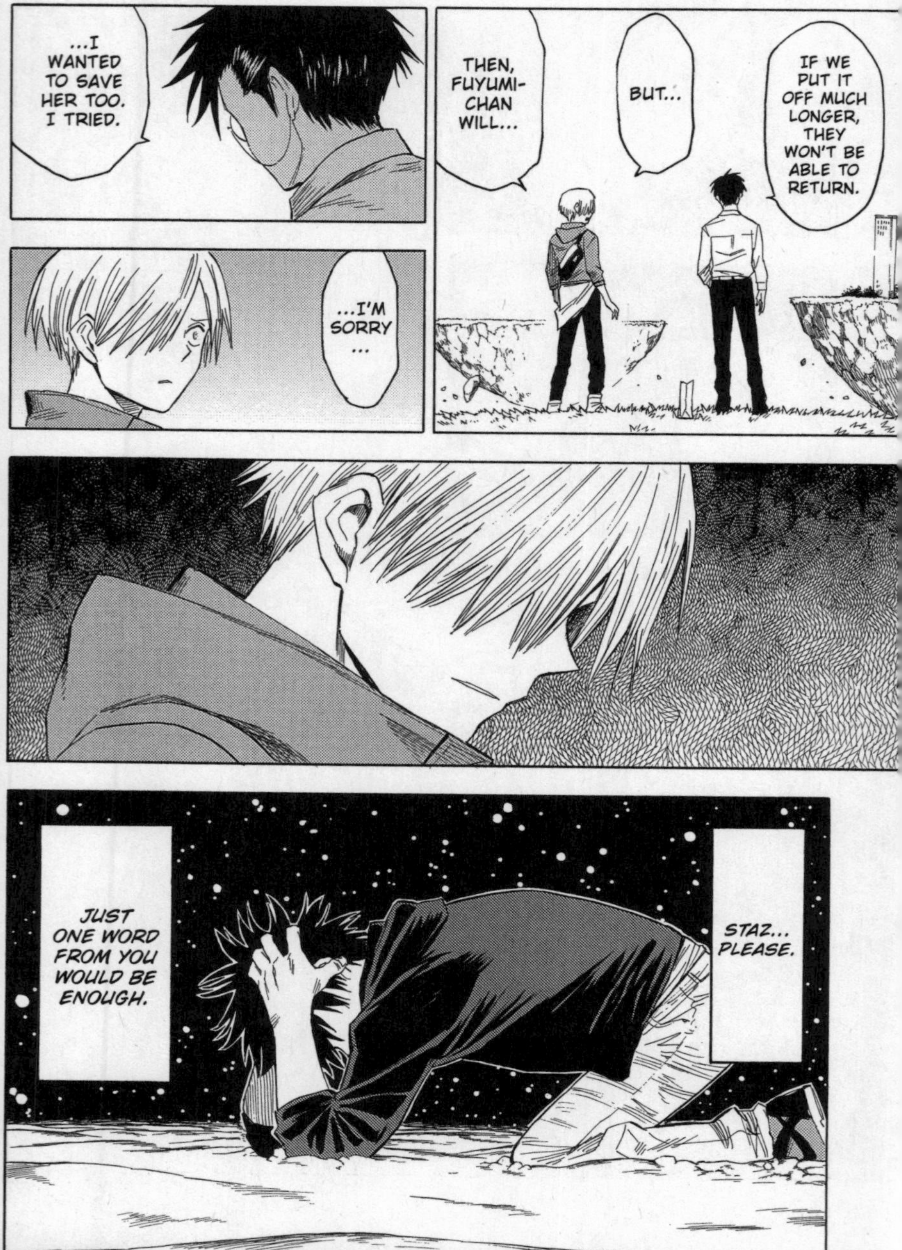
IF WE PUT IT OFF MUCH LONGER, THEY WON'T BE ABLE TO RETURN.
BUT...
THEN, FUYUMI-CHAN WILL...
...I WANTED TO SAVE HER TOO. I TRIED.
...I'M SORRY...
STAZ... PLEASE.
JUST ONE WORD FROM YOU WOULD BE ENOUGH.

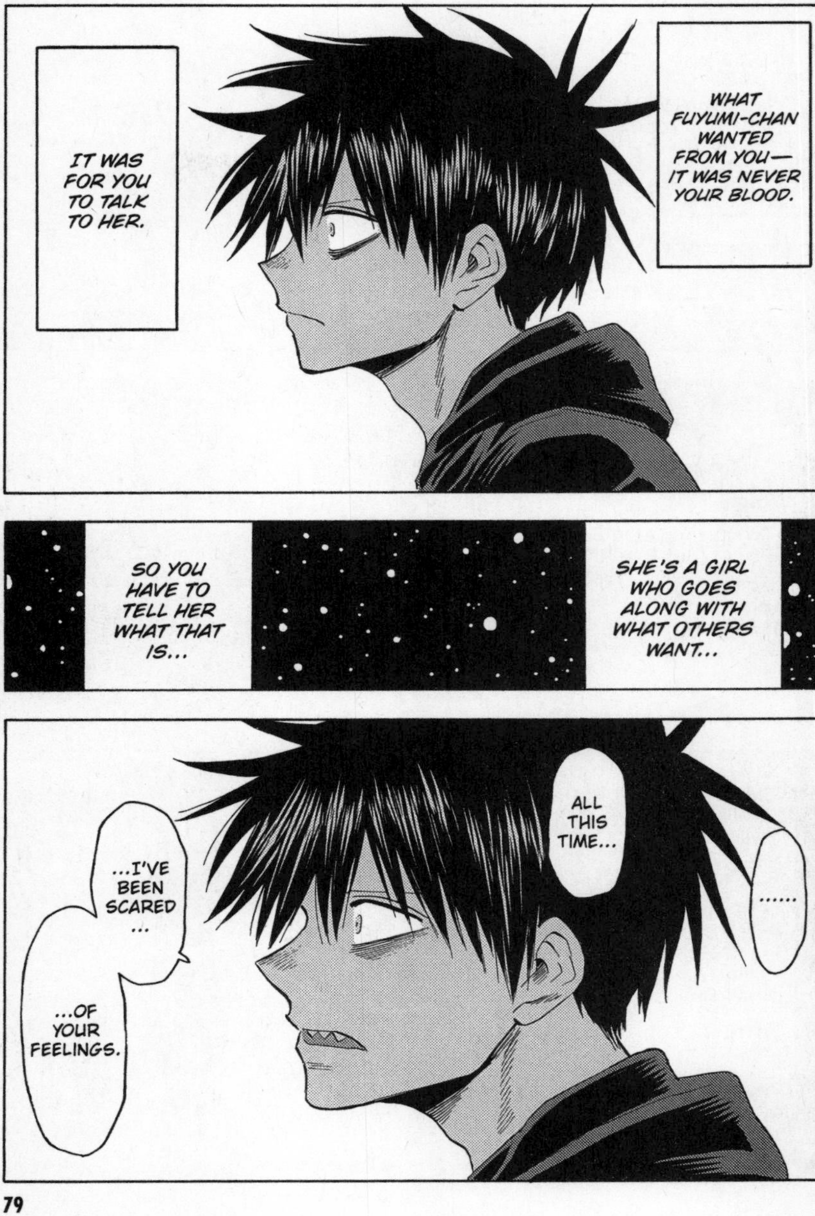
WHAT FUYUMI-CHAN WANTED FROM YOU—IT WAS NEVER YOUR BLOOD.
IT WAS FOR YOU TO TALK TO HER.
SHE'S A GIRL WHO GOES ALONG WITH WHAT OTHERS WANT...
SO YOU HAVE TO TELL HER WHAT THAT IS...
......
ALL THIS TIME...
...I'VE BEEN SCARED...
...OF YOUR FEELINGS.

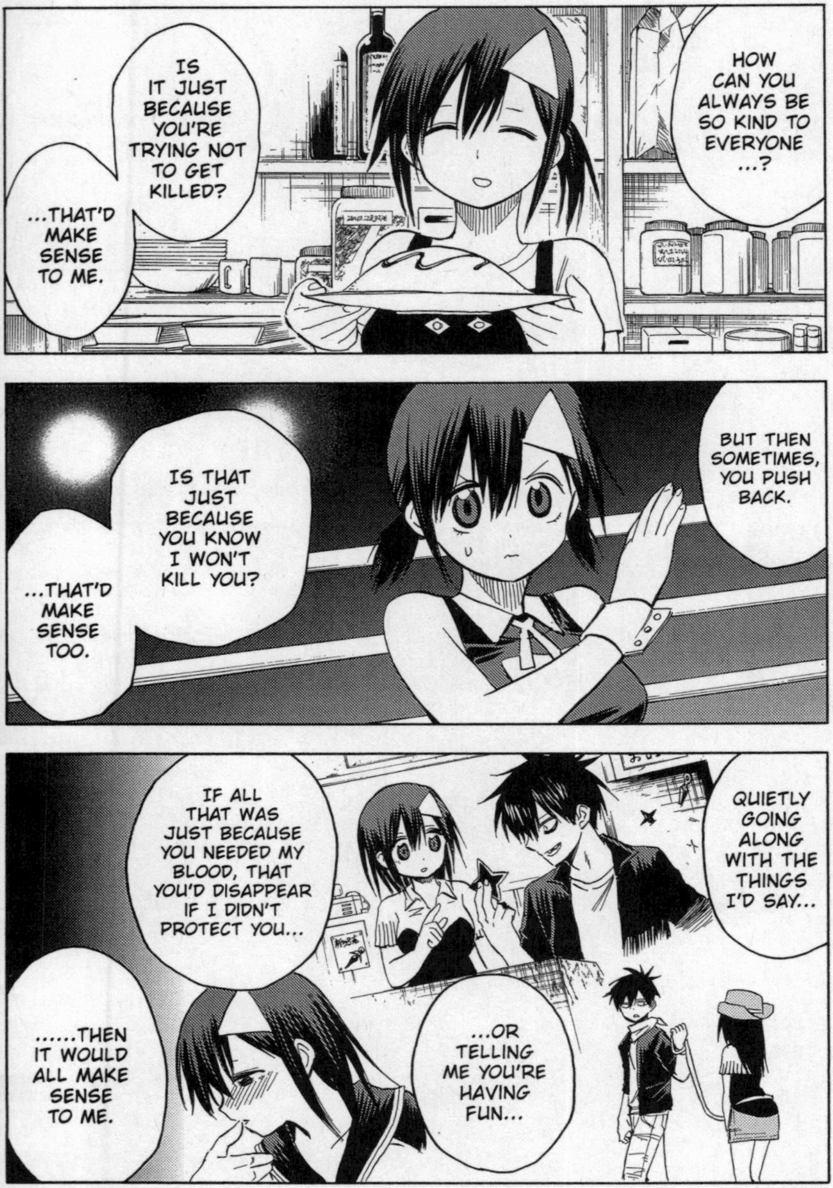
HOW CAN YOU ALWAYS BE SO KIND TO EVERYONE ...?
IS IT JUST BECAUSE YOU'RE TRYING NOT TO GET KILLED?
...THAT'D MAKE SENSE TO ME.
BUT THEN SOMETIMES, YOU PUSH BACK.
IS THAT JUST BECAUSE YOU KNOW I WON'T KILL YOU?
...THAT'D MAKE SENSE TOO.
QUIETLY GOING ALONG WITH THE THINGS I'D SAY...
...OR TELLING ME YOU'RE HAVING FUN...
IF ALL THAT WAS JUST BECAUSE YOU NEEDED MY BLOOD, THAT YOU'D DISAPPEAR IF I DIDN'T PROTECT YOU...
......THEN IT WOULD ALL MAKE SENSE TO ME.

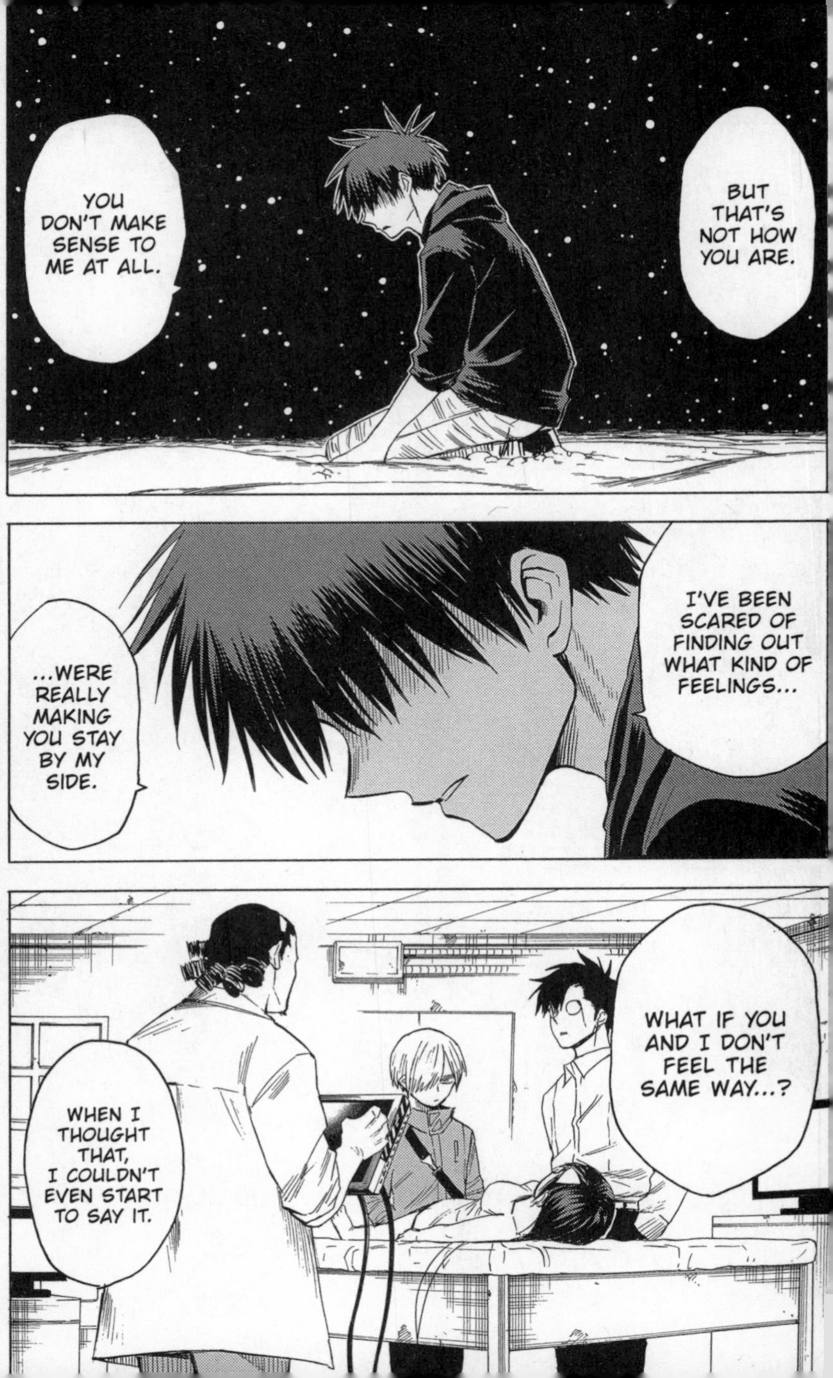
BUT THAT'S NOT HOW YOU ARE.
YOU DON'T MAKE SENSE TO ME AT ALL.
I'VE BEEN SCARED OF FINDING OUT WHAT KIND OF FEELINGS...
...WERE REALLY MAKING YOU STAY BY MY SIDE.
WHAT IF YOU AND I DON'T FEEL THE SAME WAY...?
WHEN I THOUGHT THAT, I COULDN'T EVEN START TO SAY IT.

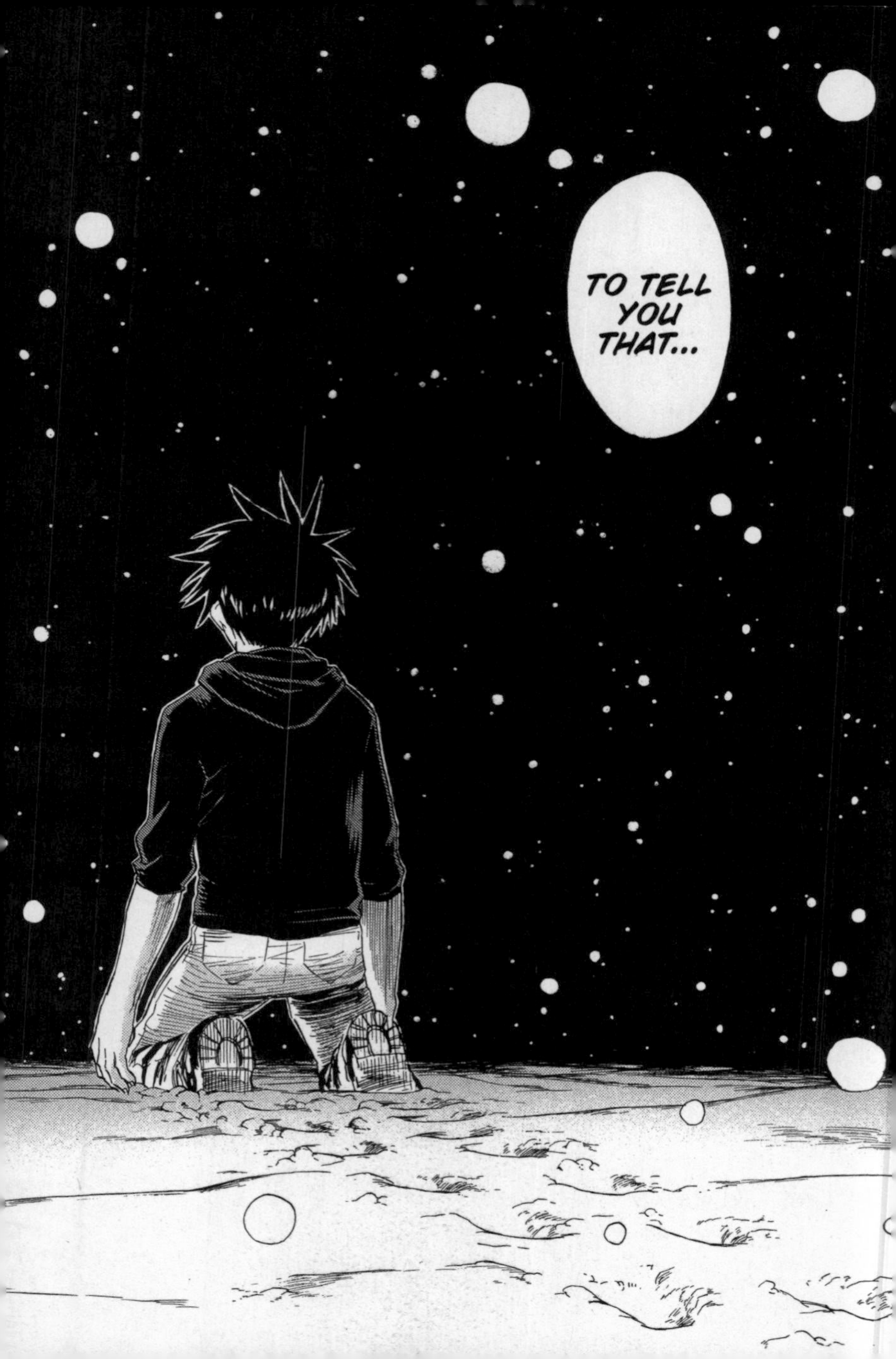
TO TELL YOU THAT...

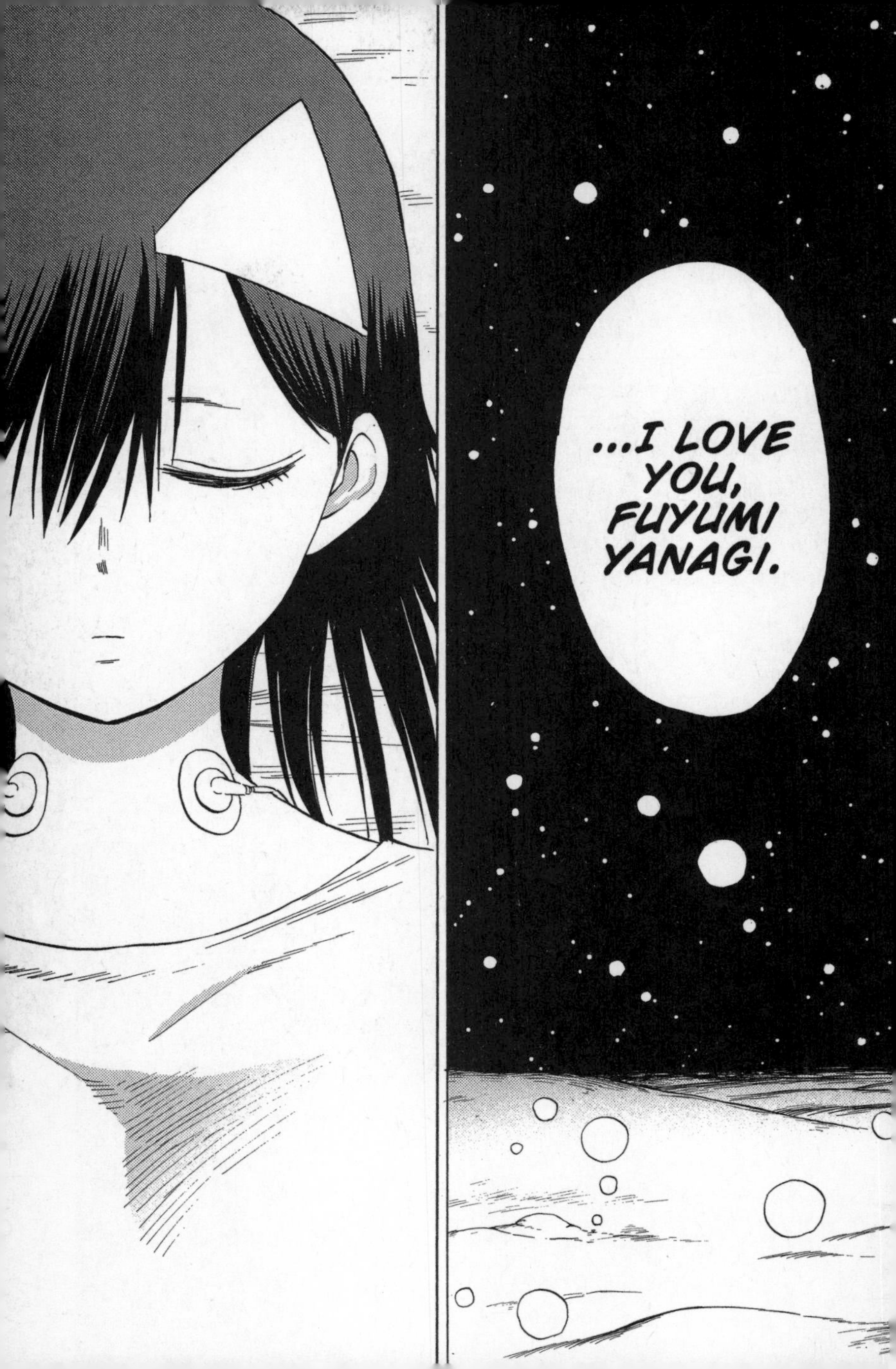
...I LOVE YOU, FUYUMI YANAGI.

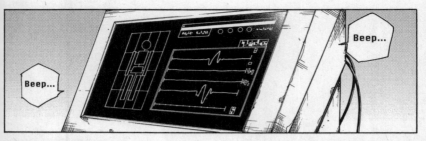

Beep...

Beep...

...SHE'S AWAKE ...!?

WAIT A SEC... THAT'S...

!

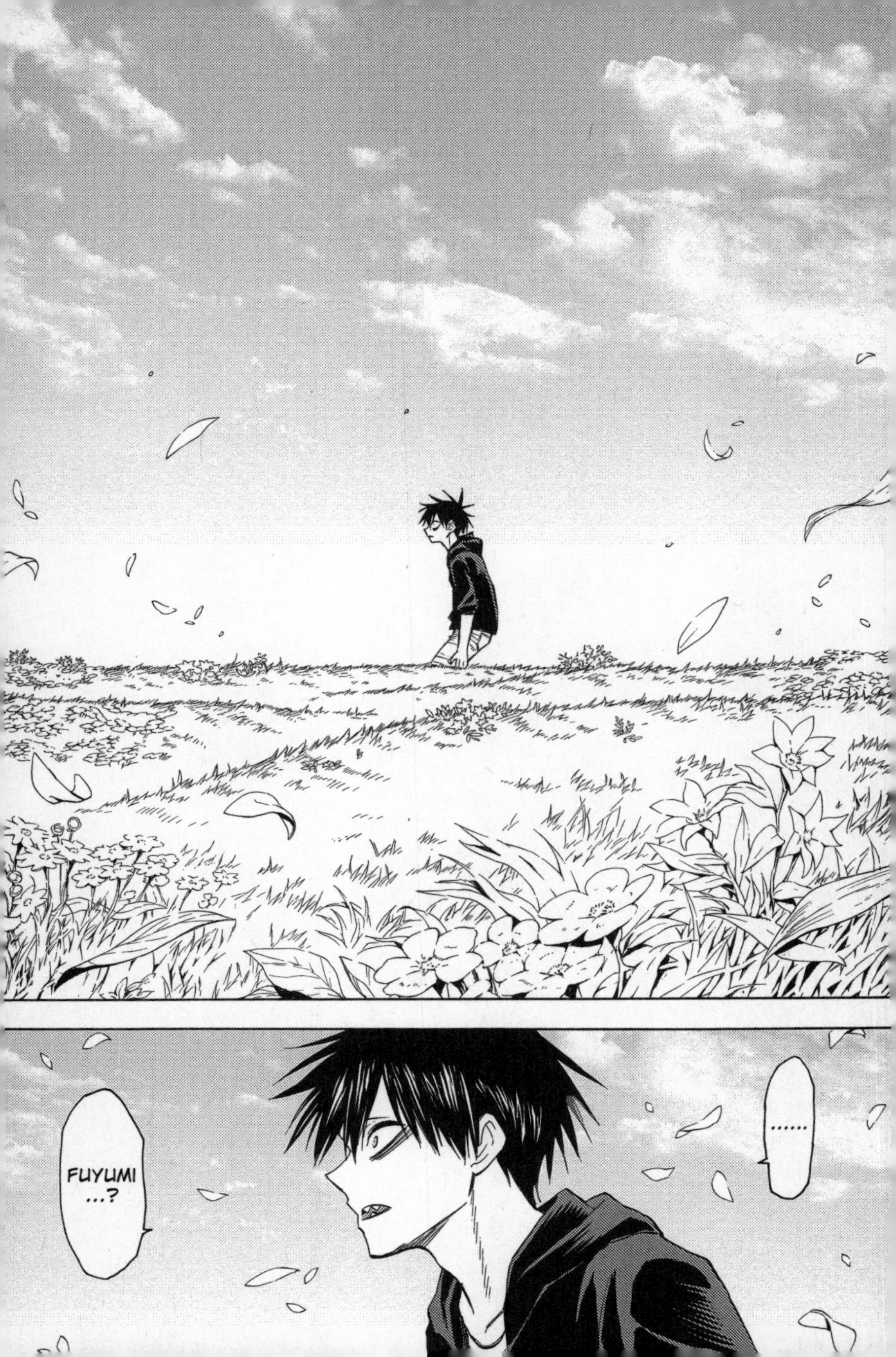
......
FUYUMI ...?

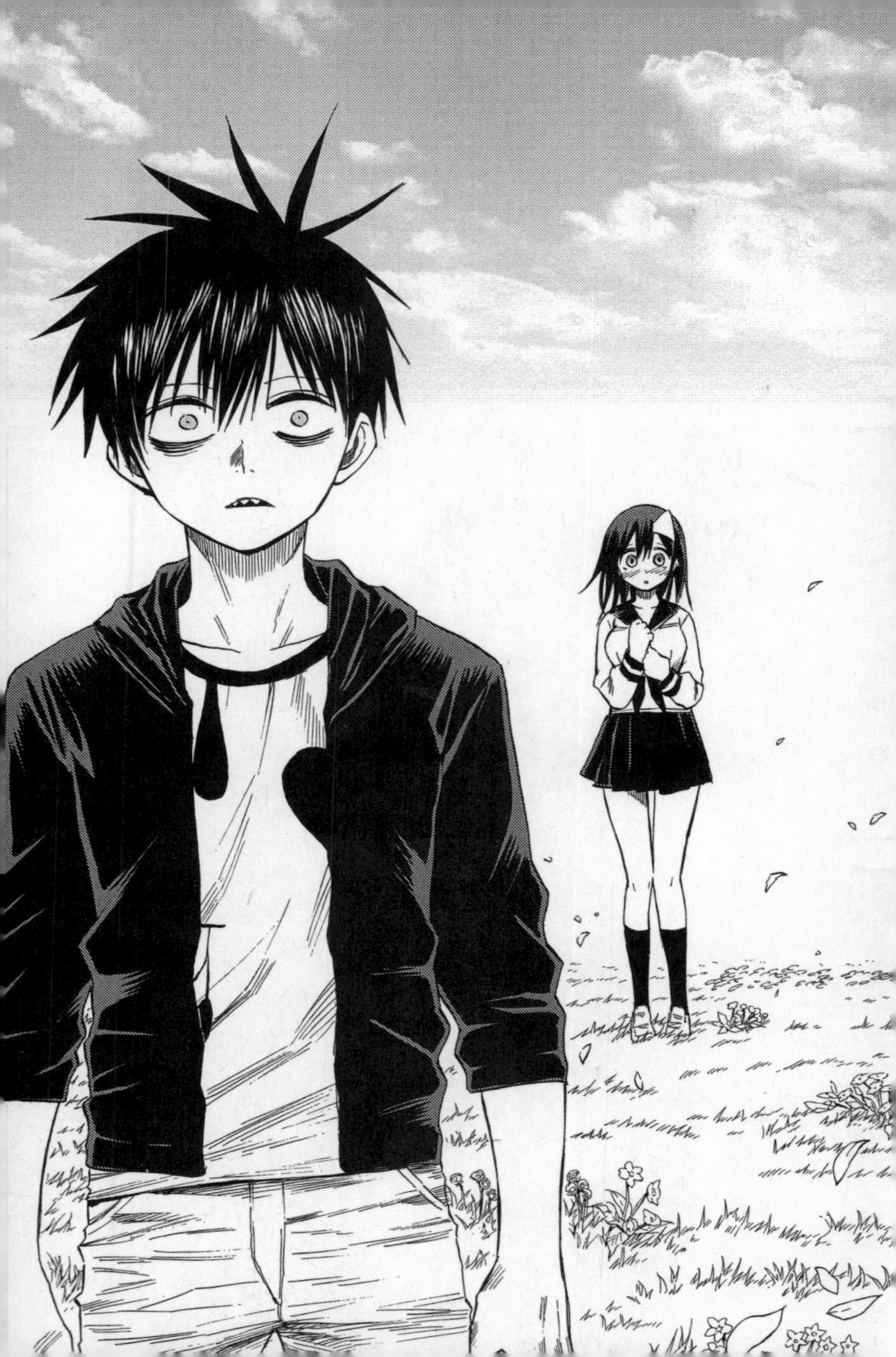

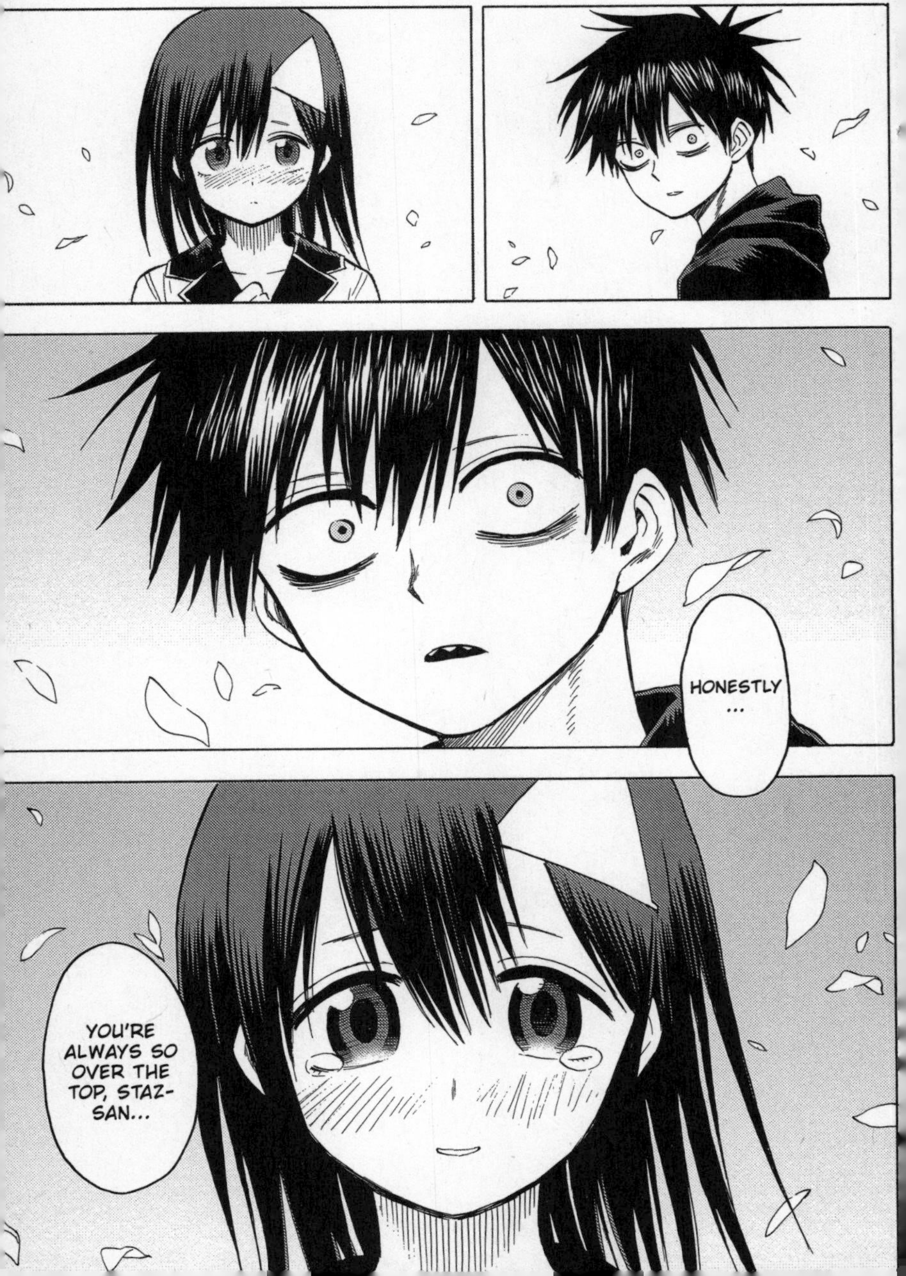
HONESTLY ...
YOU'RE ALWAYS SO OVER THE TOP, STAZ-SAN...

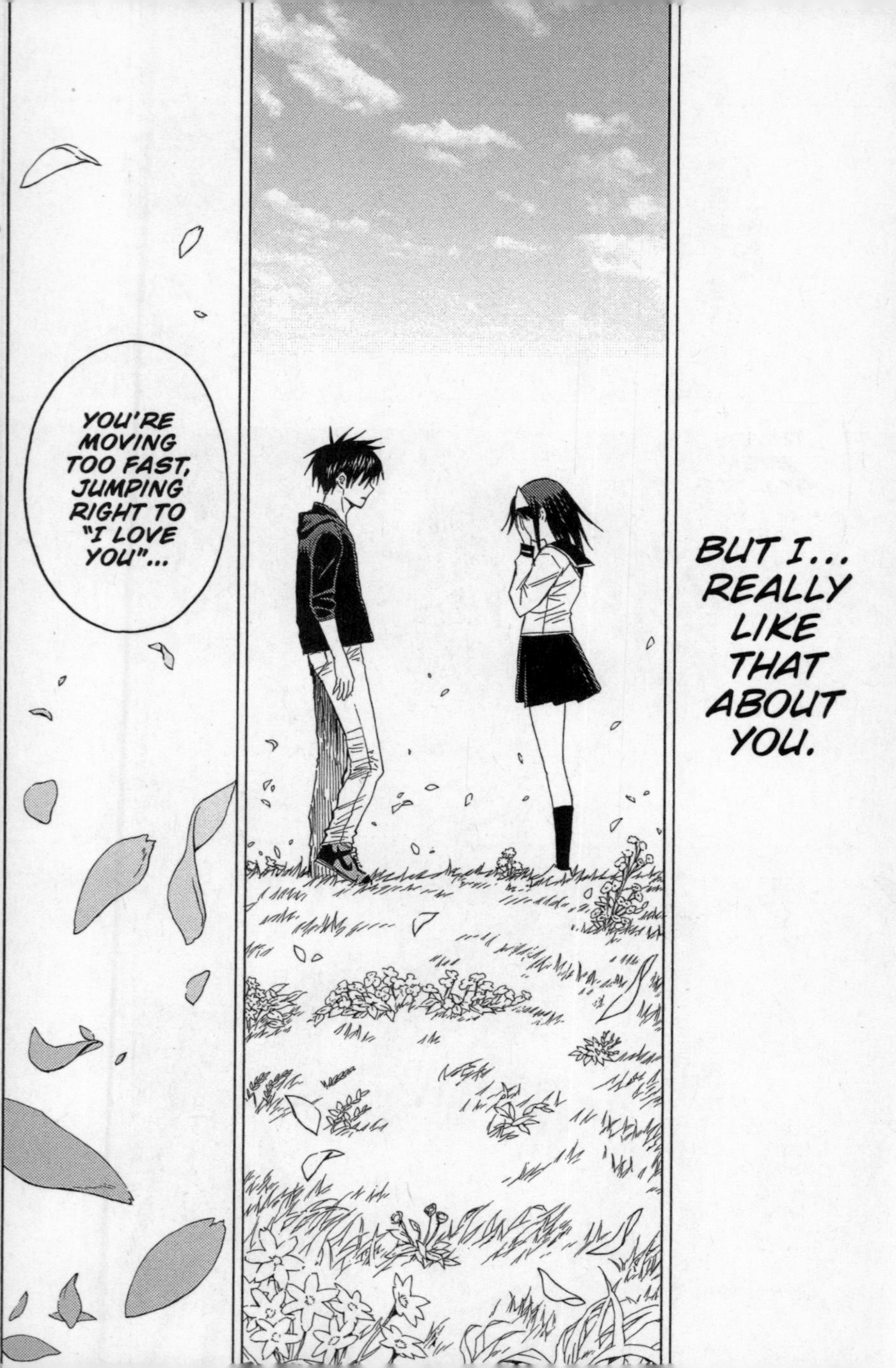
YOU'RE MOVING TOO FAST, JUMPING RIGHT TO "I LOVE YOU"...
BUT I... REALLY LIKE THAT ABOUT YOU.

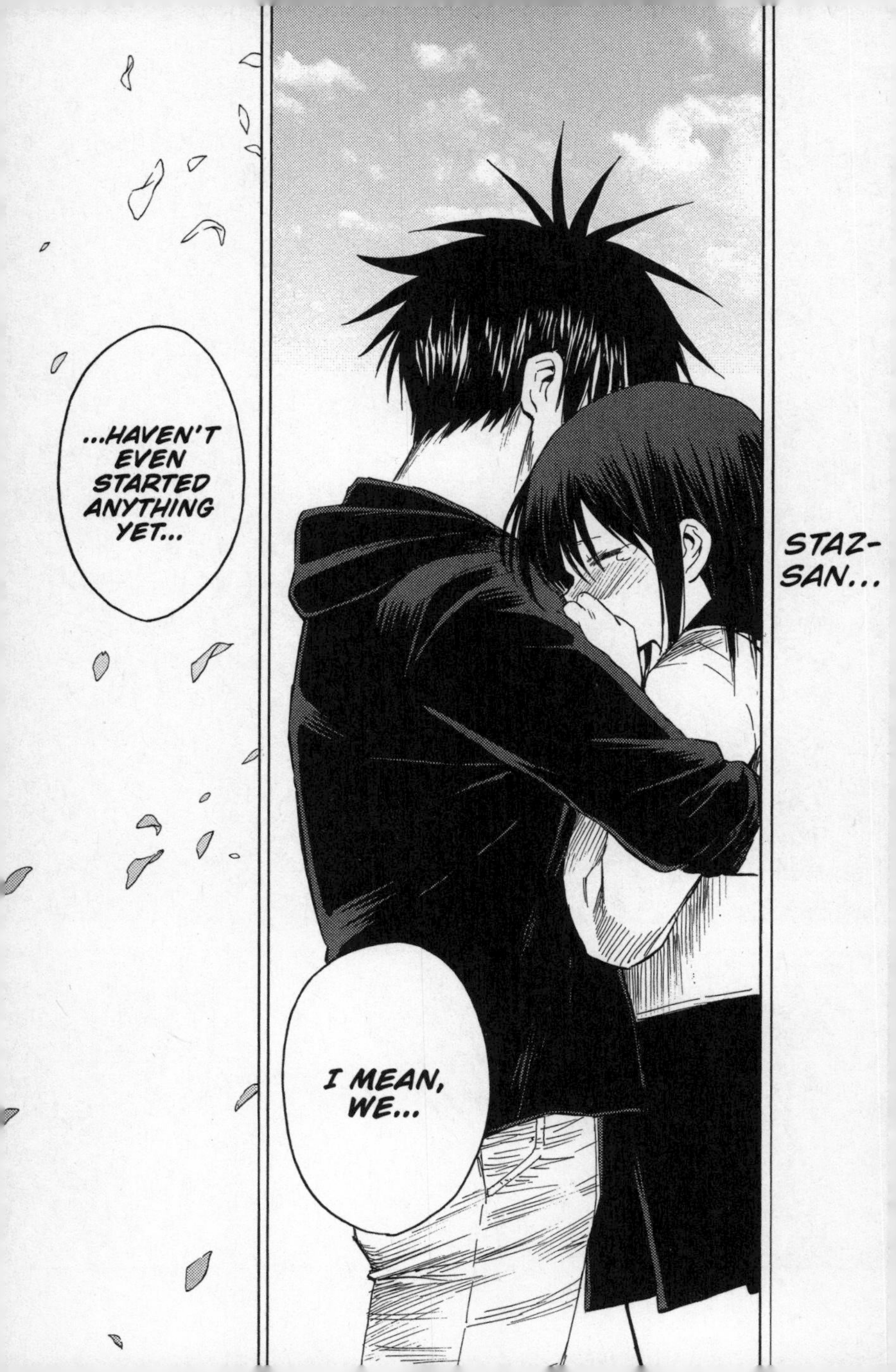
STAZ-SAN...
I MEAN, WE...
...HAVEN'T EVEN STARTED ANYTHING YET...

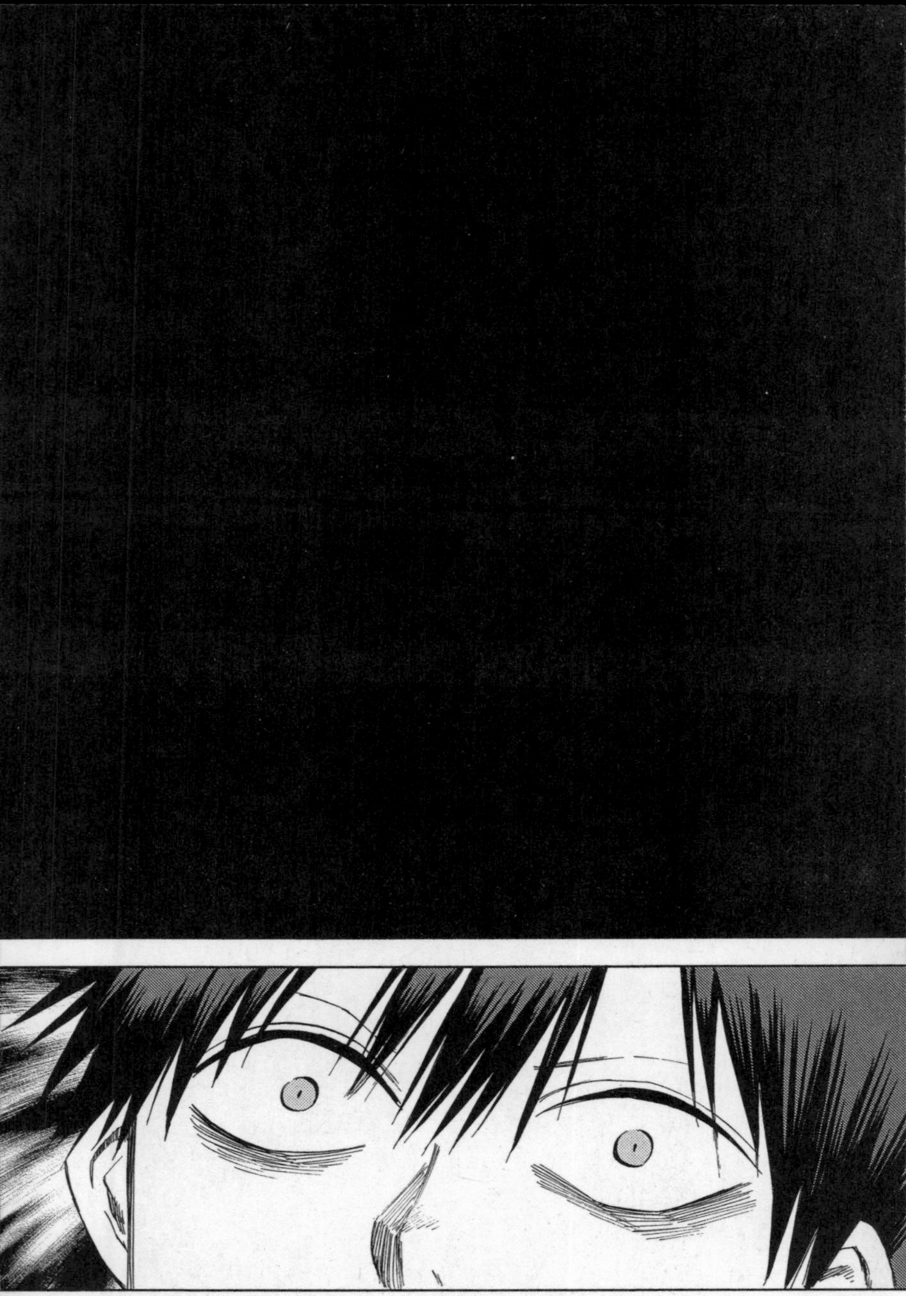

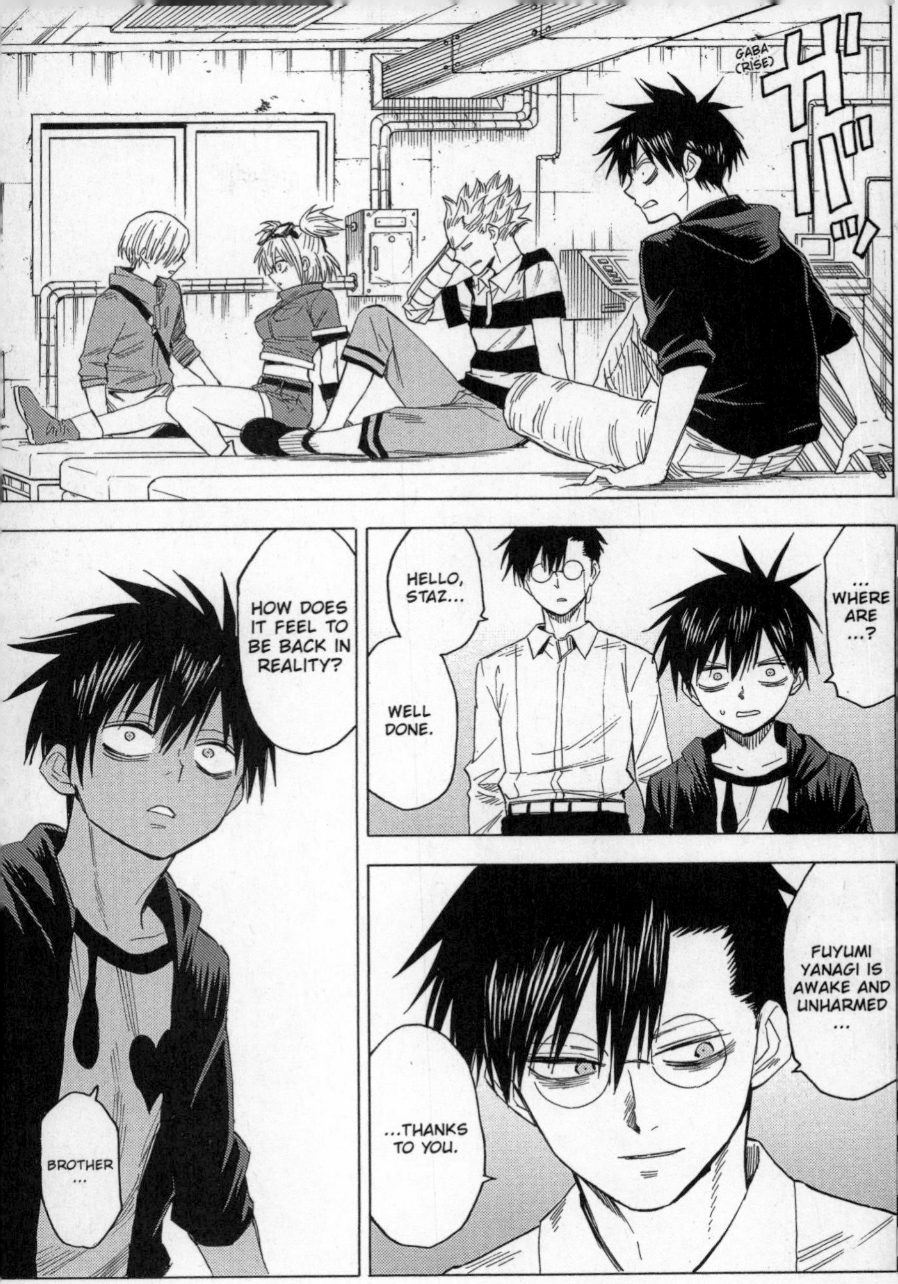
GABA (RISE)
... WHERE ARE ...?
HELLO, STAZ...
WELL DONE.
FUYUMI YANAGI IS AWAKE AND UNHARMED ...
...THANKS TO YOU.
HOW DOES IT FEEL TO BE BACK IN REALITY?
BROTHER ...

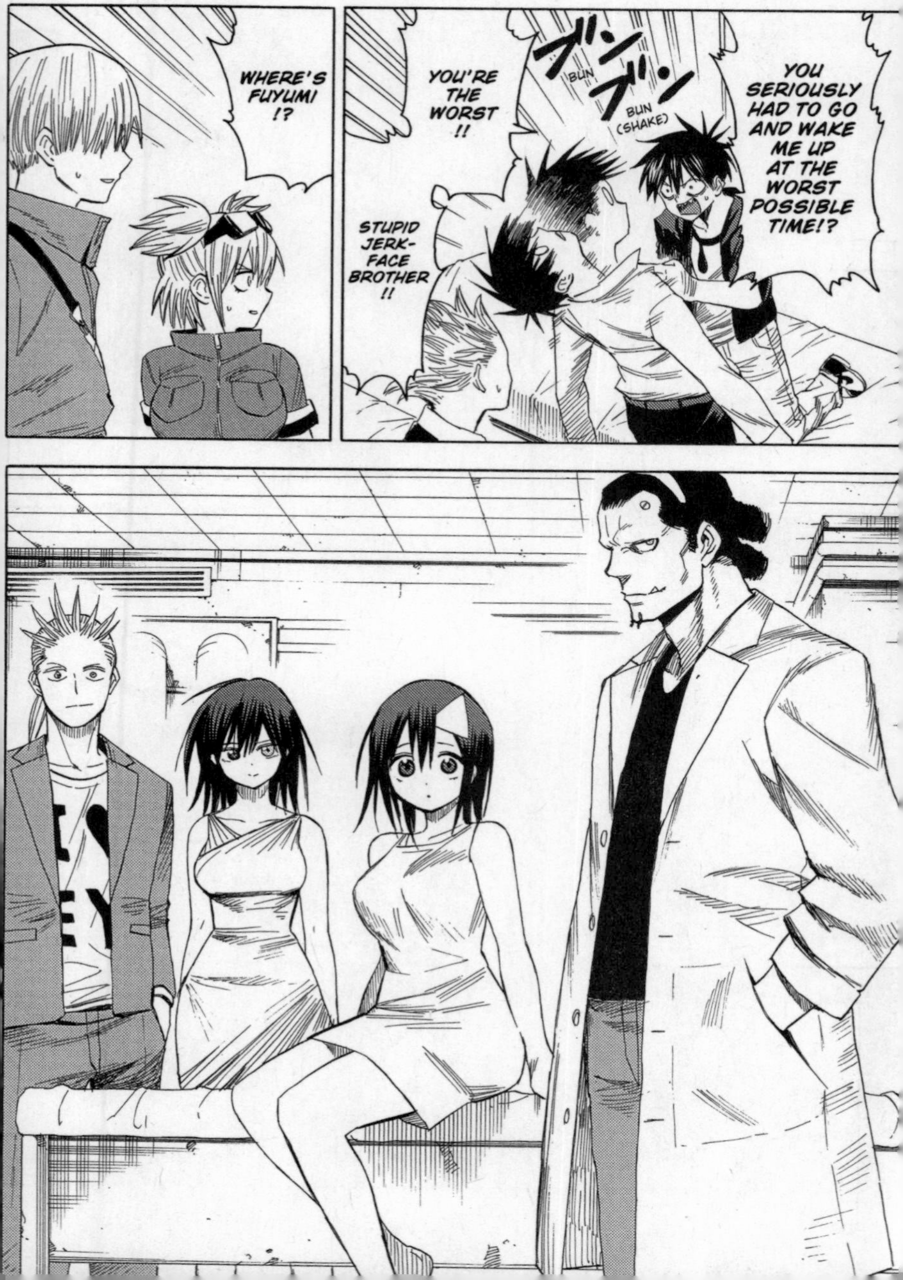
YOU SERIOUSLY HAD TO GO AND WAKE ME UP AT THE WORST POSSIBLE TIME!?
ブン BUN
ブン BUN (SHAKE)
YOU'RE THE WORST!!
STUPID JERK-FACE BROTHER!!
WHERE'S FUYUMI!?

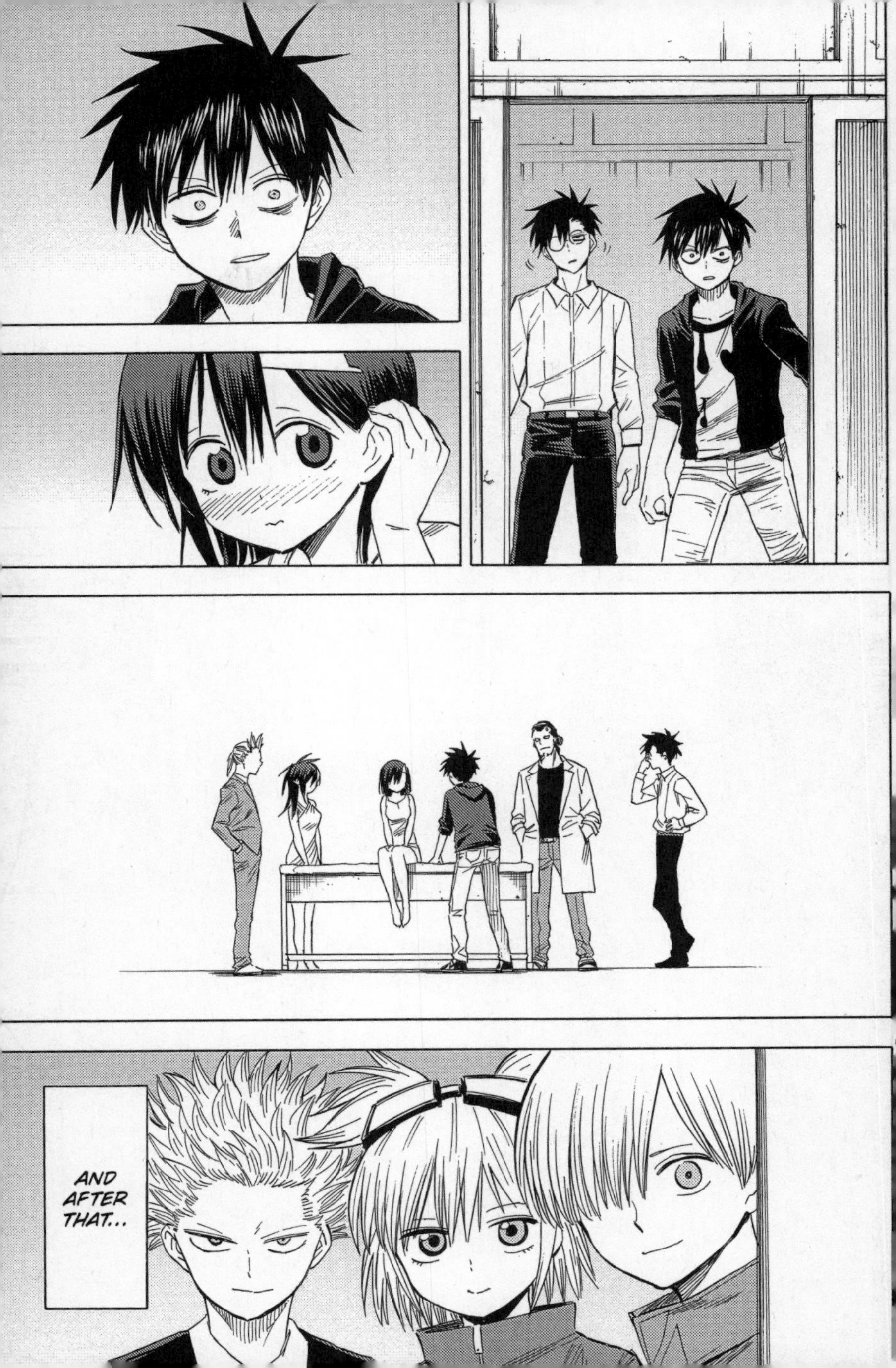
AND AFTER THAT...

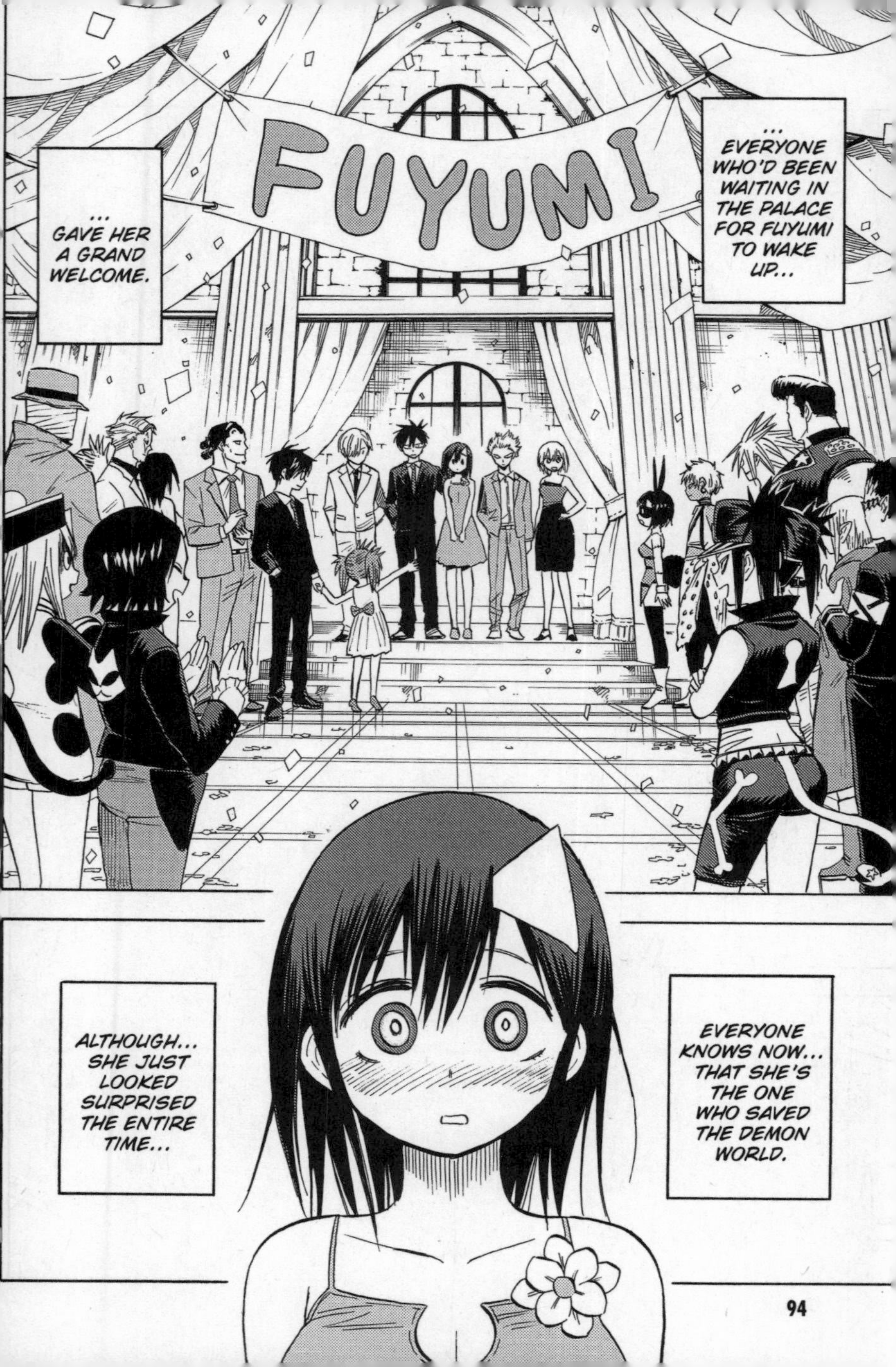

... EVERYONE WHO'D BEEN WAITING IN THE PALACE FOR FUYUMI TO WAKE UP...
FUYUMI
... GAVE HER A GRAND WELCOME.
EVERYONE KNOWS NOW... THAT SHE'S THE ONE WHO SAVED THE DEMON WORLD.
ALTHOUGH... SHE JUST LOOKED SURPRISED THE ENTIRE TIME...

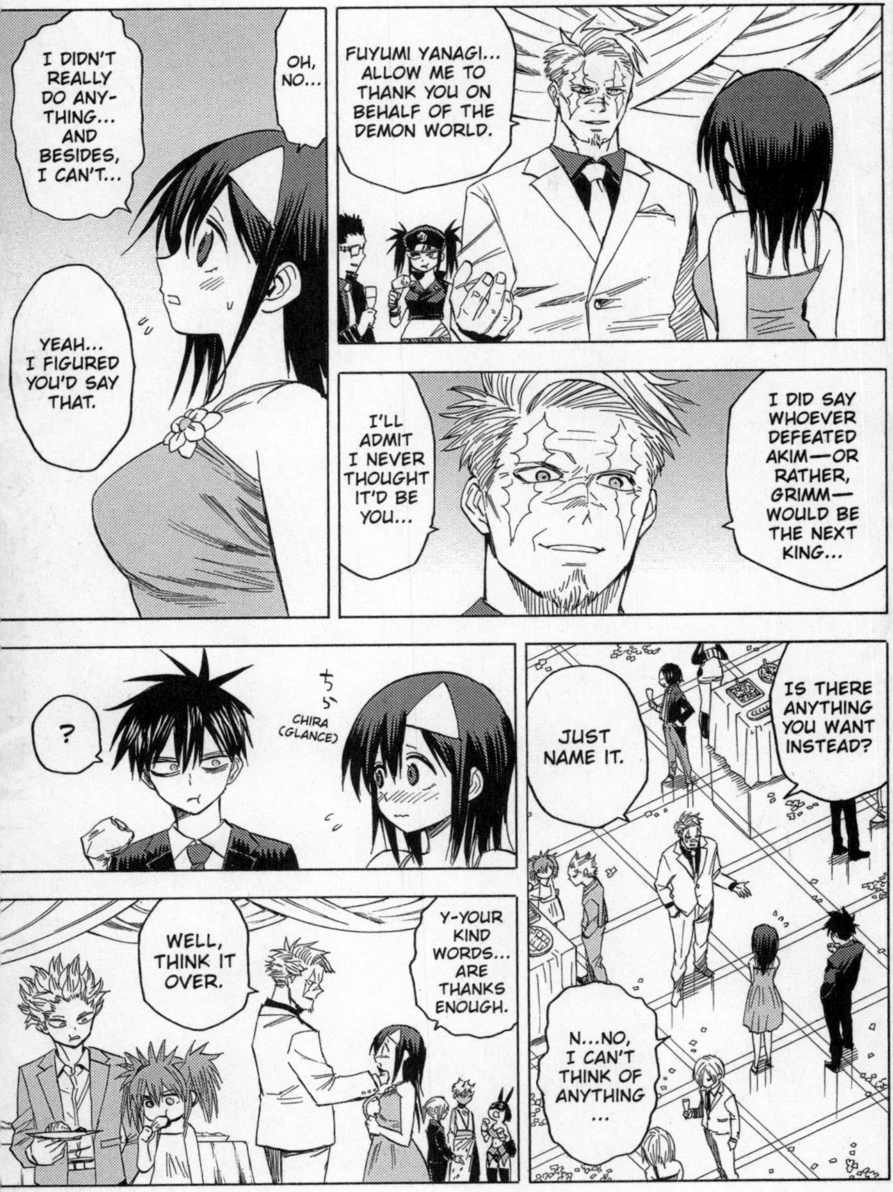
FUYUMI YANAGI... ALLOW ME TO THANK YOU ON BEHALF OF THE DEMON WORLD.
I DID SAY WHOEVER DEFEATED AKIM—OR RATHER, GRIMM—WOULD BE THE NEXT KING...
I'LL ADMIT I NEVER THOUGHT IT'D BE YOU...
OH, NO...
I DIDN'T REALLY DO ANY-THING... AND BESIDES, I CAN'T...
YEAH... I FIGURED YOU'D SAY THAT.
IS THERE ANYTHING YOU WANT INSTEAD?
JUST NAME IT.
N...NO, I CAN'T THINK OF ANYTHING ...
ちら
CHIRA (GLANCE)
?
Y-YOUR KIND WORDS... ARE THANKS ENOUGH.
WELL, THINK IT OVER.

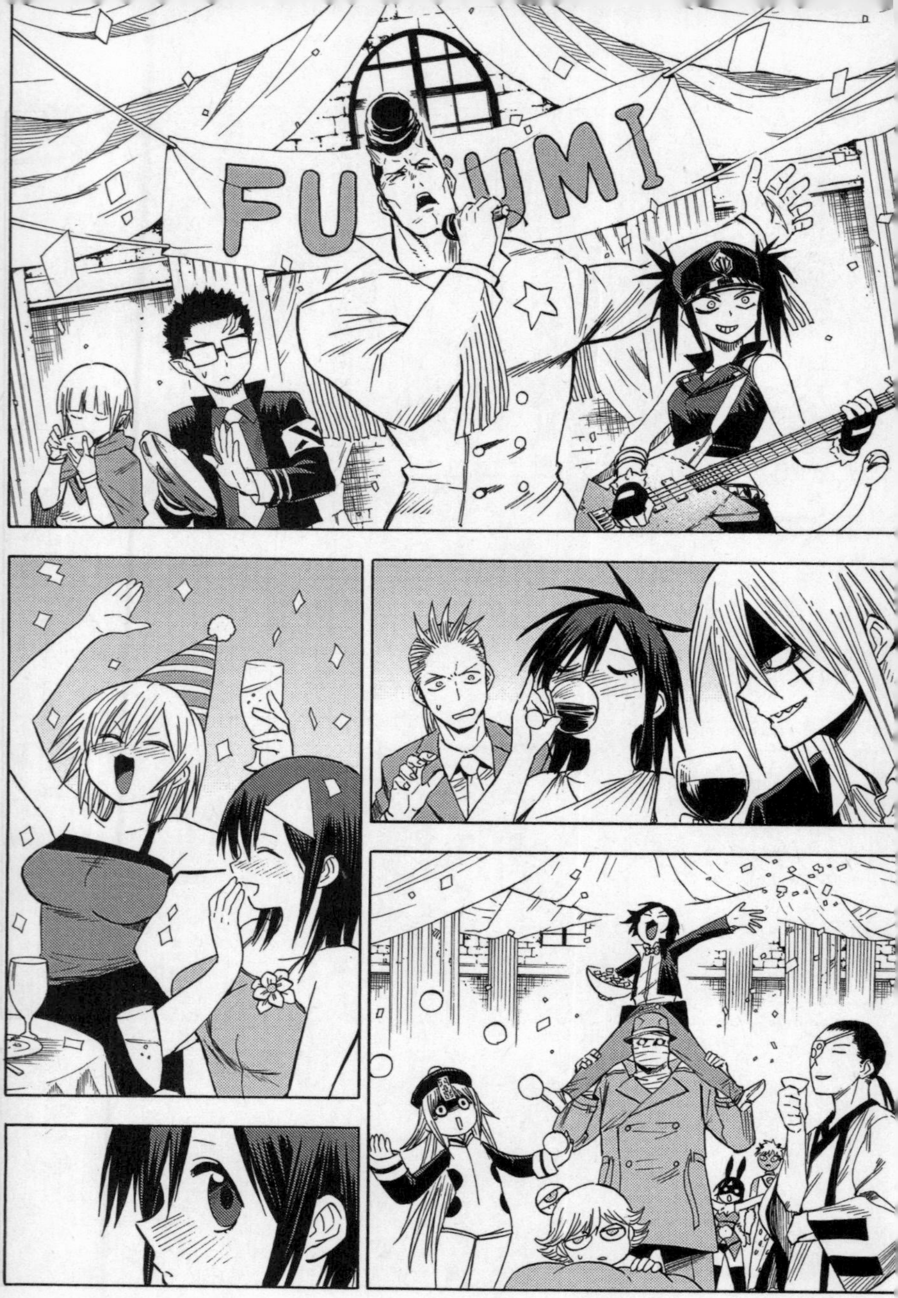
FU UMI

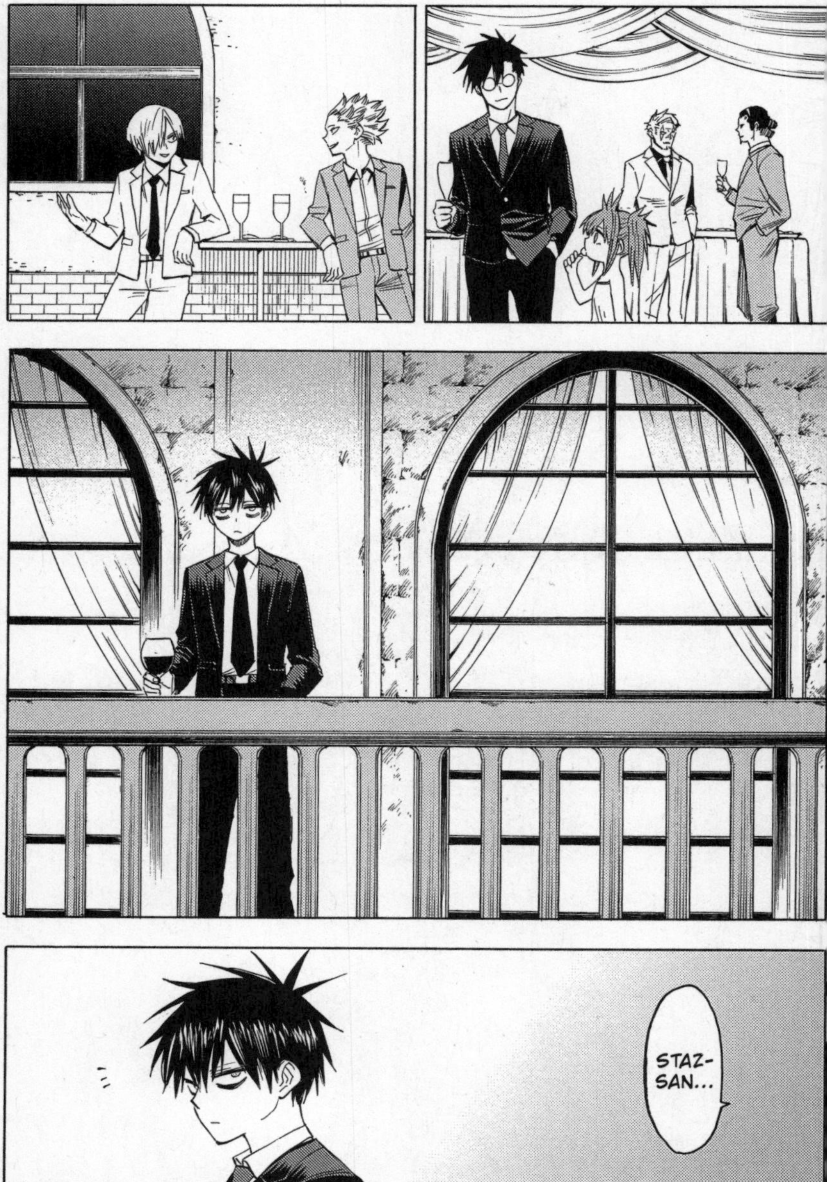
STAZ-
SAN...

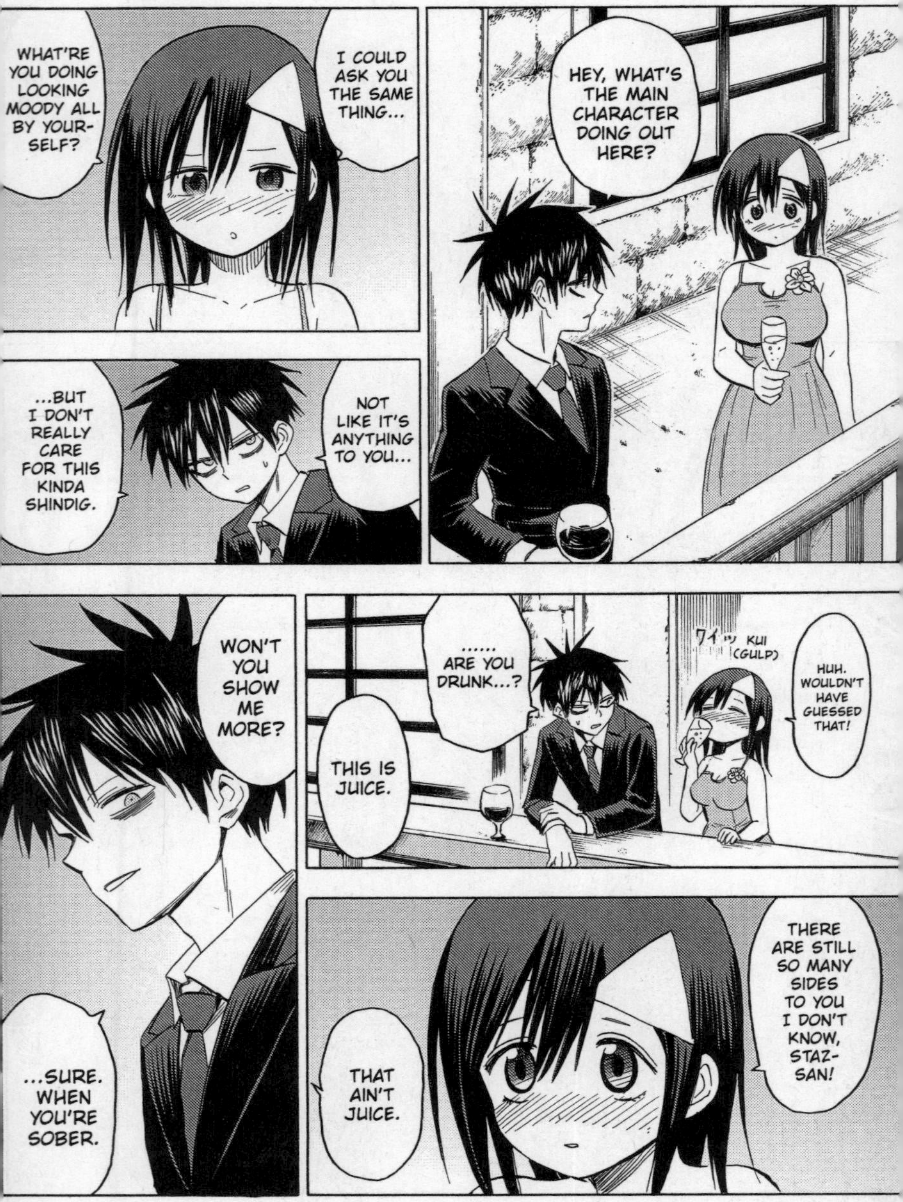
HEY, WHAT'S THE MAIN CHARACTER DOING OUT HERE?
I COULD ASK YOU THE SAME THING...
WHAT'RE YOU DOING LOOKING MOODY ALL BY YOURSELF?
NOT LIKE IT'S ANYTHING TO YOU...
...BUT I DON'T REALLY CARE FOR THIS KINDA SHINDIG.
HUH. WOULDN'T HAVE GUESSED THAT!
クイッ KUI (GULP)
...... ARE YOU DRUNK...?
THIS IS JUICE.
THERE ARE STILL SO MANY SIDES TO YOU I DON'T KNOW, STAZ-SAN!
THAT AIN'T JUICE.
WON'T YOU SHOW ME MORE?
...SURE. WHEN YOU'RE SOBER.

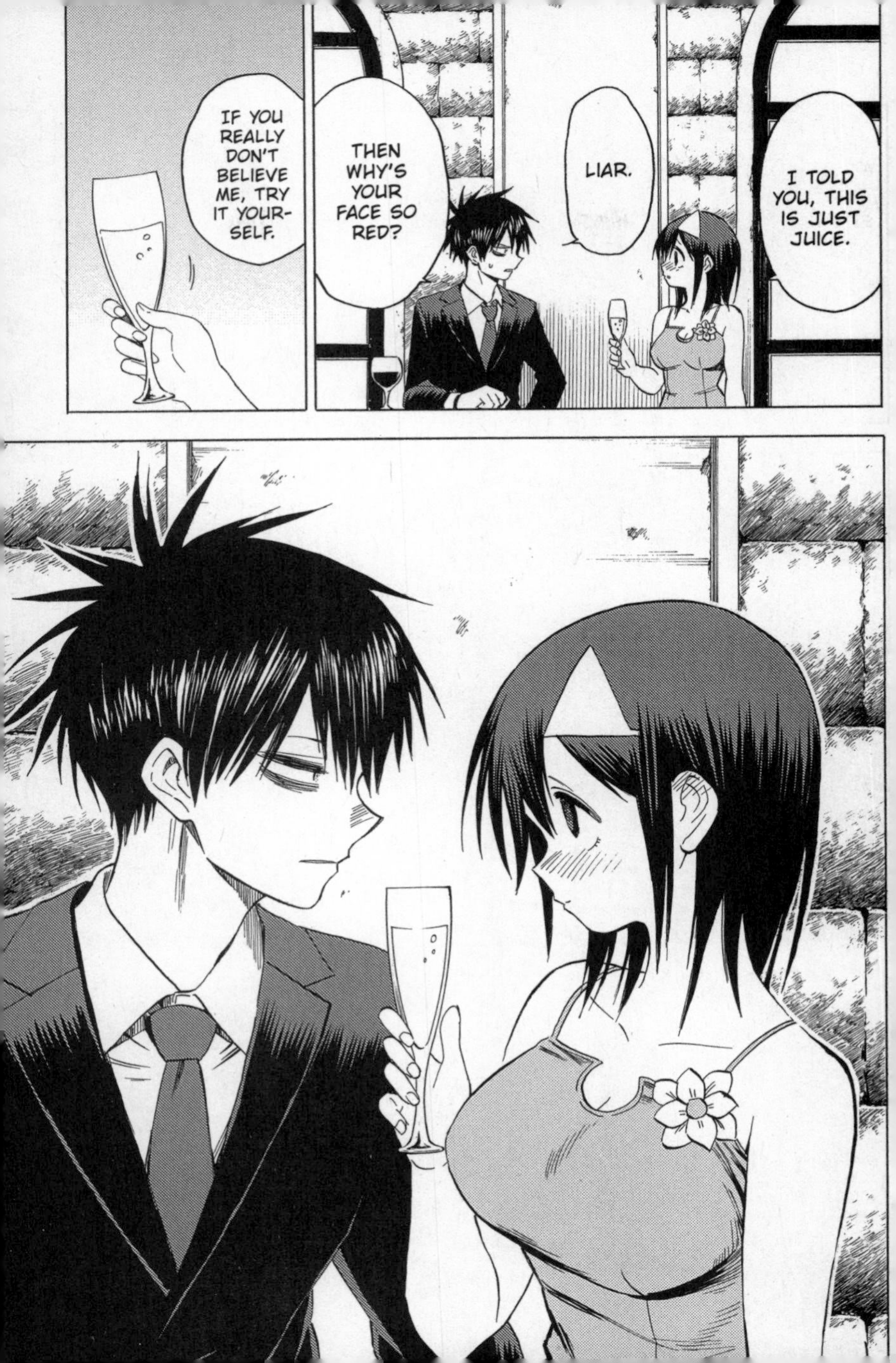
I TOLD YOU, THIS IS JUST JUICE.
LIAR.
THEN WHY'S YOUR FACE SO RED?
IF YOU REALLY DON'T BELIEVE ME, TRY IT YOUR-SELF.

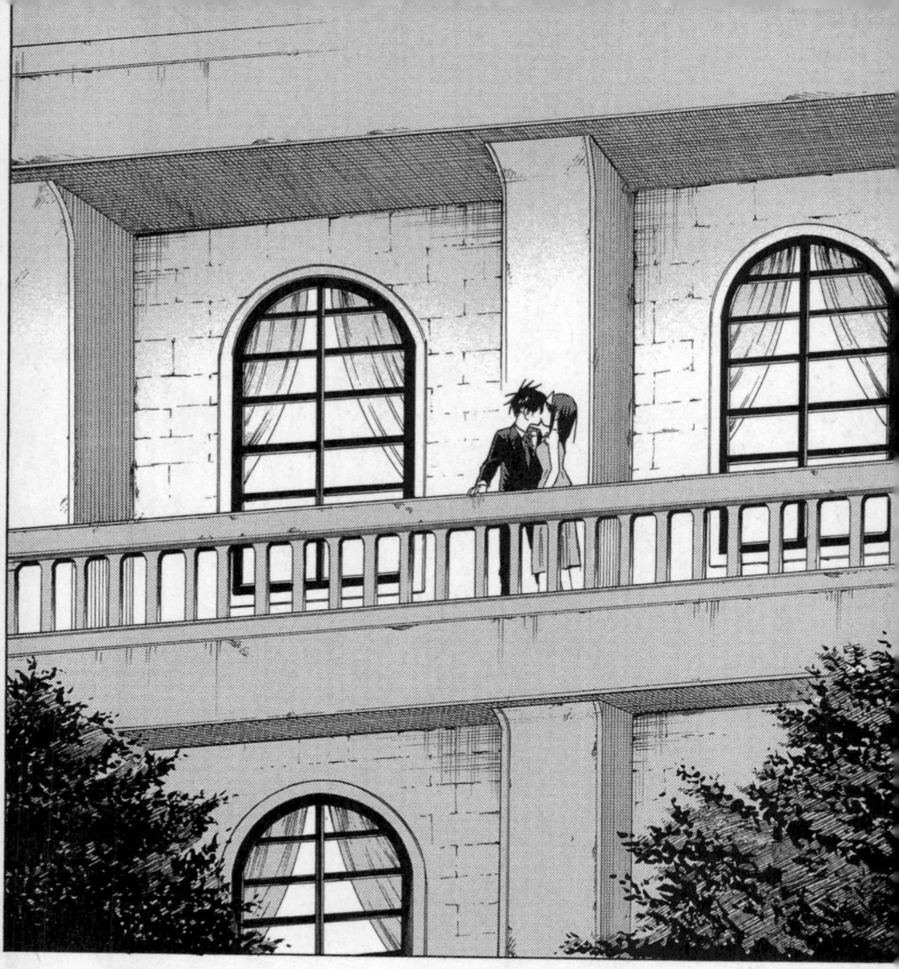
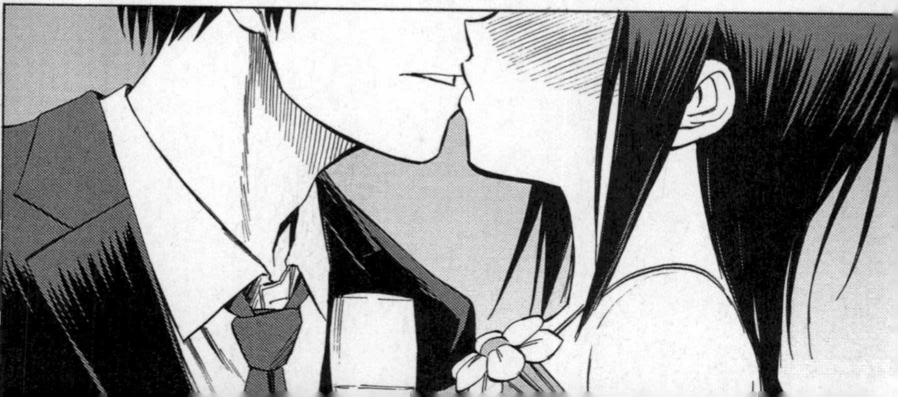

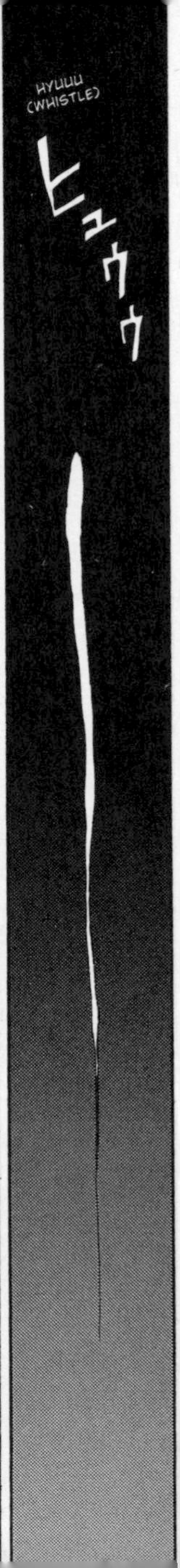
HYUUU (WHISTLE)
ヒュウウ
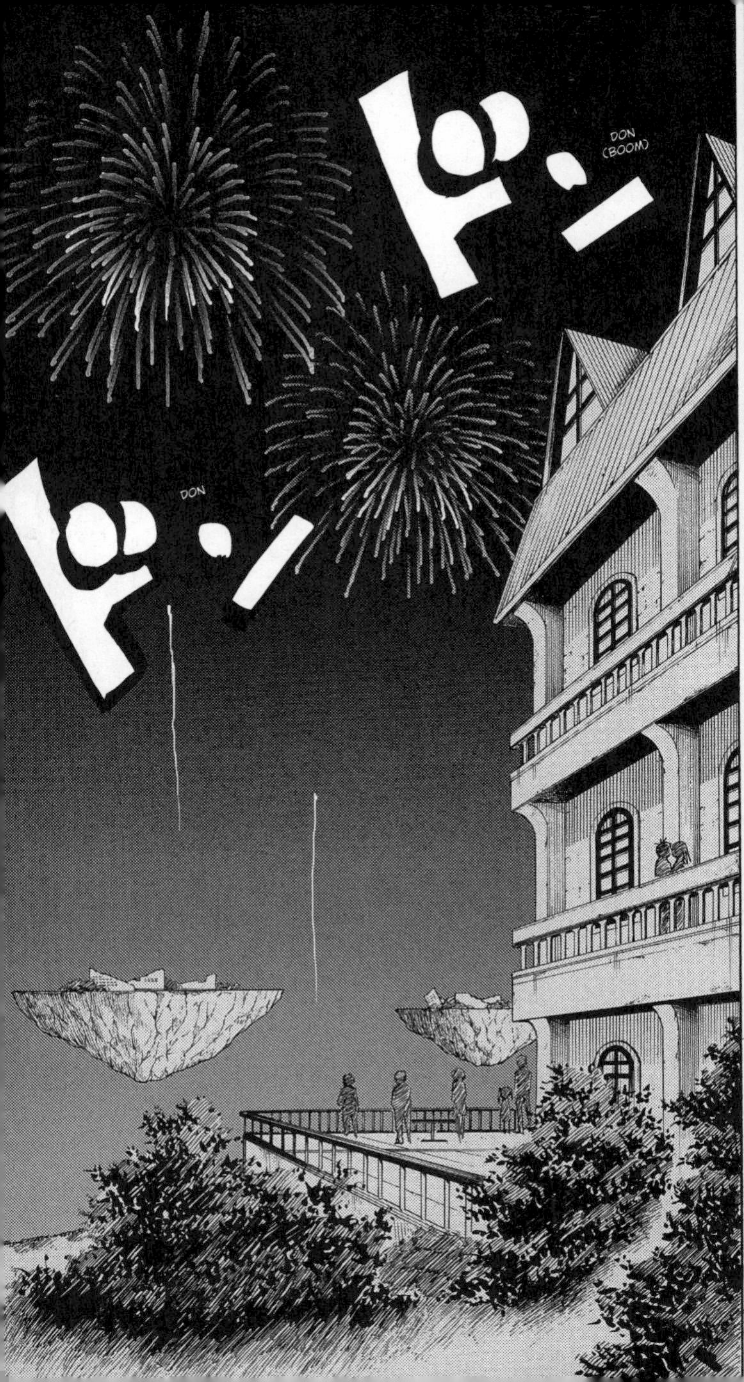
ドーン
DON (BOOM)
ドーン
DON

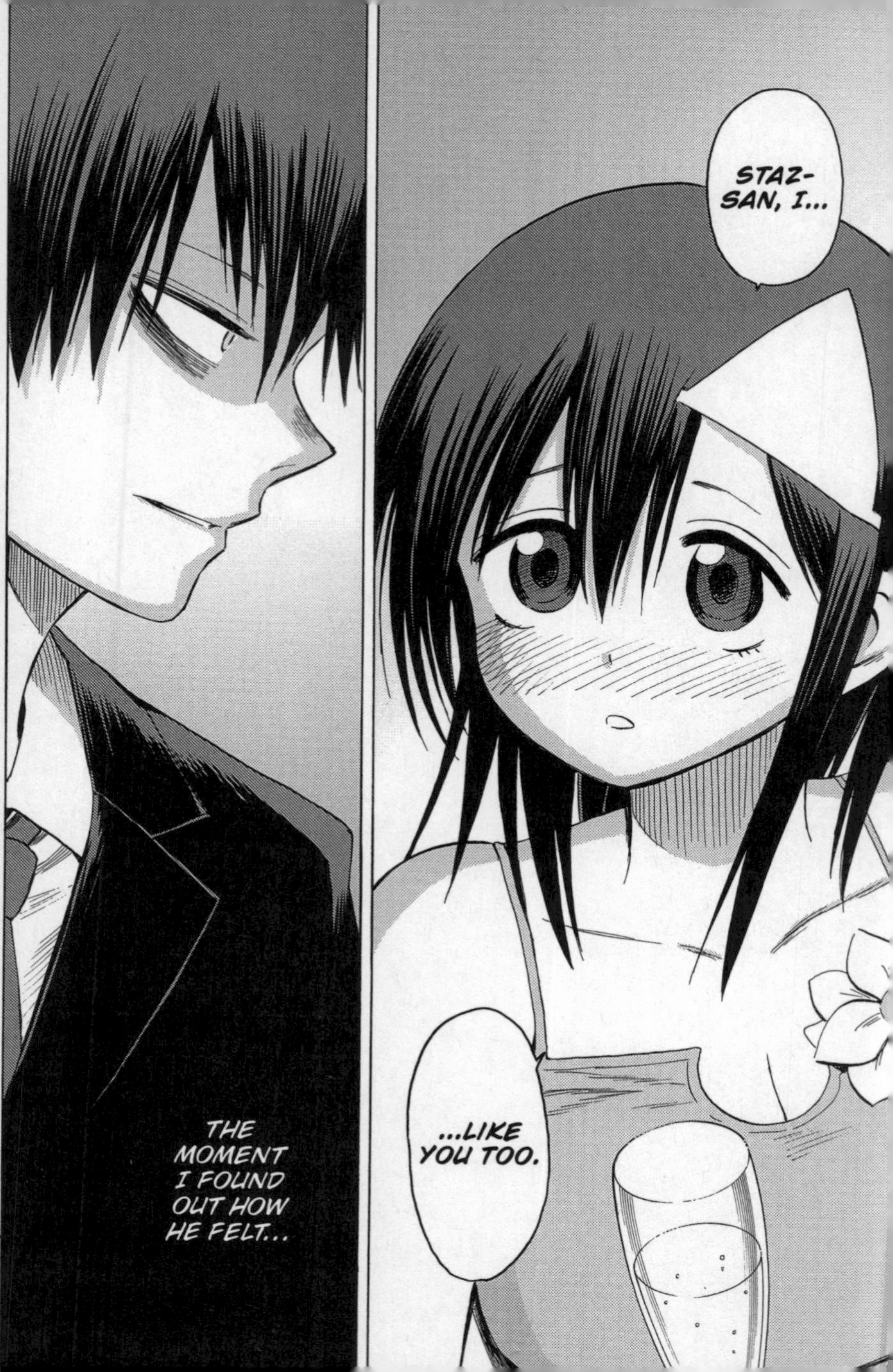
STAZ-SAN, I...
...LIKE YOU TOO.
THE MOMENT I FOUND OUT HOW HE FELT...

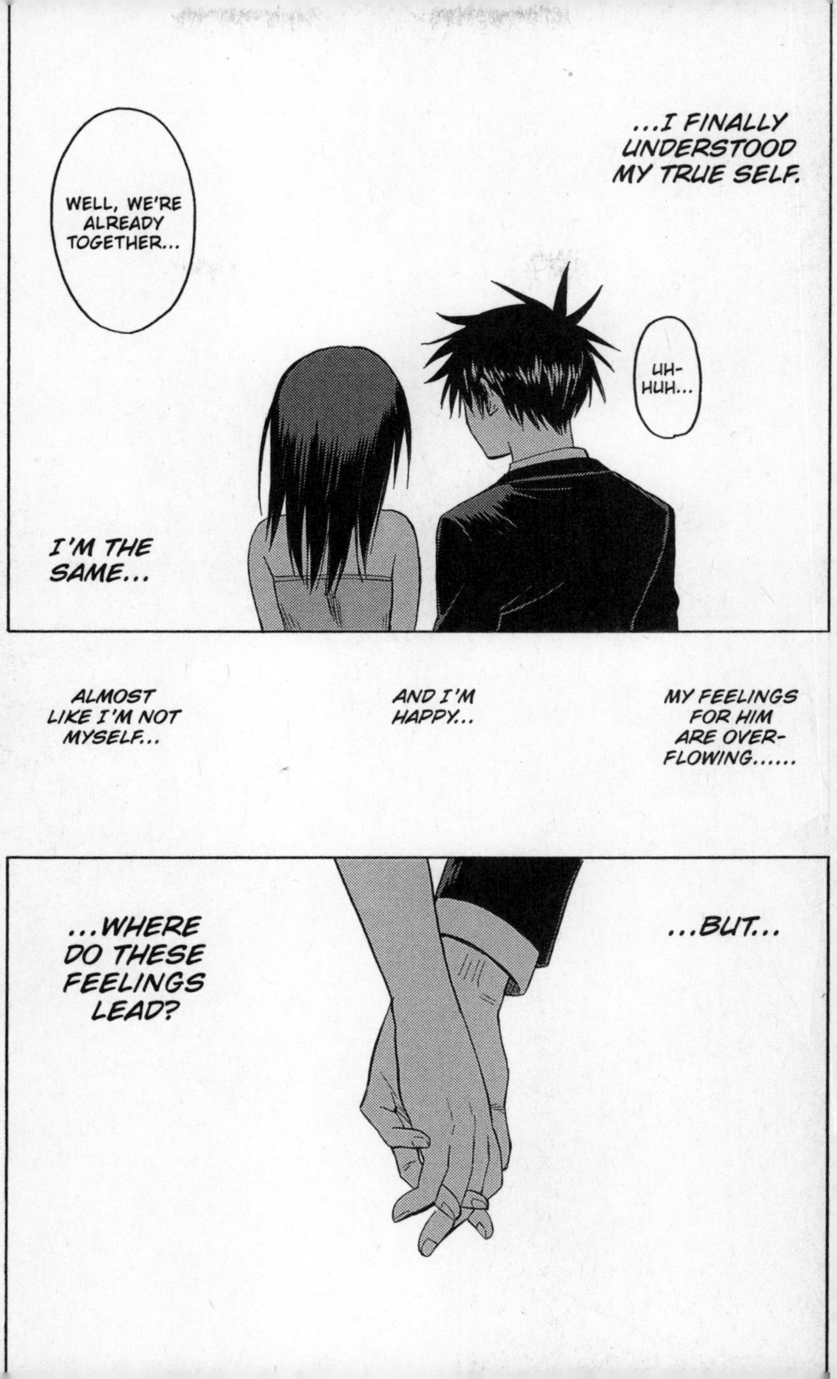
...I FINALLY UNDERSTOOD MY TRUE SELF.
UH-HUH...
WELL, WE'RE ALREADY TOGETHER...
I'M THE SAME...
MY FEELINGS FOR HIM ARE OVER-FLOWING......
AND I'M HAPPY...
ALMOST LIKE I'M NOT MYSELF...
...BUT...
...WHERE DO THESE FEELINGS LEAD?

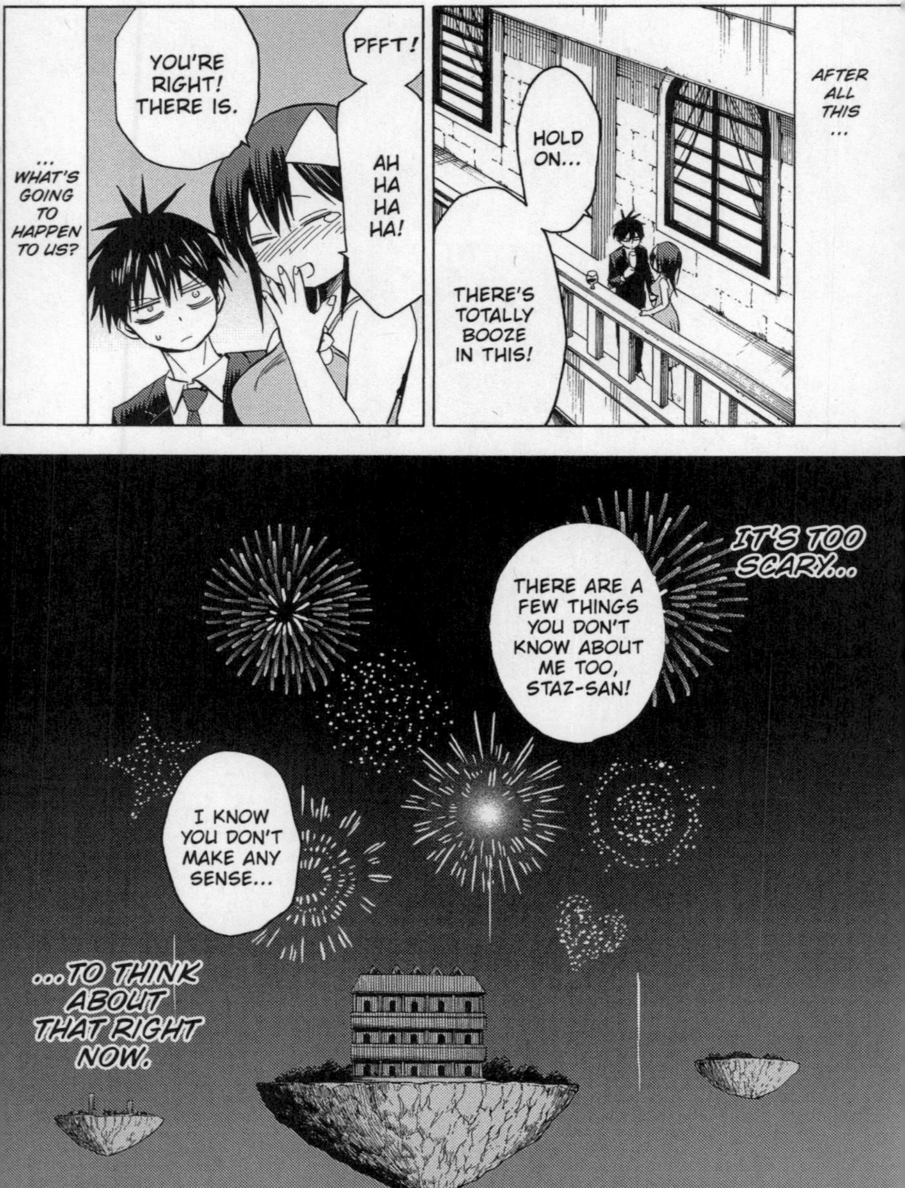
AFTER ALL THIS ...
HOLD ON...
THERE'S TOTALLY BOOZE IN THIS!
PFFT!
AH HA HA HA!
YOU'RE RIGHT! THERE IS.
... WHAT'S GOING TO HAPPEN TO US?
IT'S TOO SCARY...
THERE ARE A FEW THINGS YOU DON'T KNOW ABOUT ME TOO, STAZ-SAN!
I KNOW YOU DON'T MAKE ANY SENSE...
...TO THINK ABOUT THAT RIGHT NOW.
To Be Continued

BLOOD LAD

CHAPTER 84 ♠ BLOOD LAD

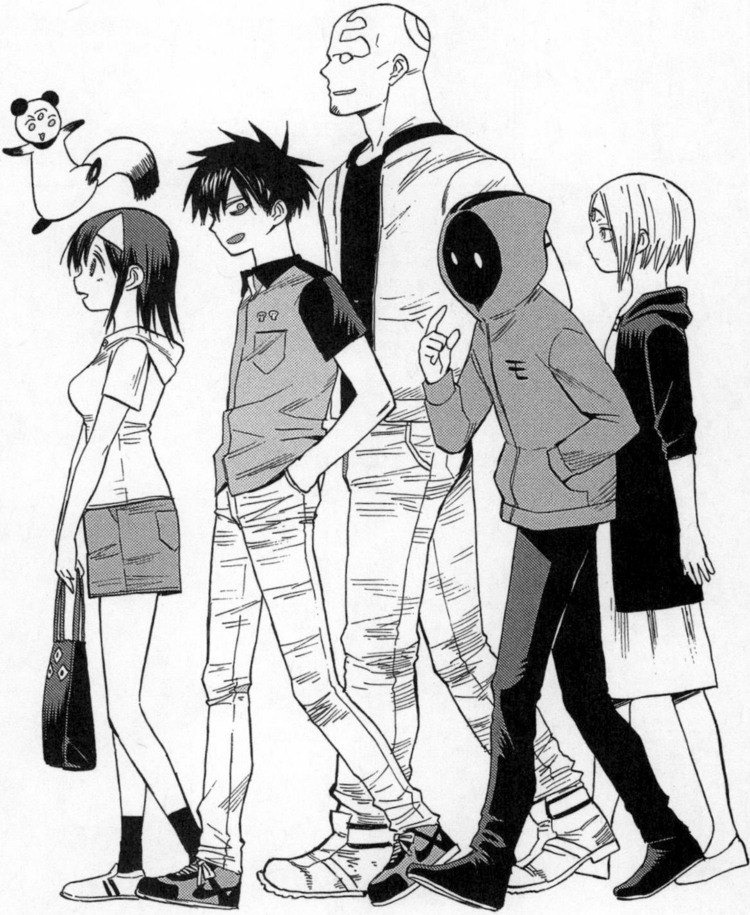

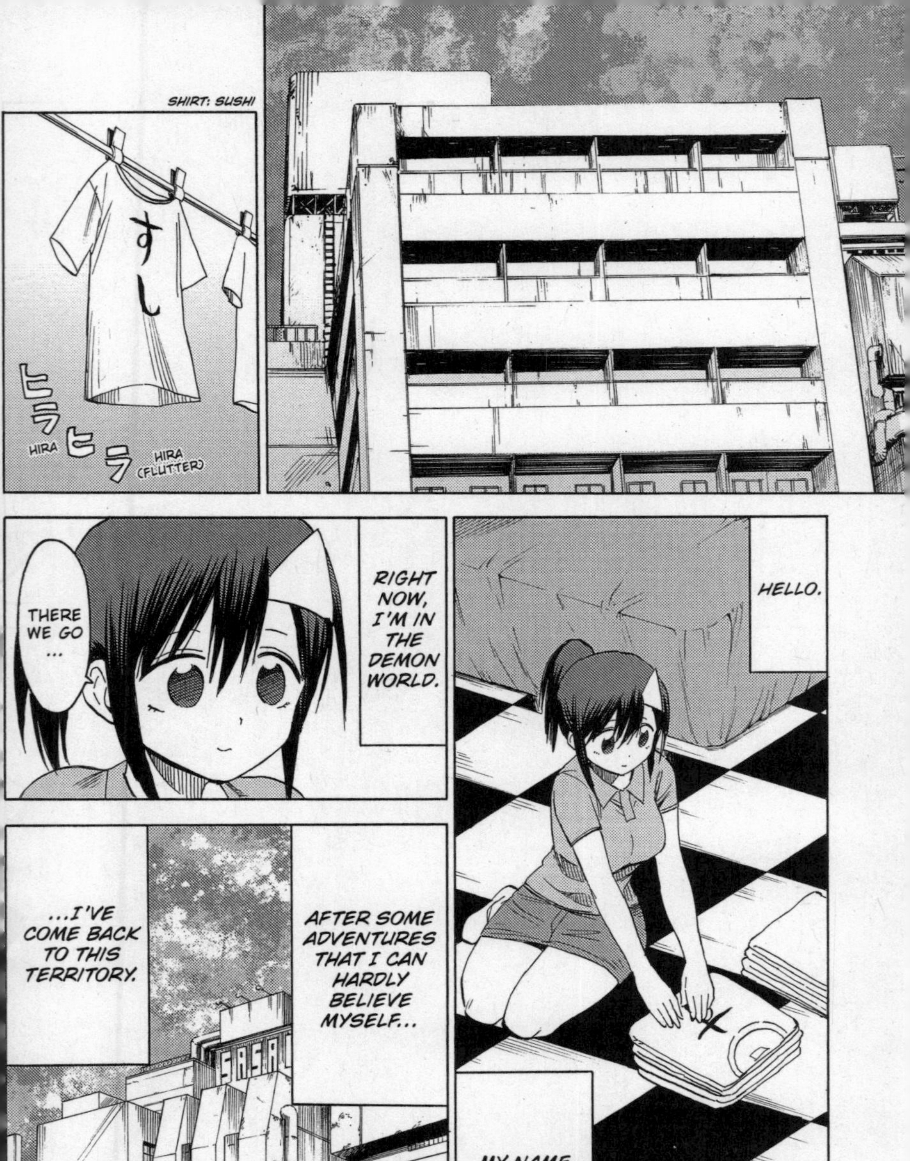
SHIRT: SUSHI
すし
ヒラ
HIRA
ヒラ
HIRA (FLUTTER)
HELLO.
MY NAME IS FUYUMI YANAGI.
RIGHT NOW, I'M IN THE DEMON WORLD.
THERE WE GO...
AFTER SOME ADVENTURES THAT I CAN HARDLY BELIEVE MYSELF...
...I'VE COME BACK TO THIS TERRITORY.

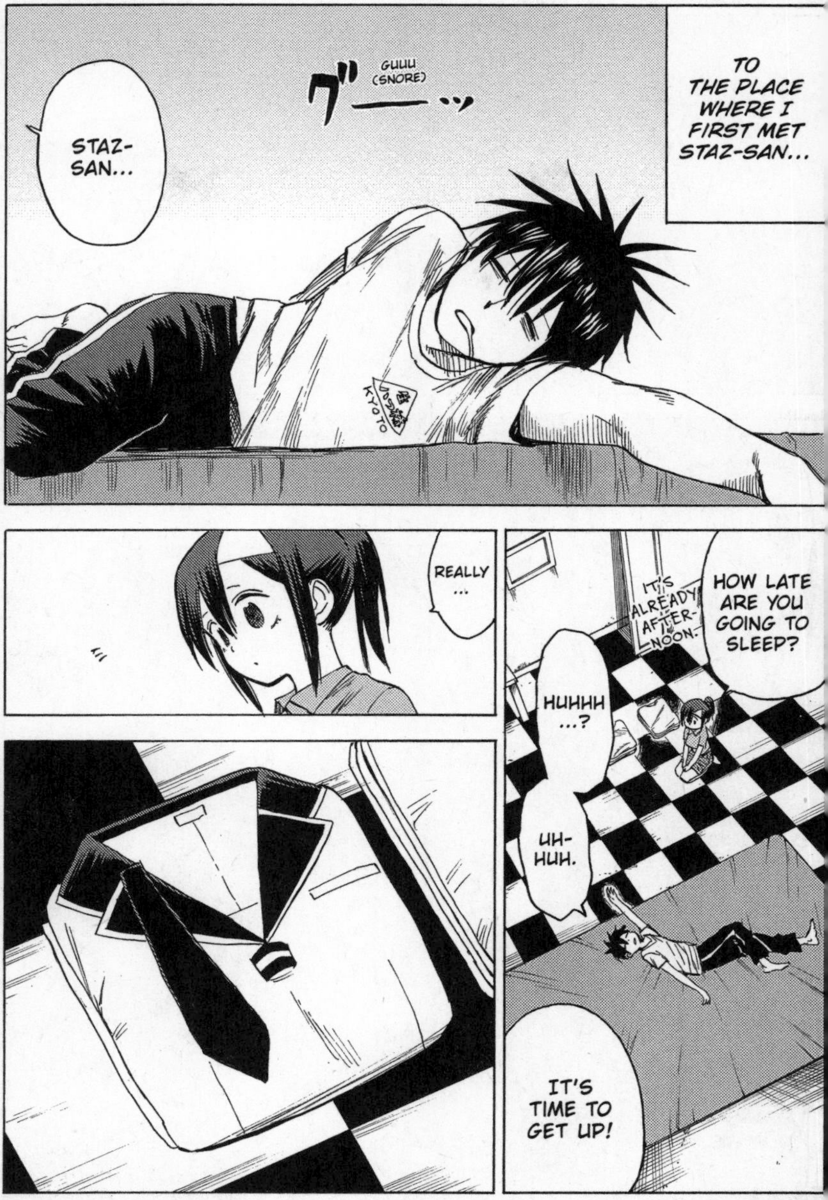
TO THE PLACE WHERE I FIRST MET STAZ-SAN...
グーーッ
GUUU (SNORE)
STAZ-SAN...
HOW LATE ARE YOU GOING TO SLEEP?
IT'S ALREADY AFTERNOON.
HUHHH...?
UH-HUH.
IT'S TIME TO GET UP!
REALLY...

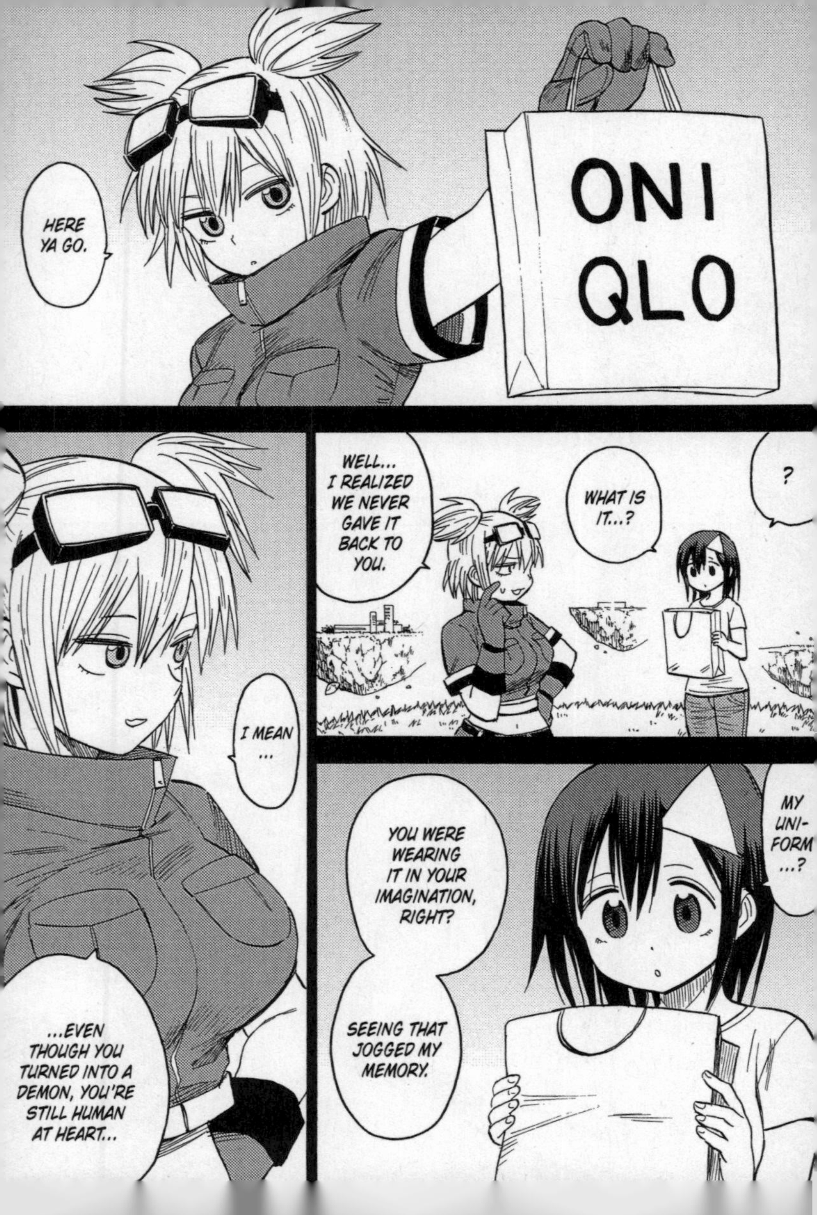
HERE YA GO.
ONI QLO
?
WHAT IS IT...?
WELL... I REALIZED WE NEVER GAVE IT BACK TO YOU.
MY UNI-FORM...?
YOU WERE WEARING IT IN YOUR IMAGINATION, RIGHT?
SEEING THAT JOGGED MY MEMORY.
I MEAN...
...EVEN THOUGH YOU TURNED INTO A DEMON, YOU'RE STILL HUMAN AT HEART...

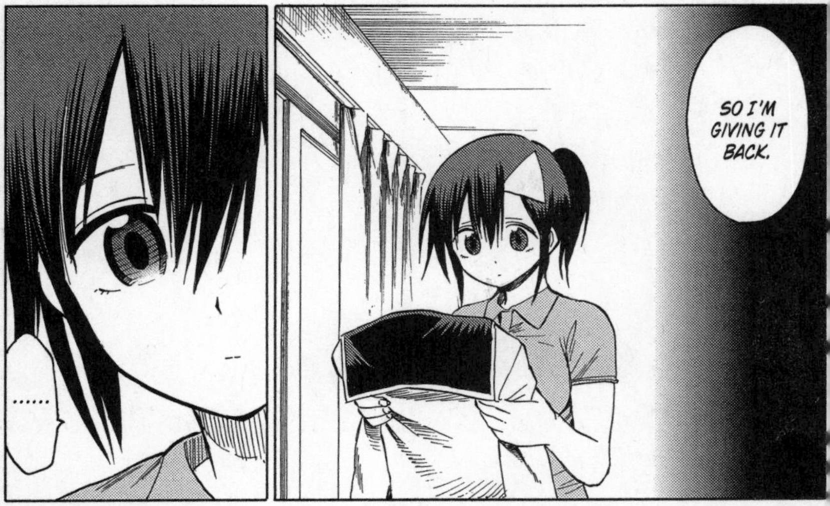
SO I'M GIVING IT BACK.
......

SIGN: CAFÉ THIRD EYE

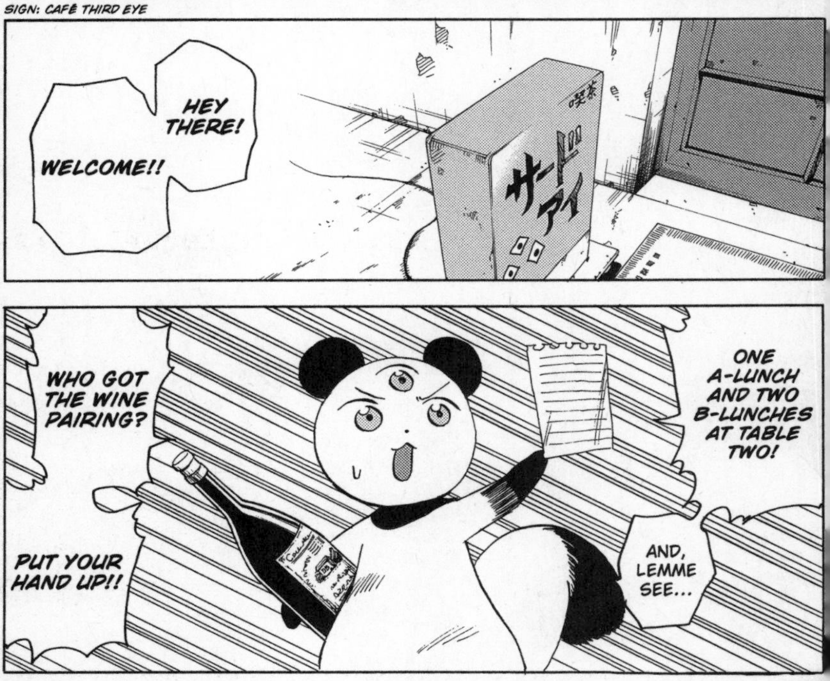
HEY THERE! WELCOME!!
喫茶
サードアイ
ONE A-LUNCH AND TWO B-LUNCHES AT TABLE TWO!
AND, LEMME SEE...
WHO GOT THE WINE PAIRING?
PUT YOUR HAND UP!!

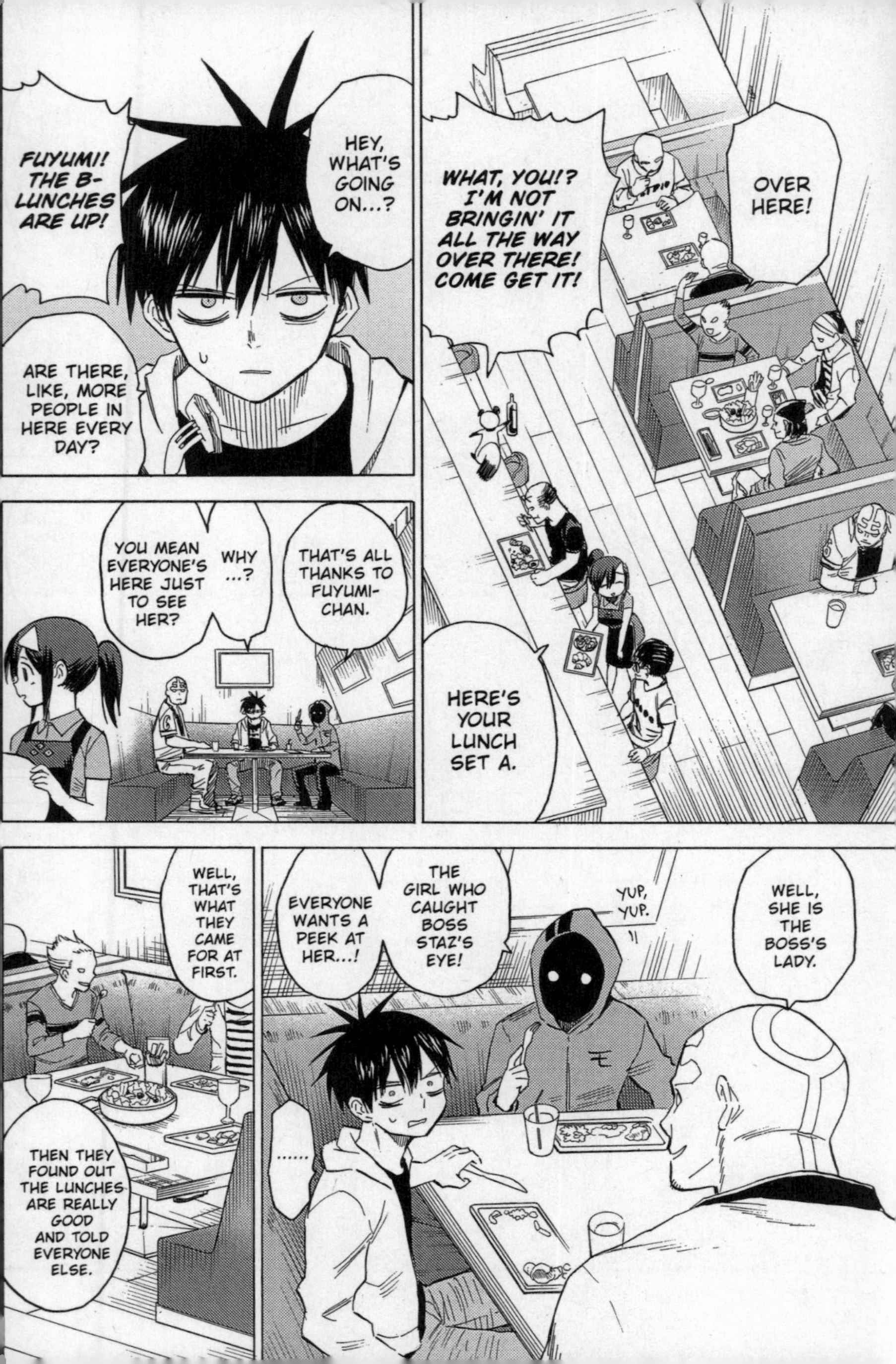
OVER HERE!
WHAT, YOU!? I'M NOT BRINGIN' IT ALL THE WAY OVER THERE! COME GET IT!
HERE'S YOUR LUNCH SET A.
HEY, WHAT'S GOING ON...?
FUYUMI! THE B-LUNCHES ARE UP!
ARE THERE, LIKE, MORE PEOPLE IN HERE EVERY DAY?
THAT'S ALL THANKS TO FUYUMI-CHAN.
WHY ...?
YOU MEAN EVERYONE'S HERE JUST TO SEE HER?
WELL, SHE IS THE BOSS'S LADY.
YUP, YUP.
THE GIRL WHO CAUGHT BOSS STAZ'S EYE!
EVERYONE WANTS A PEEK AT HER...!
......
WELL, THAT'S WHAT THEY CAME FOR AT FIRST.
THEN THEY FOUND OUT THE LUNCHES ARE REALLY GOOD AND TOLD EVERYONE ELSE.

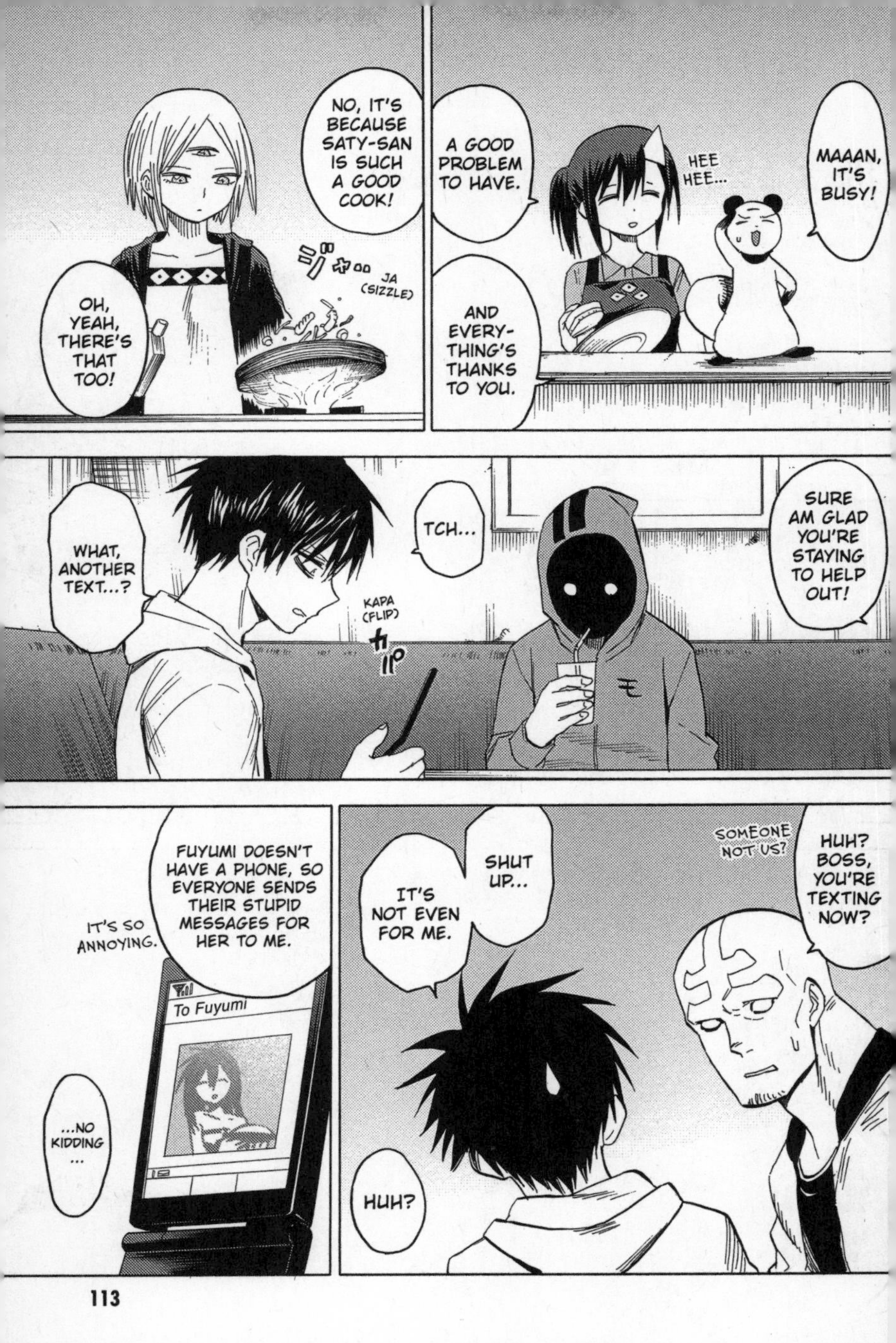
MAAAN, IT'S BUSY!
HEE HEE...
A GOOD PROBLEM TO HAVE.
AND EVERY-THING'S THANKS TO YOU.
NO, IT'S BECAUSE SATY-SAN IS SUCH A GOOD COOK!
JA (SIZZLE)
OH, YEAH, THERE'S THAT TOO!
SURE AM GLAD YOU'RE STAYING TO HELP OUT!
TCH...
KAPA (FLIP)
WHAT, ANOTHER TEXT...?
HUH? BOSS, YOU'RE TEXTING NOW?
SOMEONE NOT US?
SHUT UP...
IT'S NOT EVEN FOR ME.
HUH?
FUYUMI DOESN'T HAVE A PHONE, SO EVERYONE SENDS THEIR STUPID MESSAGES FOR HER TO ME.
IT'S SO ANNOYING.
To Fuyumi
...NO KIDDING ...

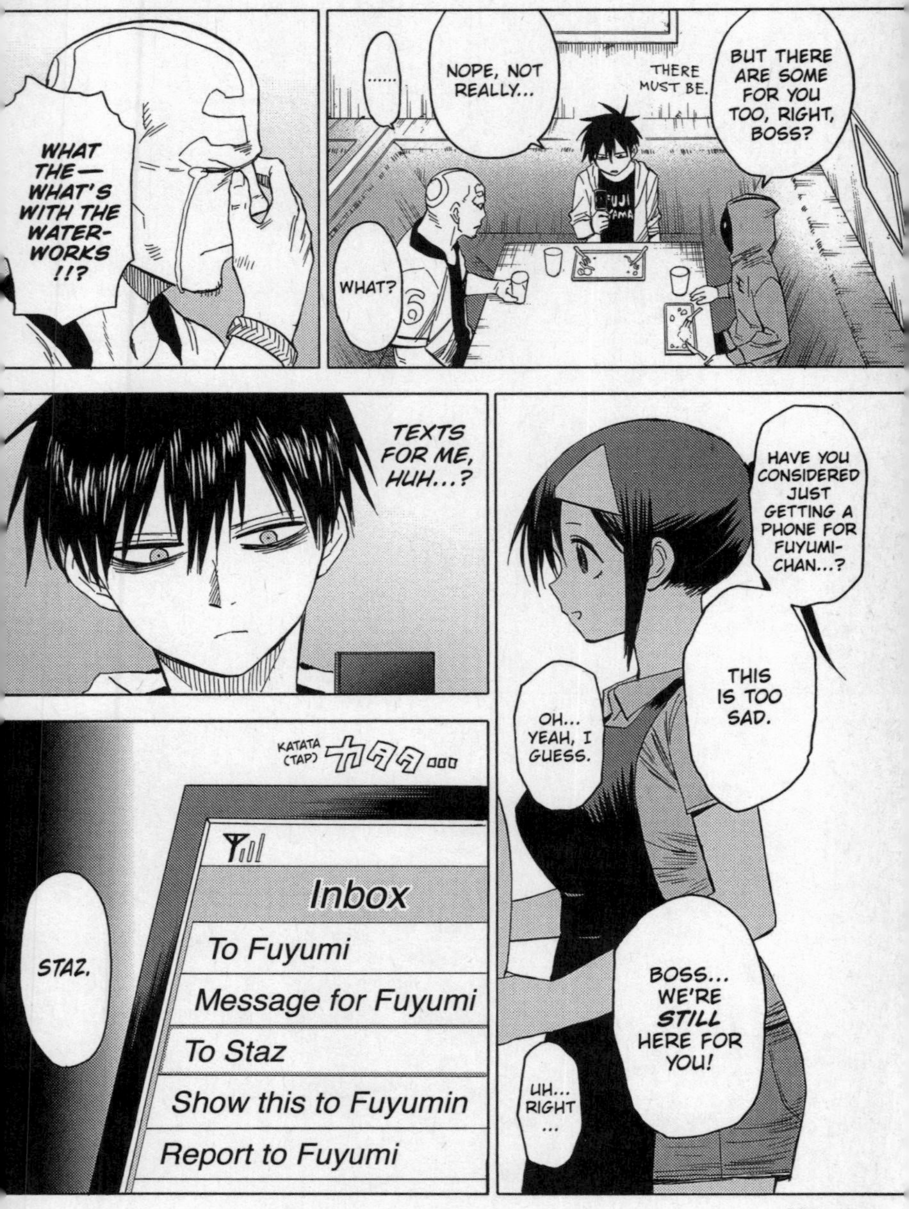
BUT THERE ARE SOME FOR YOU TOO, RIGHT, BOSS?
THERE MUST BE.
NOPE, NOT REALLY...
......
WHAT?
WHAT THE— WHAT'S WITH THE WATER-WORKS!!?
HAVE YOU CONSIDERED JUST GETTING A PHONE FOR FUYUMI-CHAN...?
THIS IS TOO SAD.
OH... YEAH, I GUESS.
BOSS... WE'RE STILL HERE FOR YOU!
UH... RIGHT...
TEXTS FOR ME, HUH...?
KATATA (TAP) カタタ
Inbox
To Fuyumi
Message for Fuyumi
To Staz
Show this to Fuyumin
Report to Fuyumi
STAZ.

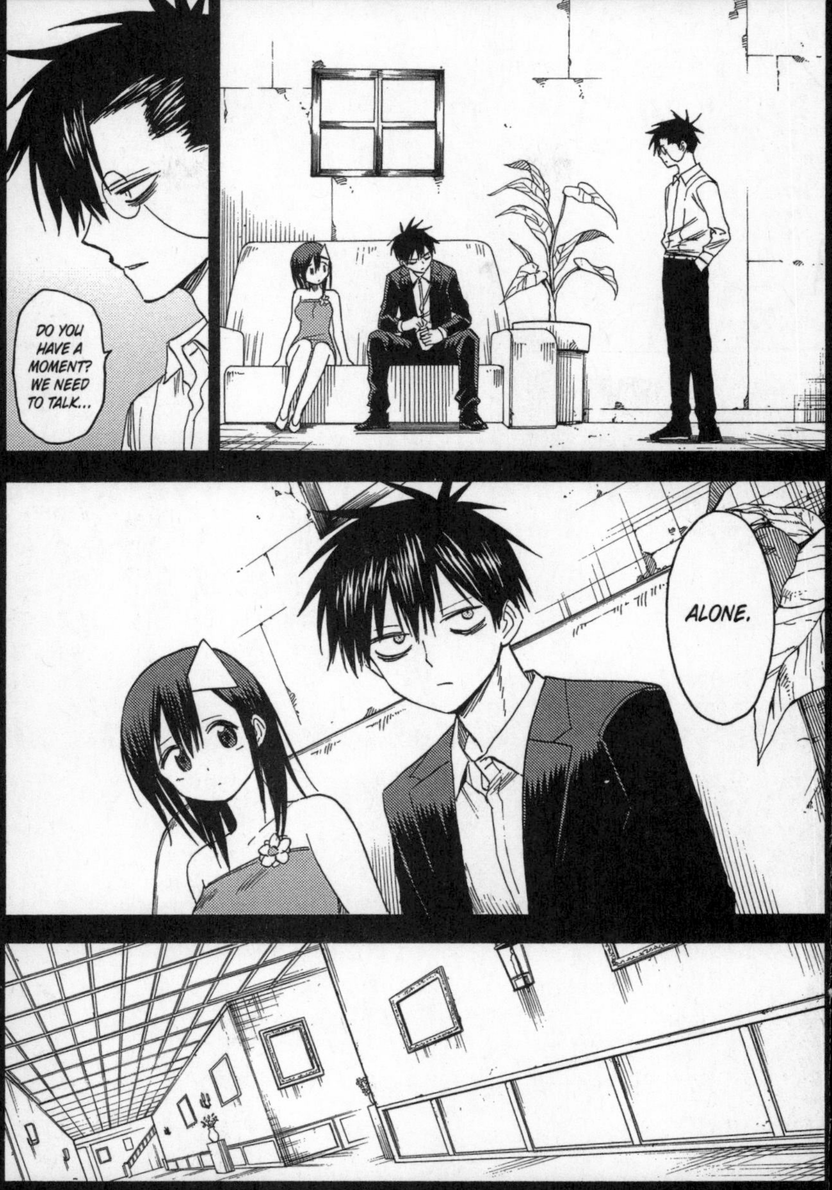
DO YOU HAVE A MOMENT? WE NEED TO TALK...
ALONE.

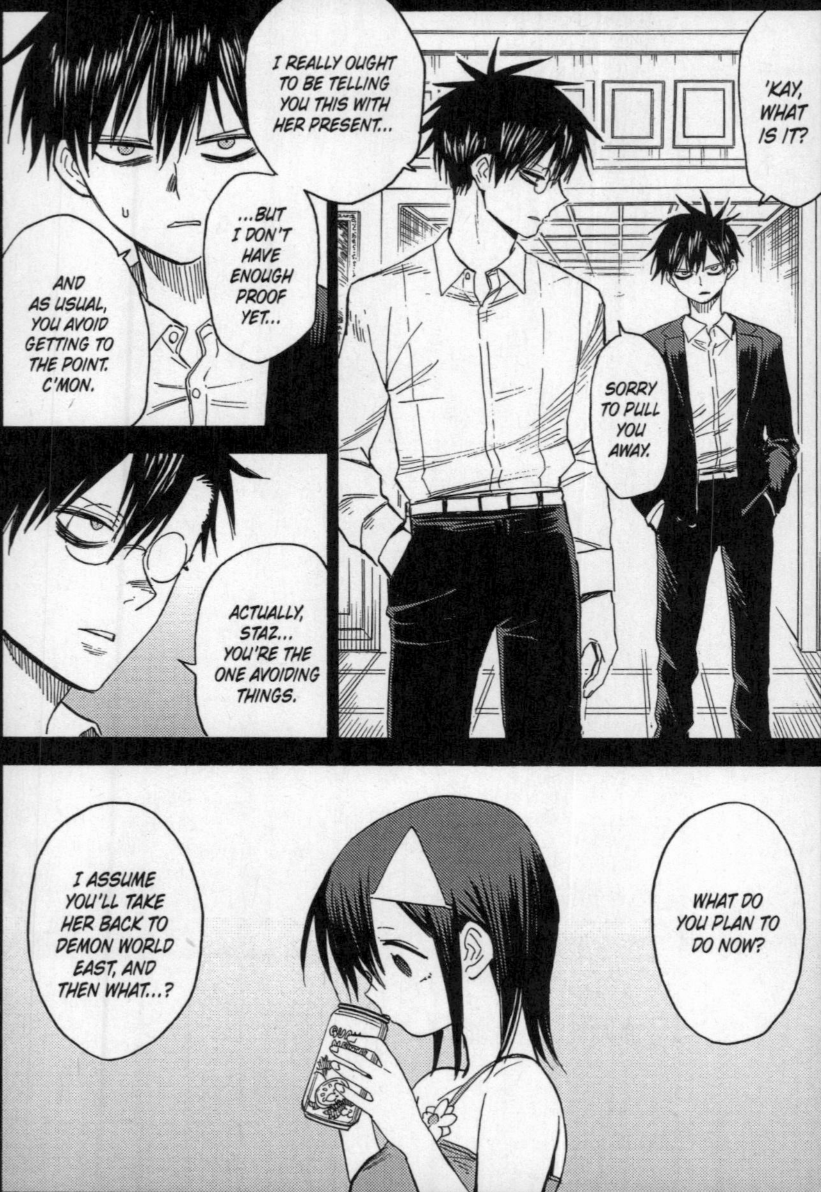
'KAY, WHAT IS IT?
SORRY TO PULL YOU AWAY.
I REALLY OUGHT TO BE TELLING YOU THIS WITH HER PRESENT...
...BUT I DON'T HAVE ENOUGH PROOF YET...
AND AS USUAL, YOU AVOID GETTING TO THE POINT. C'MON.
ACTUALLY, STAZ... YOU'RE THE ONE AVOIDING THINGS.
WHAT DO YOU PLAN TO DO NOW?
I ASSUME YOU'LL TAKE HER BACK TO DEMON WORLD EAST, AND THEN WHAT...?

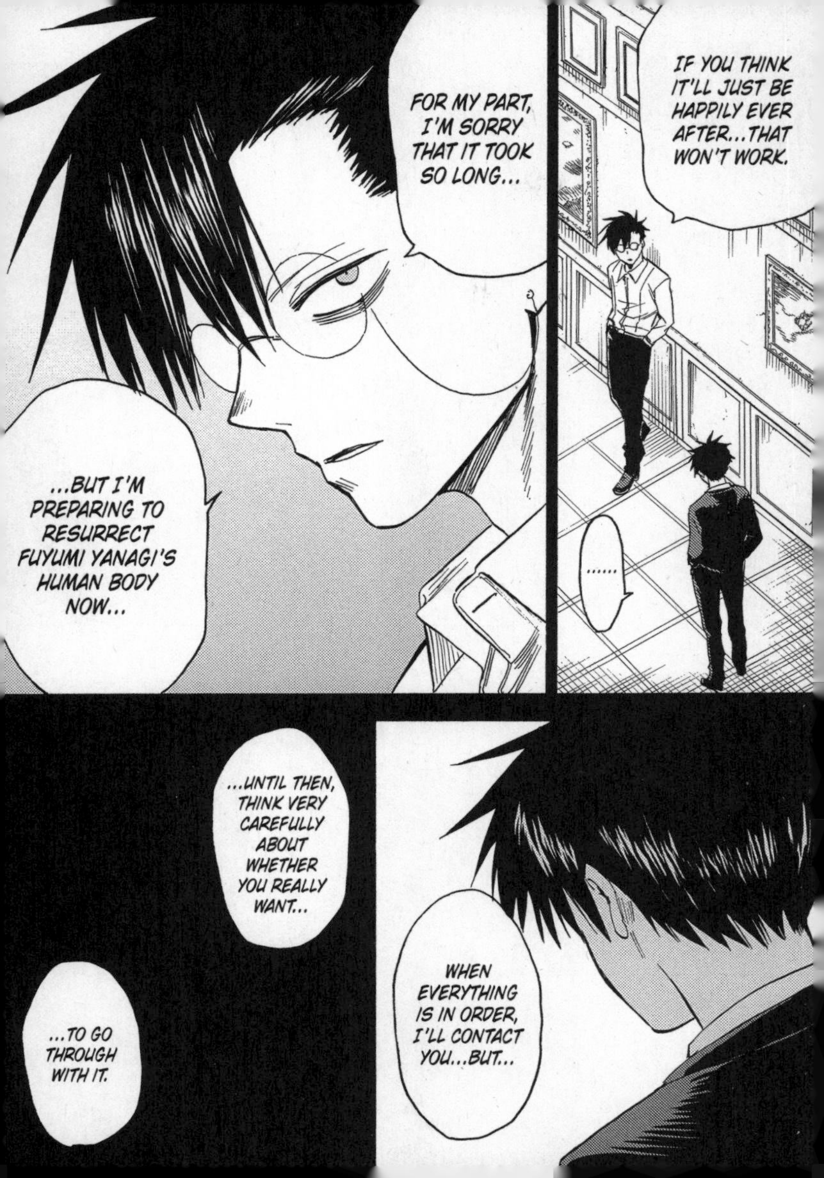
IF YOU THINK IT'LL JUST BE HAPPILY EVER AFTER...THAT WON'T WORK.
......
FOR MY PART, I'M SORRY THAT IT TOOK SO LONG...
...BUT I'M PREPARING TO RESURRECT FUYUMI YANAGI'S HUMAN BODY NOW...
WHEN EVERYTHING IS IN ORDER, I'LL CONTACT YOU...BUT...
...UNTIL THEN, THINK VERY CAREFULLY ABOUT WHETHER YOU REALLY WANT...
...TO GO THROUGH WITH IT.

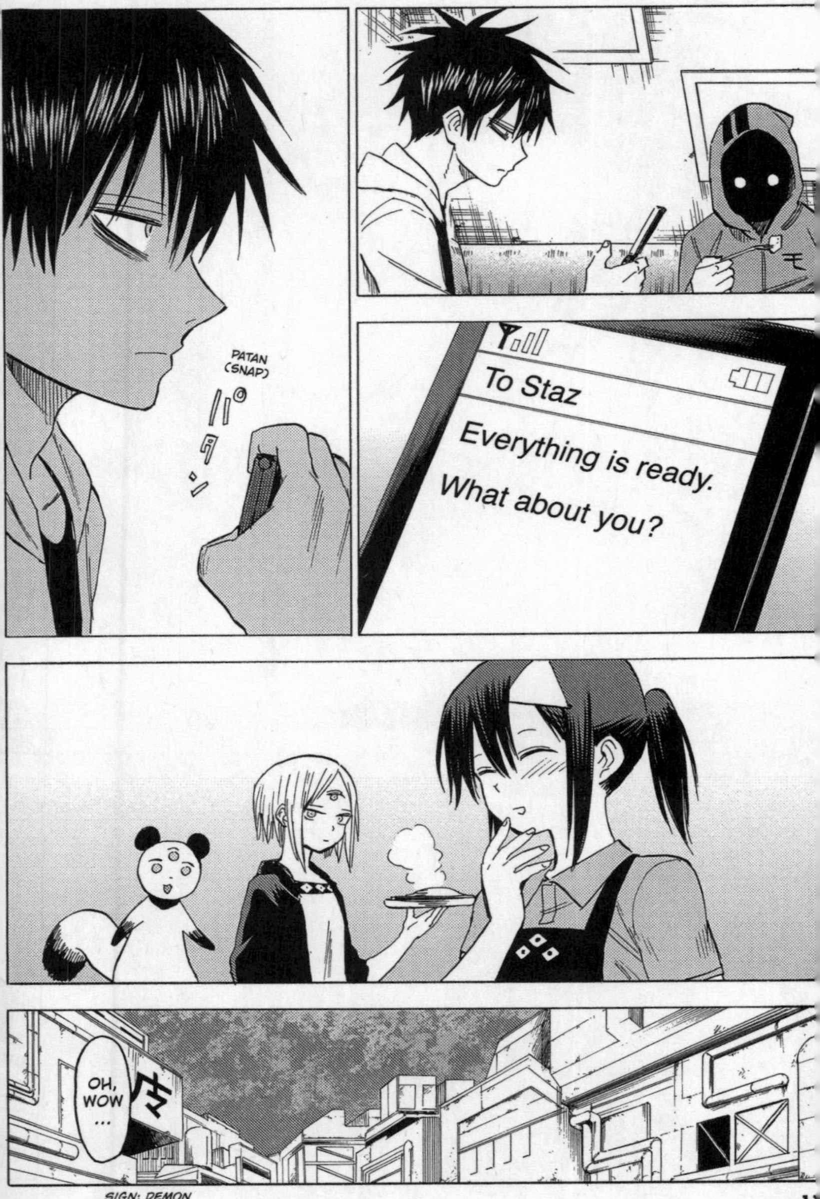
To Staz
Everything is ready.
What about you?
PATAN
(SNAP)
パタン
OH, WOW ...

SIGN: DEMON

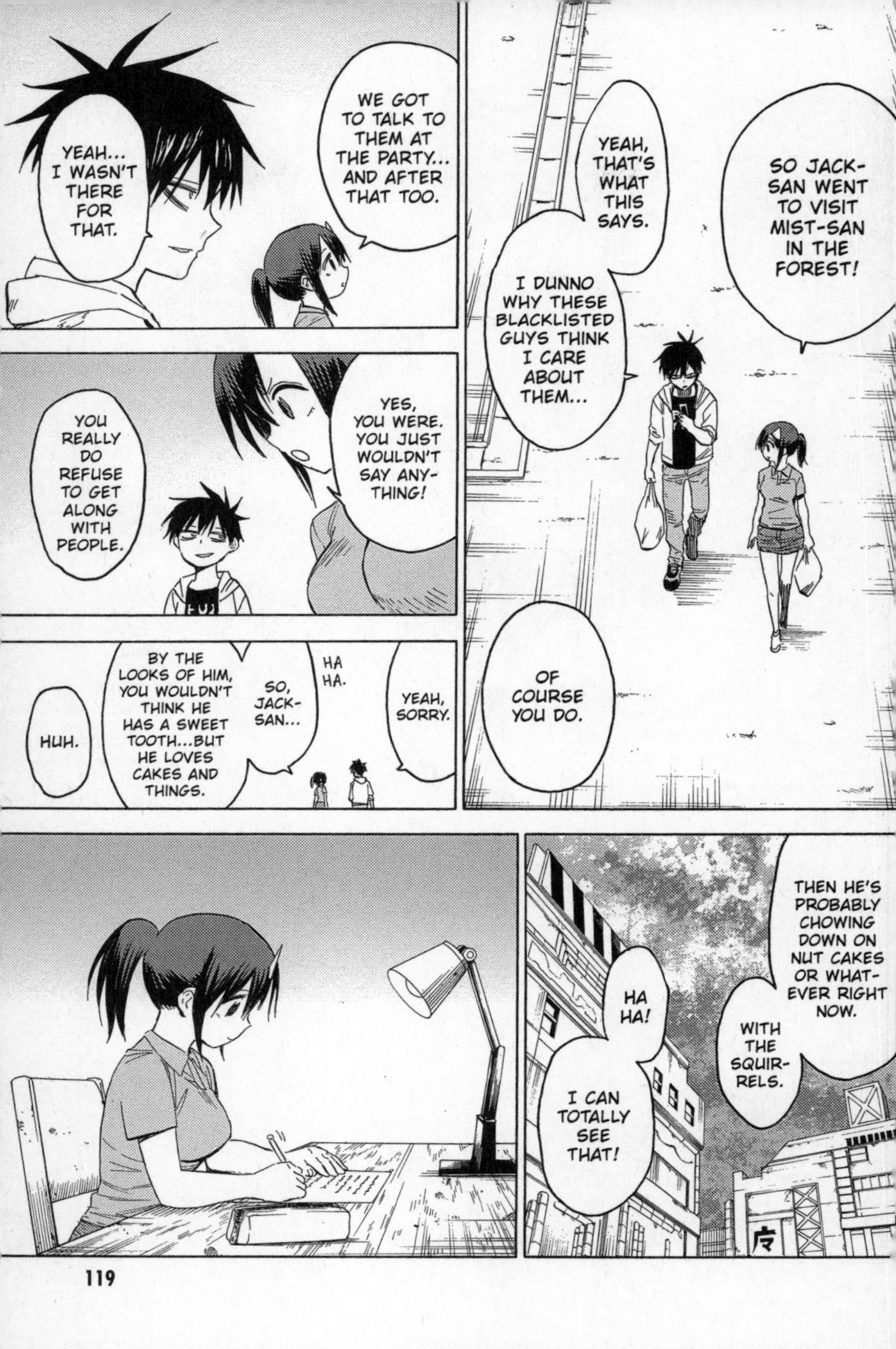
SO JACK-SAN WENT TO VISIT MIST-SAN IN THE FOREST!
YEAH, THAT'S WHAT THIS SAYS.
I DUNNO WHY THESE BLACKLISTED GUYS THINK I CARE ABOUT THEM...
OF COURSE YOU DO.
WE GOT TO TALK TO THEM AT THE PARTY... AND AFTER THAT TOO.
YEAH... I WASN'T THERE FOR THAT.
YES, YOU WERE. YOU JUST WOULDN'T SAY ANY-THING!
YOU REALLY DO REFUSE TO GET ALONG WITH PEOPLE.
YEAH, SORRY.
HA HA.
SO, JACK-SAN...
BY THE LOOKS OF HIM, YOU WOULDN'T THINK HE HAS A SWEET TOOTH...BUT HE LOVES CAKES AND THINGS.
HUH.
THEN HE'S PROBABLY CHOWING DOWN ON NUT CAKES OR WHAT-EVER RIGHT NOW.
WITH THE SQUIR-RELS.
HA HA!
I CAN TOTALLY SEE THAT!

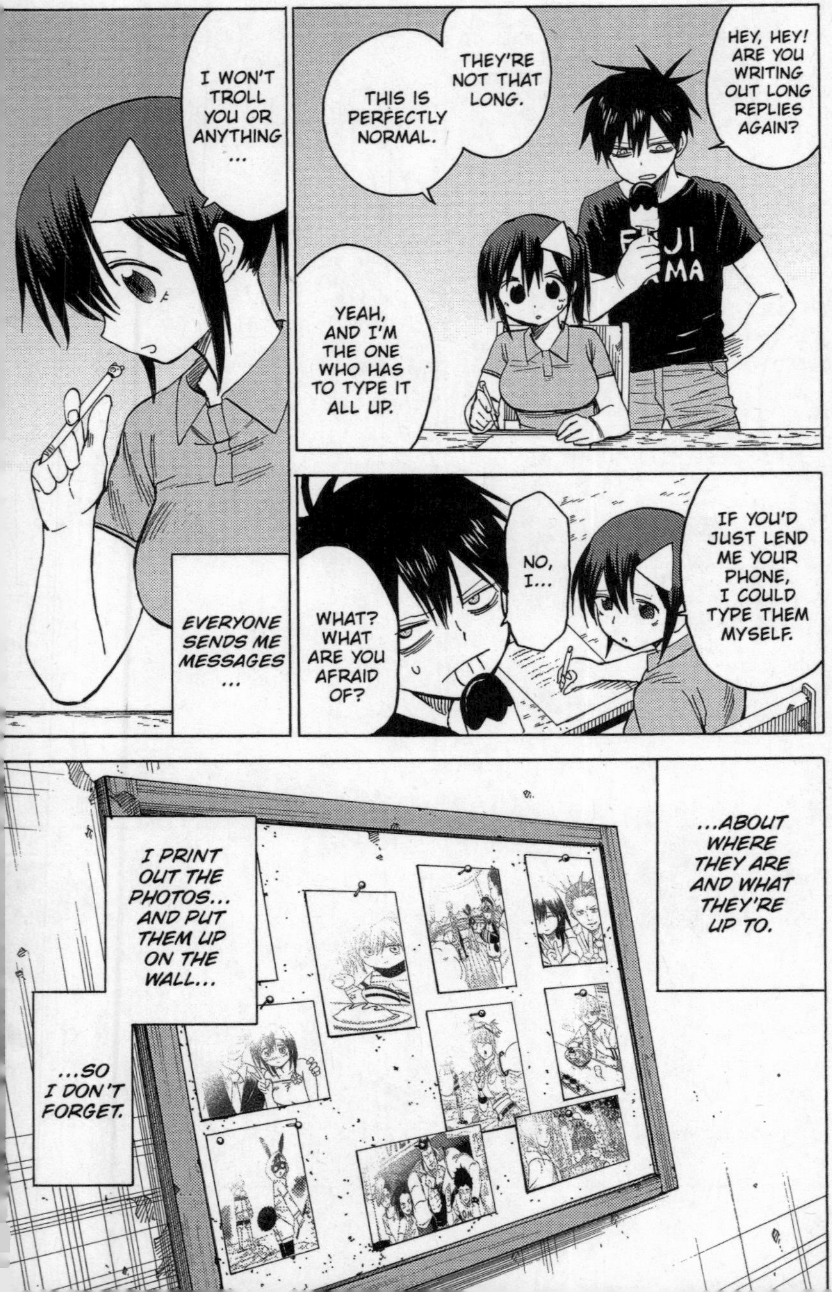
HEY, HEY! ARE YOU WRITING OUT LONG REPLIES AGAIN?
THEY'RE NOT THAT LONG.
THIS IS PERFECTLY NORMAL.
YEAH, AND I'M THE ONE WHO HAS TO TYPE IT ALL UP.
IF YOU'D JUST LEND ME YOUR PHONE, I COULD TYPE THEM MYSELF.
NO, I...
WHAT? WHAT ARE YOU AFRAID OF?
I WON'T TROLL YOU OR ANYTHING ...
EVERYONE SENDS ME MESSAGES ...
...ABOUT WHERE THEY ARE AND WHAT THEY'RE UP TO.
I PRINT OUT THE PHOTOS... AND PUT THEM UP ON THE WALL...
...SO I DON'T FORGET.

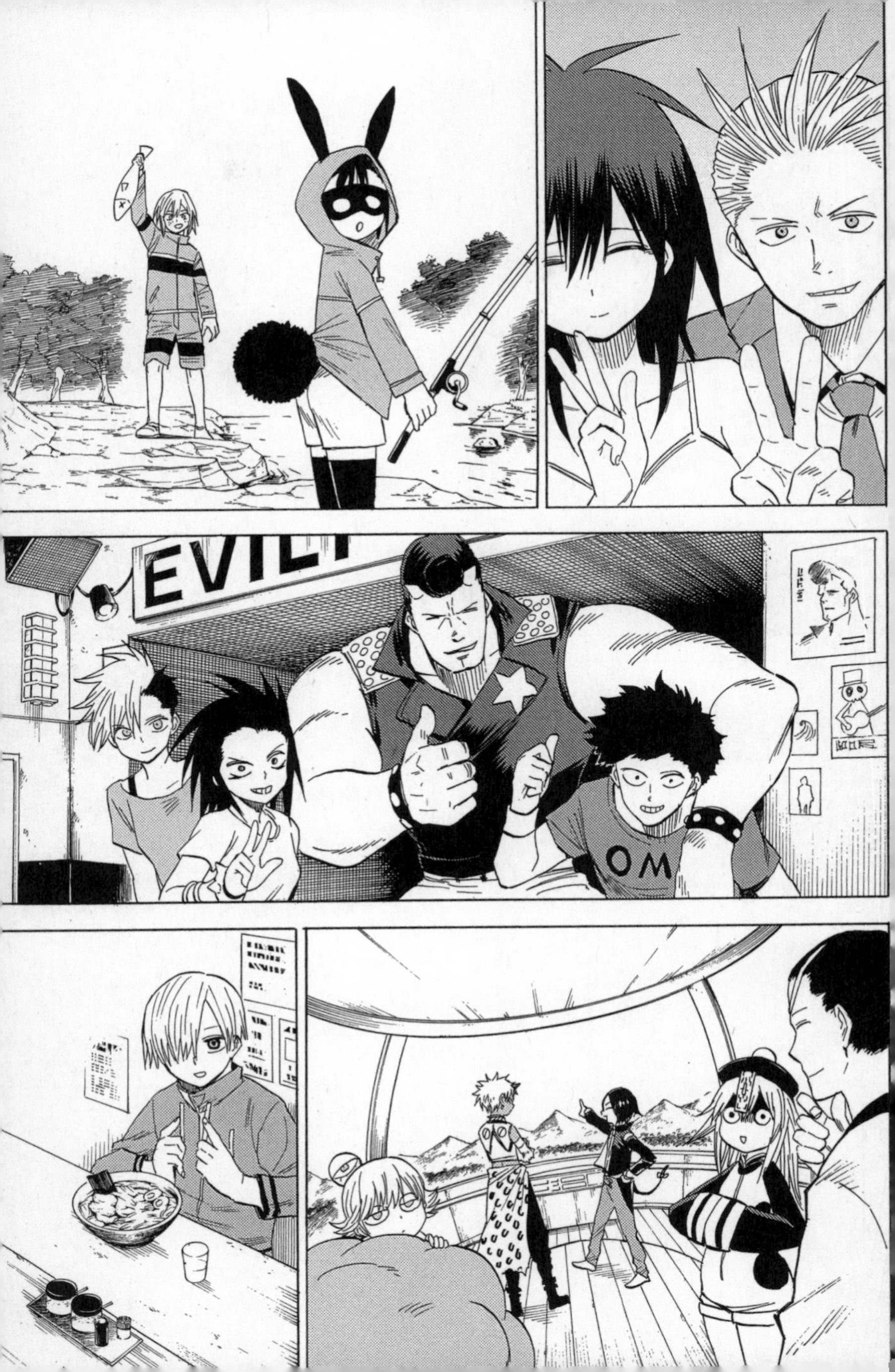
EVILI
OM

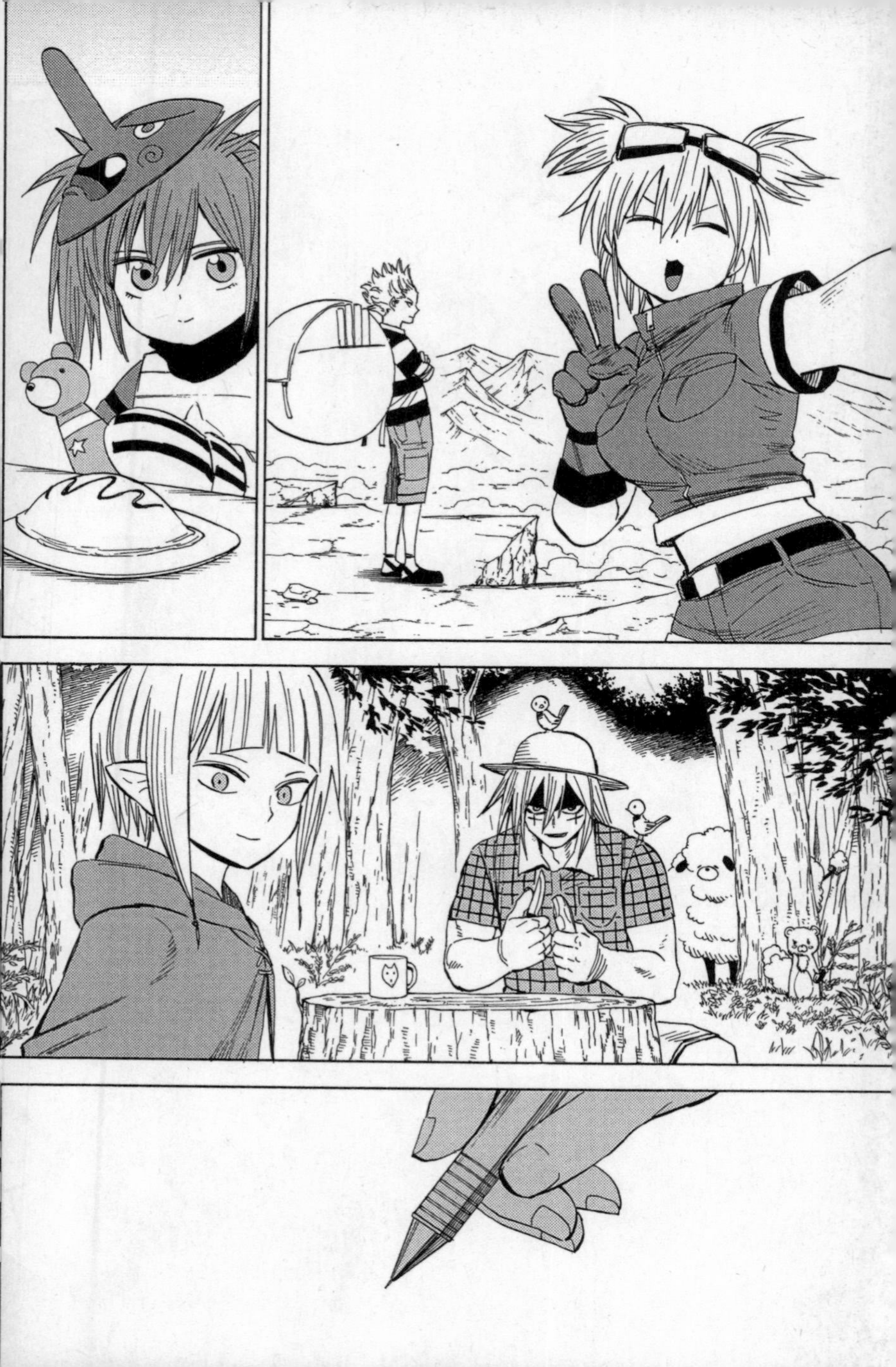

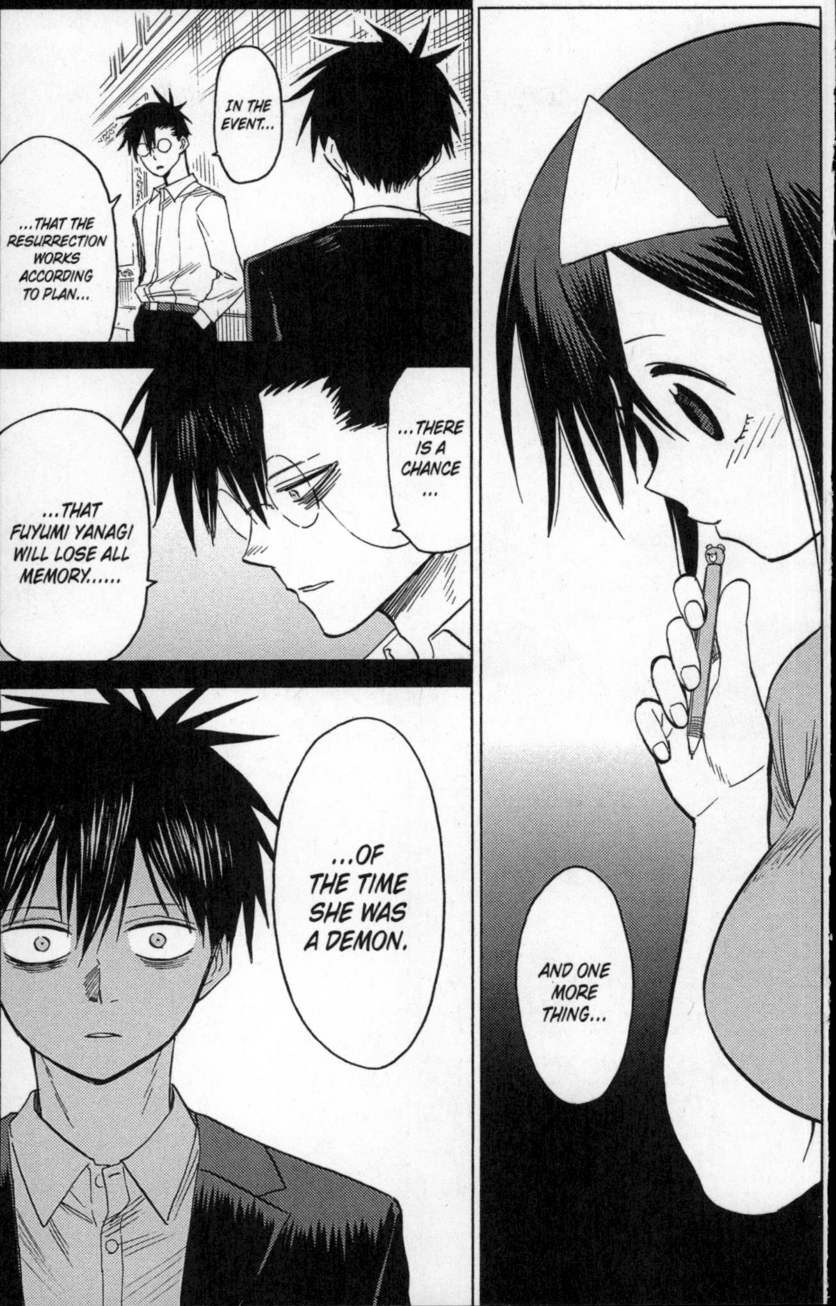
AND ONE MORE THING...
IN THE EVENT...
...THAT THE RESURRECTION WORKS ACCORDING TO PLAN...
...THERE IS A CHANCE ...
...THAT FUYUMI YANAGI WILL LOSE ALL MEMORY......
...OF THE TIME SHE WAS A DEMON.

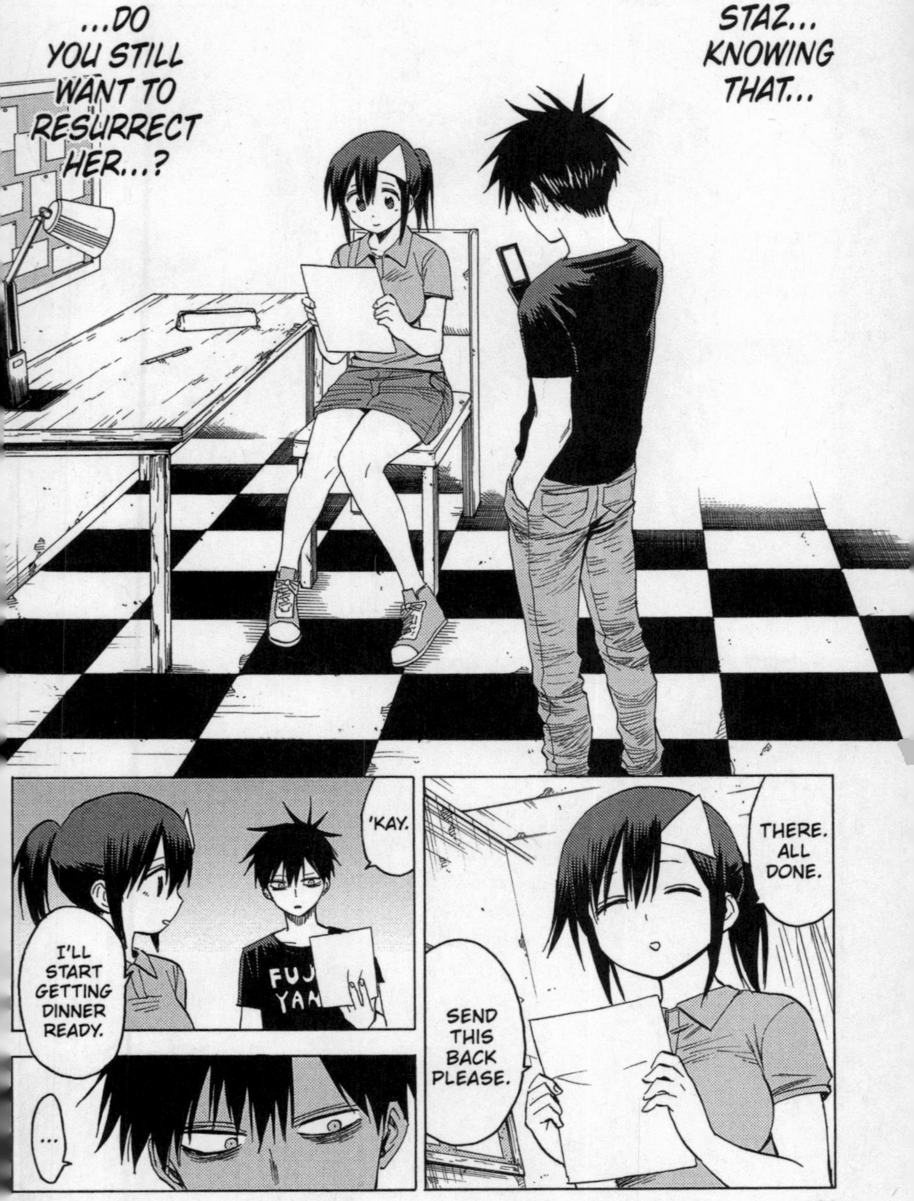

STAZ... KNOWING THAT...
...DO YOU STILL WANT TO RESURRECT HER...?
THERE. ALL DONE.
SEND THIS BACK PLEASE.
'KAY.
I'LL START GETTING DINNER READY.
...

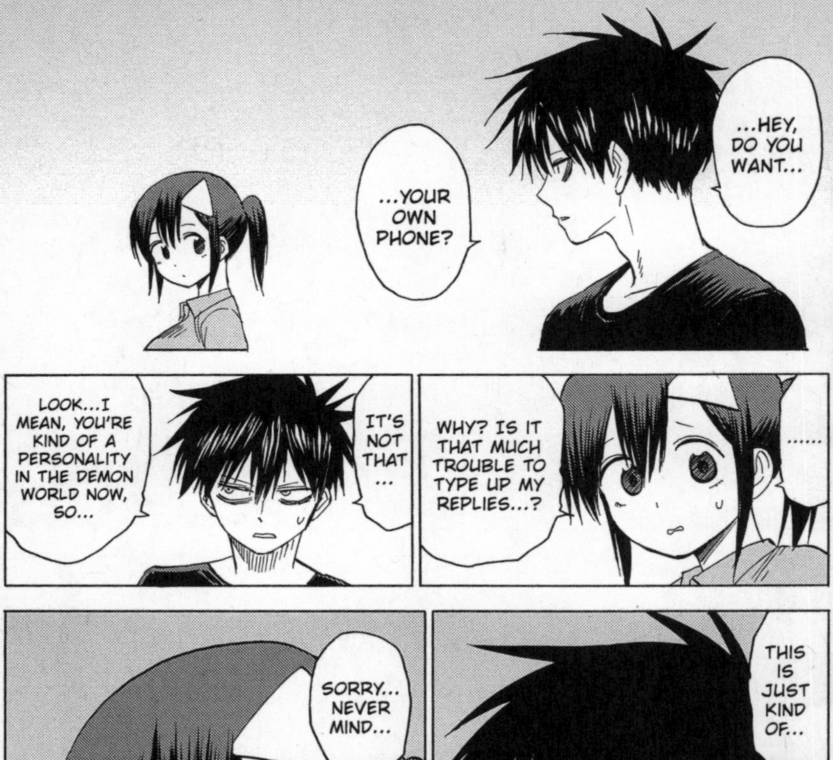
...HEY, DO YOU WANT...
...YOUR OWN PHONE?
......
WHY? IS IT THAT MUCH TROUBLE TO TYPE UP MY REPLIES...?
IT'S NOT THAT...
LOOK...I MEAN, YOU'RE KIND OF A PERSONALITY IN THE DEMON WORLD NOW, SO...
THIS IS JUST KIND OF...
......
SORRY... NEVER MIND...
... STAZ-SAN...

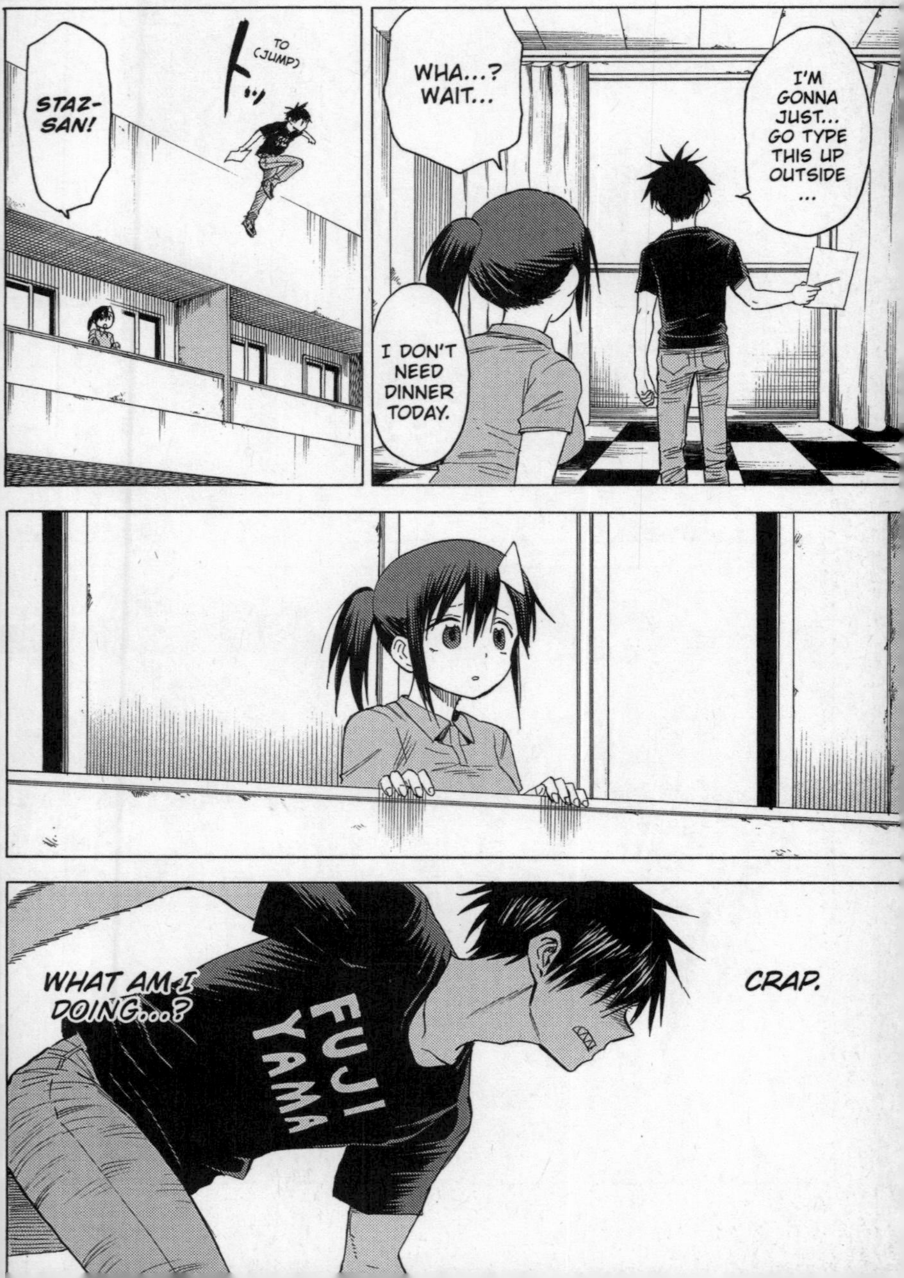
I'M GONNA JUST... GO TYPE THIS UP OUTSIDE ...
WHA...? WAIT...
I DON'T NEED DINNER TODAY.
トッ
TO (JUMP)
STAZ-SAN!
CRAP.
FUJI YAMA
WHAT AM I DOING...?

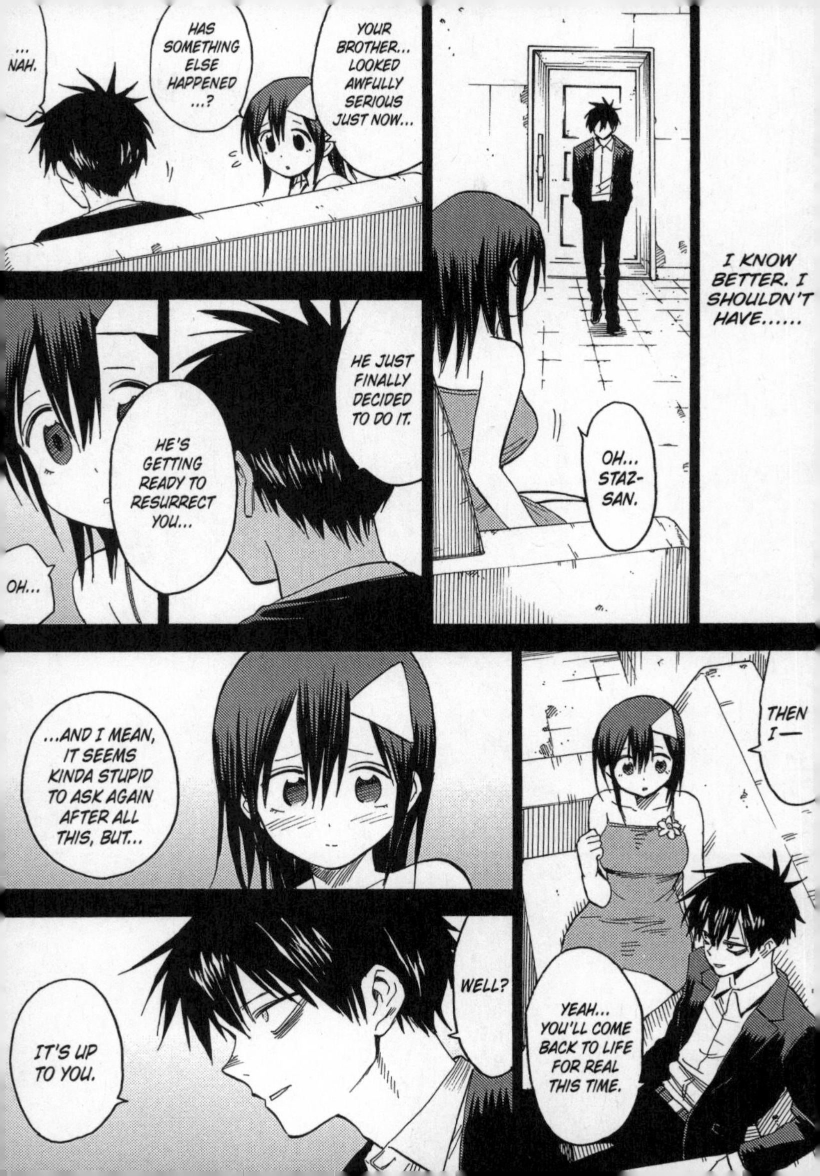
I KNOW BETTER. I SHOULDN'T HAVE......
OH... STAZ-SAN.
YOUR BROTHER... LOOKED AWFULLY SERIOUS JUST NOW...
HAS SOMETHING ELSE HAPPENED ...?
... NAH.
HE JUST FINALLY DECIDED TO DO IT.
HE'S GETTING READY TO RESURRECT YOU...
OH...
THEN I—
YEAH... YOU'LL COME BACK TO LIFE FOR REAL THIS TIME.
...AND I MEAN, IT SEEMS KINDA STUPID TO ASK AGAIN AFTER ALL THIS, BUT...
WELL?
IT'S UP TO YOU.

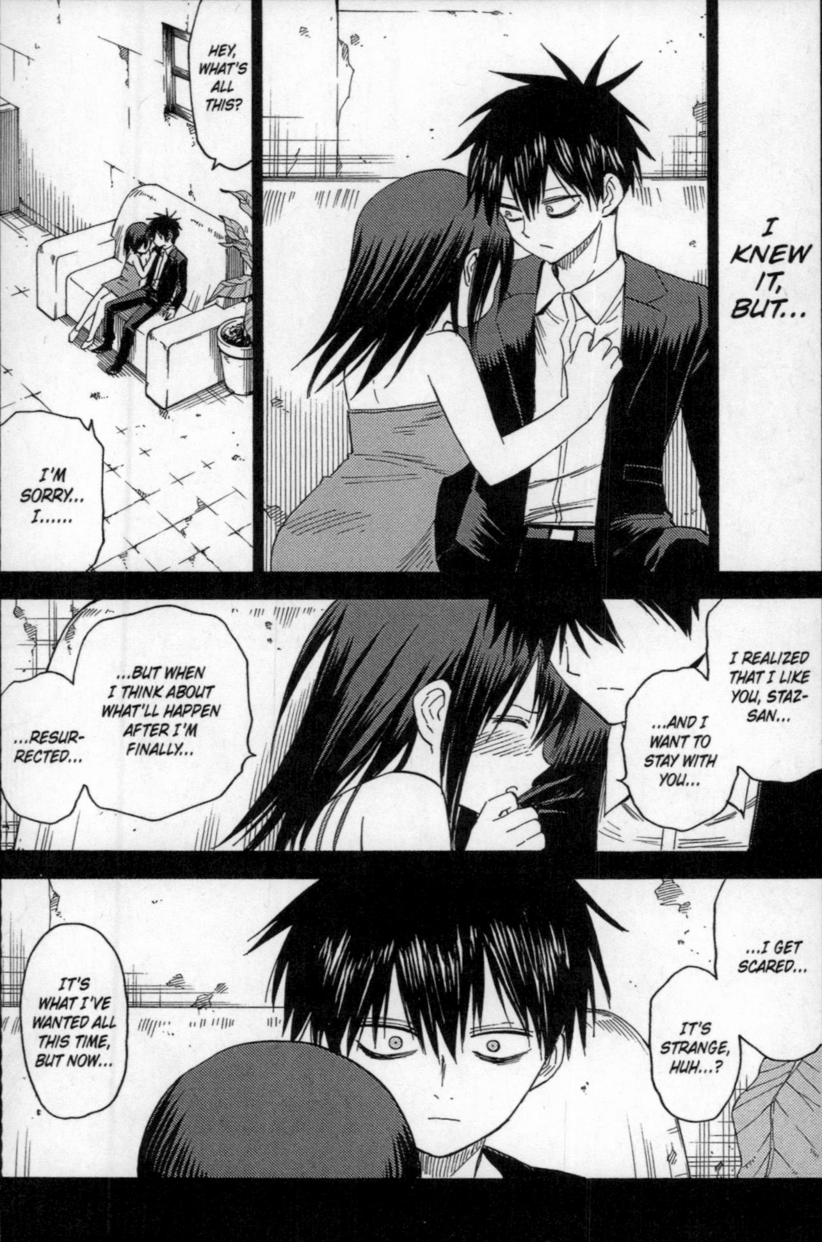
I KNEW IT, BUT...
HEY, WHAT'S ALL THIS?
I'M SORRY... I......
I REALIZED THAT I LIKE YOU, STAZ-SAN...
...AND I WANT TO STAY WITH YOU...
...BUT WHEN I THINK ABOUT WHAT'LL HAPPEN AFTER I'M FINALLY...
...RESUR-RECTED...
...I GET SCARED...
IT'S STRANGE, HUH...?
IT'S WHAT I'VE WANTED ALL THIS TIME, BUT NOW...

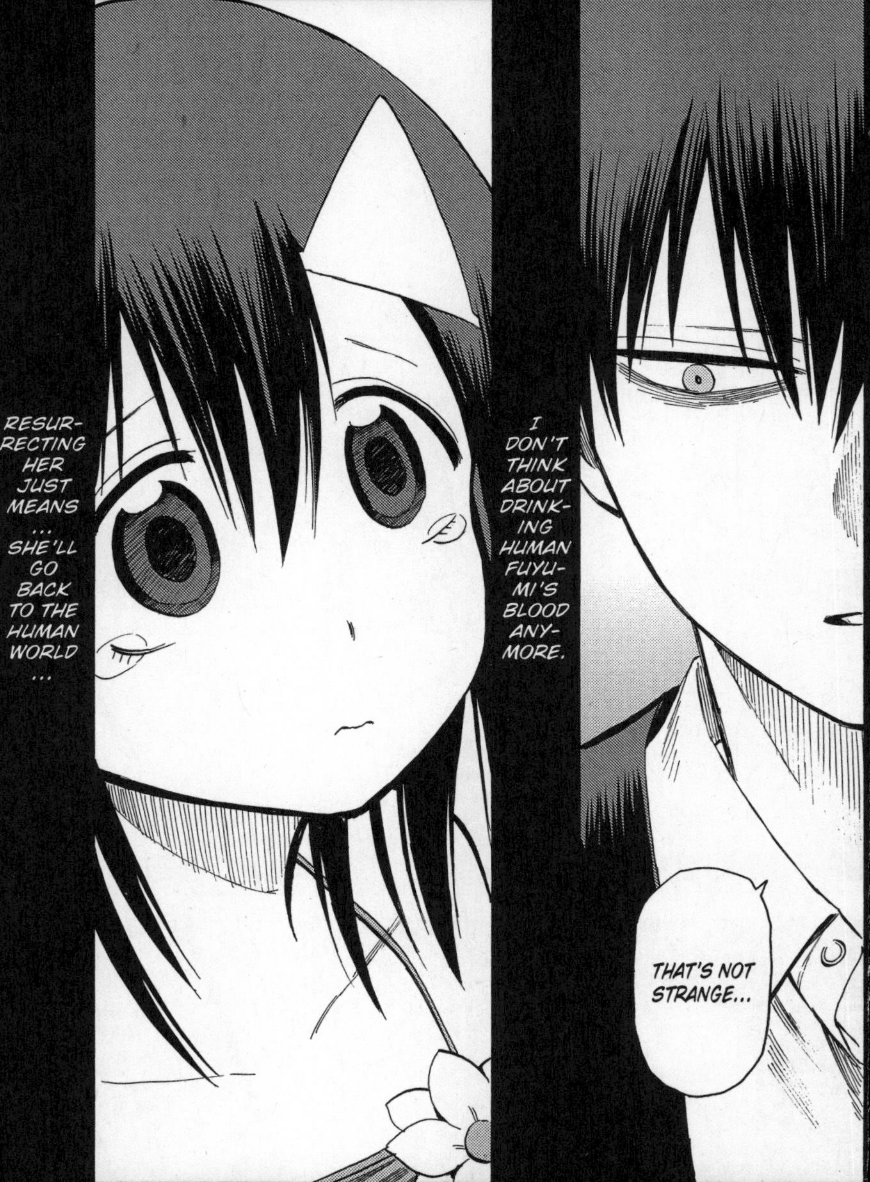
I DON'T THINK ABOUT DRINKING HUMAN FUYUMI'S BLOOD ANYMORE.
THAT'S NOT STRANGE...
RESURRECTING HER JUST MEANS... SHE'LL GO BACK TO THE HUMAN WORLD...

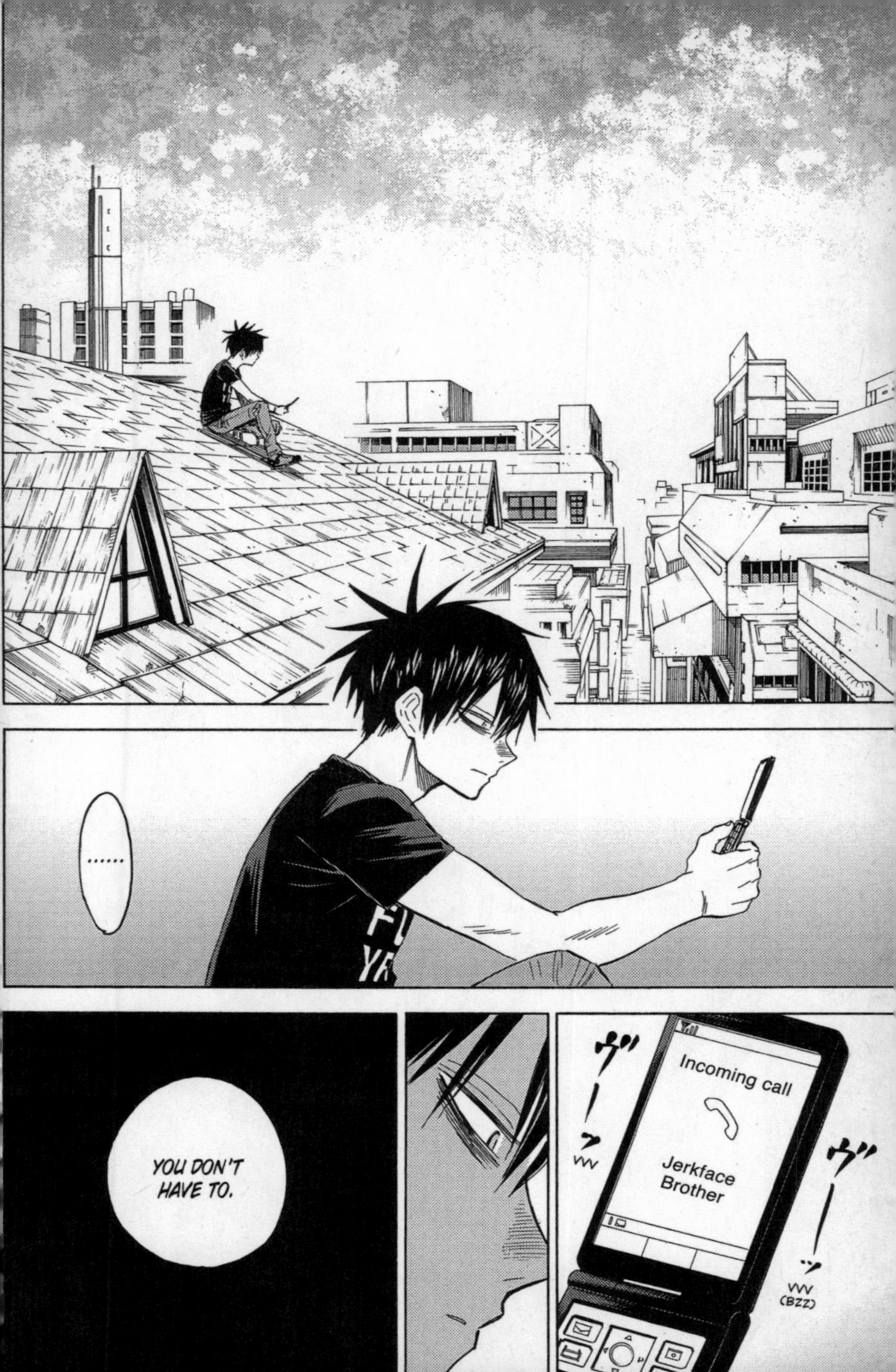
......
Incoming call
Jerkface Brother
ヴーッ
VVV
ヴーッ
VVV (BZZ)
YOU DON'T HAVE TO.

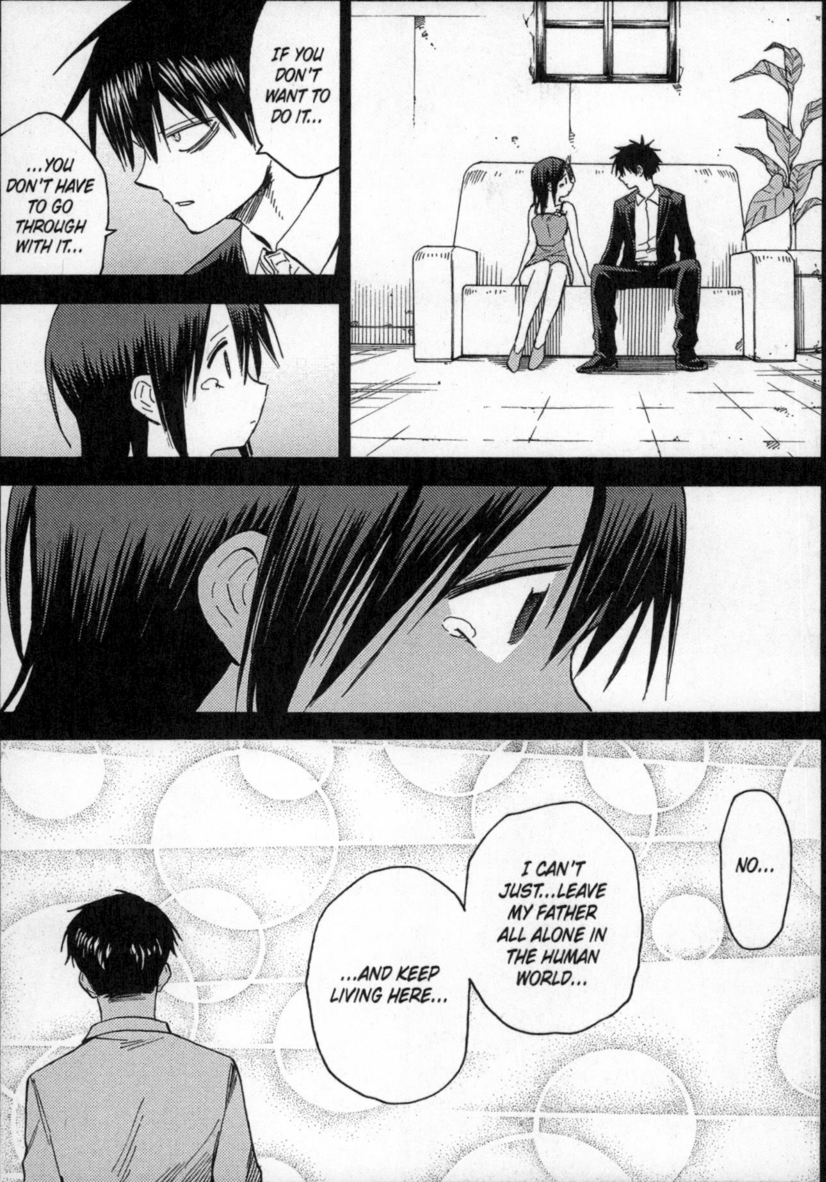
IF YOU DON'T WANT TO DO IT...
...YOU DON'T HAVE TO GO THROUGH WITH IT...
NO...
I CAN'T JUST...LEAVE MY FATHER ALL ALONE IN THE HUMAN WORLD...
...AND KEEP LIVING HERE...

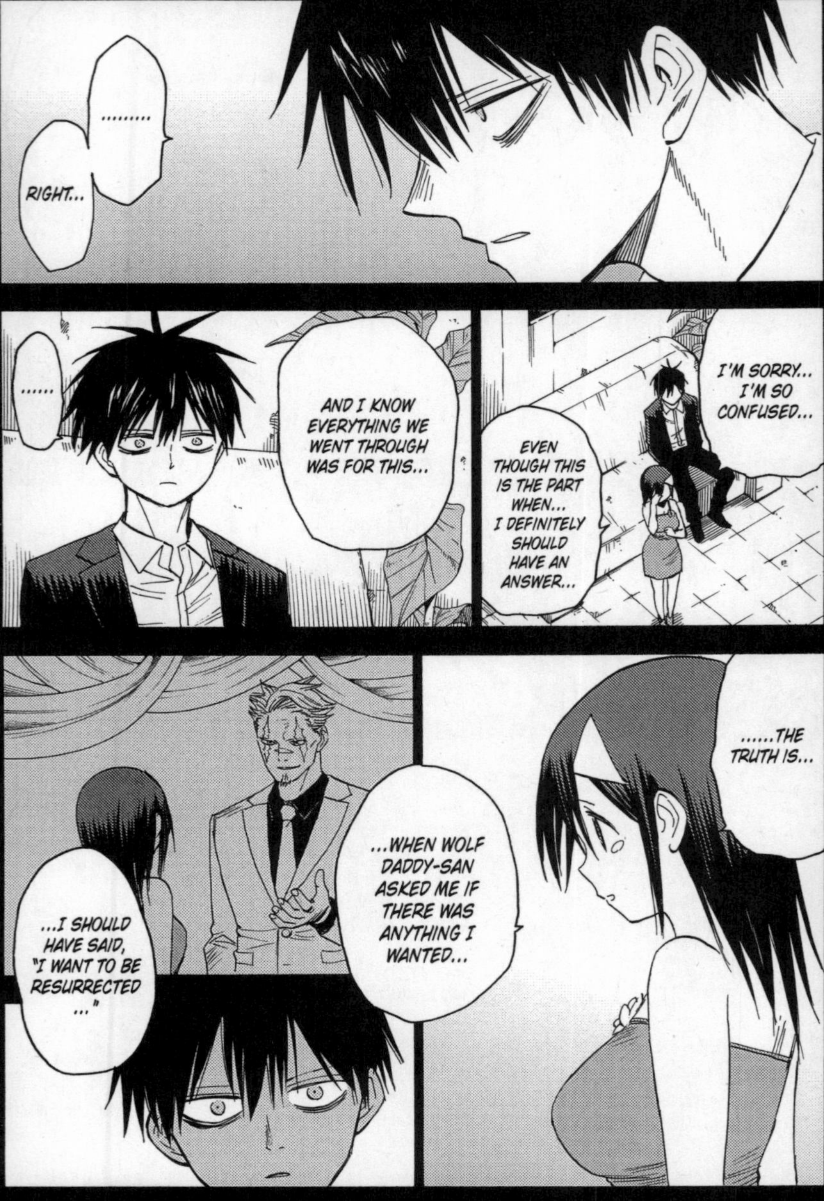
....
RIGHT...
I'M SORRY... I'M SO CONFUSED...
EVEN THOUGH THIS IS THE PART WHEN... I DEFINITELY SHOULD HAVE AN ANSWER...
AND I KNOW EVERYTHING WE WENT THROUGH WAS FOR THIS...
......
......THE TRUTH IS...
...WHEN WOLF DADDY-SAN ASKED ME IF THERE WAS ANYTHING I WANTED...
...I SHOULD HAVE SAID, "I WANT TO BE RESURRECTED..."

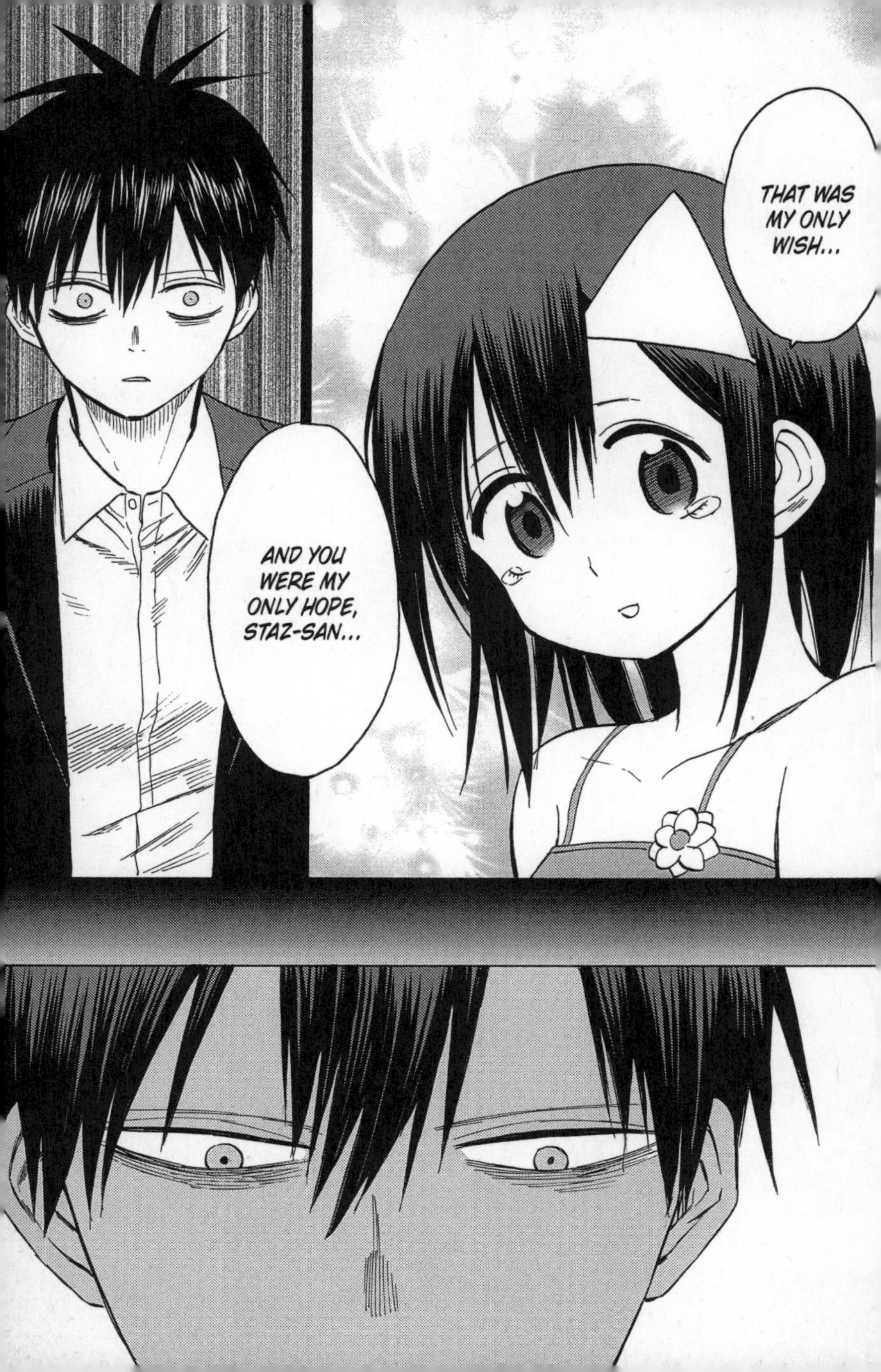
THAT WAS MY ONLY WISH...
AND YOU WERE MY ONLY HOPE, STAZ-SAN...

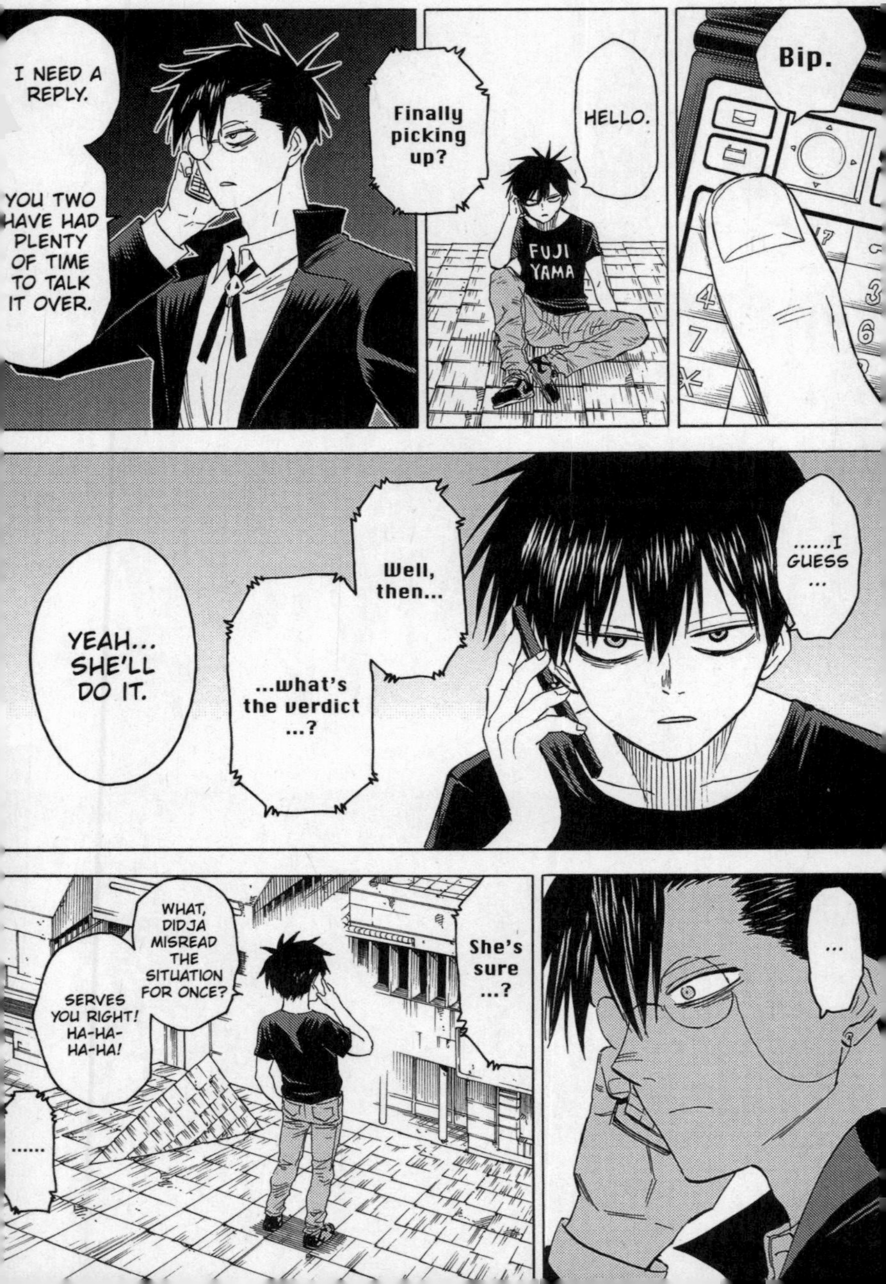
Bip.
HELLO.
Finally picking up?
I NEED A REPLY.
YOU TWO HAVE HAD PLENTY OF TIME TO TALK IT OVER.
......I GUESS ...
Well, then...
...what's the verdict ...?
YEAH... SHE'LL DO IT.
...
She's sure ...?
WHAT, DIDJA MISREAD THE SITUATION FOR ONCE?
SERVES YOU RIGHT! HA-HA-HA-HA!
......

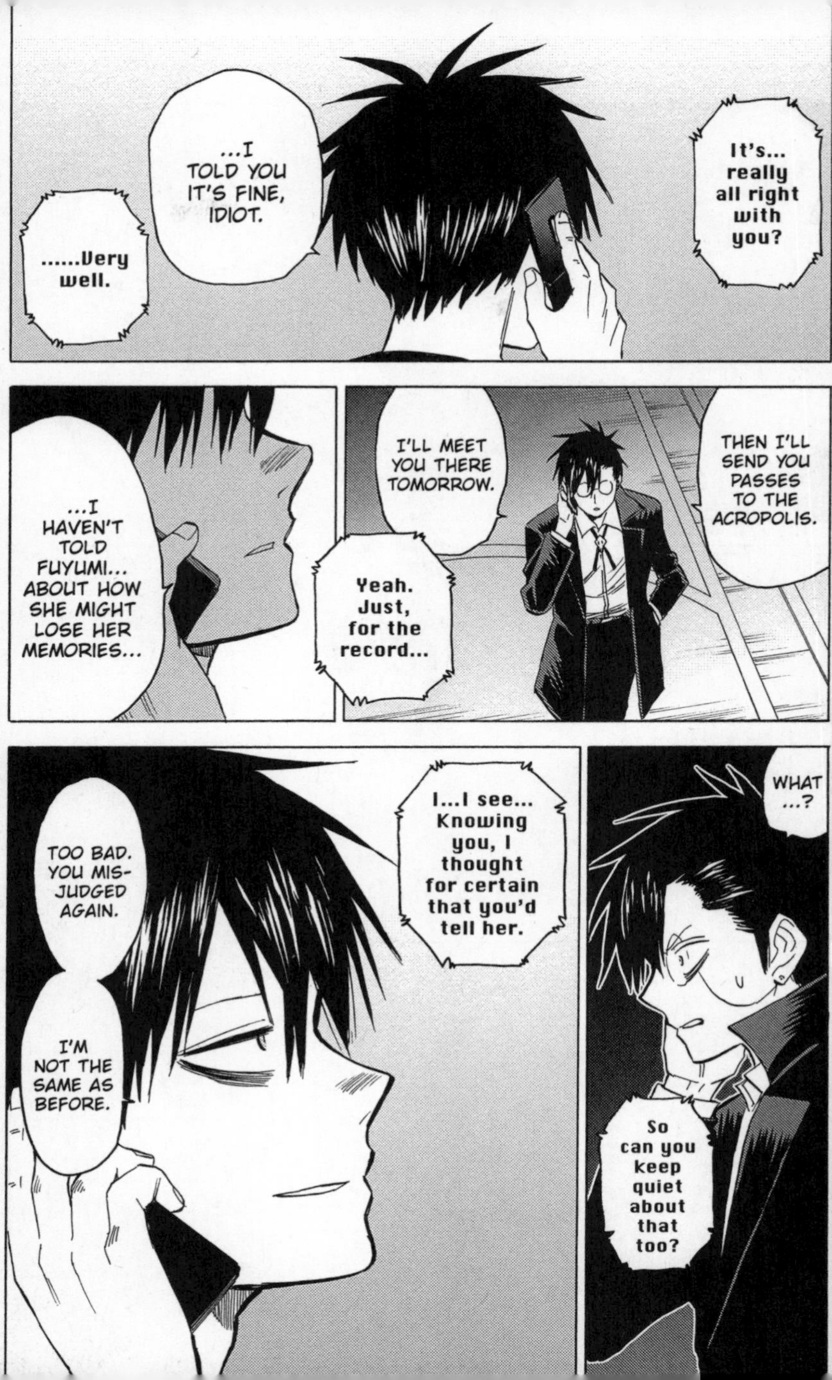
It's... really all right with you?
...I TOLD YOU IT'S FINE, IDIOT.
......Very well.
THEN I'LL SEND YOU PASSES TO THE ACROPOLIS.
I'LL MEET YOU THERE TOMORROW.
Yeah. Just, for the record...
...I HAVEN'T TOLD FUYUMI... ABOUT HOW SHE MIGHT LOSE HER MEMORIES...
WHAT ...?
So can you keep quiet about that too?
I...I see... Knowing you, I thought for certain that you'd tell her.
TOO BAD. YOU MIS-JUDGED AGAIN.
I'M NOT THE SAME AS BEFORE.

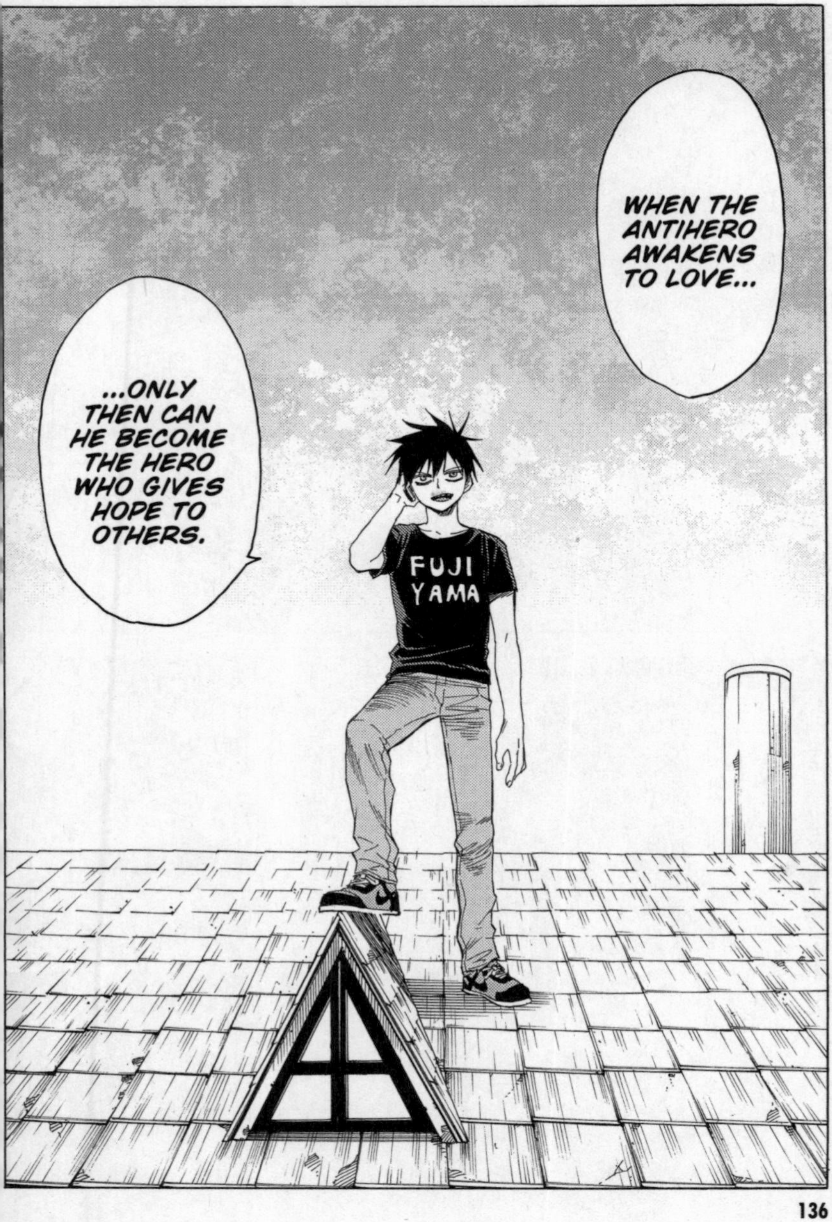
WHEN THE ANTIHERO AWAKENS TO LOVE...
...ONLY THEN CAN HE BECOME THE HERO WHO GIVES HOPE TO OTHERS.
FUJI YAMA

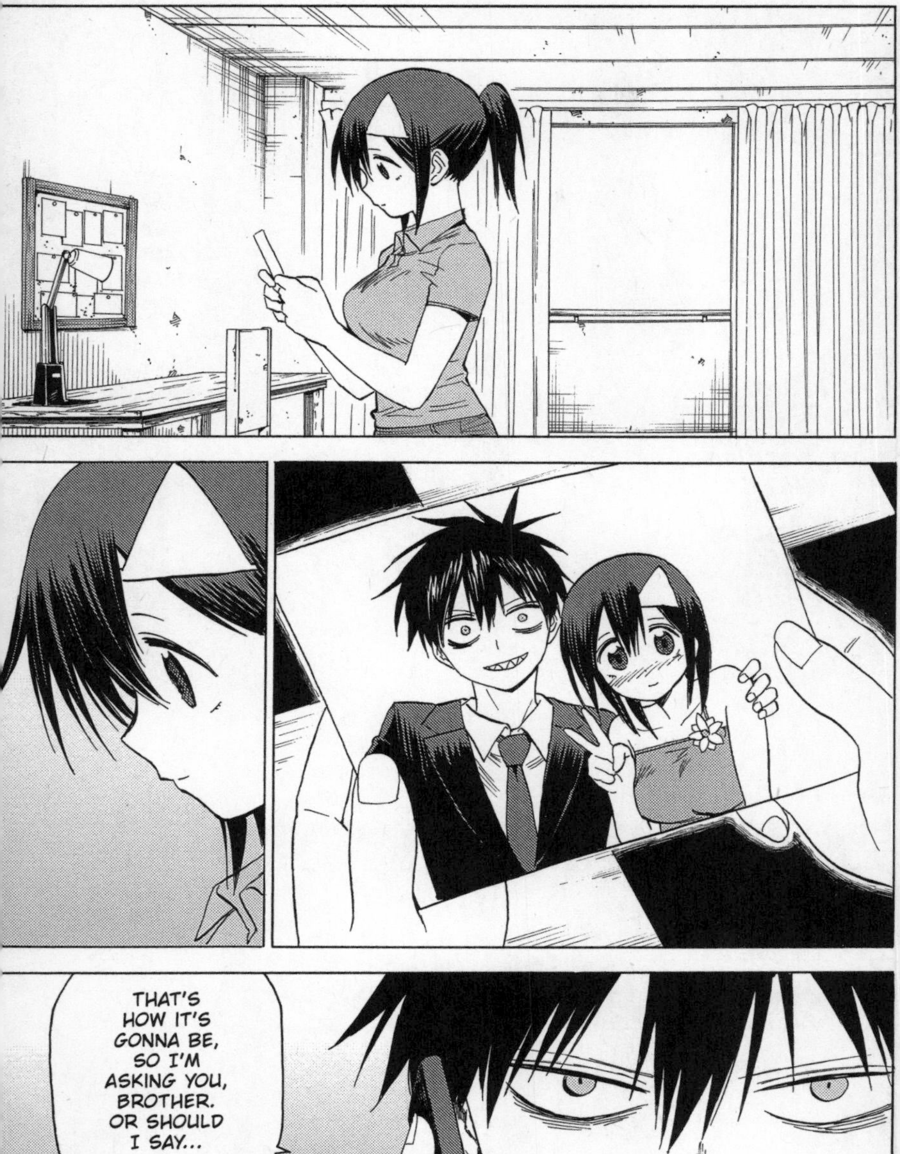
THAT'S HOW IT'S GONNA BE, SO I'M ASKING YOU, BROTHER. OR SHOULD I SAY...

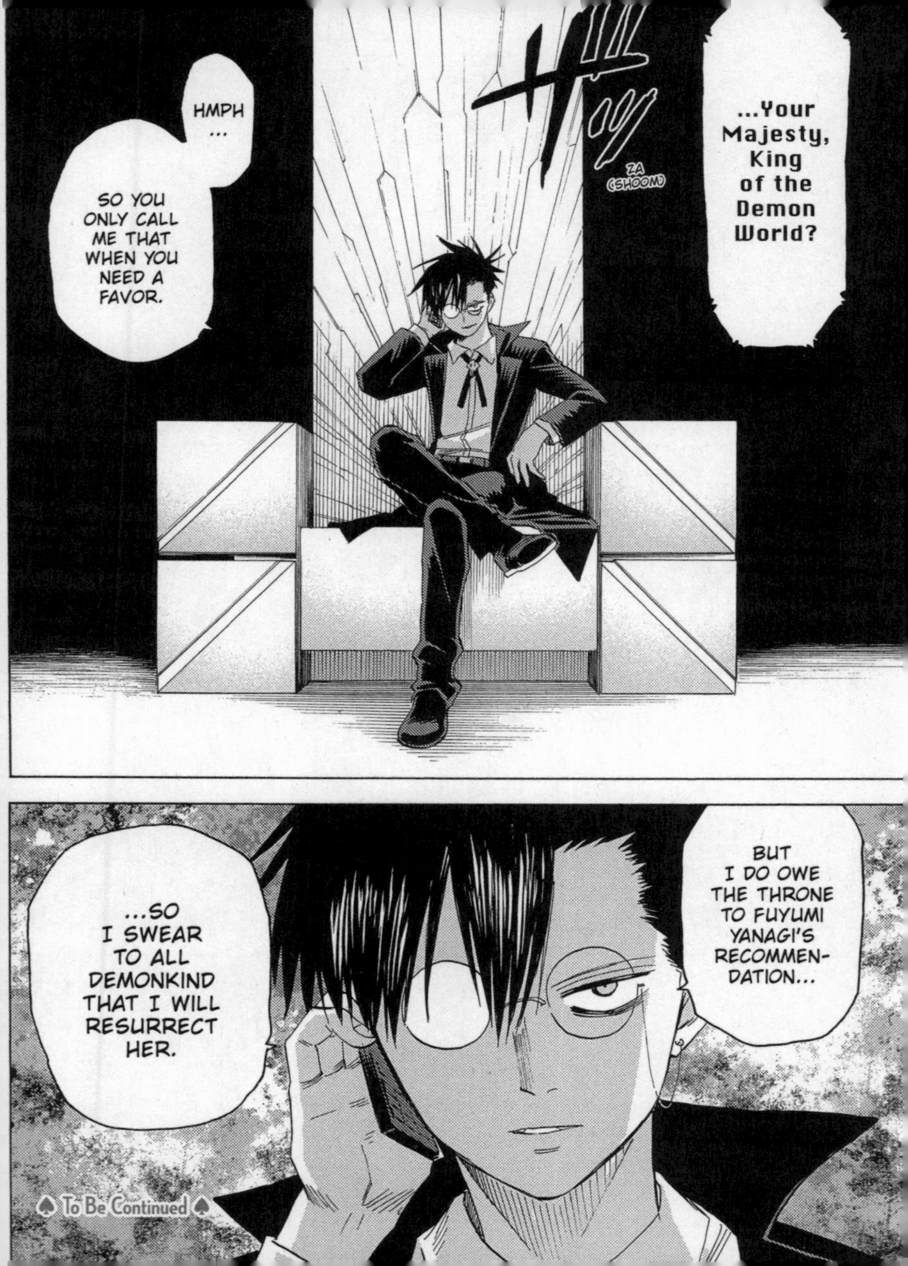
...Your Majesty, King of the Demon World?
ZA (SHOOM)
HMPH ...
SO YOU ONLY CALL ME THAT WHEN YOU NEED A FAVOR.
BUT I DO OWE THE THRONE TO FUYUMI YANAGI'S RECOMMENDATION...
...SO I SWEAR TO ALL DEMONKIND THAT I WILL RESURRECT HER.
To Be Continued

BLOOD LAD

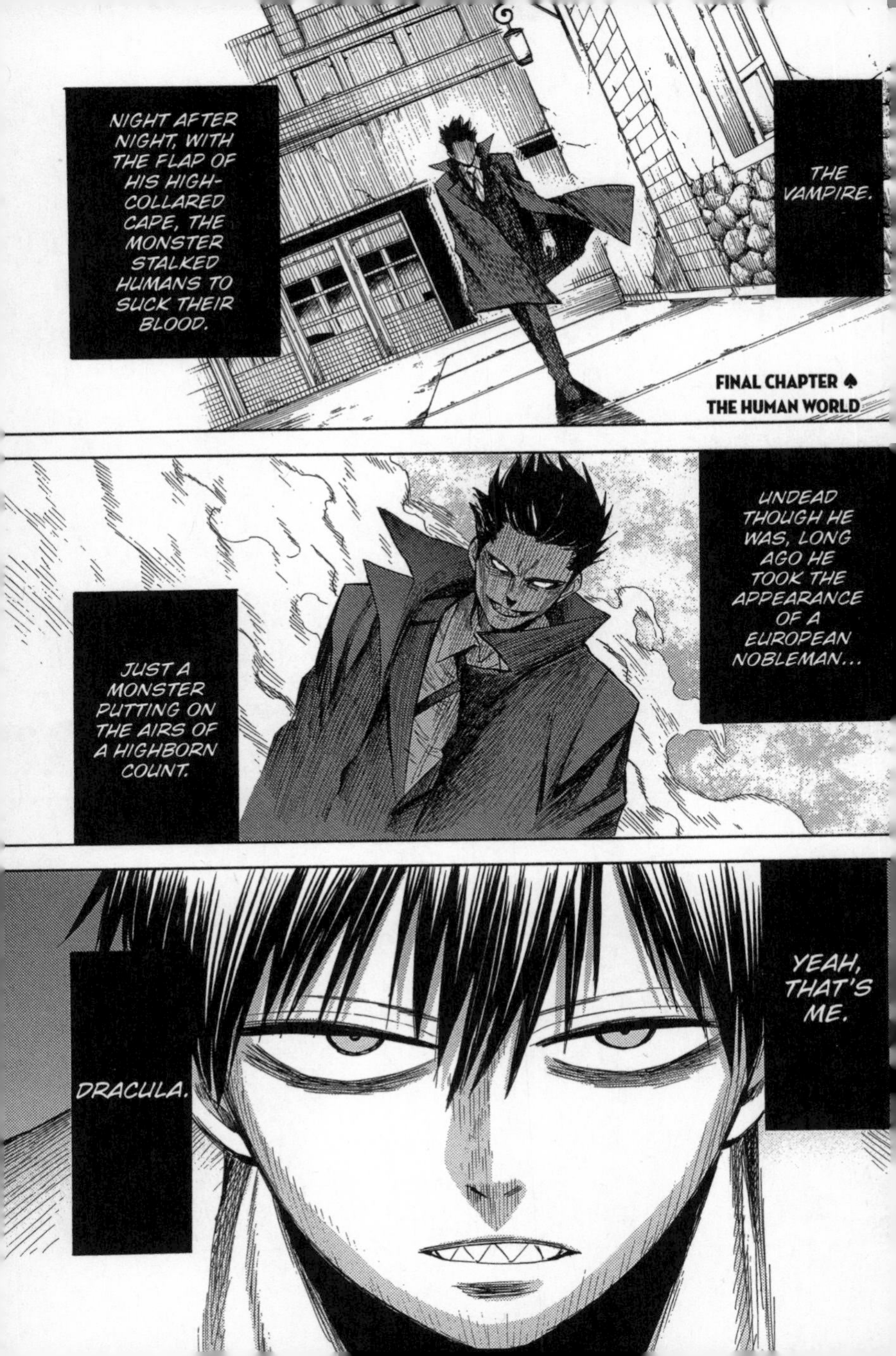

THE VAMPIRE.
NIGHT AFTER NIGHT, WITH THE FLAP OF HIS HIGH-COLLARED CAPE, THE MONSTER STALKED HUMANS TO SUCK THEIR BLOOD.
FINAL CHAPTER ♠ THE HUMAN WORLD
UNDEAD THOUGH HE WAS, LONG AGO HE TOOK THE APPEARANCE OF A EUROPEAN NOBLEMAN...
JUST A MONSTER PUTTING ON THE AIRS OF A HIGHBORN COUNT.
YEAH, THAT'S ME.
DRACULA.

FINAL CHAPTER ♠ THE HUMAN WORLD

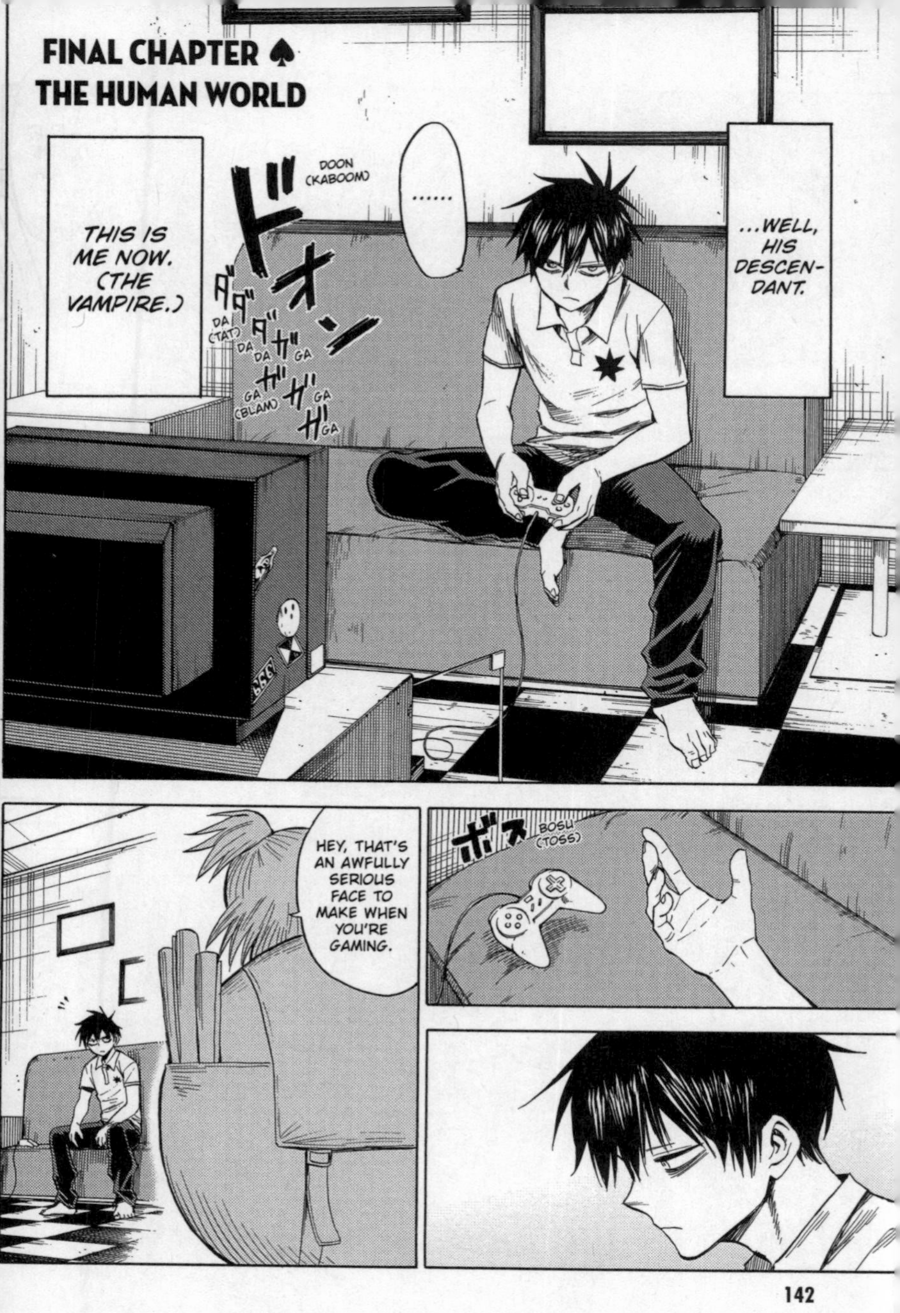
THIS IS ME NOW. (THE VAMPIRE.)
......
ドオン
DOON (KABOOM)
ダダダガガガガガ
DA (TAT) DA DA GA GA (BLAM) GA GA GA
...WELL, HIS DESCENDANT.
ボス
BOSU (TOSS)
HEY, THAT'S AN AWFULLY SERIOUS FACE TO MAKE WHEN YOU'RE GAMING.

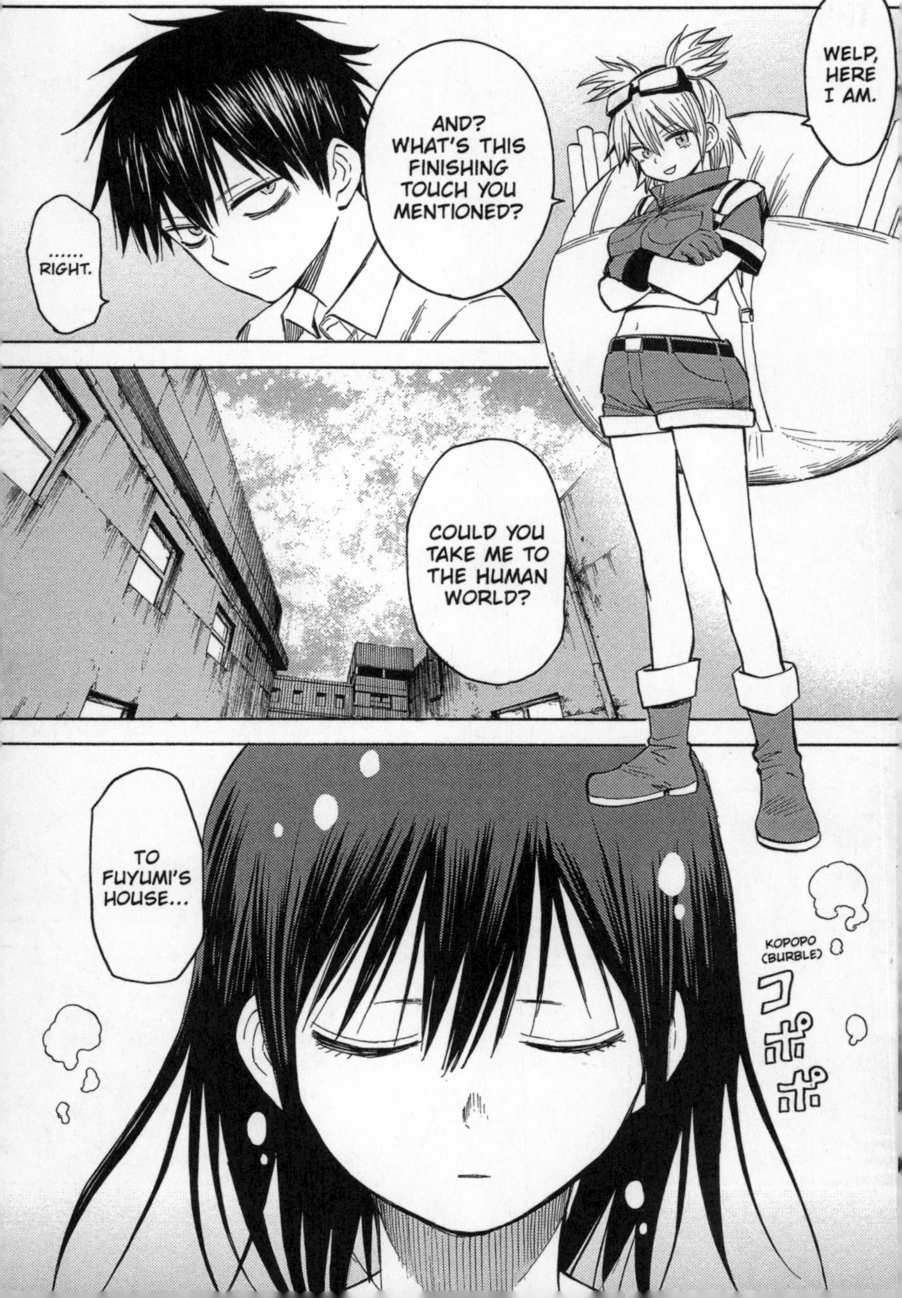
WELP, HERE I AM.
AND? WHAT'S THIS FINISHING TOUCH YOU MENTIONED?
...... RIGHT.
COULD YOU TAKE ME TO THE HUMAN WORLD?
KOPOPO (BURBLE)
コポポ
TO FUYUMI'S HOUSE...

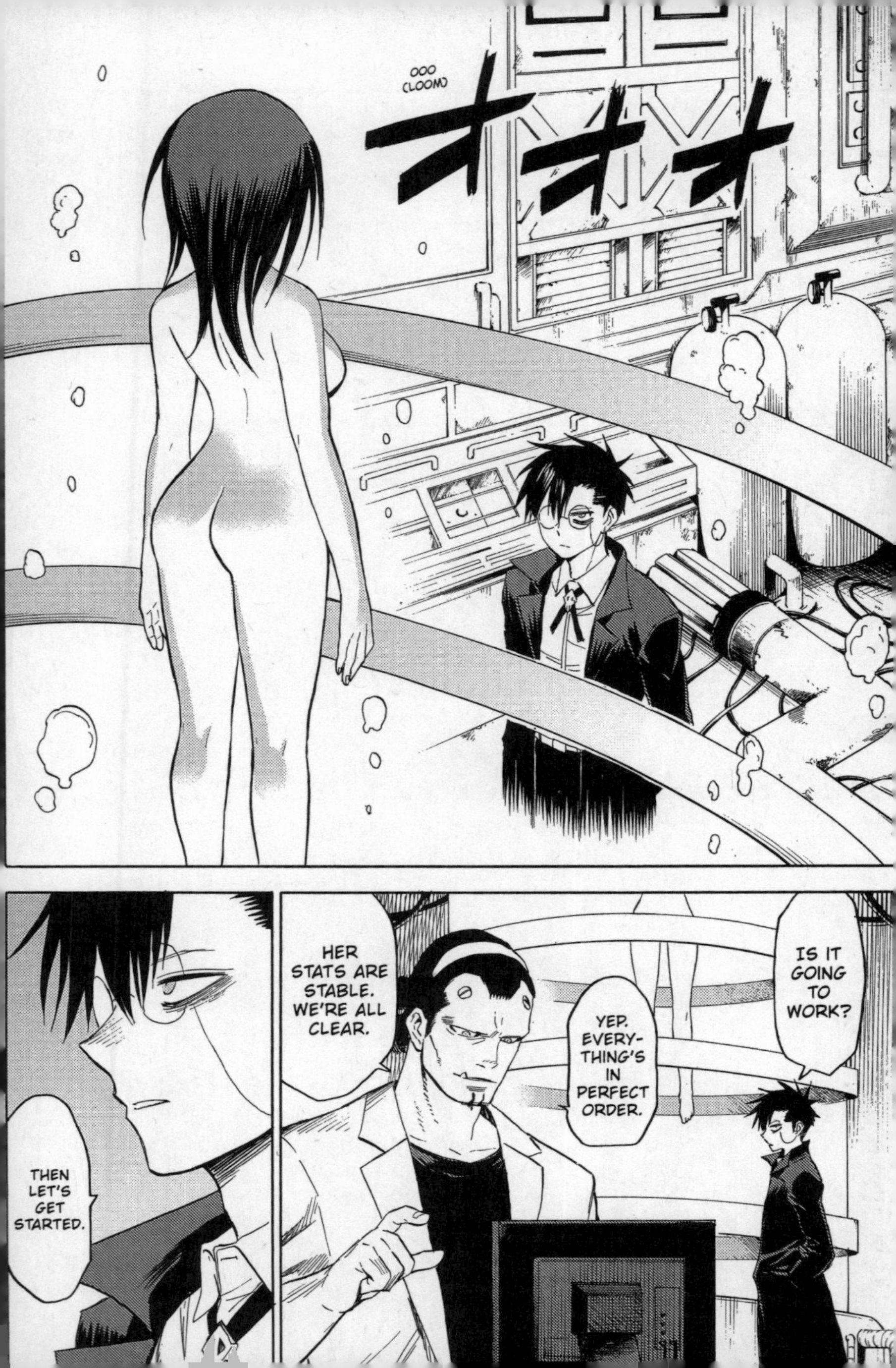
OOO (LOOM)
オオオ
IS IT GOING TO WORK?
YEP. EVERYTHING'S IN PERFECT ORDER.
HER STATS ARE STABLE. WE'RE ALL CLEAR.
THEN LET'S GET STARTED.

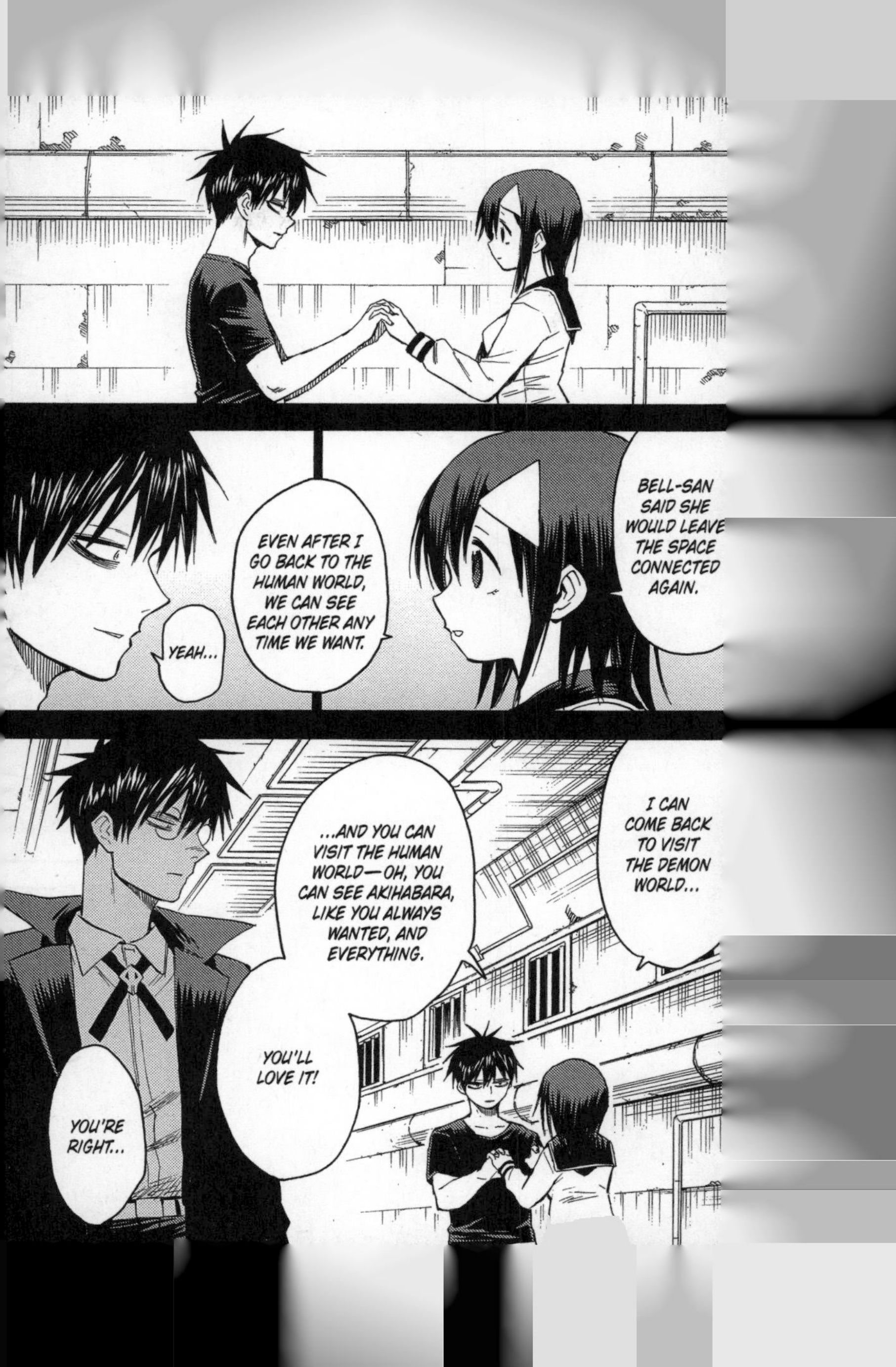
BELL-SAN SAID SHE WOULD LEAVE THE SPACE CONNECTED AGAIN.
EVEN AFTER I GO BACK TO THE HUMAN WORLD, WE CAN SEE EACH OTHER ANY TIME WE WANT.
YEAH...
I CAN COME BACK TO VISIT THE DEMON WORLD...
...AND YOU CAN VISIT THE HUMAN WORLD—OH, YOU CAN SEE AKIHABARA, LIKE YOU ALWAYS WANTED, AND EVERYTHING.
YOU'LL LOVE IT!
YOU'RE RIGHT...

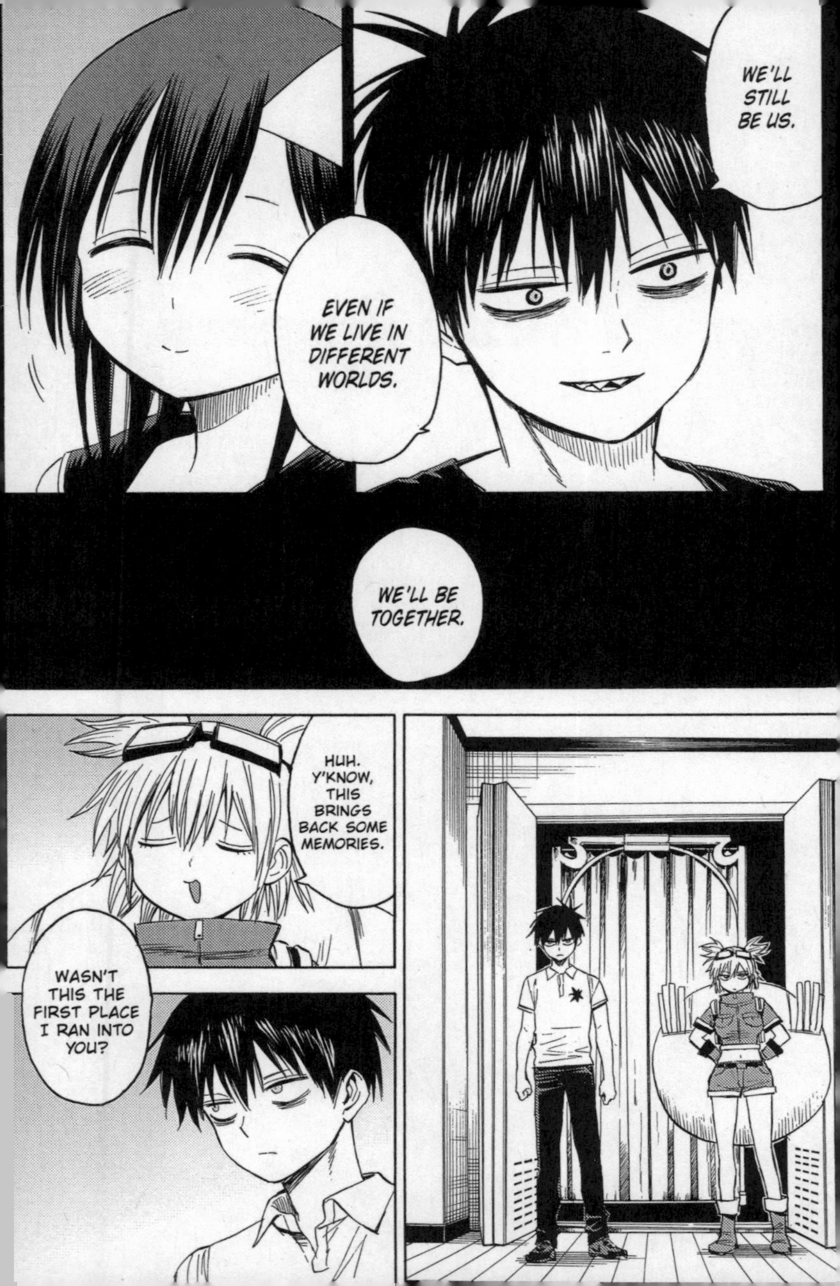
WE'LL STILL BE US.
EVEN IF WE LIVE IN DIFFERENT WORLDS.
WE'LL BE TOGETHER.
HUH. Y'KNOW, THIS BRINGS BACK SOME MEMORIES.
WASN'T THIS THE FIRST PLACE I RAN INTO YOU?

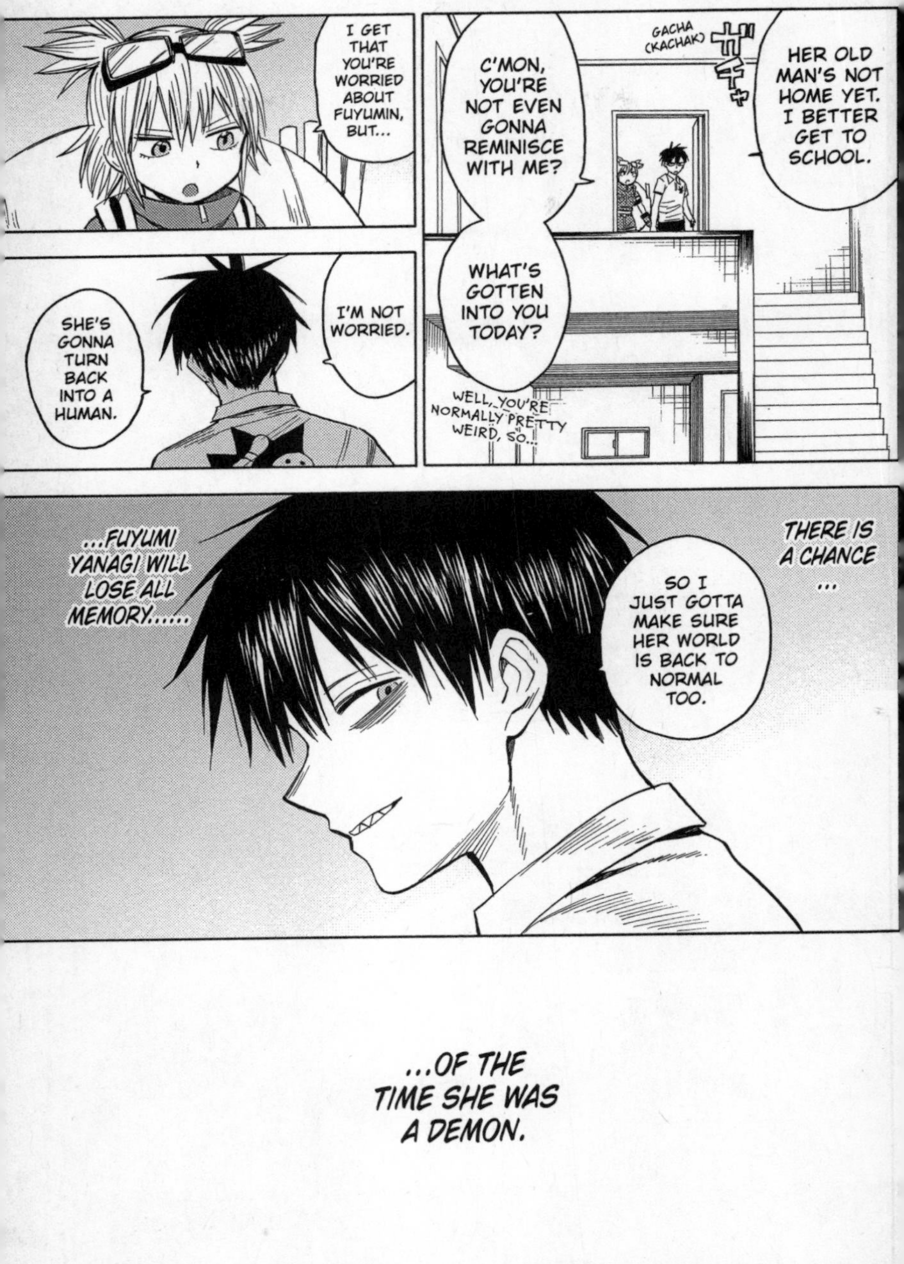
GACHA (KACHAK)
HER OLD MAN'S NOT HOME YET. I BETTER GET TO SCHOOL.
C'MON, YOU'RE NOT EVEN GONNA REMINISCE WITH ME?
WHAT'S GOTTEN INTO YOU TODAY?
WELL, YOU'RE NORMALLY PRETTY WEIRD, SO...
I GET THAT YOU'RE WORRIED ABOUT FUYUMIN, BUT...
I'M NOT WORRIED.
SHE'S GONNA TURN BACK INTO A HUMAN.
THERE IS A CHANCE...
SO I JUST GOTTA MAKE SURE HER WORLD IS BACK TO NORMAL TOO.
...FUYUMI YANAGI WILL LOSE ALL MEMORY......
...OF THE TIME SHE WAS A DEMON.

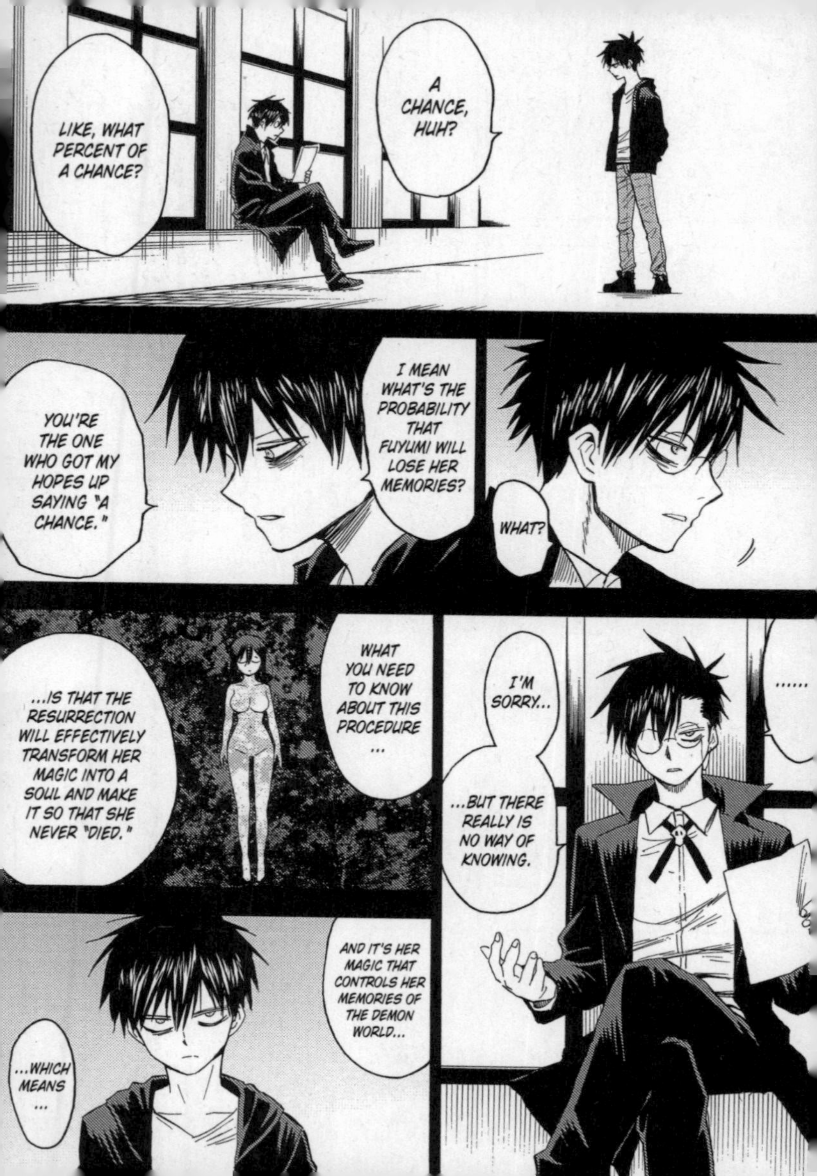
A CHANCE, HUH?
LIKE, WHAT PERCENT OF A CHANCE?
WHAT?
I MEAN WHAT'S THE PROBABILITY THAT FUYUMI WILL LOSE HER MEMORIES?
YOU'RE THE ONE WHO GOT MY HOPES UP SAYING "A CHANCE."
......
I'M SORRY...
...BUT THERE REALLY IS NO WAY OF KNOWING.
WHAT YOU NEED TO KNOW ABOUT THIS PROCEDURE ...
...IS THAT THE RESURRECTION WILL EFFECTIVELY TRANSFORM HER MAGIC INTO A SOUL AND MAKE IT SO THAT SHE NEVER "DIED."
AND IT'S HER MAGIC THAT CONTROLS HER MEMORIES OF THE DEMON WORLD...
...WHICH MEANS ...

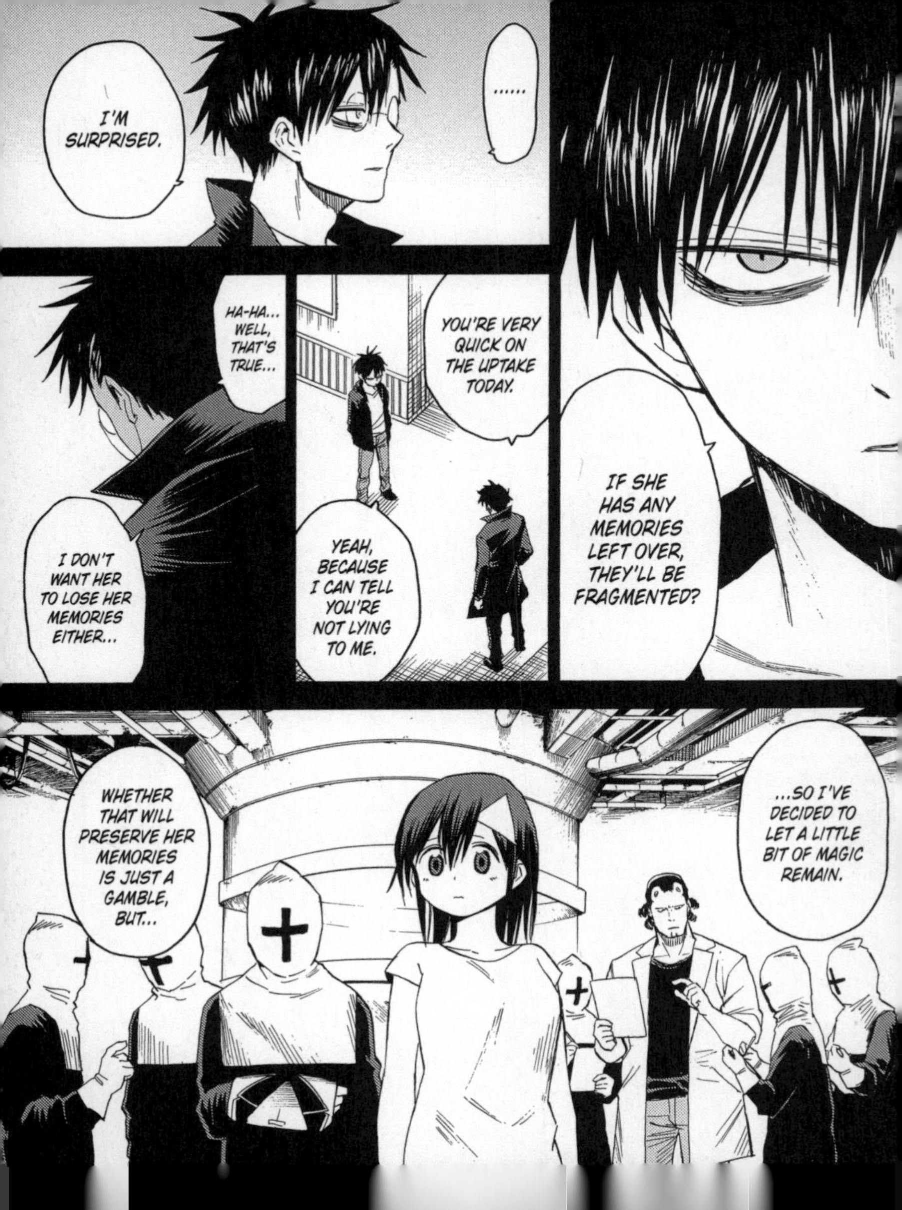
IF SHE HAS ANY MEMORIES LEFT OVER, THEY'LL BE FRAGMENTED?
......
I'M SURPRISED.
YOU'RE VERY QUICK ON THE UPTAKE TODAY.
YEAH, BECAUSE I CAN TELL YOU'RE NOT LYING TO ME.
HA-HA... WELL, THAT'S TRUE...
I DON'T WANT HER TO LOSE HER MEMORIES EITHER...
...SO I'VE DECIDED TO LET A LITTLE BIT OF MAGIC REMAIN.
WHETHER THAT WILL PRESERVE HER MEMORIES IS JUST A GAMBLE, BUT...

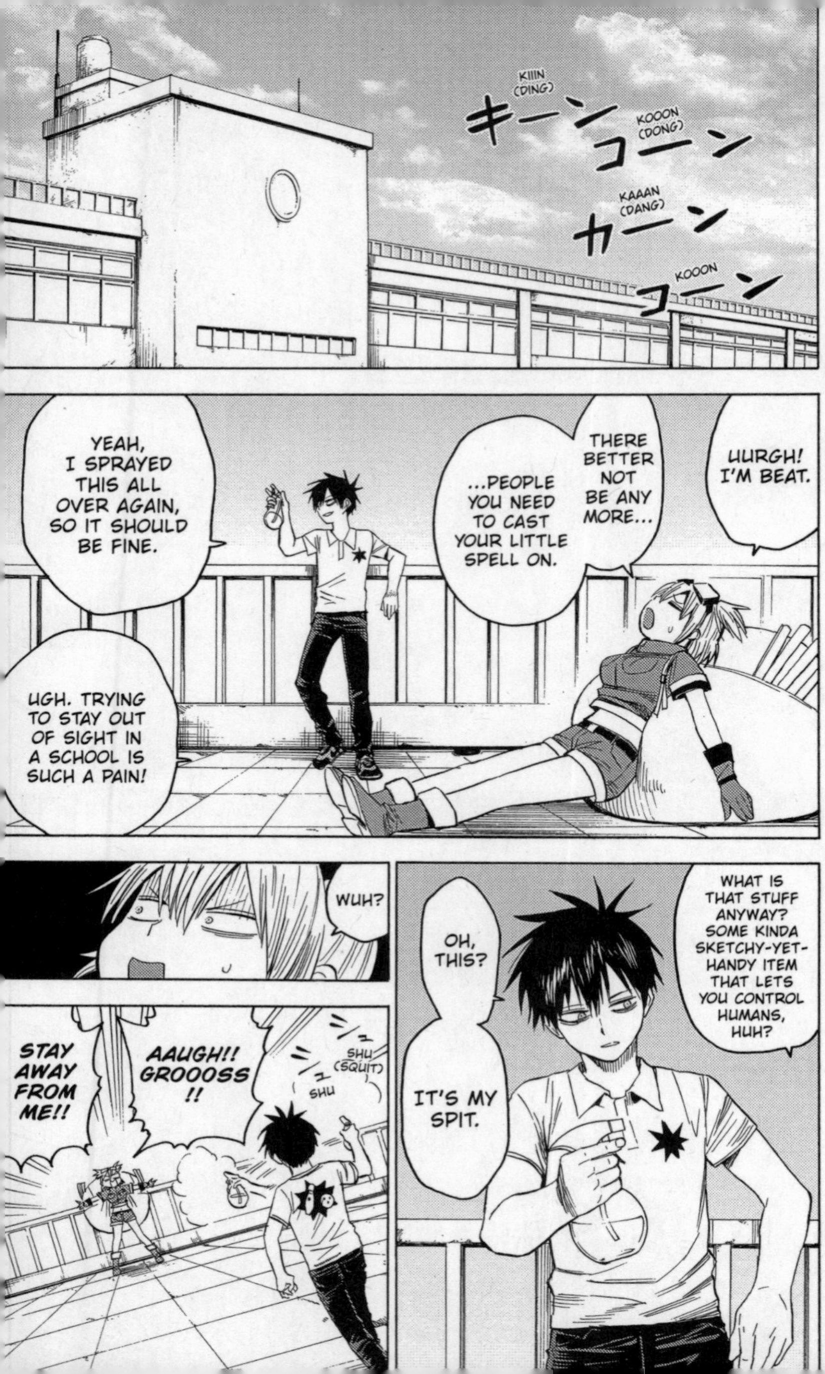
KIIN (DING)
キーン
KOOON (DONG)
コーン
KAAAN (DANG)
カーン
KOOON
コーン
UURGH! I'M BEAT.
THERE BETTER NOT BE ANY MORE...
...PEOPLE YOU NEED TO CAST YOUR LITTLE SPELL ON.
YEAH, I SPRAYED THIS ALL OVER AGAIN, SO IT SHOULD BE FINE.
UGH. TRYING TO STAY OUT OF SIGHT IN A SCHOOL IS SUCH A PAIN!
WHAT IS THAT STUFF ANYWAY? SOME KINDA SKETCHY-YET-HANDY ITEM THAT LETS YOU CONTROL HUMANS, HUH?
OH, THIS?
IT'S MY SPIT.
WUH?
SHU (SQUIT)
SHU
AAUGH!! GROOOSS!!
STAY AWAY FROM ME!!

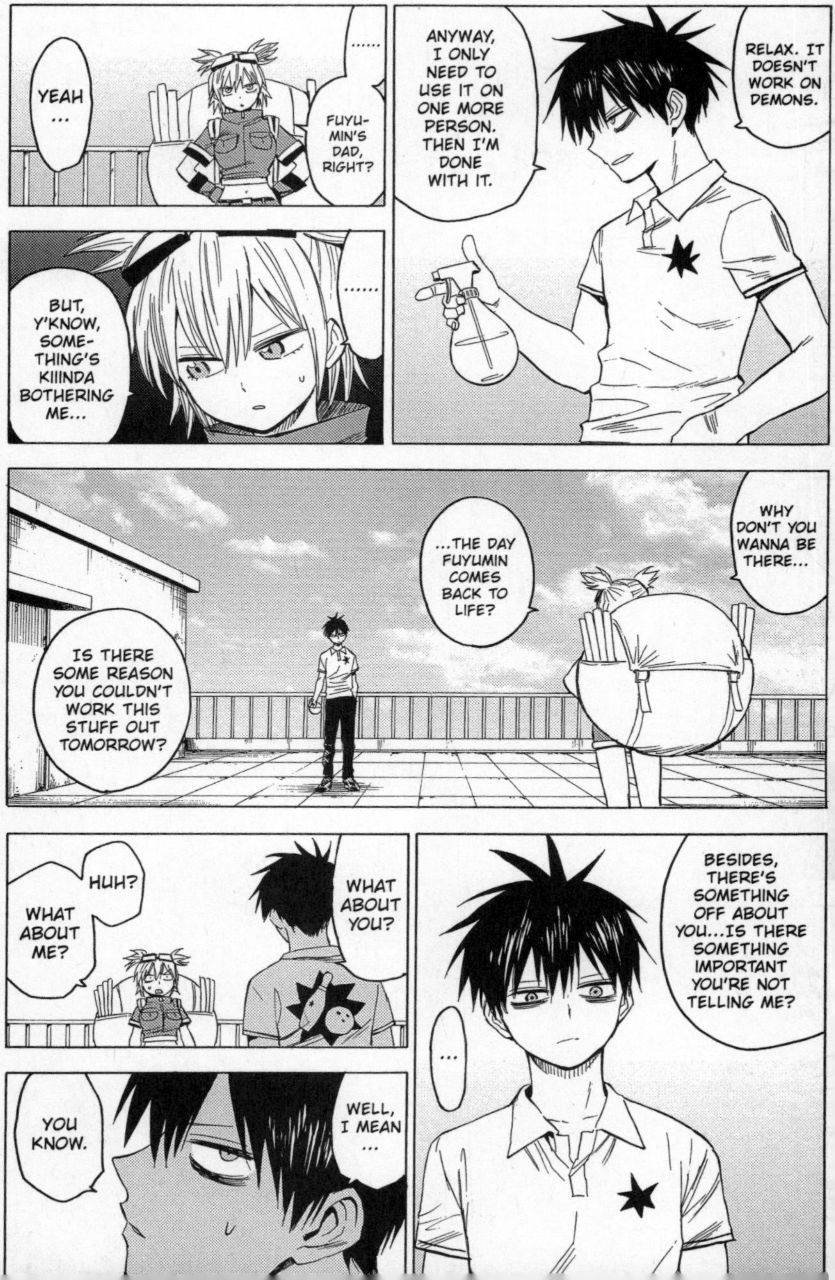
RELAX. IT DOESN'T WORK ON DEMONS.
ANYWAY, I ONLY NEED TO USE IT ON ONE MORE PERSON. THEN I'M DONE WITH IT.
......
FUYU-MIN'S DAD, RIGHT?
YEAH ...
......
BUT, Y'KNOW, SOME-THING'S KIIINDA BOTHERING ME...
WHY DON'T YOU WANNA BE THERE...
...THE DAY FUYUMIN COMES BACK TO LIFE?
IS THERE SOME REASON YOU COULDN'T WORK THIS STUFF OUT TOMORROW?
BESIDES, THERE'S SOMETHING OFF ABOUT YOU...IS THERE SOMETHING IMPORTANT YOU'RE NOT TELLING ME?
...
WHAT ABOUT YOU?
HUH? WHAT ABOUT ME?
WELL, I MEAN ...
YOU KNOW.

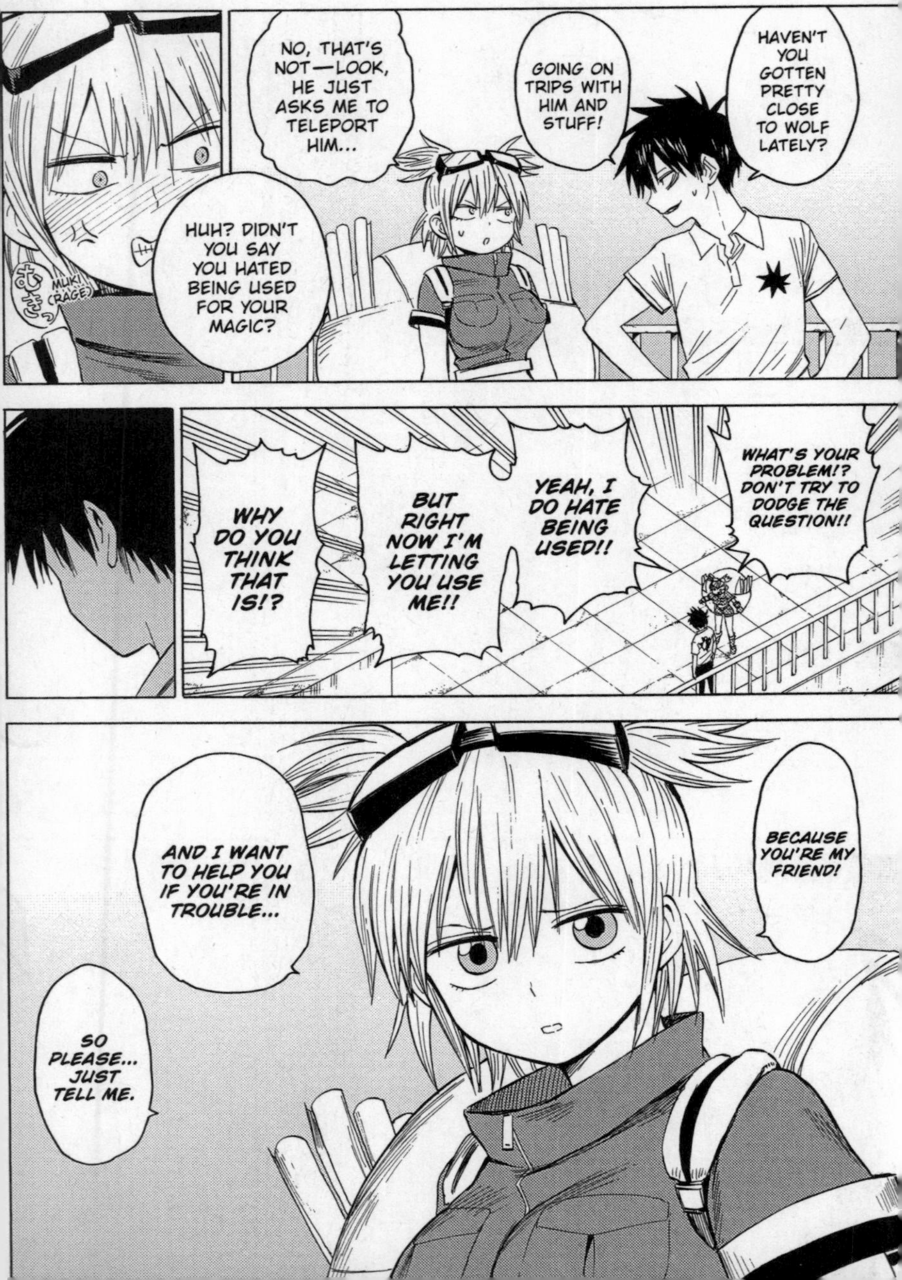
HAVEN'T YOU GOTTEN PRETTY CLOSE TO WOLF LATELY?
GOING ON TRIPS WITH HIM AND STUFF!
NO, THAT'S NOT—LOOK, HE JUST ASKS ME TO TELEPORT HIM...
HUH? DIDN'T YOU SAY YOU HATED BEING USED FOR YOUR MAGIC?
むきっ
MUKI (RAGE)
WHAT'S YOUR PROBLEM!? DON'T TRY TO DODGE THE QUESTION!!
YEAH, I DO HATE BEING USED!!
BUT RIGHT NOW I'M LETTING YOU USE ME!!
WHY DO YOU THINK THAT IS!?
BECAUSE YOU'RE MY FRIEND!
AND I WANT TO HELP YOU IF YOU'RE IN TROUBLE...
SO PLEASE... JUST TELL ME.

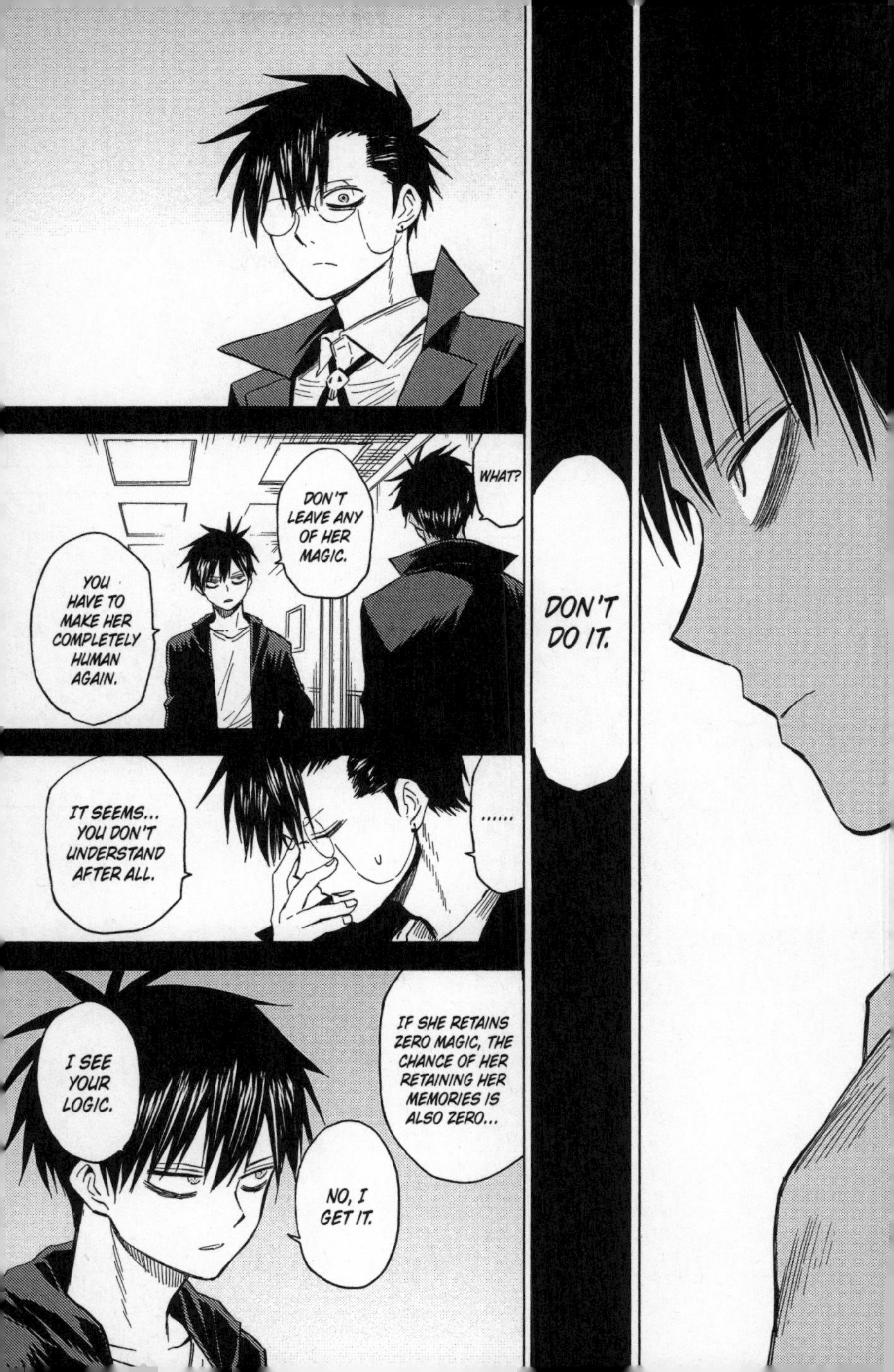
DON'T DO IT.
WHAT?
DON'T LEAVE ANY OF HER MAGIC.
YOU HAVE TO MAKE HER COMPLETELY HUMAN AGAIN.
......
IT SEEMS... YOU DON'T UNDERSTAND AFTER ALL.
IF SHE RETAINS ZERO MAGIC, THE CHANCE OF HER RETAINING HER MEMORIES IS ALSO ZERO...
NO, I GET IT.
I SEE YOUR LOGIC.

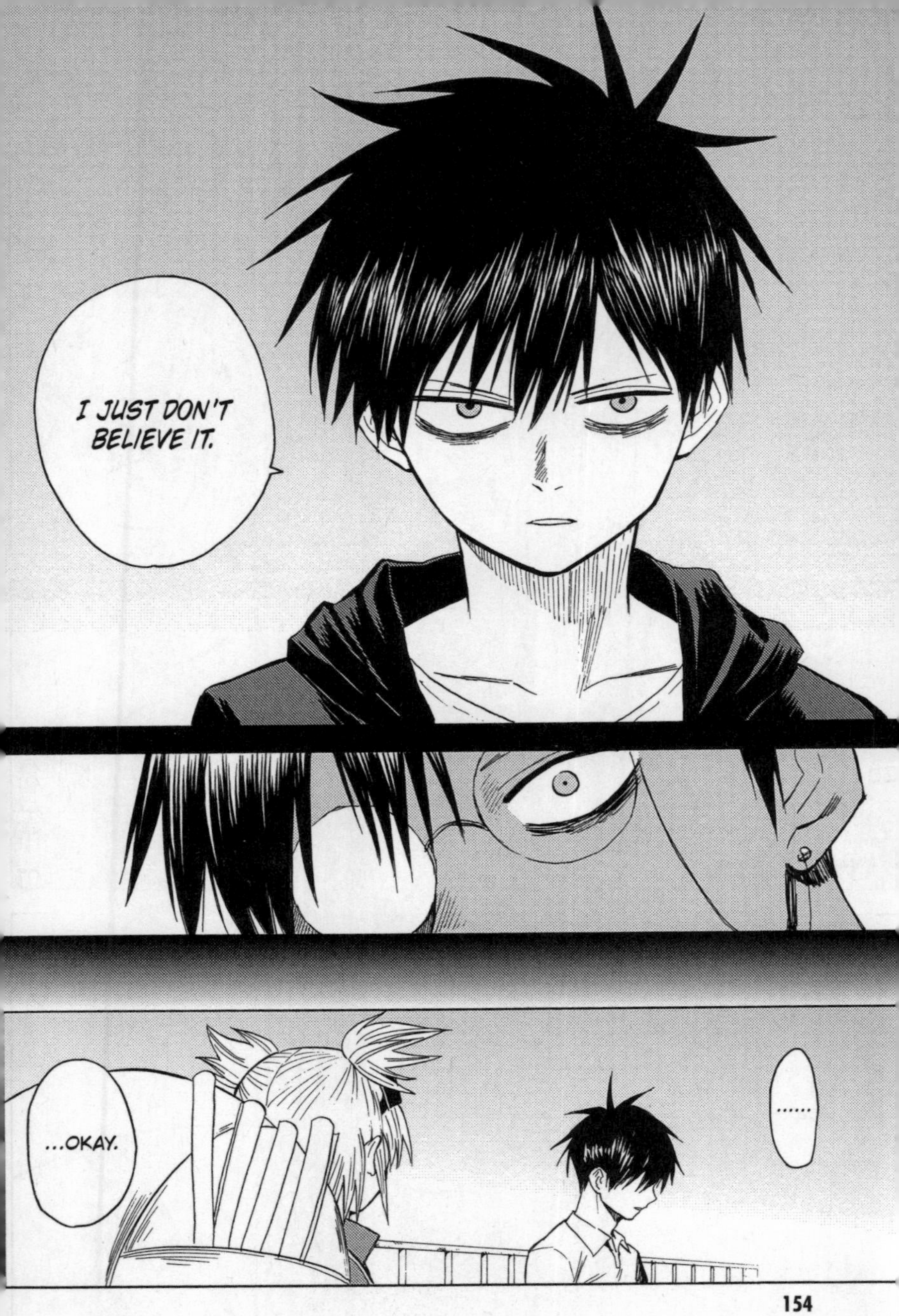
I JUST DON'T BELIEVE IT.
......
...OKAY.

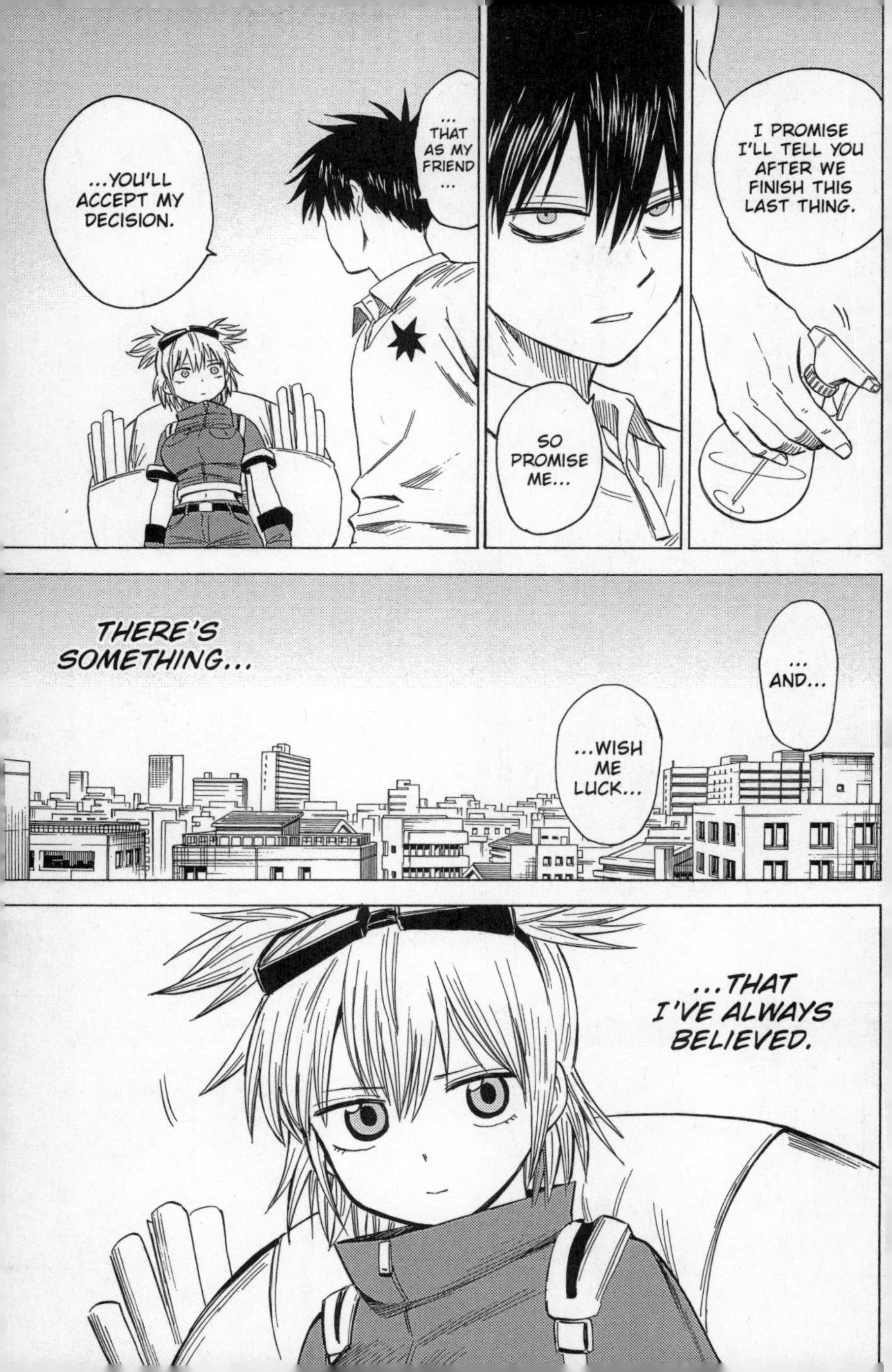
I PROMISE I'LL TELL YOU AFTER WE FINISH THIS LAST THING.
SO PROMISE ME...
...THAT AS MY FRIEND...
...YOU'LL ACCEPT MY DECISION.
...AND...
...WISH ME LUCK...
THERE'S SOMETHING...
...THAT I'VE ALWAYS BELIEVED.

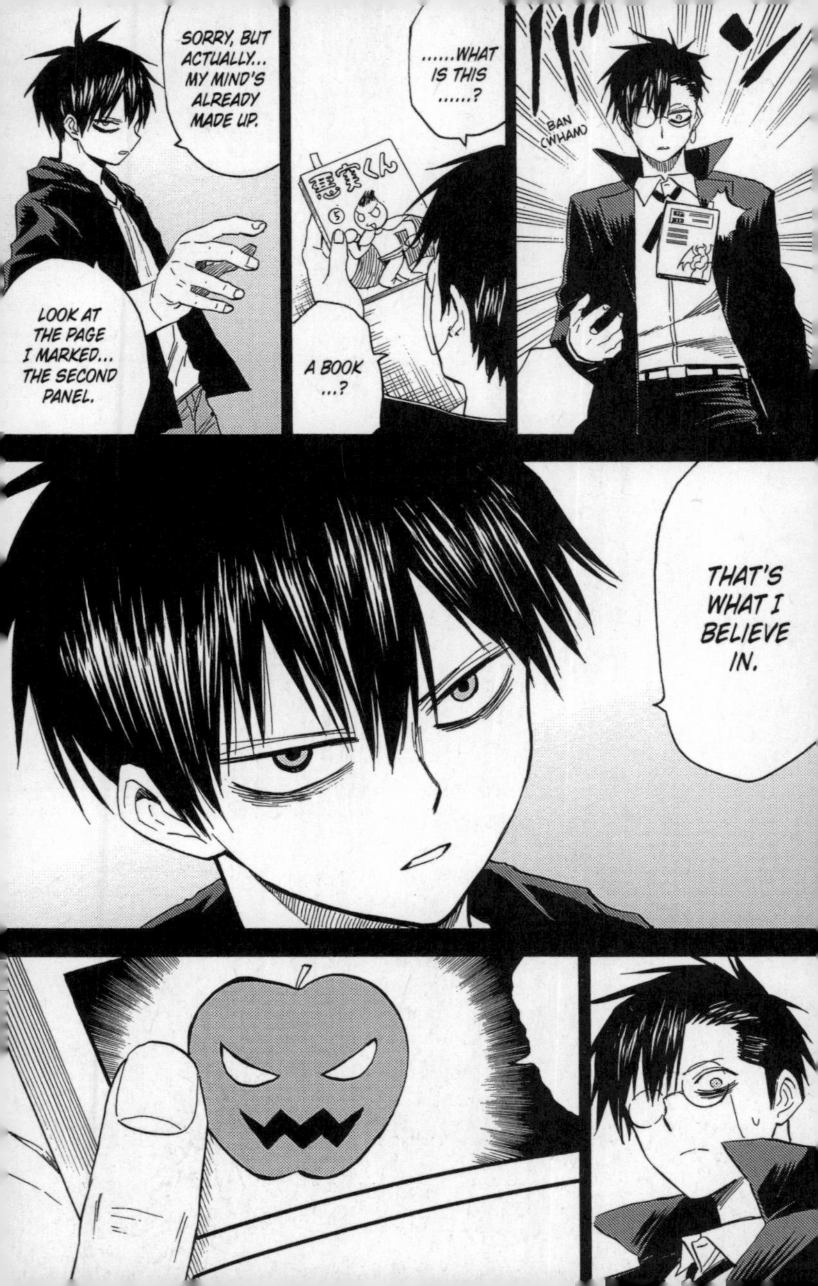
BAN (WHAM)
......WHAT IS THIS ......?
A BOOK ...?
SORRY, BUT ACTUALLY... MY MIND'S ALREADY MADE UP.
LOOK AT THE PAGE I MARKED... THE SECOND PANEL.
THAT'S WHAT I BELIEVE IN.

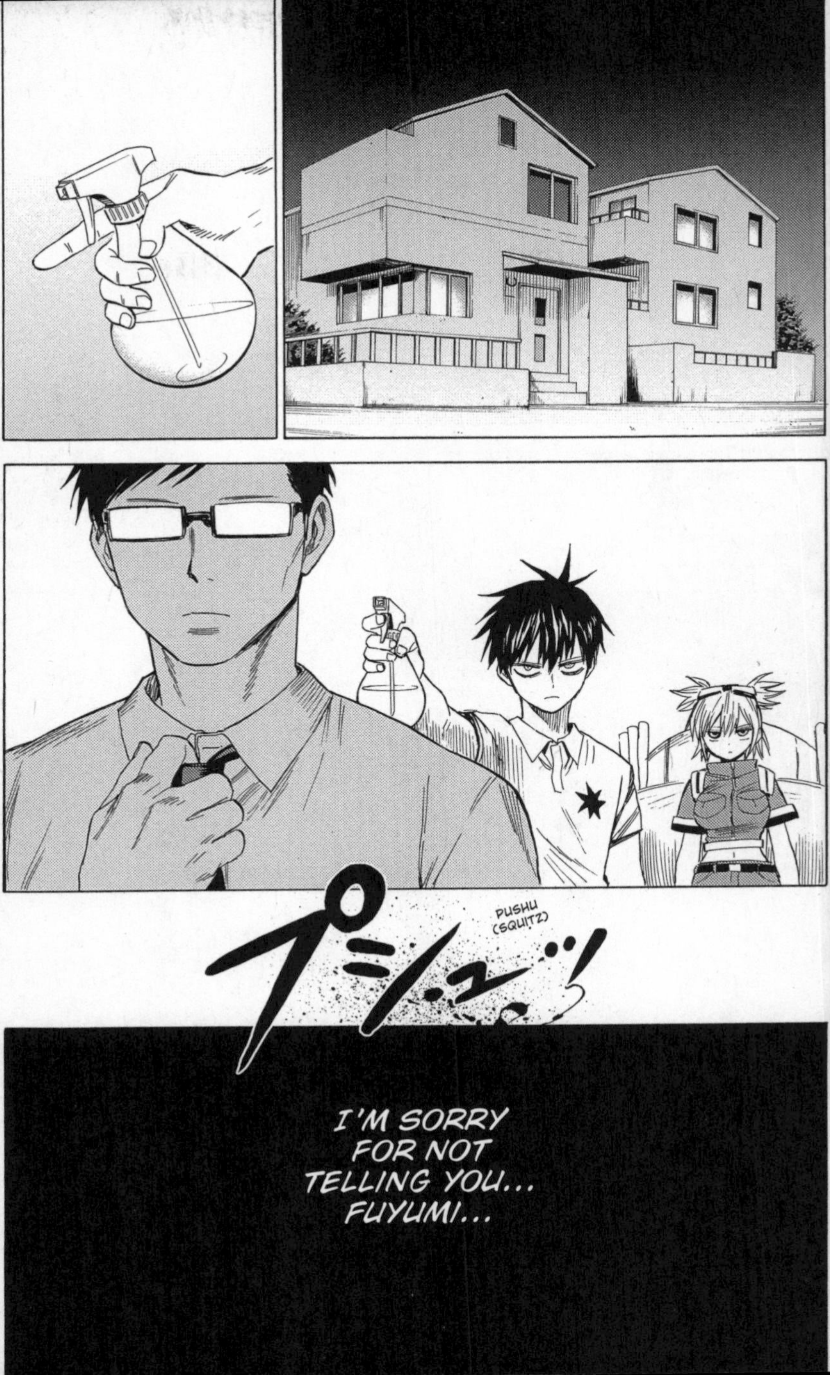
PUSHU (SQUITZ)
I'M SORRY FOR NOT TELLING YOU... FUYUMI...

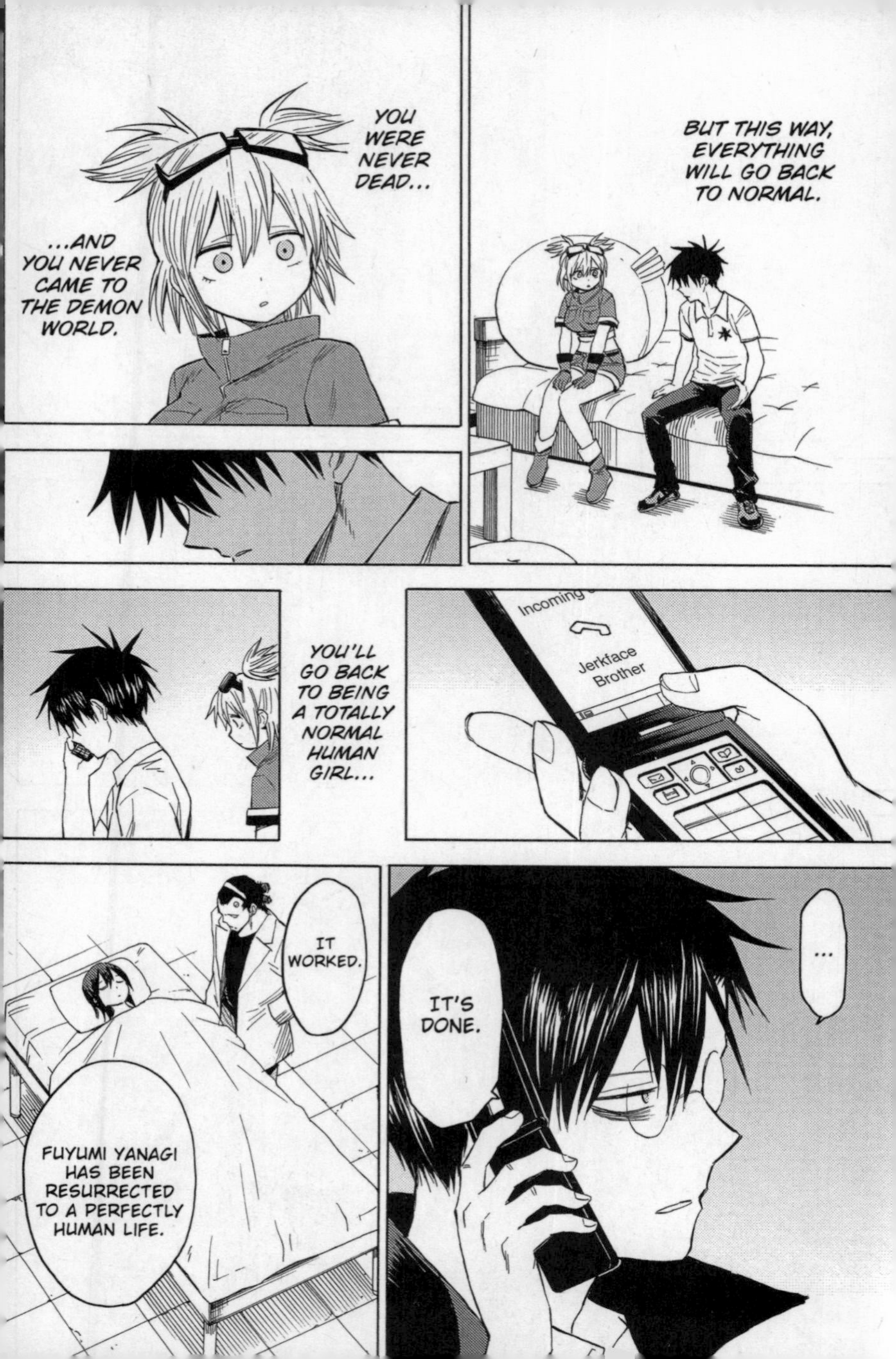
BUT THIS WAY, EVERYTHING WILL GO BACK TO NORMAL.
YOU WERE NEVER DEAD...
...AND YOU NEVER CAME TO THE DEMON WORLD.
Incoming
Jerkface Brother
YOU'LL GO BACK TO BEING A TOTALLY NORMAL HUMAN GIRL...
...
IT'S DONE.
IT WORKED.
FUYUMI YANAGI HAS BEEN RESURRECTED TO A PERFECTLY HUMAN LIFE.

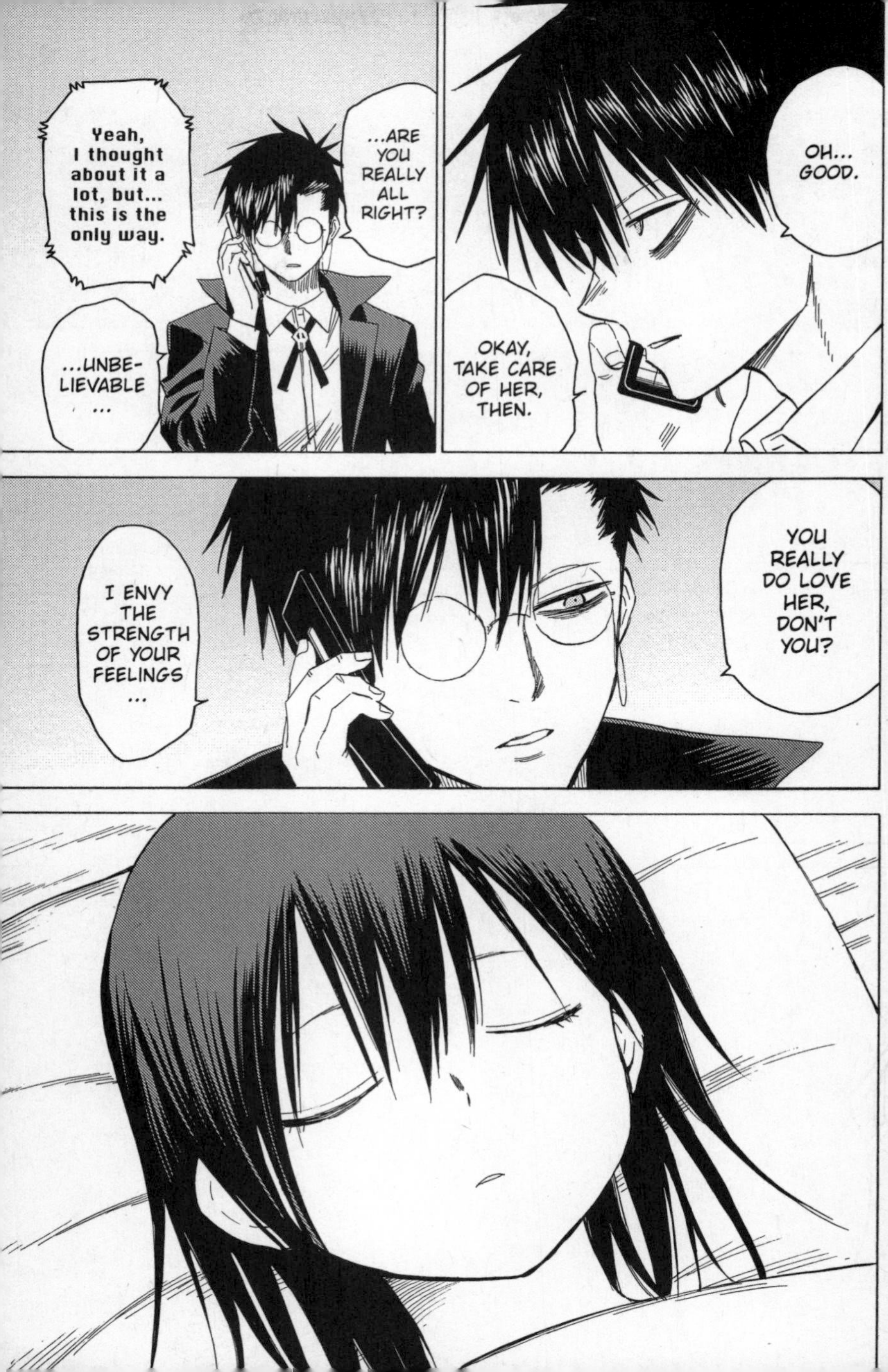
OH... GOOD.
OKAY, TAKE CARE OF HER, THEN.
...ARE YOU REALLY ALL RIGHT?
Yeah, I thought about it a lot, but... this is the only way.
...UNBE-LIEVABLE ...
YOU REALLY DO LOVE HER, DON'T YOU?
I ENVY THE STRENGTH OF YOUR FEELINGS ...

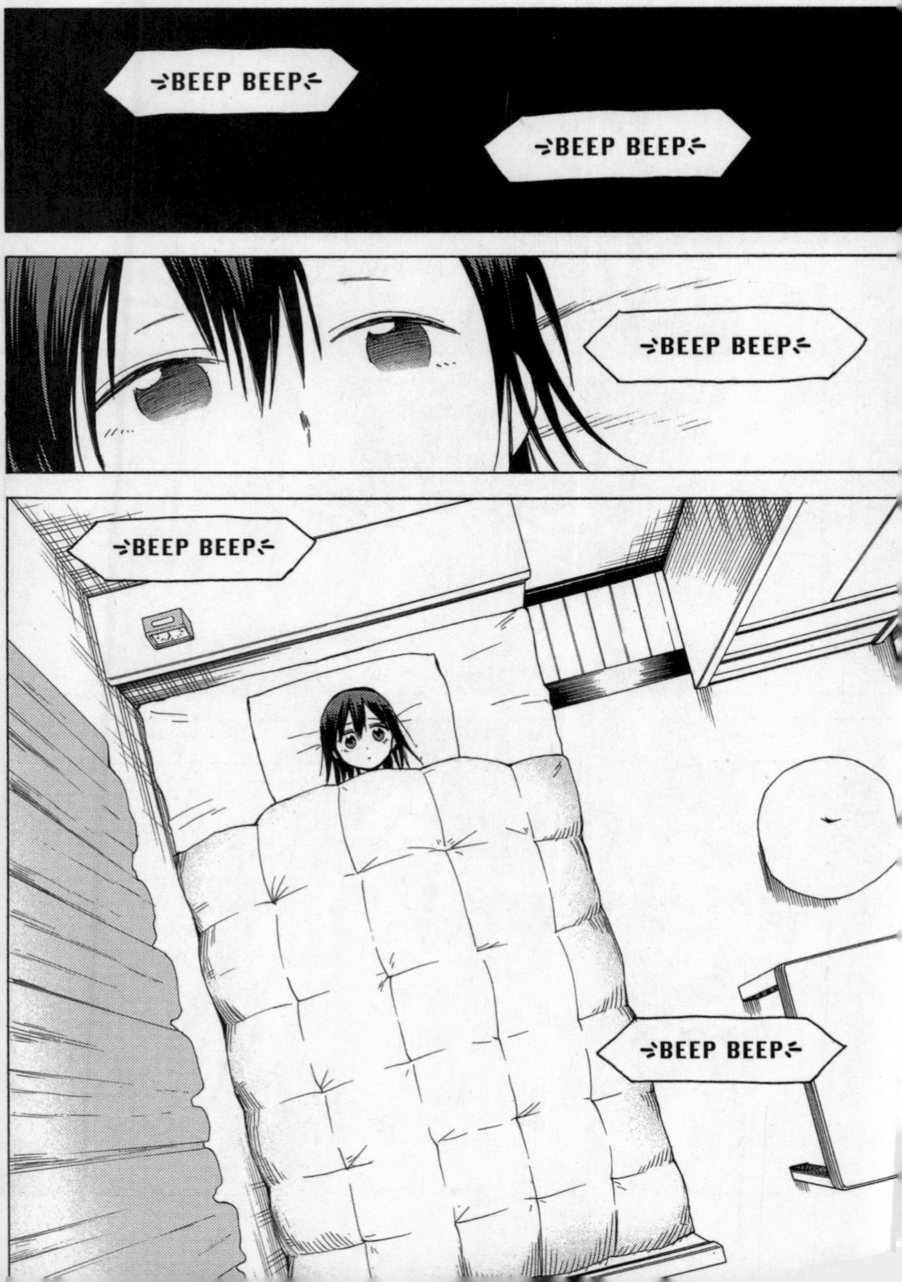
BEEP BEEP
BEEP BEEP
BEEP BEEP
BEEP BEEP
BEEP BEEP

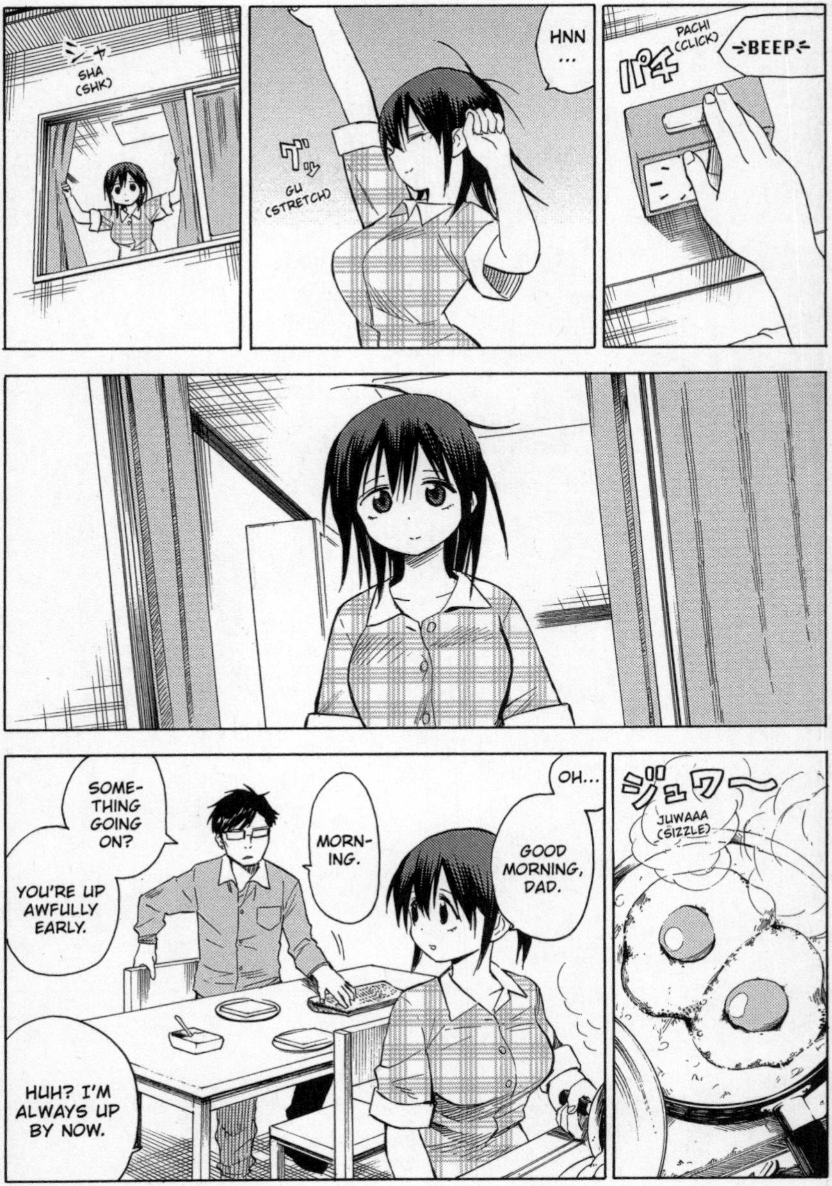

BEEP
パチ
PACHI (CLICK)
HNN ...
グッ
GU (STRETCH)
シャ
SHA (SHK)
ジュワ〜
JUWAAA (SIZZLE)
OH...
GOOD MORNING, DAD.
MORNING.
SOMETHING GOING ON?
YOU'RE UP AWFULLY EARLY.
HUH? I'M ALWAYS UP BY NOW.

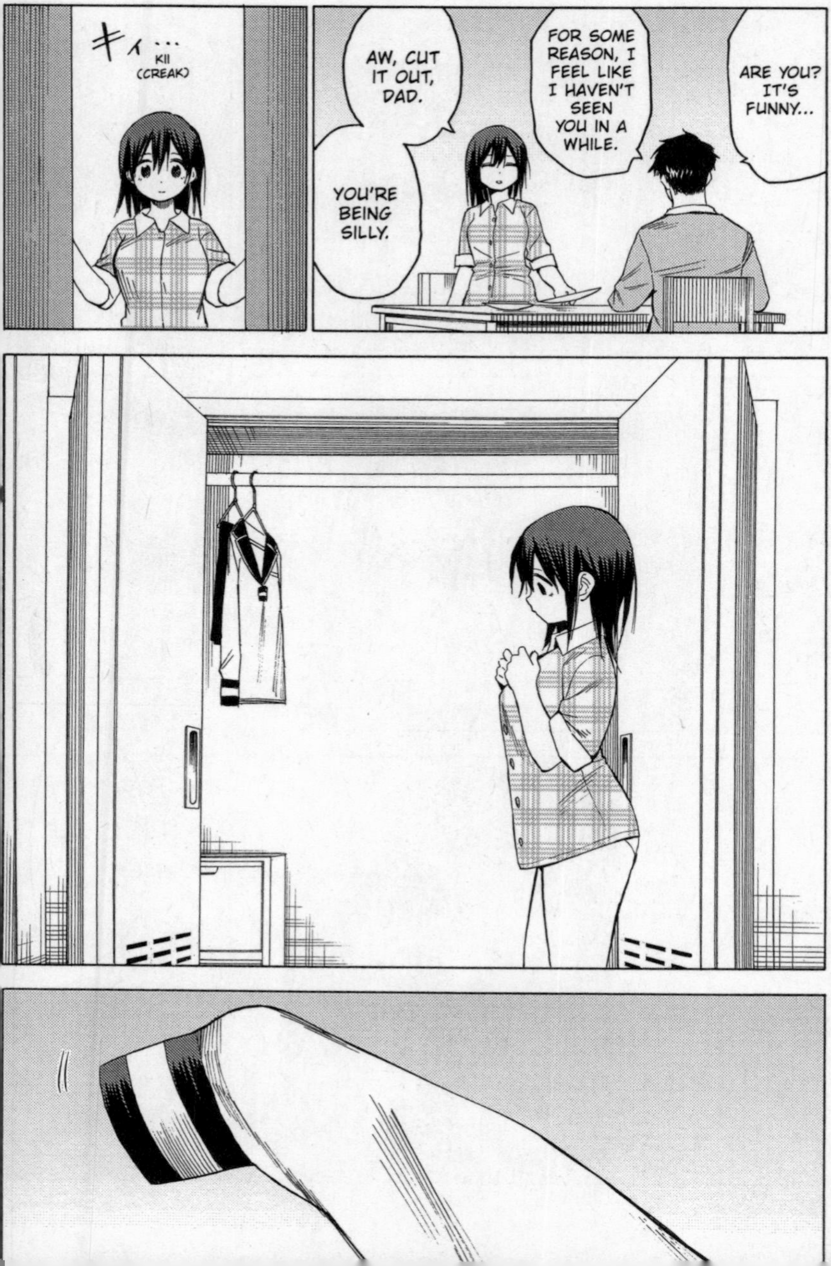
ARE YOU? IT'S FUNNY...
FOR SOME REASON, I FEEL LIKE I HAVEN'T SEEN YOU IN A WHILE.
AW, CUT IT OUT, DAD.
YOU'RE BEING SILLY.
キィ…
KII (CREAK)

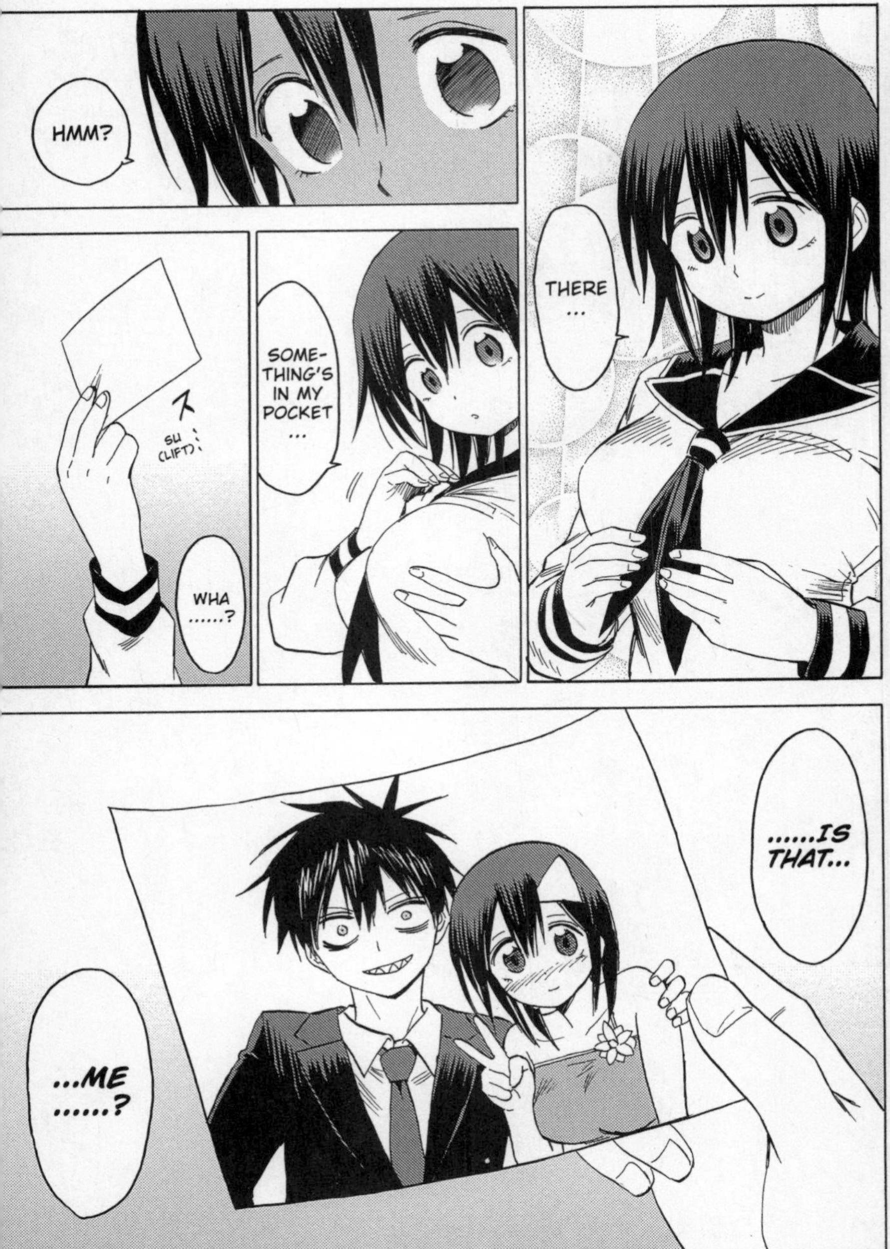

THERE ...
HMM?
SOME-THING'S IN MY POCKET ...
ス
SU (LIFT)
WHA ......?
......IS THAT...
...ME ......?

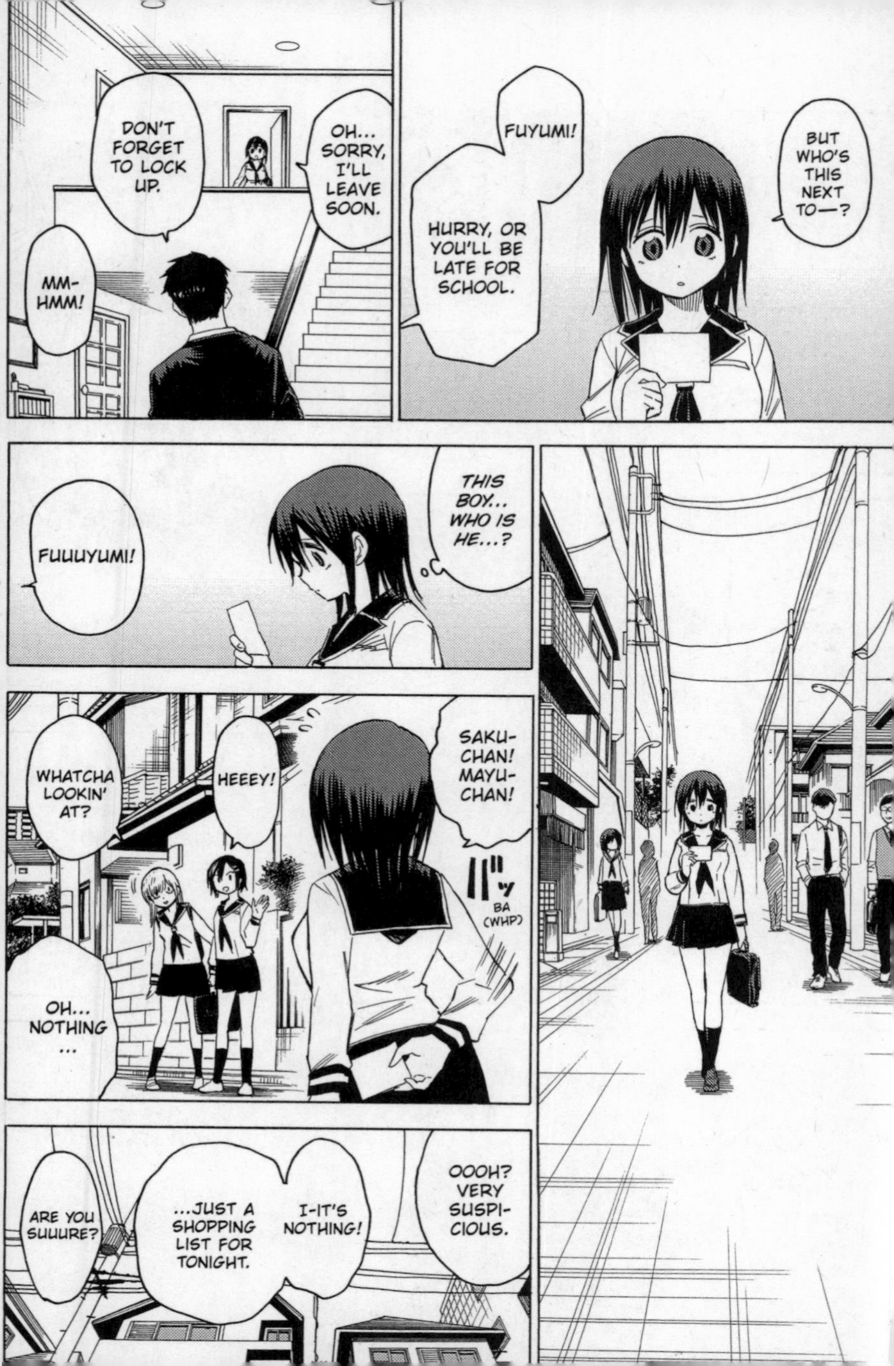
BUT WHO'S THIS NEXT TO—?
FUYUMI!
HURRY, OR YOU'LL BE LATE FOR SCHOOL.
OH... SORRY, I'LL LEAVE SOON.
DON'T FORGET TO LOCK UP.
MM-HMM!
THIS BOY... WHO IS HE...?
FUUUYUMI!
SAKU-CHAN! MAYU-CHAN!
バッ
BA (WHP)
HEEEY!
WHATCHA LOOKIN' AT?
OH... NOTHING...
OOOH? VERY SUSPICIOUS.
I-IT'S NOTHING!
...JUST A SHOPPING LIST FOR TONIGHT.
ARE YOU SUUURE?

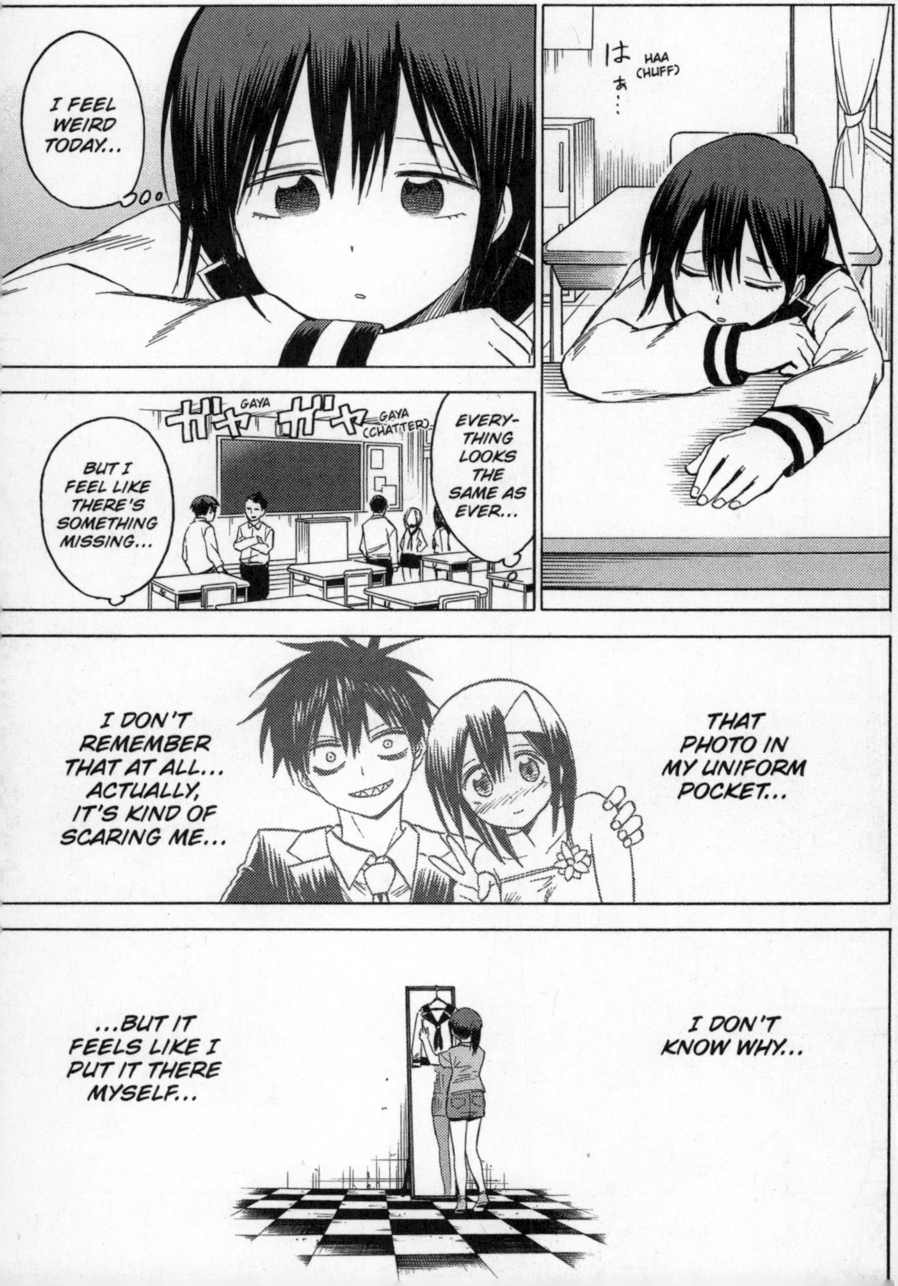
はぁ…
HAA (HUFF)
I FEEL WEIRD TODAY...
EVERY-THING LOOKS THE SAME AS EVER...
ガヤ GAYA ガヤ GAYA (CHATTER)
BUT I FEEL LIKE THERE'S SOMETHING MISSING...
THAT PHOTO IN MY UNIFORM POCKET...
I DON'T REMEMBER THAT AT ALL... ACTUALLY, IT'S KIND OF SCARING ME...
I DON'T KNOW WHY...
...BUT IT FEELS LIKE I PUT IT THERE MYSELF...

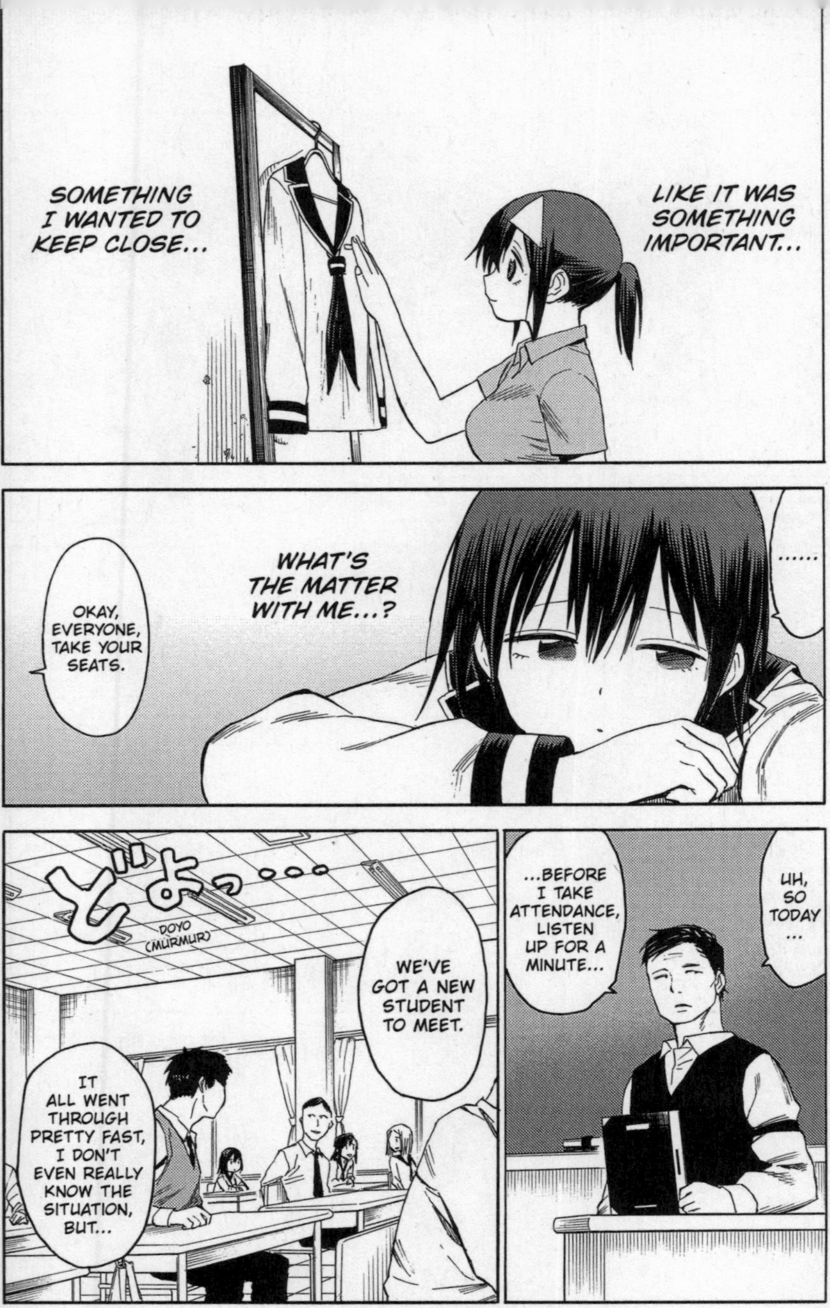
LIKE IT WAS SOMETHING IMPORTANT...
SOMETHING I WANTED TO KEEP CLOSE...
......
WHAT'S THE MATTER WITH ME...?
OKAY, EVERYONE, TAKE YOUR SEATS.
UH, SO TODAY...
...BEFORE I TAKE ATTENDANCE, LISTEN UP FOR A MINUTE...
どよっ。。。
DOYO (MURMUR)
WE'VE GOT A NEW STUDENT TO MEET.
IT ALL WENT THROUGH PRETTY FAST, I DON'T EVEN REALLY KNOW THE SITUATION, BUT...

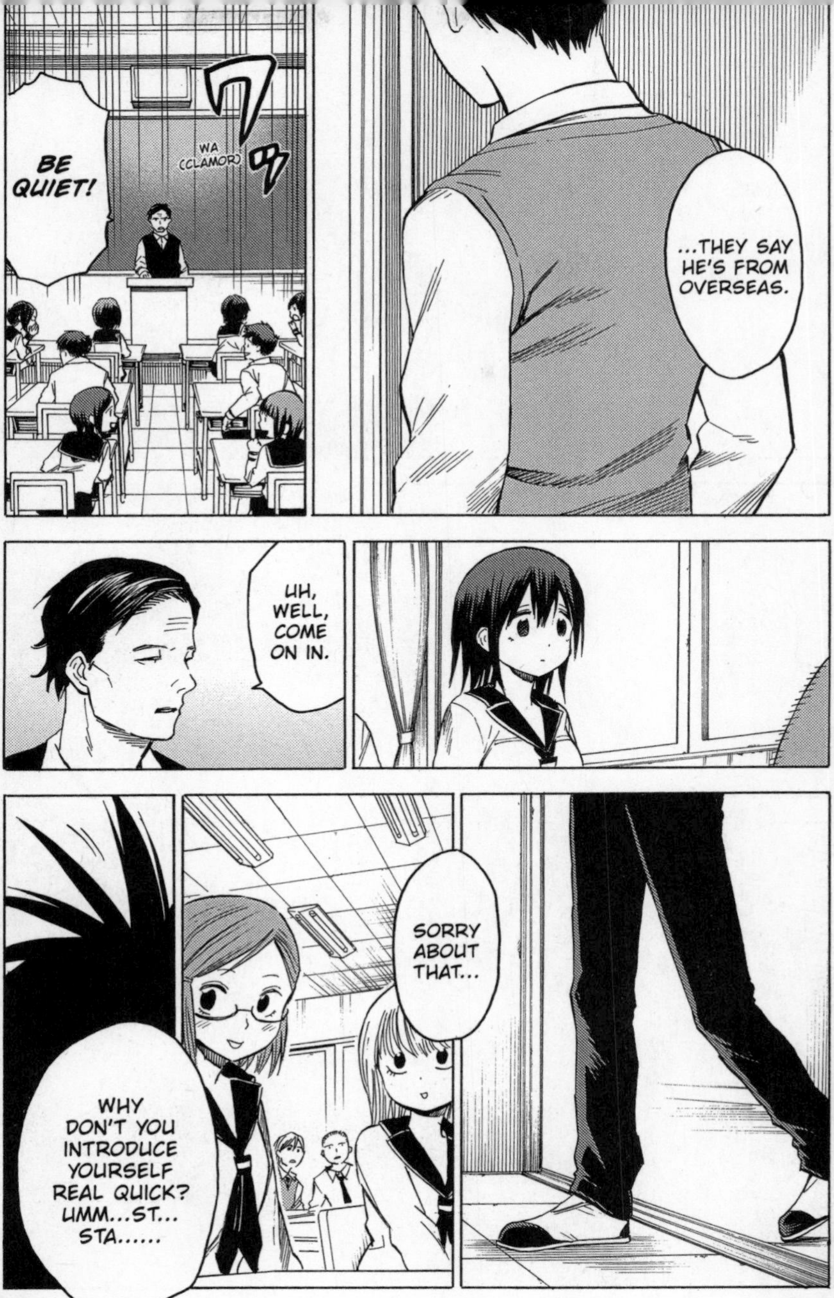
...THEY SAY HE'S FROM OVERSEAS.
ワッ
WA (CLAMOR)
BE QUIET!
UH, WELL, COME ON IN.
SORRY ABOUT THAT...
WHY DON'T YOU INTRODUCE YOURSELF REAL QUICK? UMM...ST... STA......

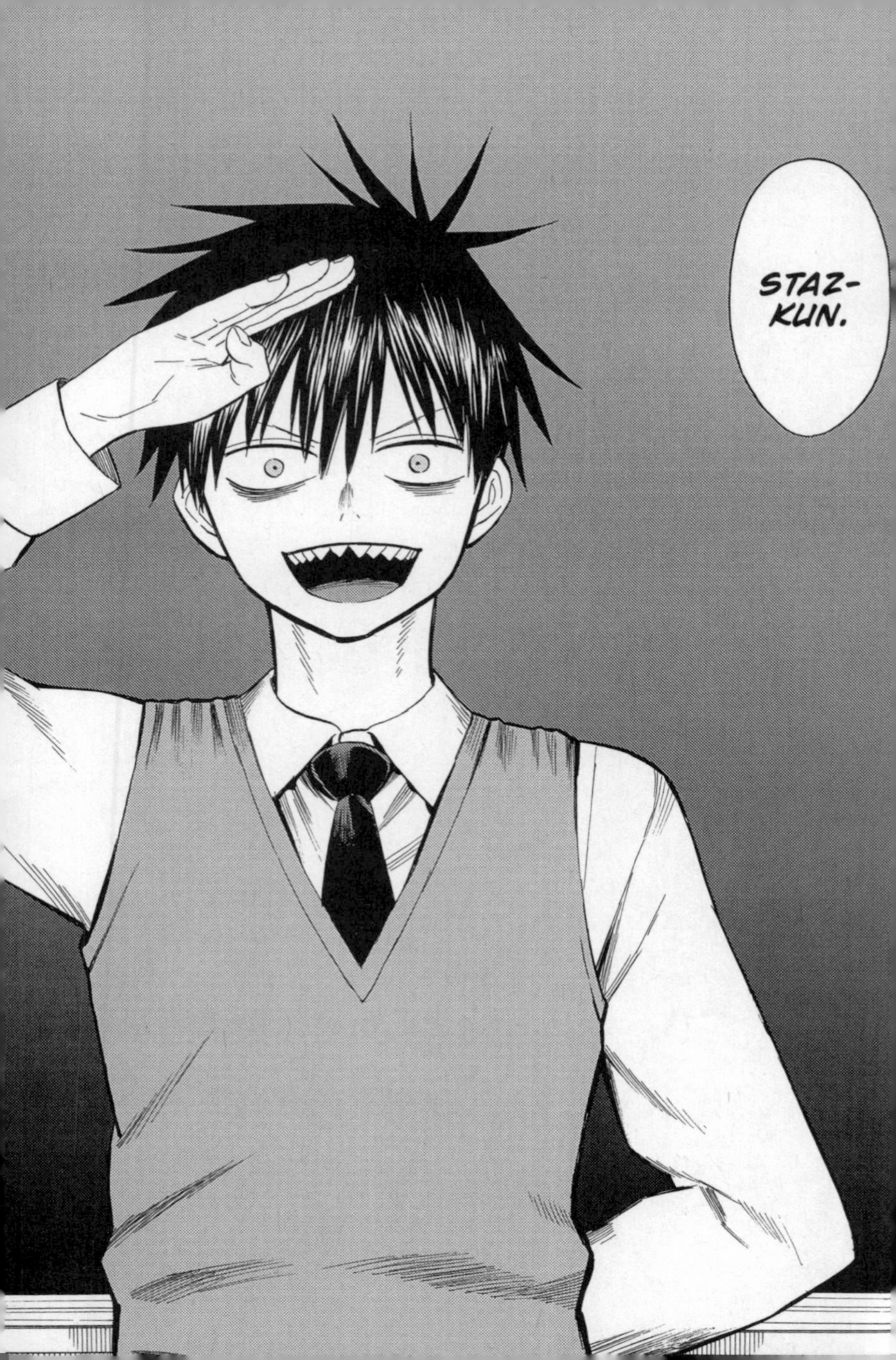
STAZ-KUN.

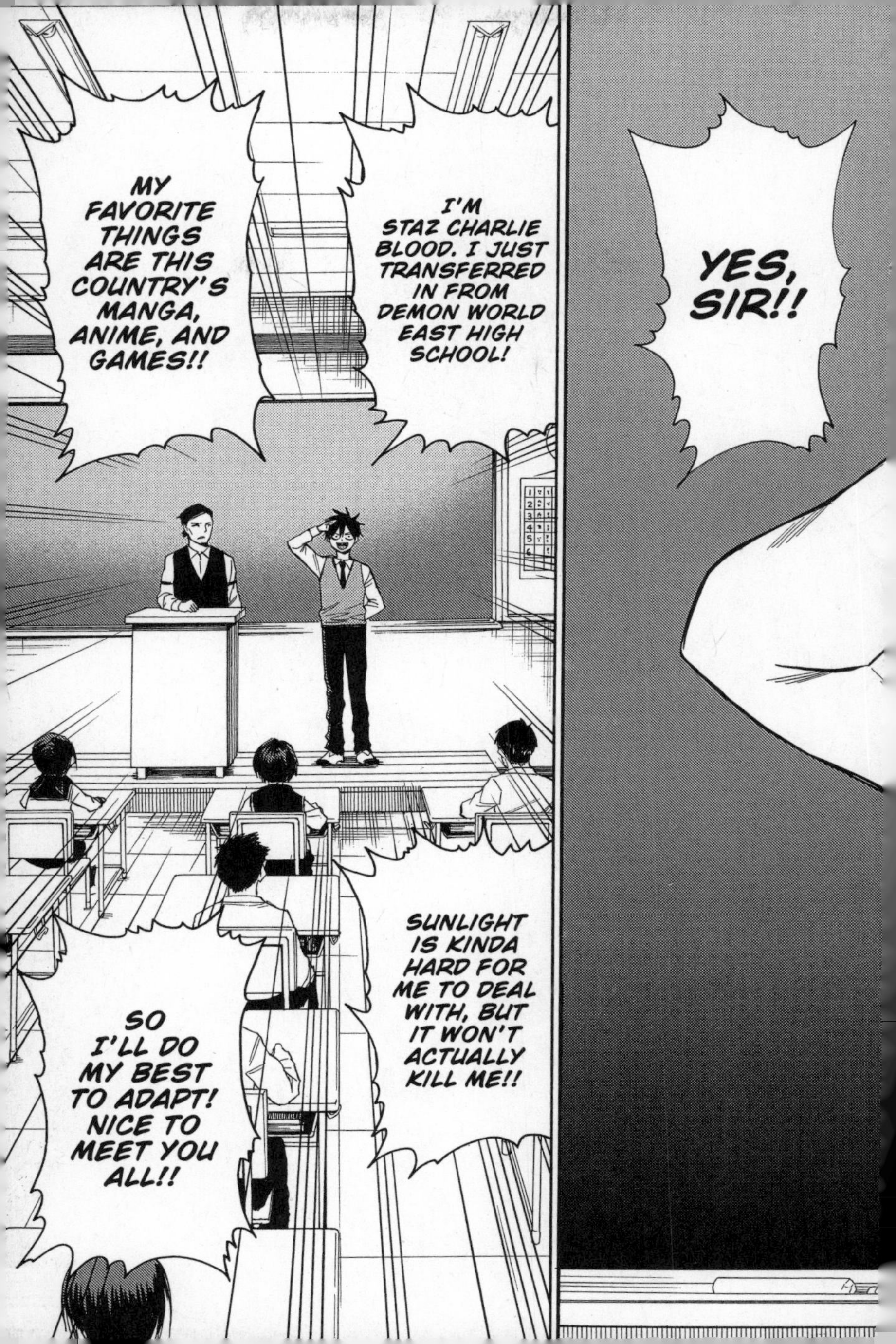
YES, SIR!!
I'M STAZ CHARLIE BLOOD. I JUST TRANSFERRED IN FROM DEMON WORLD EAST HIGH SCHOOL!
MY FAVORITE THINGS ARE THIS COUNTRY'S MANGA, ANIME, AND GAMES!!
SUNLIGHT IS KINDA HARD FOR ME TO DEAL WITH, BUT IT WON'T ACTUALLY KILL ME!!
SO I'LL DO MY BEST TO ADAPT! NICE TO MEET YOU ALL!!

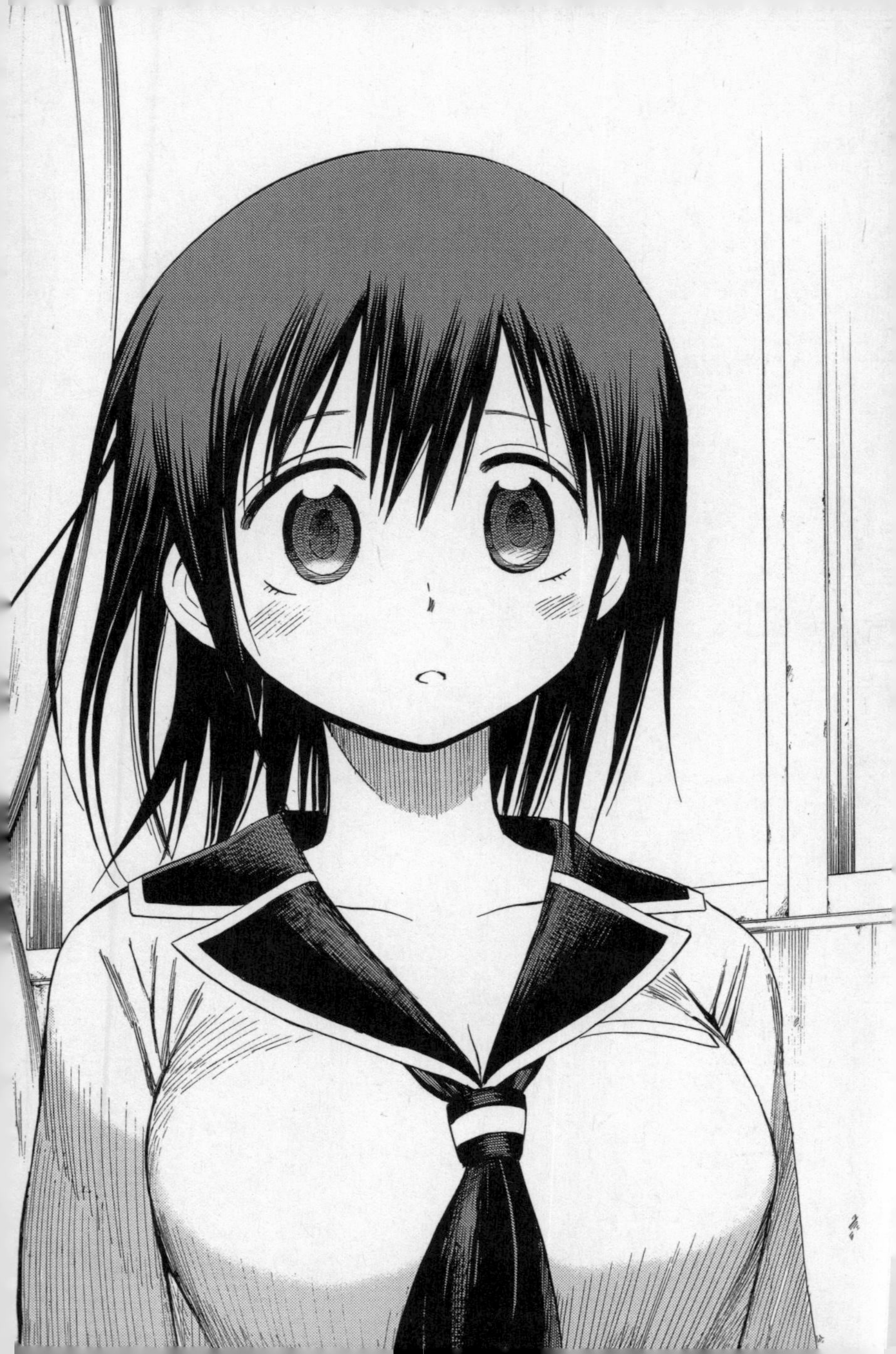

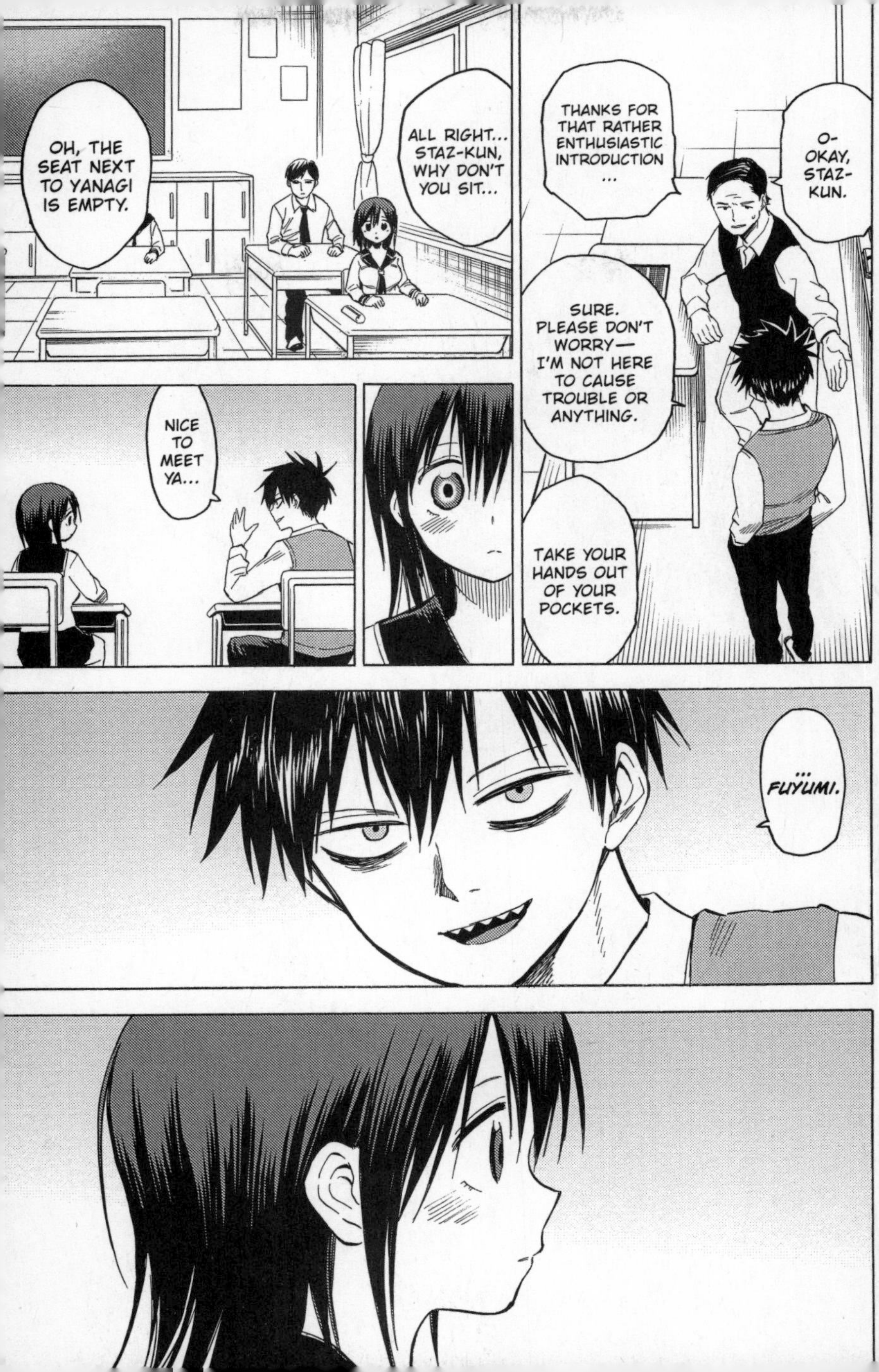
O-OKAY, STAZ-KUN.
THANKS FOR THAT RATHER ENTHUSIASTIC INTRODUCTION...
SURE. PLEASE DON'T WORRY— I'M NOT HERE TO CAUSE TROUBLE OR ANYTHING.
TAKE YOUR HANDS OUT OF YOUR POCKETS.
ALL RIGHT... STAZ-KUN, WHY DON'T YOU SIT...
OH, THE SEAT NEXT TO YANAGI IS EMPTY.
NICE TO MEET YA...
...FUYUMI.

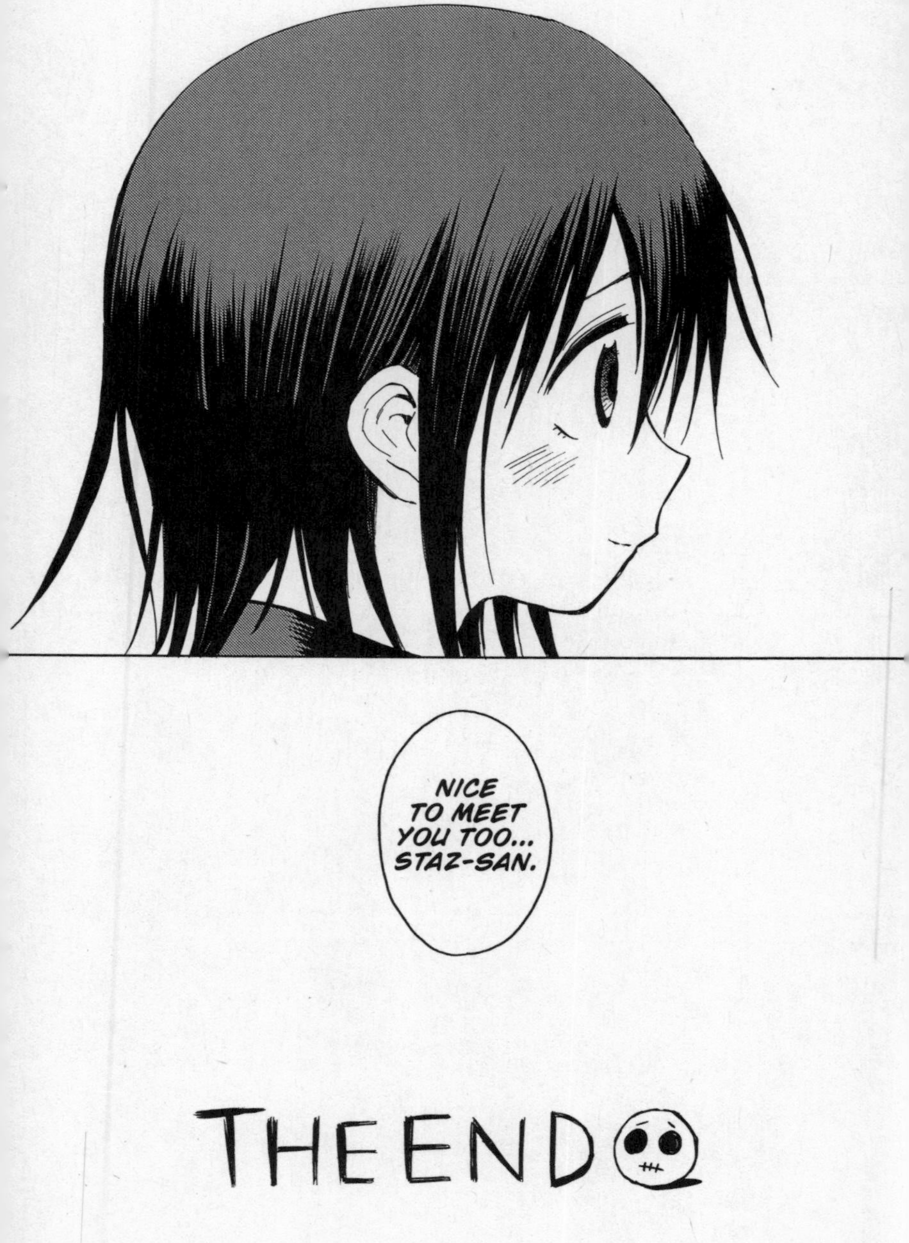
NICE TO MEET YOU TOO... STAZ-SAN.
THE END

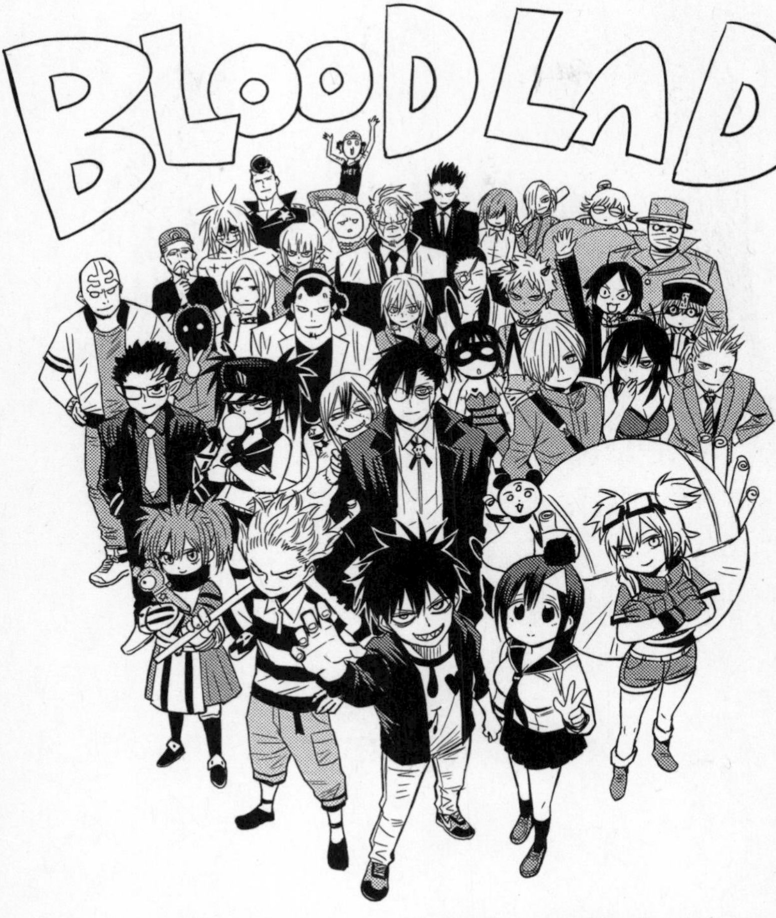
BLOOD LAD

THANK YOU FOR READING
BYE BYE

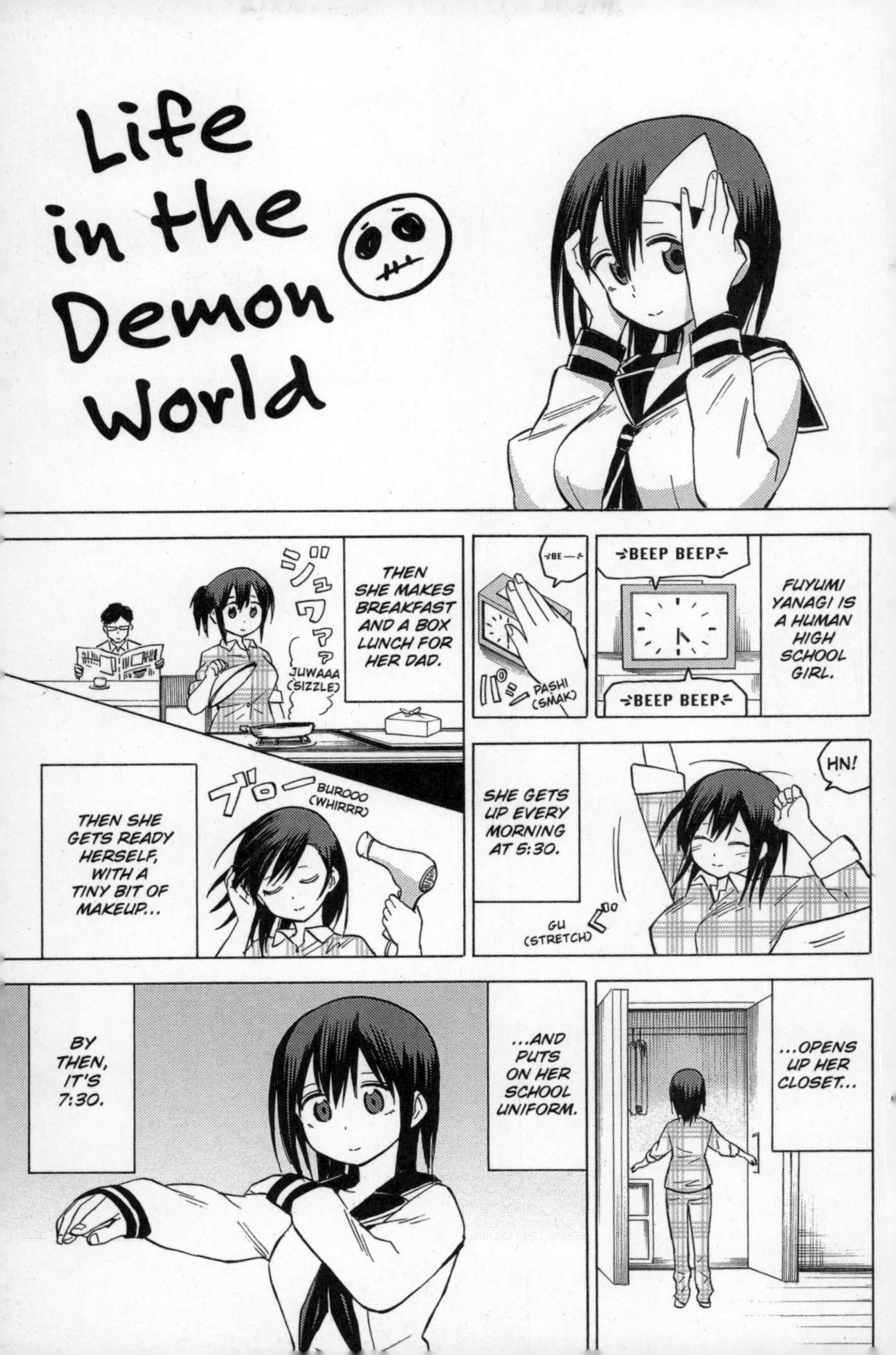

Life in the Demon World
FUYUMI YANAGI IS A HUMAN HIGH SCHOOL GIRL.
BEEP BEEP
BEEP BEEP
BE—
PASHI (SMAK)
HN!
SHE GETS UP EVERY MORNING AT 5:30.
GU (STRETCH)
THEN SHE MAKES BREAKFAST AND A BOX LUNCH FOR HER DAD.
JUWAAA (SIZZLE)
BUROOO (WHIRRR)
THEN SHE GETS READY HERSELF, WITH A TINY BIT OF MAKEUP...
...OPENS UP HER CLOSET...
...AND PUTS ON HER SCHOOL UNIFORM.
BY THEN, IT'S 7:30.

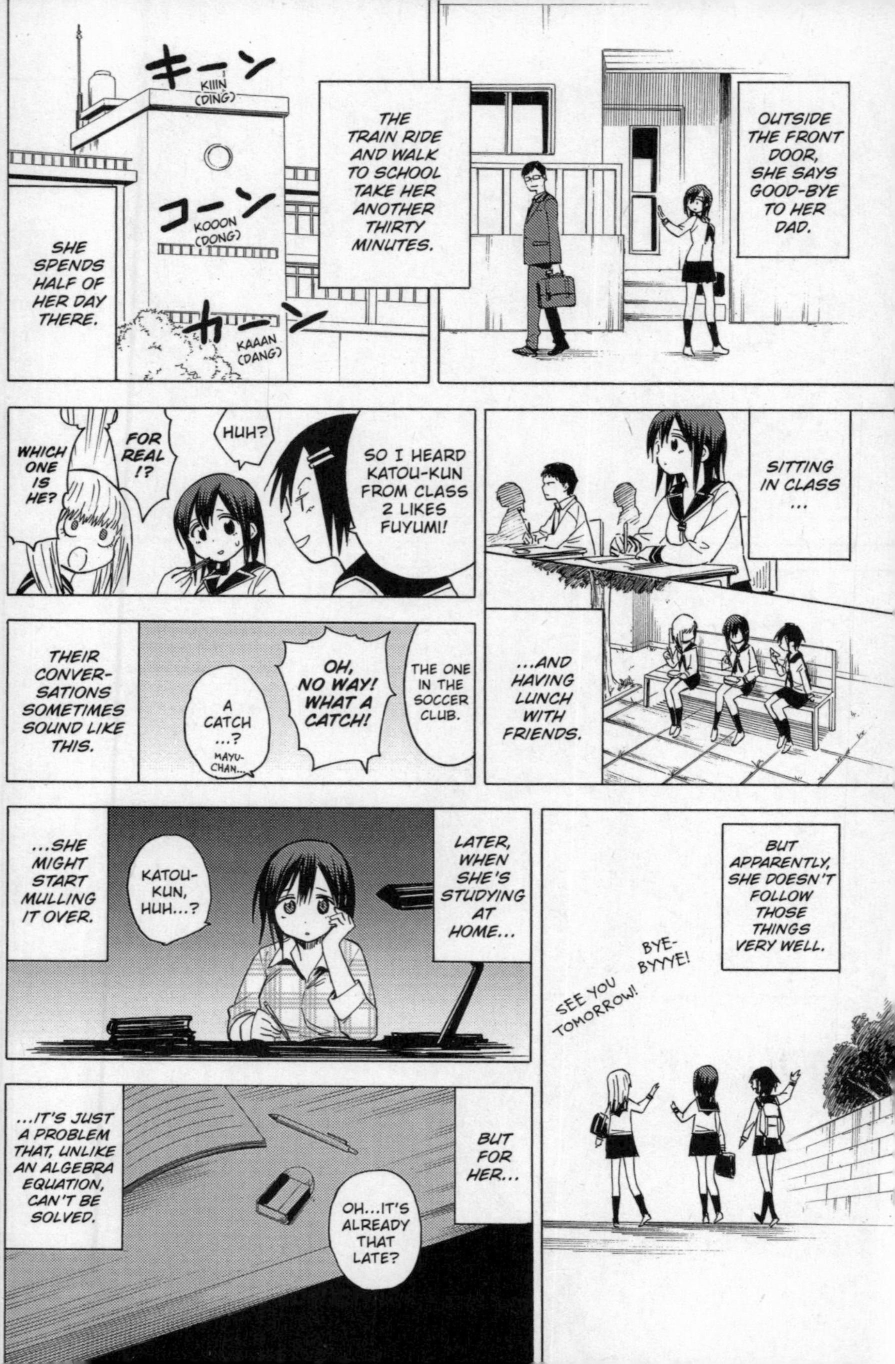
OUTSIDE THE FRONT DOOR, SHE SAYS GOOD-BYE TO HER DAD.
THE TRAIN RIDE AND WALK TO SCHOOL TAKE HER ANOTHER THIRTY MINUTES.
キーン
KIIIN (DING)
コーン
KOOON (DONG)
カーン
KAAAN (DANG)
SHE SPENDS HALF OF HER DAY THERE.
SITTING IN CLASS...
...AND HAVING LUNCH WITH FRIENDS.
SO I HEARD KATOU-KUN FROM CLASS 2 LIKES FUYUMI!
HUH?
FOR REAL!?
WHICH ONE IS HE?
THE ONE IN THE SOCCER CLUB.
OH, NO WAY! WHAT A CATCH!
A CATCH...?
MAYU-CHAN...
THEIR CONVERSATIONS SOMETIMES SOUND LIKE THIS.
BUT APPARENTLY, SHE DOESN'T FOLLOW THOSE THINGS VERY WELL.
BYE-BYYYE!
SEE YOU TOMORROW!
LATER, WHEN SHE'S STUDYING AT HOME...
KATOU-KUN, HUH...?
...SHE MIGHT START MULLING IT OVER.
BUT FOR HER...
OH...IT'S ALREADY THAT LATE?
...IT'S JUST A PROBLEM THAT, UNLIKE AN ALGEBRA EQUATION, CAN'T BE SOLVED.

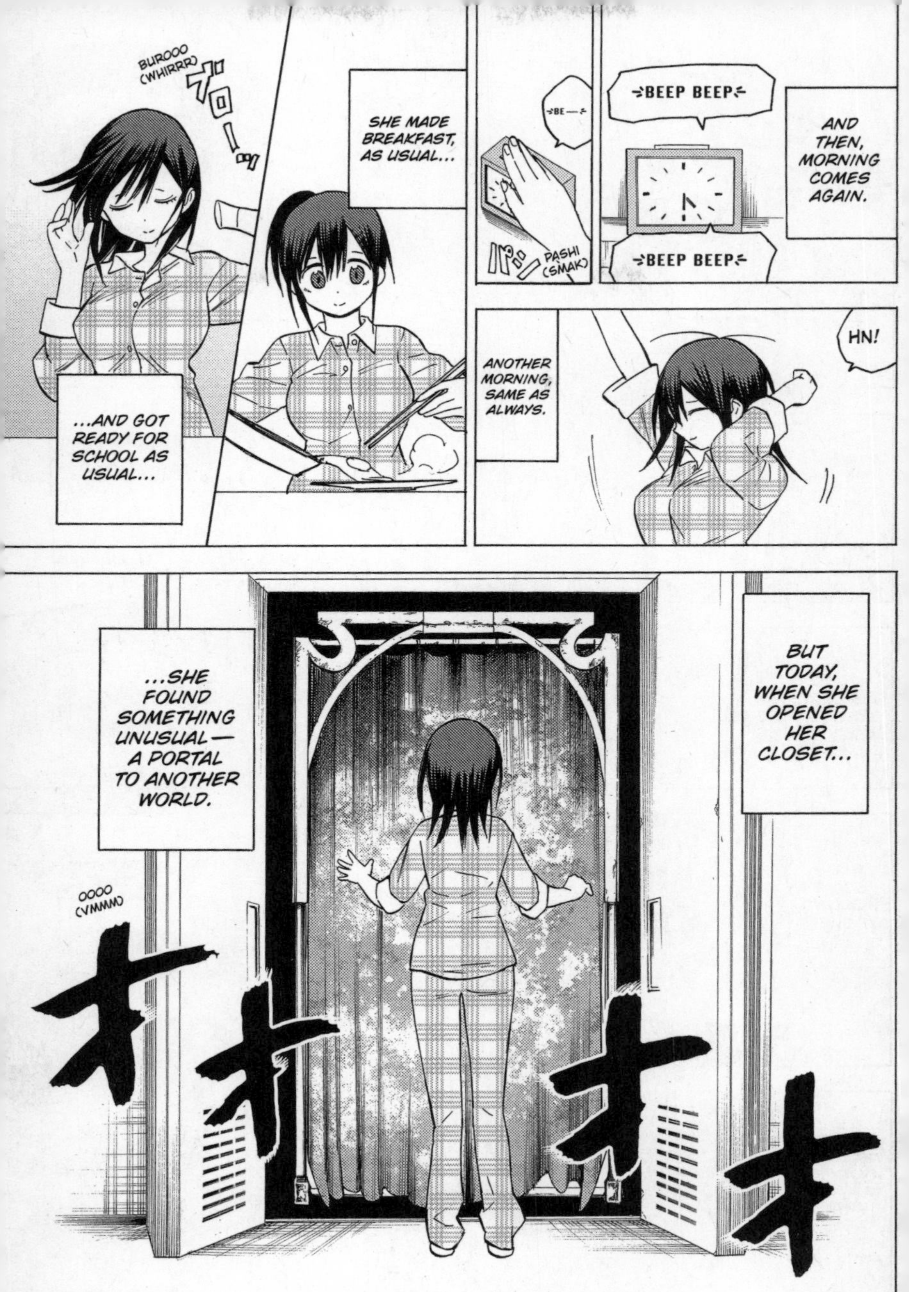
AND THEN, MORNING COMES AGAIN.
BEEP BEEP
BEEP BEEP
BE—
PASHI (SMAK)
HN!
ANOTHER MORNING, SAME AS ALWAYS.
SHE MADE BREAKFAST, AS USUAL...
BUROOO (WHIRRR)
...AND GOT READY FOR SCHOOL AS USUAL...
BUT TODAY, WHEN SHE OPENED HER CLOSET...
...SHE FOUND SOMETHING UNUSUAL—A PORTAL TO ANOTHER WORLD.
OOOO (VMMMM)

END

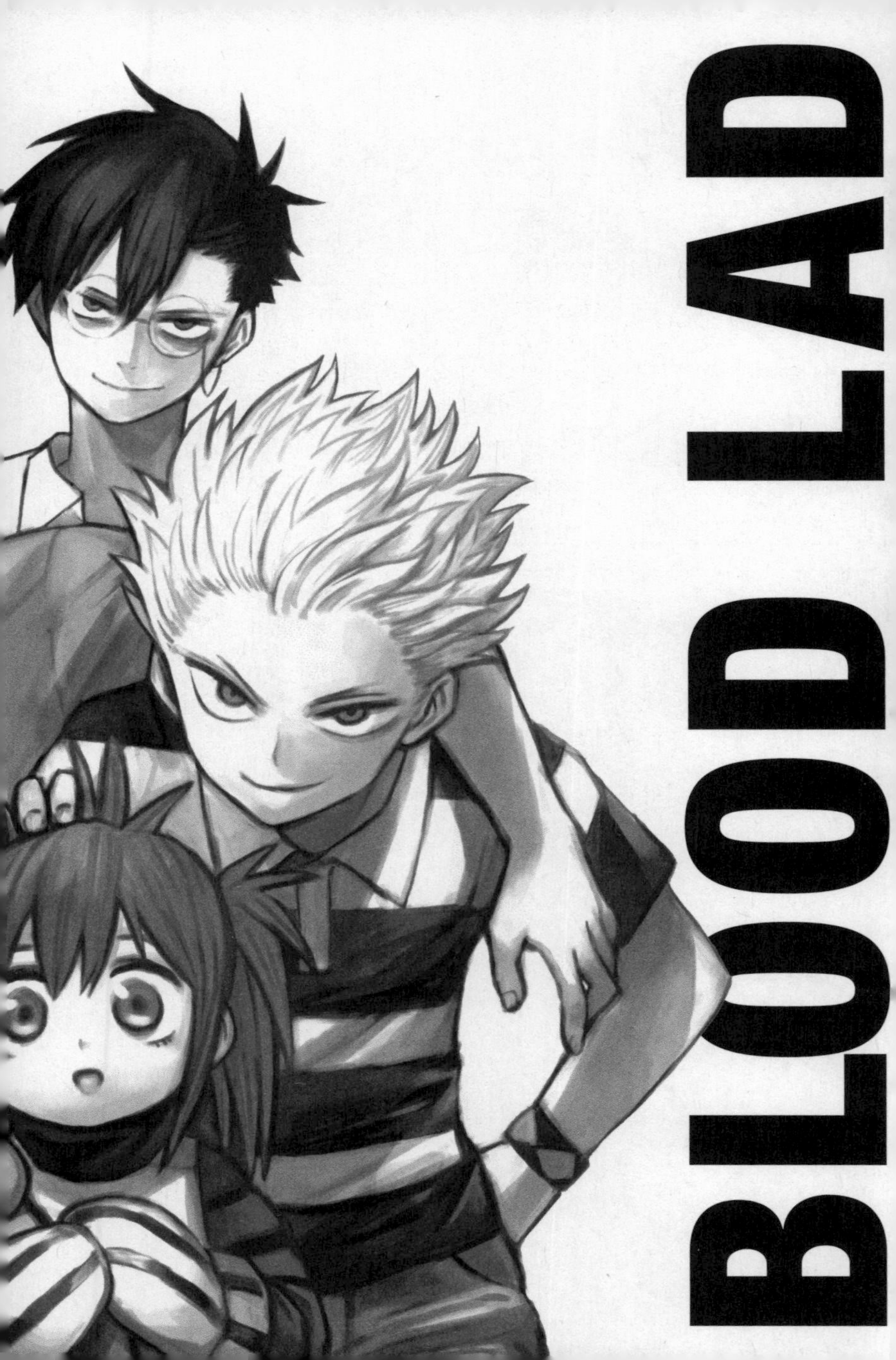
BLOOD LAD

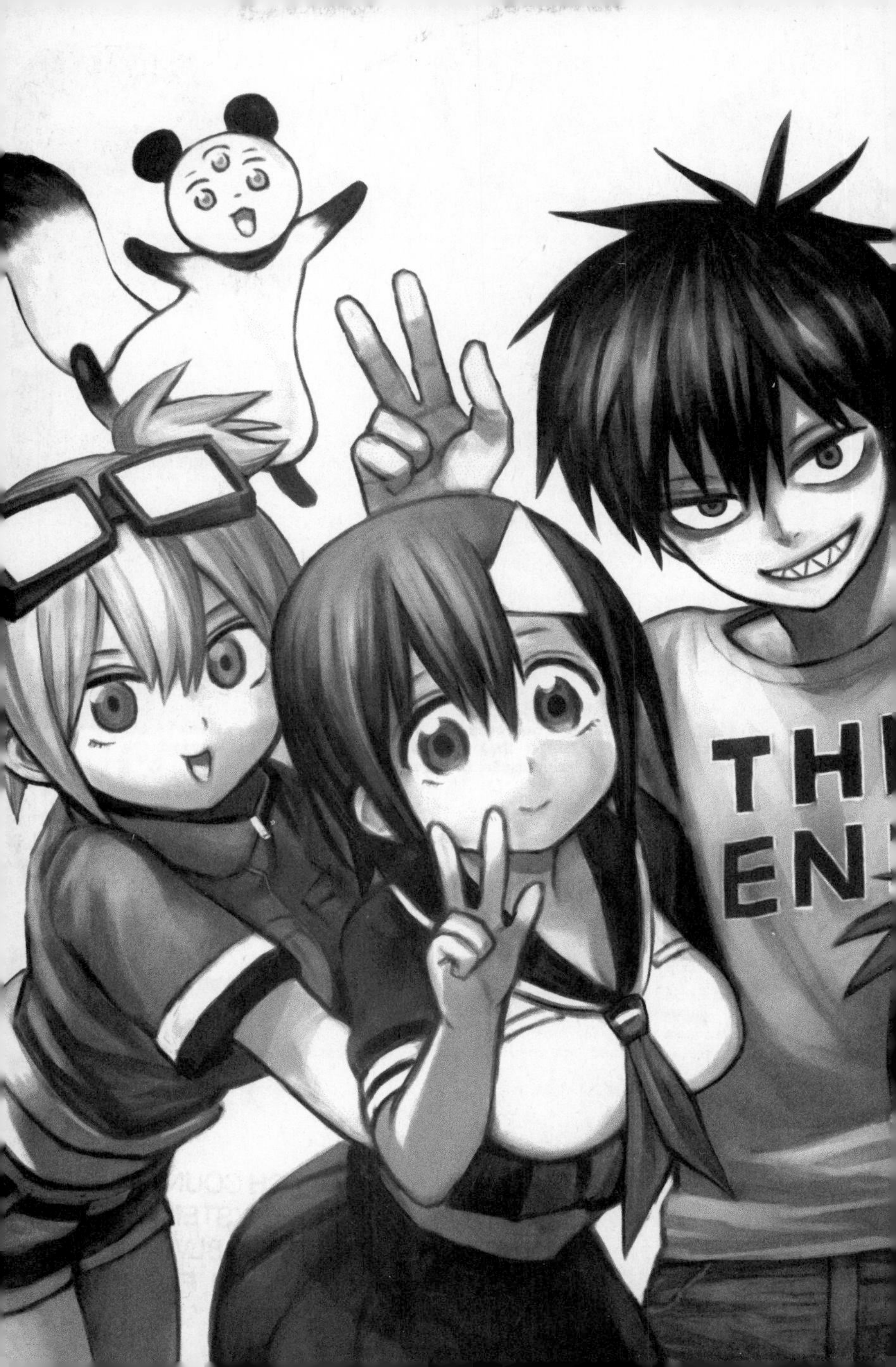
TH
EN

YUUKI KODAMA

Translation: Melissa Tanaka

Lettering: Alexis Eckerman

BLOOD LAD Volume 17 © Yuuki KODAMA 2016. First published in Japan in 2016 by KADOKAWA CORPORATION, Tokyo. English translation rights arranged with KADOKAWA CORPORATION, Tokyo, through TUTTLE-MORI AGENCY, INC., Tokyo.

English translation © 2017 by Yen Press, LLC

Yen Press
1290 Avenue of the Americas
New York, NY 10104

Visit us at yenpress.com
facebook.com/yenpress
twitter.com/yenpress
yenpress.tumblr.com
instagram.com/yenpress

First Yen Press Edition: August 2017

Yen Press is an imprint of Yen Press, LLC.
The Yen Press name and logo are trademarks of Yen Press, LLC.

Library of Congress Control Number: 2014504627

ISBN: 978-0-316-47392-7

10 9 8 7 6 5 4 3 2 1

BVG

Printed in the United States of America